HISTORY OF RUSSIA

HISTORY OF RUSSIA

FROM THE EARLIEST TIMES TO THE RISE OF COMMERCIAL CAPITALISM

BY

PROFESSOR M. N. POKROVSKY

Mikhail Nikolaevich

TRANSLATED AND EDITED BY

J. D. CLARKSON, Ph.D.

ASSISTANT PROFESSOR OF HISTORY, BROOKLYN
COLLEGE, AND

M. R. M. GRIFFITHS, M.A.

NEW YORK / RUSSELL & RUSSELL

1966

FIRST PUBLISHED IN 1931
REISSUED, 1966, BY RUSSELL & RUSSELL
A DIVISION OF ATHENEUM HOUSE, INC.
L. C. CATALOG CARD NO: 66—24751

PRINTED IN THE UNITED STATES OF AMERICA

CONTENTS

EDITORS' PREFACE

THERE are available in English a number of valuable histories of Russia, covering a wide range of varying interpretations. The products of the "old masters," from the pioneer and arch-conservative work of the landlord Karamzin, through the monumental volumes of the Hegelian Solovyev, to the brilliant synthesis of Klyuchevsky, have all undergone translation. Nor have writers still living been neglected: the secondary school text of the conservative Platonov, Academician and tutor to the brother of Nicholas II, and the essays of the liberal Milyukov, sometime professor of the history of law and prominent leader of the Constitutional Democratic Party, have likewise been made accessible to the Western reader. It is true that these translations and the numerous books of English-speaking authors based on these and other Russian writers afford but fleeting and unsatisfactory glimpses into the wealth of historical literature produced in Russia since the dawn of "scientific history" some four generations ago. It is, however, no less true that the English reader can, from material already published in English, acquaint himself with at least the general outlines of Russian history as it appears to most of the various Russian schools of thought.

Yet there is one viewpoint from which the English reader cannot survey the sweep of Russian history, namely, the viewpoint of the present rulers of Russia, the Marxists. This circumstance is the more curious and the more regrettable since there exists in Russian a carefully conceived and elaborated Marxist interpretation of the whole of Russia's history, written by a competent scholar, a pupil of (Sir) Paul G. Vinogradov. Professor Pokrovsky's *History of Russia from the Earliest Times* is the outstanding Marxist synthesis of Russian history. The editors have therefore deemed it worth while to undertake the translation of this work, which, they feel, merits equal consideration with those of other Russian historians writing from conservative, liberal, or other viewpoints; it is not to be compared with the all too numerous books on Russian history written, from whatever viewpoint, by untrained historians. Professor Pokrovsky's life and scholarly activity are summarised in the appended Biographical Sketch; the editors therefore are here confining themselves to a few comments on the mechanics of the translation.

This *History of Russia* was published in 1910-1912, in five volumes, including some chapters by collaborators; in subsequent editions these chapters were omitted, and the work appeared in four volumes. In the English translation these volumes have been compressed into two; the author is preparing additional material to bring the story through the Revolution of 1917 and the establishment of the Soviet régime. The English edition has been prepared in close collaboration with the author, no abridgements or alterations having been made without his specific authorisation. The original Russian text was naturally addressed to a public familiar with many details of Russian history and life unknown to the foreign reader. The editors have therefore been confronted with the problem of allusions to persons, events, or literary works that might puzzle the American or English reader; such passages they have striven to eliminate altogether, where they felt them unessential to the text, or to explain in notes. In either case the author was consulted, to the end that the final product might be authentically Professor Pokrovsky's interpretation, uncoloured by the prejudices of the authors. As all footnotes, whether author's or editors', have been accepted by the author, no distinction has been made between them; footnote references to Russian texts have been omitted as superfluous to the English reader.

Certain Russian terms have been retained in the text; in forming plurals these terms have been treated as English words. Each has been italicised the first time it occurs, and, where its meaning is not clear from the context, an explanation has been inserted in square brackets. For the convenience of the reader such terms have been brought together in a Glossary. Russian weights and measures have been retained, and their English equivalents have been included in the Glossary. Brief notes on persons, institutions, events, etc., mentioned in the text have been added if for the English reader more information seemed desirable; these notes are not intended to take the place of the Index for general reference. Dates are, of course, old style. The system of transliteration employed is that of the Library of Congress with slight departures: *ya* has been used for $\widehat{ia}$, *yu* for $\widehat{iu}$ (*ye* only initial or after vowels); *-y* for final *-ii*.

The editors do not, of course, disclaim responsibility for any failure on their part to convert ideas expressed in Russian into the exactly corresponding ideas expressed in English; it may, however, give the reader more confidence to know that the complete English translation has been carefully read by the author, and that modifications have been made to meet his criticisms.

The editors desire to express their appreciation of the aid of all those who have generously given assistance or encouragement in the various stages of the preparation of this translation.

THE EDITORS.

AUTHOR'S PREFACE TO THE ENGLISH TRANSLATION

EVERY historical work reflects a certain philosophy of life and a certain period of time. The first book on Russian history to be widely read and to influence the historical views of the ruling social classes in Russia was the *History of the Russian State* by Karamzin (1765-1826); it was written by a noble and landlord at the period when economy based on obligatory labour—the art of extracting the surplus product from the peasant by means of extra-economic compulsion—had reached the zenith of its evolution. But, on the one hand, extra-economic compulsion presupposes as its political integument absolutism; on the other hand, the estate based on obligatory labour was closely linked with merchant capital, the intermediary between this estate and the market; to become merchandise what was extracted from the peasant must fall into the hands of a merchant. Karamzin's central ideas were the formation of the autocracy and the formation of the united realm, *i.e.*, the formation of an absolute state authority and the formation of a market.

Karamzin profoundly believed that the order of things, the origin of which he was describing, was eternal and immutable. It did not enter his head that what had had a beginning must also have an end. Yet this end was already in sight less than twenty years after Karamzin's death. The appearance of Russian grain on the world market and the necessity for the Russian landlord to compete with bourgeois economy soon disclosed that compulsory labour was disadvantageous. At the same time peasant revolution, suppressed but not liquidated when the Pugachev rebellion was crushed, continued to seethe in the depths, and one tsar after another—Alexander I, Nicholas I, and especially Alexander II—was forced to remind his nobility that at any moment the volcano might erupt anew. Preservation of that order of things which to Karamzin had seemed so stable was manifestly threatening the stability of the rule of the nobility. If the landlords' state was not to fall victim to foreign competition and peasant revolt, it must renounce extra-economic compulsion in its cruder forms—obligatory labour and the right to sell men like cattle, so much per head.

The historical literature of the 'forties, 'fifties, and 'sixties of the nineteenth century begins to perceive what Karamzin had not seen: what has had a beginning must also have an end. Parallel with projects for the liquidation of serfdom arise animated controversies as to the origin of serfdom. This question—the origin of serfdom—becomes the cardinal question in Russian history for a number of decades. The autocracy continues to be the hero of the whole historical process, but it is no longer the basic force of extra-economic compulsion; it is rather the enlightened guide of national economy, the basic factor of progress. From the time of Solovyev (1820-1879) every tsar is transformed into a reformer, and his importance is measured by the number and scope of the reforms he effected. In these reforms is embodied the whole evolution of Russia. Of revolution nothing is said; the masses of the people are not the subject but the object of action. In essence the Russian historiography of the middle of the past century is very reminiscent of the philosophy of history of the period of the Enlightenment. Enlightened men with the tsar at their head—a tsar who loves and fosters enlightenment—do for the people all that is needful. The people have only to bow down and give thanks.

The estate based on obligatory labour and downright slavery are replaced by the *Junker* estate of Prussian type and by exploitation with the aid of economic compulsion in its crudest forms. It is still a far cry to a bourgeoisie of European model, and Russian historical literature of this period—the period of the "reforms" of Alexander II— may only very conditionally be called bourgeois. Solovyev, Chicherin (1828-1904), and Kavelin (1818-1885) are bourgeois only by comparison with the serf-owning Karamzin. In actual fact they are merely liberal landlords or their ideologists (Solovyev was not personally a landlord). The few democrats or semi-democrats of this time—Chernyshevsky (1828-1889), Shchapov (1830-1876), Kostomarov (1817-1885)—had no influence on the development of Russian academic learning. Klyuchevsky (1841-1911) and Milyukov (1859—) proceed from Solovyev and Chicherin, in less degree from Kavelin, and only in certain details from Shchapov. Valuing the autocracy, these historians value in no less degree the united realm. The formation of the Russian empire is for them, too, the basic fact of Russian history, and they see only its bright sides. They give no picture of the barbarous enslavement of tens of peoples, but only the triumphal progress of enlightenment, expanding the area of landlord exploitation over one-sixth part of the land area of the globe.

In Russian history the period of bourgeois democracy lasted only eight months [March-November, 1917]. Moreover, it came very late, when there already existed a revolutionary movement of the workers and socialist parties. This is the reason why landlord historiography was in Russia not replaced by a bourgeois-democratic historiography, as might have been expected and as was the case in other countries—in France, for example. Russian historiography knows no Michelet. In Russia landlord historians are succeeded by historians of a new class, thrust into Russian history by the stormy evolution of Russian capitalism in the course of the second half of the past century. Almost without transitional stages the philosophy of the nobility is replaced by the philosophy of the proletariat. There sets in the *Marxist* period of Russian historiography.

In the course of forty years this philosophy—in the form in which it has been reflected in historical books—has passed through a series of stages. Marxism is not, as bourgeois publicists think, a dead dogma. It is the most revolutionary, that is, the most living doctrine in the world. The Marxism of the 1890's, especially in the form in which it was permitted by the tsarist censorship and which has therefore received the name of "legal Marxism," is almost as alien to us now as is the Catholic religion. Even the revolutionary Marxism of that time has almost ceased to be Marxism for us: examples are Kautsky and Cunow, from whose books we all studied thirty years ago, and whom no one now in the U.S.S.R. counts as Marxists. It is true that while history has gone forward, and very rapidly, these writers have moved backward, and none too slowly, either. Yet it was not without reason that the works of Kautsky in his best period seemed to Lenin obsolescent even in 1923. "Doubtless the textbook Kautsky wrote was a very useful thing for its time," wrote Lenin in *On our revolution,* one of his last articles. "But it is time to renounce the idea that this textbook anticipated all forms of the evolution of further world history."

Marxism is not a dogma but a guide to action, said the founders of Marxism; and the experiences of this action have in the most powerful way been reflected on the guidance. Not in the sense of principles: fundamentally we all to this day stand firmly on the Communist Manifesto of 1848. But history has taught us a far wider application of these principles to the interpretation of concrete historical facts. For which of us in 1905 was it not an axiom that the most advanced capitalist countries would be the first to become the theatre of socialist revolution? History has shown that it was easiest to effect this revolution in a country where capitalism already existed but had not yet attained ultimate dominance. We expected that socialism would come from Europe to Russia, whereas, on the contrary, it is going from Russia to Western Europe.

Revolution has been the great teacher which *ex cathedra* has taught us how history is to be understood. In 1905 we attended only the first part of the course; the second part of the course began in 1917. Until 1905 the class struggle existed for us in books; in 1905 we experienced it on our own skins. There was no living historian for whom the experience of our first revolution was not a break in his life as a scholar, not excluding the most academic of the Academicians, who after 1905 set about assiduously to expunge from their works whatever materialistic explanation of history they contained (many had sinned in this respect in their youth). But this experience is not to be compared with what we lived through in 1917-1921. In 1905 we, bookmen, saw with our own eyes what revolution is. In 1917 we became active participants in one of the greatest revolutionary catastrophes in the world. And this was reflected equally on both sides of the barricades. Is the Milyukov of the 1920's, the author of *The Ruin of Russia*, the same Milyukov who wrote *Essays on the History of Russian Culture?* Compare the two books!

During this period were manifested in sharp relief the root differences between Marxist Russian historiography and its predecessor, the historiography of the landlords, whether landlord partisans of serfdom or liberal landlords. Both of the latter were in reality far closer to each other than we are to them. We alone have properly appraised the significance of the *masses* in history—because we have seen these masses in action. We alone have fully understood the state as a *class* state—because we ourselves have destroyed the state of one class and erected the state of another class; even in the literature of the "legal" Marxism of the 1890's it was possible to find the state defined as an extra-class "organisation of order." We alone, finally, have abandoned the idyllic picture of the unification of a mass of "backward" peoples under the "enlightened" guidance of the Russian tsars—because it has become possible for these peoples to tell how the "propagators of enlightenment" tortured, oppressed, and exploited them, and because the rule of the proletariat has at last opened the way for the genuine enlightenment of the non-Russian majority of the population of the former "Russian empire."

In the realm of historical conceptions there is nothing for us to borrow from our predecessors. For us their writings are but collections of facts. Fortunately, not anticipating our appearance, they did not omit from their works facts that might be of use to us—as their successors are doing to-day. But even in the realm of facts we are ever less and less dependent on them. In recent years there has been among us a very wide development of the work of editing documents, from the sixteenth to the twentieth century—and soon we shall be in a position to write a social history even of Muscovite Rus without giving any thought to what Solovyev or Chicherin wrote about it; they did not know what we know. As for modern and recent history there is no argument. The history of Russia in the nineteenth century was really created by Marxists; the landlord historians and their epigones had scarcely touched it. The number of documents for this period edited by Marxists is to the number previously published as ten is to one.

Russian Marxist historiography—the child of the proletariat and of two revolutions, 1905 and 1917, in which the proletariat was the principal actor—is the second basic stage in the study of the Russian historical process. The first runs from Karamzin to Klyuchevsky. The second can by no means be considered concluded; the evolution of Russian historical literature is now proceeding parallel with the evolution of the Russian Revolution. The author began to write this book as a political exile at the height of the Stolypin reaction, about 1910. He concludes it as one of the participants in the socialist reconstruction of the country which, in 1910, was the Russian empire, and which is now the first Union of Socialist Republics on our planet. But this socialist reconstruction itself is only in its infancy. During the period of time in which this book has been written the author has more than once had to correct his whole outline. Who shall predict what form this outline will take after the final triumph of socialism? One thing may be certain: every new explanation of the Russian historical process will be more materialistic, more sustainedly *Marxist,* than its predecessor. To the historiography of the master class, which treated contemptuously the muzhik and the "non-Russian subject," unwilling to recognise revolution and speaking only of "reforms," we shall never turn back.

BIOGRAPHICAL SKETCH

MICHAEL NICHOLAEVICH POKROVSKY was born in 1868 and attended one of the best classical gymnasia in Moscow. After the completion in 1891 of his courses under the Historical-Philological Faculty in the University of Moscow, he taught history in Moscow secondary schools; from 1895 to 1902 he was lecturer in pedagogical courses in Moscow, taking an active part in the work of the Pedagogical Society. Between 1896 and 1899 he contributed a number of articles on the history of Western Europe to *Readings on the History of the Middle Ages,* edited by (Sir) Paul G. Vinogradov. Like most historians of the period Pokrovsky was somewhat under the influence of economic materialism, though only slowly attracted to Marxism. In 1903 he was forbidden by the police to give public lectures and in the following year contributed to the Bolshevik newspaper, *Pravda,* an article on *Idealism and the Laws of History.*

In 1905, roused by the events of that year of revolution, he became actively affiliated with the Bolshevik Fraction of the Social-Democratic Party, abandoning formal instruction for revolutionary literary work. In the winter of 1906-1907 he was elected a member of the Moscow Committee of the Party, and in 1907 attended the London Congress, where he was elected a member of the Bolshevik Centre. At the same time he continued his historical studies, contributing a number of articles to Granat's *History of Russia in the Nineteenth Century,* notably the ones on Alexander I, on foreign policy, on the peasant reform of 1861, and on the Decabrists. In 1908 he was compelled to emigrate, joining the "Forward" group in Paris. As an émigré he lectured in the Party schools at Capri (1909) and Bologna (1911); during the war he collaborated on the newspapers *Golos* [*Voice*] and *Nashe Slovo* [*Our Word*].

His chief work, *A History of Russia from the Earliest Times,* was written during this period of exile. The original edition (published at Moscow, 1910-1912) was in five volumes, including articles on religion and the Church written by N. M. Nikolsky and V. N. Storozhev; in the fourth (Moscow, 1922-1923) and subsequent editions all but Pokrovsky's own work is eliminated; the English edition is based on the seventh edition (Moscow, 1924-1925). In this same period Pokrovsky contributed numerous articles to Granat's *Encyclopædic Dictionary* [in

Russian] and to various periodicals; in 1914 he published the first volume of *An Outline of the History of Russian Culture.*

Pokrovsky returned to Moscow in the summer of 1917, taking an active part in revolutionary work there. Shortly after the "October" Revolution he was elected president of the Moscow Soviet of Workers' Deputies. Since the Revolution he has figured prominently in the reorganisation of higher education in Russia, having served as Vice-Commissar of Education since May, 1918. He is the organiser (1919) and president of GUS (State Council of Scholarship in the Commissariat of Education), president of the Communist Academy and editor of the *Marxist Historian* [in Russian], initiator of the *Rabfaks* [Workers' Faculties] and of the Institute of Red Professors. In 1929 he was elected a member of the Russian Academy of Sciences. Under his direction have been published a great number of documents and monographs, particularly on the history of the revolutionary movement and on foreign policy.

Among his own post-revolutionary publications may be mentioned: *Outline of the History of Russian Culture,* 2 vol., 1914-1918 (2nd ed., 1923); *France before and during the War* (a collection of articles), 1918 (3rd ed., 1924); *Russian History in its most concise outline* (a textbook highly commended by Lenin), Pts. 1-2, 1920 (7th ed., 1929), Pt. 3, 1923 (3rd ed., 1928); *The Diplomacy and Wars of Tsarist Russia in the Nineteenth Century* (a collection of articles), 1923; *The Struggle of Classes and Russian Historical Literature* (lectures), 1923 (2nd ed., 1927); *Outline of the History of the Revolutionary Movement of Russia in the Nineteenth and Twentieth Centuries,* 1924 (2nd ed., 1927); *Marxism and the Peculiarities of the Historical Evolution of Russia* (a collection of articles), 1925; *The Decabrists* (a collection of articles), 1927; *The Imperialist War* (a collection of articles), 1928.*

Not the least important of Pokrovsky's services to historical scholarship has been his reorganisation of the Central Archives, the journal of which (*Krasny Archiv*) he edits.

---

* An attempt at a complete bibliography may be found in *The Marxist Historian* [in Russian], vol. VII (September, 1928), pp. 215-231.

CHAPTER I

THE origin of the early inhabitants of Russia and the level of material civilisation to which they had attained at the dawn of Russian history offer problems that have divided historians for generations. One school of thought has held that the early Slavs were utterly uncivilised; the opposing school has maintained that they had already attained a high degree of civilisation. The controversy goes back to the eighteenth century. At that time pessimists, like Prince Shcherbatov or Schlözer, were ready to depict the Russian Slavs of the tenth century in colours borrowed from the palette of the travellers who were then creating the classic "savage," a creature little better than a quadruped. Shcherbatov pronounced the early inhabitants of Russia "a nomadic people." "Of course, there were people here," Schlözer gravely reasoned, "God knows from what times and whence; but they were people without governance, living like the birds and beasts that filled their forests." The early Russian Slavs were so much like birds and beasts that the commercial treaties which they were said to have concluded with the Greeks were deemed by Schlözer to be forgeries as naïve as any to be found in history. But other scholars regarded these same early Russian Slavs almost as enlightened Europeans in the style of their own eighteenth century. "It is not true," optimists like Boltin replied to Shcherbatov and Schlözer; "the Russians lived in an ordered society; they had towns, governance, industries and trade, intercourse with neighbouring peoples, letters and laws." And Storch, the well-known economist of the beginning of the nineteenth century, not only acknowledged that the Russian Slavs of Rurik's time had carried on trade, but even based his explanation of the rise of the Russian state on this trade and on the political order it created. Its "first beneficial consequence" was "the building of towns, which were, perhaps, indebted exclusively to it both for their rise and for their prosperity." "Kiev and Novgorod soon became entrepôts for the Levantine trade; even from the earliest period of their existence, foreign merchants settled in both these towns." This same trade

1

provoked a second and incomparably more important change, from which first arose a stable political organisation. "The enterprising spirit of the Northmen, their trade connections with the Slavs, and their frequent journeys through Russia laid the foundation for the celebrated union, which subjected a great and numerous people to a handful of foreigners." And the subsequent history of the Rus of Kiev, the expeditions of the princes to Constantinople and their struggle with the nomads of the steppe, Storch explains by these same economic factors, citing Constantine Porphyrogenitus, whose description of the trade caravans annually directed from Kiev to Constantinople has been popularised by the *Lectures* [1] of Professor Klyuchevsky.

The newly founded and closely reasoned views of Storch have in our day acquired great popularity, but they by no means convinced contemporary pessimists. Schlözer declared Storch's theory "not only an unscholarly, but a monstrous idea"; his only concession was that he began to compare the Russian Slavs with American Indians, "Iroquois and Algonquins," instead of with birds and beasts. Thus the controversy passed unsettled to the succeeding generation, in which the Slavophils took the optimistic side, while the Westerners appeared as the successors of Schlözer and Shcherbatov. "According to the testimony of all writers, both native and foreign, the Russians of old were an agricultural and settled people," says Belyaev. "In the words of Nestor, they paid tribute on *hearth* and *plough, i.e.,* on dwelling-house and on agricultural implement." The Westerners did not, it is true, go so far as either to avow the Russian Slavs to be nomads or to compare them with American Indians. But one cannot fail to note with what manifest sympathy Solovyev quotes the chronicle's characterisation of the Eastern Slavonic tribes. "Excluding the Polyans," says Solovyev, "whose customs were mild and peaceful, . . . the manners of the remaining tribes are described by him [the chronicler] in dark colours: the Drevlyans lived like cattle, slew each other, ate everything unclean, and had no marriage but the rape of maidens. The Radimiches, Vyatiches, and Severyans had similar customs; they lived in the forest like wild beasts, ate everything unclean, spoke shameful things before their fathers, and before their daughters-in-law; they had no marriage, but at games between villages the young men persuading the maidens, ravished them." Solovyev himself was probably well aware that this was not an objective description of the life of the Drevlyans and Severyans, but a malicious satire of the pagans by a monkish chronicler, and of the Polyans' hostile neighbours by a Polyan. Yet he could not resist the temptation to repeat these accusations, for they agreed much

[1] Translated by C. J. Hogarth as *A History of Russia*, by V. O. Klyuchevsky, London and New York, 1911-1926.

too well with his own picture of the Slavs. "As is evident," he says in another passage, "towns were few [among the Russian Slavs]. We know that the Slavs liked to live dispersed, in clans, for which the forests and swamps served in place of fortified towns; on the whole way from Novgorod to Kiev, along the great river-route, Oleg found but two towns—Smolensk and Lyubech. There is no mention of towns in the central tract among the Radimiches, the Dregoviches and the Vyatiches. . . ."

If any dispute be long protracted, it is usually not the disputants alone who are to blame, but the subject of dispute itself. The historical sources supplied arguments enough, both in favour of a comparatively high level of economic development and with it of every other phase of the civilisation of the early Slavs, and equally in favour of a low level of that civilisation; from one and the same chronicle we learn of the savagery of the Vyatiches with their brethren, and of the commercial treaties between the ancient Rus and the Greeks. What is to be taken as the rule, what the exception? What was merely an individual peculiarity of one tribe, and what the common inheritance of all the Slavonic tribes? In order to answer, we must draw back somewhat from the arguments exchanged by the two opposing schools. The initial chronicler, Nestor, or whatever his name, began his narrative with a catalogue of the scattered Slavonic tribes. Could we reconstruct the picture of the economic phases of the civilisation of the Slavs before they became dispersed, while they still lived together and spoke one language, we should get a certain minimum, common, of course, to all the Russian Slavs; before us would be the background on which Greek and Scandinavian influences, Christian preaching, and Levantine trade embroidered such multi-coloured patterns. With the aid of comparative philology we can to a certain degree restore this background. Cultural terms common to all the Slavonic dialects indicate their common cultural heritage and give some idea of their mode of life, not only "before the coming of Rurik," but even before the time when the "Volokhi," *i.e.*, the Romans, dislodged the Slavs from the Danube.

Philological data indicate, first of all, one characteristic feature of that archaic mode of life. The Slavs of old were predominantly, if not exclusively, engaged in the acquisition of forest products. In all Slavonic languages the words for bee, honey, and hive sound alike. Apparently, apiculture is a primitive Slavonic occupation. Indirectly this suggests the primitive habitat of the Slavs, for apiculture is conceivable only in wooded country. This forest origin of the Slavs is wholly in accord with other philological indications. The Slavonic name for a dwelling, *dom,* is unquestionably related, even though remotely, to the Medieval High German *Zimber* [building timber] and connotes, of course, a wooden structure. Masonry, on the other hand, seems to have been altogether unknown to the Slavs before their dispersion. All terms referring to it are borrowed. Russian *kirpich* [brick] is the Turkish word *kerpidz;* the ancient Slavonic *plinfa* [tile] is Greek, as are also the words for lime, the ancient *vapno* (from the Greek βαφή) and the modern *izvest* (from the Greek ἄσβεστος, unquenchable). And, whereas southern and western Europeans have a special word to designate a stone wall (Latin *murus,* whence the German *Mauer*), in Slavonic languages even to this day no special term for it exists.

Agricultural terms—to plough, to reap, to mow, the words for plough and harrow and the names of the more important kinds of grain (oats, barley, rye, and wheat)—are common to all the Slavonic stocks. Common to them also is the word for bread (*zhito*) ; most striking of all, this term (from the same root as *zhizn* [life]) is used to designate all food in general. That is to say, not only did they eat bread, but, as with the Russian peasant of to-day, bread constituted the basis of early Slavonic diet, was food *par excellence.* Should we stop here, the question of early Slavonic civilisation would no doubt have to be decided in favour of the optimistic school. But this same study of comparative philology ruthlessly destroys that pleasant illusion. The enlightened Slav agriculturists were to all appearances living in the Stone Age. All the names of metals among the Slavs are either descriptive [2] or, like the nomenclature of stone construction, borrowed.[3] The earliest Slavonic burial-places in Galicia all reveal stone implements; only in the later ones are the implements of metal.

Here, from the old point of view, we are face to face with an irreconcilable contradiction. According to that view agriculture was one of the higher economic stages of civilisation; it presupposed two earlier stages—hunting and cattle-raising. How could the Slavs have passed through this long evolution without changing even the primitive means of preparing implements from stone? Modern economic archæology and ethnology enable us to settle this seeming contradiction very easily. Observation of contemporary savages has shown quite conclusively the fallacies in the old view of economic development: hunting, cattle-raising, agriculture. The old idea was based on the perfectly sound general proposition that man first engages in those forms of economic activity that demand from him the least expenditure of energy, gradually passing to ever more and more difficult forms. But the authors of this theory had in mind only those methods of hunting, cattle-raising,

[2] *Ruda* [ore], something red, whence this word denotes both blood and hematite; *zlato* [gold], something yellow and glittering; etc.

[3] *Serebro* [silver], from the old North German *silfr*—modern German *Silber; med* [copper], from the Mediæval High German *Smide* [metal ornament]; etc.

and agriculture that are met with among so-called "historic," *i.e.*, more or less civilised, peoples. From the fact that something is easy or difficult for civilised man they deduced that it was easy or difficult for primitive man, *i.e.*, for a savage. But the savage doubtless first secured his food by means easier than the easiest of our means; he began by gathering nature's free products, the obtaining of which generally demanded no labour; he began by gathering wild fruits, roots, and similar objects. Like the higher anthropoids, man was at the outset a "frugivorous" animal. His animal food probably consisted originally of shell-fish, snails, and similar food resources, which could likewise be procured without labour. Certain Brazilian tribes, low in the scale of civilisation, have to this day not advanced beyond this "collectional" stage. The sole indication of the activity of the littoral tribes of southern Brazil consists in enormous heaps of empty shells, stretching in long rows along the seashore. At ebb-tide the natives go out on the dry sandy shore, collect the shell-fish brought in by the flood-tide, and have to be content until the following ebb-tide. This is the sum of their "hunting." In the amount of labour expended this method of securing food admits of no comparison with the present-day hunting of bird and beast or with fishing by the aid of net, hook, and other devices. Present-day fowlers and hunters by no means belong to the "lower" tribes. The inhabitants of Western Europe in the Stone Age apparently were hunters, but their implements as found in excavations astonish us by the perfection and even beauty of their finish; their representation of an elk's head or of a drove of horses on a single staff or the carving of a mammoth in bone would do honour to civilised people. Hunting is undoubtedly simpler than our agriculture with its application of animal labour; but the use of horses or oxen is not essential to agriculture, nor is it even generally customary.

Much more usual among uncivilised peoples is another form of tillage, which German investigators have christened *Hackbau* [hoe culture]. Its distinctive peculiarity lies in the fact that it is carried on entirely by human hands, almost without implements, since the primitive "hoe" was nothing more than a forked bough with which the earth was loosened before the seed was sown. Such an implement is much simpler than the bow and arrow or the sling and probably was the very earliest of man's mechanical inventions; the amount of energy demanded by hoe culture on virgin soil is, of course, considerably less than the amount of strength that must be exerted to overcome a wild beast. Hoe culture being easier than hunting, there is every reason to believe that it was the earliest of the regular methods of obtaining food. It is quite unconnected with a settled mode of life; on the contrary, it necessarily presupposes a migratory existence. Since the top soil, which alone is accessible to such cultivation, is quickly exhausted, this method of cultivation demands a comparatively vast extent of land. In early times hunting was probably auxiliary to hoe culture. The geographical environment determined further development. Tribes living in regions abounding in game or fish speedily came to regard hunting or fishing as a basic occupation and agriculture as auxiliary. On the other hand, wherever there was a rich supply of vegetative food, agriculture developed. The theory that cattle-raising grew out of hunting, serving originally as a means of having a supply of meat constantly on hand, is false. Hahn has very clearly demonstrated that the domestication of cattle of the largest and most valuable kind was connected, not with hunting but with agriculture, and that the ox served, at first, not as a meat but as a draught animal. The patriarchs of agriculture who tamed the ox did not even eat beef; to this day the very oldest agricultural peoples, the Hindus and the Chinese, do not eat it.

If we turn from these analogies and from the indirect evidence of philology to the earliest written testimony about the Eastern Slavs, to the earliest texts, we find that they fully bear out our characterisation of the early Slavs as an agricultural but culturally rather backward people. Of more or less civilised peoples the very first to come into contact with the Eastern Slavs were the Arabs, who visited Russia even earlier than did the Greeks. At least, the first eyewitnesses to describe the Slavs' manner of life and culture were Arab travellers, whose narratives may be found in the compilations of the Arab geographers. One of the most important pieces of testimony of this sort occurs in the *Book of Precious Treasures,* by the compiler Ibn-Dasta, who wrote in the first half of the tenth century, though his sources are considerably earlier. In view of the importance of this text, we shall quote from it to illustrate the economic aspects of the civilisation of the Eastern Slavs, the name of whose capital town is given by Ibn-Dasta as "Kuyaba," *i.e.,* Kiev. "The country of the Slavs is a level and forested country; they live in the forests. They have neither vineyards nor ploughed fields. From a tree they prepare a kind of pitcher in which they have hives for bees, and the bees' honey is preserved. Among them this is called *sidzh,* and one pitcher contains about ten cups. They pasture swine after the manner of sheep. . . . [The narrative continues with a description of the burial customs prevalent among the Slavs.] For the most part they sow millet. . . . They have few draught animals, while riding-horses belong only to the one man mentioned [the serene ruler]. . . . In their country the cold is so severe that every one digs out for himself in the earth a kind of cellar, to which he adds a wooden sharp-pointed roof like [the roof] of a Christian church; and on the roof he lays earth. Into these cellars they move with their whole family; taking firewood and stones, they kindle a fire, heating the stones red-hot. When the stones are aglow, they pour water on them which gives off steam, making the dwellings so warm that they take off their clothes."

Some things in this tale, which evidently were not sufficiently clear to the author himself, can be ascribed to simple misapprehension. Thus, writers have long since noted that for the Slavonic mead Ibn-Dasta adopts the name given to this beverage among the Bolgars of the Volga, the nearest intermediaries of the Arabs in their relations with the Eastern Slavs. Quite obvious, too, is the confusion, in the last lines, of the Slavonic dwelling, the mud hut, with the bath-house so well known to us from other contemporary descriptions. At first glance it may seem that the sharp contradiction of the two phrases, "they have no ploughed fields" and "they sow millet," springs from a similar mis-apprehension. But the mention of "vineyards" in connection with ploughed fields shows clearly that from Ibn-Dasta's point of view this was no misapprehension. By "ploughed fields" the Arab writer under-stood fields on which agriculture is carried on year in and year out, as vineyards are cultivated year in and year out. He did not find such permanent ploughed fields among the Slavs, who lived in the forest and sowed their millet on new ground each year. This circumstance explains also our author's statement concerning the backwardness of cattle-raising among the Slavs. As yet it was only in the initial stage, though for the twelfth century we have indubitable evidence of the fact that ploughing with the aid of horses was universal in southern Rus. The late introduction of cattle-raising and the consequent high price of cattle have left an interesting trace in early Russian codes of law. In certain articles of the *Russkaya Pravda* the word "cattle" is used in the sense of "money" (analogous is the ancient Roman *pecunia*); but we know that usually the articles that become money, or units of exchange, are those for which the demand is great, but of which the supply is limited. Consequently, in ancient Greece the first coin was an iron bar (*obol*), a metal then still rare and costly. In Russia draught cattle were just as rare and costly in the ninth and tenth centuries as they had been in the Greece of Homer; in both instances, therefore, all values were reckoned in terms of cattle. It was for this reason that the *Russkaya Pravda* gave so much attention to the increase of cattle [4] and in addition allotted a conspicuous place [5] to the swine Ibn-Dasta men-tioned.

The characteristics of the Slavs as a *forest* people, living primarily

[4] In the so-called "Karamzin" copy this subject is allotted no less than eight distinct articles.

[5] Three articles out of eight.

by *apiculture,* are brought out in strong relief by the Arab geographer. Yet, curiously enough, Ibn-Dasta does not even mention hunting, another occupation that would seem no less natural in a "forested" country. It is, of course, difficult to imagine that before the beginning of the tenth century the Russian Slavs did not hunt at all, but it is obvious that bee-keeping, swine-raising, and nomadic agriculture truly constituted the basis of their economy; hunting as an occupation did not attract such notice as it did in the case of the neighbouring Bolgars, concerning whom the Arab writer noted that "among them marten pelts constitute the chief wealth." The Bolgars were already much more active in Eastern trade, and furs were their principal export. It is probable that, in connection with this Eastern trade, hunting was acquiring serious economic importance among the Eastern Slavs. But to make hunting the basis of their whole economy, as certain authors have done in recent times, would be rash in the face of direct evidence to the contrary both from comparative philology and from Arab writers, the source of the earliest systematic information about the Russian Slavs.

Earliest social organisation is closely related to the means of obtaining food. This organisation is described by the *Initial Chronicle* in a famous passage: "Living alone with his own clan in their own locality, and ruling alone his own clan"—a characterisation which has served as the point of departure for many of the more or less fantastic hypotheses about the primitive social organisation of the Russian Slavs. It was obvious that this passage referred to some sort of union of relatives, but it was not so clear what bound the members together, apart from blood relationships, which in themselves do not prevent people from living apart and occupying themselves with various matters. Especially did the idealistic viewpoint of Russian historians—their habit of explaining all historical changes by changes in the thoughts and feelings of the historical actors—prevent them from forming a concrete and precise idea of the "clan" of the *Initial Chronicle.* Such an intelligent historian as Solovyev, for example, indulges in long arguments about the rôle played in primitive society by the sense of kinship, its gradual decline, and the consequences. The inadequacy of such discussions was too obvious, and the "theory of clan life" gave way to other hypotheses no more valuable. But even before the materialistic viewpoint had gained the upper hand in the social sciences, the method of historical analogy, an example of which we have seen above, had permitted considerable clarification of the whole subject. In certain parts of the Russian plain the natural environment of the ninth and tenth centuries was preserved almost inviolate until comparatively recently. Such were: the Great Russian North (the modern province of Archangel) until the seventeenth century and West Russian Polesia until approximately the sixteenth century. It is very significant that in these two localities, quite remote from each other and never in communication, we find the basic unit of economic, and of social organisation in general, absolutely identical; in the North it bears the name *"pechishche,"* in the West *"dvorishche."*

"Dvorishche" and "pechishche" alike are primarily forms of collective landholding, but quite unlike the types of collective landholding known to us, such as the Great Russian village-commune (*mir*). In the *mir*, as it existed until the beginning of the twentieth century, collectivism was confined to juridical and financial relationships; the peasant members of the commune were joint holders of the land and were jointly responsible for the taxes and dues imposed on it, but they carried on their economy individually. In dvorishche landholding we have a survival of genuine communism. Originally all the inhabitants of the North Russian dvorishche, sometimes many tens of workers of both sexes, lived together under one roof in that large two-storied hut still to be seen in the North, in the provinces of Olonets or Archangel. This hut was "a real palace compared with the South Russian hovels," according to Alexandra Yefimenko, the scholar to whom Russian science is indebted for the first accurate description of the earliest form of Russian landholding. Later, perhaps, the group might distribute itself among several huts, but without changing the economic basis of the organisation. As before, the whole dvorishche jointly cultivated the land as a common holding, and all the workers jointly enjoyed the products. Its economy was not confined to agriculture. In extant documents the "dvorishche" is always mentioned "with fields, hay-meadows, and with woods and pineforest, and with a bee-tree, with rivers and lake . . . , with the catching of fish and birds. . . ." Everything necessary for the maintenance of life was secured by common labour; but the most durable bond of union of the entire population of the dvorishche was undoubtedly agriculture, since the group could have no task more difficult than the clearing away of a piece of forest for plough-land; in historic times a field of the customary type was cultivated, not with a forked bough but with a plough, and not by manual labour alone but with the aid of a horse. Neither "fish- and bird-catching" nor apiculture in themselves required or could create communism; communism could arise only parallel with agriculture, and it became more stable as the latter became more complicated and more difficult. Wandering hunters, as the Russian Slavs have sometimes been depicted, would have proved great individualists.

Every primitive social organisation grows up on the basis of a common economic interest. It would be very naïve to think of primitive men as peaceful toilers reverently respecting the fruits of others' labour. No family could be sure of enjoying the produce of its labour unless it could defend it by force from the attacks of neighbours; to use present-day terminology, the relations between neighbours were "international." "And there was no law among them, and clan rose against clan, and there was great dissension among them, and wars against each other most frequently," is the *Chronicle's* description of the condition of the Slavs before the "calling of the princes." [6] In actual fact these conditions remained the norm of inter-family relations even after the coming of the princes, until economic interests appeared wider than those of the family and on the basis of which a wider organisation could be formed. The *Russkaya Pravda* ascribed the abolition of blood vengeance to the sons of Yaroslav the Wise (died 1054), which means that in the time of Yaroslav, *i.e.*, down to the middle of the eleventh century, blood vengeance existed; in other words, private warfare between families was tolerated. Thus, economic organisation of the family presupposed military organisation for protection of the products of the family's economy. Survivals of this military family organisation can be clearly seen in the *Chronicle*. For example, in narrating how Svyatoslav (964-972) vanquished the Greeks and took tribute from them, the chronicler notes: "he took tribute also for his slain, saying, 'this their clan takes.' "

If we add that, besides visible and tangible foes, primitive man saw behind every phenomenon inimical to his economy foes invisible, "forces not of this world," we can form a fairly clear idea of what the primitive great family, the dvorishche or pechishche, was like at the dawn of historic times. The members of such a family were workers in one economy, soldiers of one detachment, and, finally, worshippers of one and the same family gods, participants in a common cult. This gives us the key to the position of the father of such a family. Least of all was he the "father" in our sense of the word. The direction of the whole family economy and the necessary maintenance of military discipline put tremendous power in his hands. To this real authority his position as priest of the family cult added all the force of primitive superstition. The father alone walked with the gods, *i.e.*, with the spirits of ancestors; his authority "of this world" was augmented by all the colossal force of those members of the family "not of this world." Resistance to the master of the house was out of the question; the father-master was an autocrat in the broadest sense of the word. He disposed of all the members of the family as of his own property; he could slay or sell son or daughter, as one might sell pig or goat. Hence, in the primitive family there was no possibility of drawing a line of demarcation between the members of the family and the slaves, and there was a common name

[6] The conventional term for the "invitation" to Rurik and his brothers (862); this incident used to be regarded as the starting point of Russian history. *Cf. infra.*

for both. The ancient Roman *familia* really denoted "slaves of one master"; the ancient Russian household was called *chad, chadi* [children] of their lord; and even now the word *domochadtsy* applies not only to the relatives of the master of the house, but also to his servants. The serfs used to call their landlord "little father"; similarly, in the ancient Russian family the son addressed his father as "lord little father," as the ancient Russian bondsman styled his master "lord." And for him the master actually was a lord in our sense of the word; he judged and punished his bondsman, not only for delinquencies and negligence in the seignorial economy, but also for offences against society. The representatives of public authority could not pronounce sentence on a bondsman without consulting his lord and master. On the other hand, they did not feel that they had the right to interfere with a sentence pronounced by the lord upon his own bondsman. "And whatsoever lord, becoming angry, strikes his bondsman or bondsmaid, and death ensues, the *namestniks* [local agents of the prince] shall not try him, nor find him guilty," says the Dvina Charter (fourteenth century). Written law preserved traces of such rights of the father in respect to his children down to the time of Peter the Great; his *Military Article* did not consider as murder the whipping to death of one's child. Popular psychology is even more archaic than written law; among Siberian peasants as late as the middle of the nineteenth century the conviction prevailed that for the murder of a son or daughter the parents were liable only to penance inflicted by the Church.

The oldest type of state authority developed directly from paternal authority. Though ramifying naturally, the family might under favourable circumstances preserve its economic unity or, at least, its former military and religious organisation. Thus was formed the tribe, the members of which were linked by common kinship and consequently by common authority. This natural growth was often aided artificially by fate, for, given the constant quarrels, one family might subdue one or several others. If the victory was complete and decisive, the vanquished were without much ado converted into slaves; but if they preserved some means of resistance, the conquerors made a concession. The vanquished family preserved its own organisation but accepted a subordinate relationship to the conqueror; it was subjected to certain obligations, *viz.*, tribute (*dan*), and was converted into the conqueror's subjects (*poddannye*—i.e., men under tribute). Similar relations might, of course, be formed in exactly the same way between two tribes. In this case, the power of the father-master of the conquering tribe extended also over the members of the vanquished tribe.

The princes of the twelfth century were not the descendants of local patriarchal rulers, but newcomers. Whence they came is evident enough from their names; in the Rurik, Igor, and Oleg of the *Chronicle* it is not difficult to recognise Hrörekr, Ingvar and Helgi. As late as the tenth century they spoke a language different from that of the native population, a language which they called "Russian." Constantine Porphyrogenitus cites a number of such "Russian" names for the cataracts of the Dnieper; they may all be explained through the Swedish language.[7] The philological evidence is so complete that it is quite superfluous to resort, as many polemicists have done, to the more than doubtful testimony of mediæval chroniclers; the "Rus" were certainly of Scandinavian origin.

According to the *Chronicle* the relations of the "Rus" with the Slavs began with the Varangians who came from beyond the sea and took tribute from the northwestern tribes, Slavonic and Finnish. At first the population submitted. Later they drove out the Northmen, but apparently did not feel sufficiently strong to keep them out. The Slavs were constrained to invite one of the Varangian *kunnings* with his band to defend them from other bands of Northmen. This cannot be characterised as anything but conquest in its mildest form, where the vanquished tribe were not exterminated but converted into "subjects." The story of how Igor (912-945) collected tribute from the Drevlyans is enough to destroy any doubt as to the nature of his rule. "Behold, prince," said the *druzhina* [retinue] to Igor, "what rich vestments and arms the men of Sveneld have. Let us go for tribute, and thou shalt gain, and we." This means that it was possible to demand tribute at any time—as soon as the taker of tribute felt a void in his pocket. Appetite grows with eating; Igor was unwilling to retire when he had collected the usual tribute. "Do you go home," he said to the druzhina, "while I go [for tribute], I will go again." In this case the measure of the tribute was the patience of the local inhabitants, and for once it did not endure. "Does the wolf keep company with the lambs," said the Drevlyans, "he carries off the whole flock if he be not killed; so also this man, if he be not slain, will ruin all of us." And they sent to him to say: "Why dost thou come again? Didst thou not take all the tribute?" Igor did not heed the warning and was slain. His widow avenged his death cruelly but did not venture to continue his policy. Reconquering the Drevlyan land, she "established regulations and terms"; the amount of the tribute was fixed.

The history of Igor gives us an extraordinarily clear picture of the "rule" of an Old Russian prince over his "subjects." We see that there can be no talk of any "beginnings of the state," supposedly imported by the princes from beyond the sea. The Russian princes, in

---

[7] *Cf.* V. Thomsen, *The relations between ancient Russ and Scandinavia, and the origin of the Russian state*, Oxford, London, 1877.

their homeland beyond the sea, had been patriarchal rulers like their Slavonic contemporaries. Their Scandinavian name, *kunning,* means precisely "father of the big family," from *kunne,* family. And they came to the Slavs "with their kin"; this was an emigration of a whole tribe, small though it was. It was quite natural that the authority of these newly arrived princes should assume a clearly patriarchal character, which persisted not only in the Kievan period but much later also. The tsar of the Muscovite Rus in the sixteenth and seventeenth centuries displays many traits of the "master-father," the Varangian *kunning* originally called "to rule the Rus."

With the rôle of the prince in tribal religion we shall not deal here. Nor is there need to dilate on the military significance of the Old Russian prince, or, in later times, of the Muscovite tsar; this aspect bulks too large in the elementary text-books. Far more important and better defined for Old Russian law is the peculiarity by which the prince (and later the Muscovite sovereign) was the proprietor of his whole state in his private capacity, just as the father of the patriarchal family was the proprietor of the family itself and of everything pertaining to it. In the wills of the princes of the fourteenth and fifteenth centuries this is such a marked feature that it would be impossible to ignore it; and it has long been known that Ivan Kalita (1328-1341) made no distinction between his suzerainty over his capital town of Moscow as prince and his property rights in his table service as a private individual. But it would be a great mistake to suppose that this confusion resulted from decline of the "state significance" of the prince's authority during the obscure "appanage period" between the fall of Kiev in the thirteenth century and the rise of Moscow in the fifteenth century. Juridically this condition held throughout all Old Russian history.

From this blending of private and public right ensued the consequence that the prince was the proprietor in private right of all the territory of his principality. Since they were constantly moving from one place to another, the princes paid little attention to this aspect of their rights. But when, in northeastern Rus, they had become fixed in definite localities, this right immediately found practical application. When a Muscovite peasant of the fifteenth and sixteenth centuries was asked on whose land he lived, the usual answer was: "This is the land of the sovereign grand prince, but of my holding," or, "The land is God's and the sovereign's, but the ploughed land and the rye are ours." A private individual could have only a temporary land tenure, for the prince was the proprietor.

CHAPTER II

FEUDALISM IN EARLY RUS

THE social order considered in Chapter I was more primitive than that existing in Russia at the dawn of historic times. Of that primitive order only vestiges had been preserved, obstinate and tenacious enough, it is true, and surviving in out-of-the-way corners almost to our own day. But the every-day life of early Rus belonged to a later stage of social development. This later stage, which arose directly from the relationships which we have called "primitive," Western European historians and sociologists long ago christened "feudalism." Nationalistic Russian historians, striving to prove that in the history of Russia everything was "unique," original, and unlike the history of other nations, have even denied the existence of feudalism in Russia and have succeeded in instilling into more than one generation of the reading public the celebrated and now classical antithesis of the Europe of stone and the Russia of wood—Europe cut up by mountains and seas into many tiny fragments, in every corner of which sat its "feudal robber," stubbornly and successfully resisting every attempt at centralisation; Russia, level, uniform over its whole expanse, knowing no feudal castles, as it knows neither seas nor mountains, and by its very nature, it seemed, destined to form a single state. This antithesis undoubtedly arose from contemplation of the landscape gliding past the window of a railway carriage rather than from scientific study of the social order. It needed but to ask what feudalism was and what were its distinctive characteristics for the comparison between the stone castle of the Western European baron and the wooden mansion of the Russian *votchinnik* [hereditary landholder] to fall away. The contemporary science of history considers neither the building-material nor the presence or absence of a mountain chain in the landscape as at all significant in defining the fundamental characteristics of feudalism. It does assign to feudalism, in the main, three fundamental characteristics: (1) the dominance of large landholding; (2) the combination of landholding and political power—a combination so stable that in feudal society it is impossible to imagine a landholder who was not in some degree a lord and a lord who was not a landholder; and (3) the peculiar relations that existed between these landholding lords, namely, a fixed hierarchy of landholders, according to which on the greatest depended lesser ones,

14

on these still lesser ones, and so on, the system as a whole resembling a ladder. The question whether feudalism existed in Russia comes down, then, to the question: Were these three fundamental characteristics present in old Russian society? If so, then one can talk as much as one likes about the uniqueness of the Russian historical process, but the existence of feudalism in Russia must be acknowledged.

Large landholding existed in Russia at a very early period. The bulk of the *Russkaya Pravda* was composed certainly not later than the thirteenth century, while individual articles are much older. Yet in it we find the large boyar's estate (*votchina*) with its indispensable attributes —steward, domestics (menials and craftsmen), and peasants bound by indebtedness to work on the lord's land (*"zakups"*). The "boyar" of the *Russkaya Pravda* is, first and foremost, a large landholder. The indirect evidence of the *Pravda* is directly confirmed in separate documents; at the end of the twelfth century a pious Novgorodan bestowed on the Monastery of the Holy Saviour two whole villages "with the domestics and with the cattle," with the livestock both four-legged and two-legged. For later centuries indications of the existence of large estates become so numerous that it is unnecessary to prove the prevalence of this phenomenon. Yet it is worth while to note the size of estates of that time and to compare them with those of our own times. In the registers of Novgorod of the fifteenth century are recorded holdings of 600, 900, and even 1,500 *desyatinas*[1] of arable land alone, not counting meadows, woods, etc. If we take into account that the woods were frequently measured, not in desyatinas but in *versts*,[2] and that the arable comprised only a small part of the whole area, we must conclude that estates of tens of thousands of desyatinas were not rare in old Novgorod. In the middle of the following (sixteenth) century the Troitsa-Sergiev Monastery had, in one locality alone, in the county of Yaroslavl, 555½ desyatinas of arable, which under the three-field system, even then prevalent in central Russia, comprised in all more than 1,600 desyatinas; in addition, it had meadows which yielded annually some 900 ricks of hay and "woods 9 versts in length and 6 versts in breadth." And this was by no means the monastery's largest holding; on the contrary, it was only a small part of its holdings; in the neighbouring county of Rostov the same monastery had, also in a single estate, some 5,000 desyatinas of arable alone, and 163 square versts of woods. At the same time in the county of Tver we find a *pomeshchik* (*i.e.*, a proprietor, not by inheritance, but of recent creation), Prince S. I. Glinsky, who held, besides the village in which his mansion stood, 65 hamlets and 61 clearings, in which there were altogether 273 peasant

[1] 1 *desyatina* = 2.7 acres.
[2] 1 *verst* = 0.66 miles.

homesteads, more than one and a half thousand desyatinas of arable, and meadows yielding some ten thousand ricks of hay. Glinsky was an important lord, a relative of the grand prince; but two of his neighbours, bearing names quite unrenowned, had 22 hamlets and 26 hamlets and 6 clearings, respectively; while in the county of Rostov we find a man, not a nobleman but a simple *dyak* [a minor official], who held 35 homesteads of peasants and cottars ploughing altogether some 500 desyatinas of land.

Not without reason have we passed from the number of desyatinas to the number of homesteads and hamlets belonging to this or that lord; otherwise the comparison would not be sufficiently clear. The point is that we should be greatly mistaken if we supposed that all these hundreds and thousands of desyatinas belonging to a single proprietor were ploughed by him for his own use, and that they constituted a single or even several large-scale economies. Nothing of the sort. Each individual hamlet, each individual peasant homestead [3] ploughed its individual portion of land, while the estate-owner himself with his bondsmen was content with a single "hamlet," or with not much more. The wealthiest landholder mentioned in the registers of Novgorod maintained an economy of his own only in the village where his mansion stood and where the amount of land under cultivation was only 20-30 desyatinas. On that estate of some 5,000 desyatinas, belonging to the Troitsa Monastery, the monastic arable proper comprised less than 200 desyatinas, although monasteries carried on what was for those times most intensive cultivation and were more progressive than other landed proprietors. Here we approach a fundamental characteristic of feudal large landholding—the combination of large-scale ownership with small-scale economy. The revenue of a wealthy lord of that time consisted for the most part, not in the products of his own arable but in what was furnished to him by peasants who, each on his own portion, carried on independent economies. The registers, especially those of Novgorod, give us an extremely realistic picture of this piecemeal collection of the large revenues of that time. One landholder received from one of his homesteads: "of grain a quarter, an equal measure of barley, an equal measure of oats, ½ ram, 1 cheese, 2 handfuls of flax, 10 eggs." Another, of a more progressive type, took from a similar peasant homestead "4½ *dengas* [4] or a fifth of grain, a cheese, a ram's shoulder, ½ sheep, 3½ handfuls of flax." Not only the products of rural economy in the narrow sense were thus obtained by the holder of the land, but

---

[3] "Homestead" and "hamlet" were often synonymous; a one-homestead hamlet was even typical. The word "homestead" is used in the broad European sense, not in the American legal sense of 160 acres.

[4] 100 *dengas* = 1 ruble.

also products that we should consider industrial; homesteads of smiths paid in axes, scythes, ploughshares, frying-pans. It is still more significant that personal services were secured in the same way; in the registers we find whole settlements, not only of grooms and huntsmen (who might be relatively large landholders) but also of actors and actresses. The dues (*obrok*) of these mediæval artists apparently consisted in the amusements they furnished their lord. The most striking example of personal services as dues from land, both in Russia and in the West, was the requirement of military service in return for land. To refuse to take note of this form of feudal due was impossible; but, treating it as different in nature from other dues, Russian historians have painted the extensive and complicated picture of the so-called "*pomestye* system." But the pomestye system represents only an especially vivid detail of the feudal system in general; the essence of the latter consisted in the fact that the landholder ceded to others his right to land in return for all manner of services and dues in kind.

Ultimately these dues took the form of money; in the registers of Novgorod we can clearly trace the conversion of natural obligations into money payments, the initiative being taken by the largest landholder, the grand prince of Moscow. Simultaneously with the appearance of money, or only a little earlier, the labour of the peasants on the lord's arable begins to play a conspicuous part in the series of natural obligations; as the demesne becomes too large to be worked by bondsmen alone, obligatory labour (*barshchina*) appears. Both money payments and labour obligations denote the rise of an entirely new phenomenon, unknown to, or playing a very secondary rôle in, early feudalism—the rise of the market, where everything could be bought and sold for money, and in any quantity desired. Only the appearance of a domestic grain market could force the landlords of the sixteenth century (whether votchinniks or pomeshchiks), to apply themselves seriously to independent economy, just as at the turn of the eighteenth century the appearance of an international grain market gave their great-great-grandsons a fresh impetus in the same direction. Only now did each extra *pud* [5] of grain become valuable, because it meant extra silver in the pocket, and because with silver one could now satisfy all one's wants, in such quantity and quality as was impossible with dues in kind. When feudalism was taking root, buying and selling were the exception, not the rule; men sold, not for gain but from need; men sold, not the products of their economy but the property which until then they had themselves enjoyed. Sale was often disguised ruin, while purchase was usually the buying of articles of luxury, since men already had articles of prime necessity and therefore did not need to purchase them; buying was not

---

[5] 1 *pud* = 36 lbs. avoirdupois.

rarely the first step on the road to ruin. Once upon a time the economic order in which men strove to get along by themselves, buying nothing and selling nothing, bore the name of "natural economy." The absence or limited circulation of money and the acquisition of all goods in kind were taken as its specific characteristics. But the absence of money was only a derivative characteristic; the essential point was the absence of exchange as a constant daily phenomenon, without which it is impossible to imagine economic life as it is to-day. The cardinal point was the isolation of individual economies and, in application to large landholding, this period is called by modern scholars the period of isolated votchina, or pomestye, economy ("manorial," as it is also sometimes called, from the name of the English mediæval votchina, the manor).

We see that this type of economy has one essential resemblance to the pechishche or dvorishche which we examined in Chapter I. In both cases a given economic group strives to satisfy all its wants from its own resources, without resorting to or needing outside assistance. But there is also a very essential difference: in the pechishche the fruits of common labour went to those who laboured, producer and consumer being fused in one narrow circle; in the votchina producer and consumer are divorced, individual petty economies producing and a special group (the votchinnik and his household of children and domestics) consuming.

How could such relationships have arisen? The basis of feudalism as a universal phenomenon has long since been pointed out by the historical literature of Western Europe. Long, long ago it described the process of the feudalisation of landed property, approximately as follows. At the very beginning of settled agriculture the land is found in the hands of those who cultivate it. The majority of scholars agree that the agricultural population then carried on its economy, not individually but by groups, and that the land belonged to these groups, that the initial form of landed property was not personal but communal property. Little by little, however, communal property disintegrated, giving way to individual property; parallel with this disintegration developed differentiation among the inhabitants of the commune. The more powerful families seized ever more and more land; the weaker lost what was originally in their hands and fell into economic, and later into political, dependence on powerful neighbours. Thus arose large feudal proprietorship with its distinctive characteristics. For certain countries— England, for example—the existence of the free commune as the primary phenomenon, of the feudal estate as the secondary, later phenomenon, is to-day considered proved. In the case of Russia the existence of the landed commune has long been disputed, and until recent times data for the settlement of the dispute have remained extremely scanty.

One of the most typical characteristics of the commune is, as is well known, redistribution. Inasmuch as in the commune not one square inch of land belongs as property to an individual person, the communal land is redistributed from time to time according to the movement of population. But in Russia until the sixteenth century only one case of land redistribution can be shown, and that was effected by a steward on the initiative, not of the peasants but of the local proprietor. In other words, feudal relationships already existed here. What preceded them? The most plausible answer will be that in Russia feudalism developed directly out of that collective landholding which we have defined as "primitive"—pechishche or dvorishche landholding. We shall remember that this peculiar "commune" was by no means that association of free and equal agriculturists depicted by certain scholars, the commune of the early Germans, for example. In the pechishche there was no individual property, for there was no individual economy; but when the latter appeared, the remembrance of equality disappeared. If two brothers formerly constituting "one family" separated, the pechishche was divided into two equal halves. But one brother might have three sons, the other one. In the following generation three of the grandsons of the one grandfather would each hold one-sixth of the hamlet, but the fourth grandson would hold a whole half. Such clear-cut examples, it is true, are rare. In view of the abundance of forest-land [6] any one who felt cramped in his native pechishche could establish a new "clearing," which soon developed into an independent hamlet. But cases in which one-third of the hamlet is found in the hands of one villager and the remaining two-thirds in the hands of another are quite common in the registers. The notion of the equal right of every one to an equal portion of land finds no support, and, we repeat, there was as yet no economic necessity for such equality.

There are any number of survivals of pechishche landholding on votchina lands in the sixteenth century. First of all, as might have been expected, the juridical form of collective family ownership proved far more persistent than its economic content. Votchina, or hereditary, land very rarely appears in the registers as the property of a single individual; far more frequently we find the land held by a group of

---

[6] It has long since been pointed out that the least settled parts of present-day Siberia offer the best analogy to early Russia in point of the extent of land. In both cases, to enter into full possession of a portion of land in the midst of the uncleared, virgin, forest, it was sufficient to "trace round" this portion, putting marks on the trees surrounding it. Such "tracing" is found both in the *Russkaya Pravda*, with its "boundary oak," for the felling of which a large fine was imposed, and in documents of the sixteenth century, in which this very word "tracing" occurs.

persons, usually near relatives, but sometimes distant ones. How un-usual in Muscovite Rus of the sixteenth century was the idea of personal land ownership is attested by the curious fact that when the grand prince began to distribute lands as pomestyes in return for service, it did not enter his head to distribute the land to individual persons, although the service itself, of course, was personal. The idea of a personal service-allotment took form only very gradually. In most cases a pomestye was held originally by a father and his sons, an uncle and his nephews, or by several brothers, jointly. Sometimes it so happened that an allotment liable to service was held by a mother and son, and, although the son was but three years old and obviously could not serve, the land was left him "until he shall ripen into service"; it was not possible to deprive the whole family of land because at the moment no member of it was capable of discharging the military obligation.

But though the juridical form remained, actually, as we have already seen, the pechishche had long since begun to crumble; signs of this crumbling are an index of the means by which the large votchina own-ership of early Russia arose no less significant than the survivals of collective holding. We have seen how in the course of a few generations a former "hamlet" is split up into fractions held by members of one family; but the colossal votchinas of the "princelings" were sometimes made up of just such fractional, tiny "morsels." [7] Sometimes, thanks to this crumbling process, the ownership of a piece of land became divided among persons of the most diverse social position. It would be very erroneous to imagine that sixteenth-century votchinniks were al-ways important lords, for a priest, a dyak, a bondsman of yesterday or even of to-day, might be a landed proprietor. The landowner, as well as the peasant, might, to rid himself of debt, give himself up in pay-ment. In such cases, to be sure, not only was the votchinnik not an eminent man, but he was, of course, not even a large landholder, else such a fate would not have overtaken him. We have seen that large-scale ownership was already dominant in the sixteenth century, but this did not at all mean that every votchina of those times was a large estate. At the time the registers were composed small property was still far from having been finally swallowed up, and in these registers at every step we meet votchinniks, independent, full, hereditary propri--etors of their land, holding no more land than a peasant might, 10 or 12

---

[7] In the county of Tver, according to the register of 1539-1540, a third of the hamlet of Bykovo belonged to Prince Boris Shchepin while two-thirds remained in the hands of the former proprietors, the Davidovs. Mitya Ryskunov had half the hamlet of Korobyno, while Prince Dmitry Punkov had the other half. Half of the hamlet of Popovo was in the hands of Fedor Rzhevsky while the other half was the "votchina of Princess Ulyana Punkova."

desyatinas of arable in three fields. Such a "landlord" could be converted into a proletarian just as could any peasant.[8]

Large-scale ownership in Russia, as everywhere in Europe, grew up on the ruins of small-scale ownership. What course did this process take? How were the small proprietors expropriated in favour of the divers Princes Mikulinsky, Punkov, and other landed magnates, of the Troitsa, Kirillov-Belozersk, and other monasteries? In the sixteenth century we see only the last links of the long chain; it is natural that they should strike us first, concealing older and perhaps far more widespread forms of expropriation. In the later period one of the most obvious forms of expropriation was the granting by the sovereign of settled lands as a votchina. Over a mass of petty, independent economies was set up one large proprietor, able to appropriate any part of the revenue of these economies. How simply this was done, a single example will show. In 1551 Tsar Ivan IV granted to the abbess of the Pokrovsky Monastery (in the county of Vladimir) twenty-one "black" hamlets, i.e., lands belonging in full ownership to peasants who paid nothing but state taxes. By one stroke of the pen these twenty-one free hamlets were converted into the feudal property of the Abbess Vasilisa and her sisters.

This wholly juridical (arch-legal, so to speak) form of the origin of large-scale ownership is so clear, so simple, and so well known to all, that there is no need to dwell on it. On the other hand, the love of the older Russian historians for everything pertaining to the "state" (not in vain were most of them pupils of Hegel, directly or indirectly) makes it necessary to emphasise the fact that forcible seizure of the land of others was by no means always clothed in such a correct garb, juridically irreproachable. One might have long to wait before the sovereign granted land; a powerful and influential man could appropriate it far more quickly by dispensing with this juridical formality. Through the registers of the sixteenth century runs a long series of such cases. For example, two brothers Dmitriev, grooms of the grand prince, petty landholders, possessed in all a single hamlet. "That hamlet had a grain field . . . and that grain field G. V. Morozov took away by force, and now Prince S. I. Mikulinsky has that grain field." The same hamlet had a piece of waste ground; "and that waste ground I. M. Shuisky took." Or, "the hamlet of Sokevitsyno . . . is deserted, and it was made desolate by Prince M. P. Repnin."

[8] In this same county of Tver the registrars found a hamlet belonging to a certain Vasyuk Fomin of which they "gave no description" for a very remarkable reason: there was nothing to describe. There not only was no economy carried on, but there was not even any building, and the votchinnik Vasyuk Fomin went around the homesteads and was fed in the name of Christ.

A judicial decision of the 1540's sheds very vivid light on these dry excerpts from Muscovite treasury records. Complaint is made by the Spassky Monastery of Yaroslavl, itself of course a large landholder, but smaller and weaker than Prince I. F. Mstislavsky, the neighbour sent it by fate. This neighbour's man, Ivan Tolochanov, having descended on the monastery's hamlets, "cast out the monastery's peasants from the hamlets"; he himself settled in one hamlet and imposed dues on the others in his own favour. But, "casting out" the peasants themselves, the new landholder by no means wished to part with their property; this he kept for himself, driving out the proprietors almost naked.

Thus, the existence of the first of the fundamental characteristics of feudalism—the dominance of large landholding—can be proved for early Rus, including the pre-Muscovite period, just as satisfactorily as for Western Europe of the eleventh and twelfth centuries. Even more indisputable is the existence of the second characteristic—the union of landholding and political authority in one indissoluble bond.

That the great hereditary-landowning aristocracy not only carried on economy and collected dues but also administered justice and collected taxes on its own lands is a fact which has never been denied in the literature of Russian history, for long since too much documentary confirmation of it was published; but, owing to the point of view usual to Russian legal-historical literature, with its emphasis on the "state," these rights have always been represented as exceptional privileges, the granting of which was an exceptional act of state authority. "These privileges were extended, not to a whole class but to individuals, and each time on the basis of special charters," says Prof. Sergeyevich in the last edition of his *Antiquities of Russian Law* [in Russian]. Nevertheless, two pages further on this same scholar finds himself compelled to draw his reader's attention to the fact that among those endowed with such privileges were, not only great men whose names were written with a "-vich" [9] but likewise mere "Dicks and Harrys." From this he quite correctly infers that "such grants constituted the general rule, not the exception," *i.e.*, that the privilege did belong to the "whole class" of landholders, not to "individuals" as a special favour of the sovereign. Still another two pages further on this same author discloses the still more curious fact that the grant might issue, not from the state authority at all but from any votchinnik. With the charter of the Metropolitan Jonas to a certain Andrew Afanasyev

[9] The suffix to the Russian patronymic. The Christian name and patronymic constitute the usual form of address in Russia; use of the Christian name alone, especially the diminutive, is derogatory. A servant would address his master as Ivan Ivanovich, where the master would call the servant Ivashka.

(1450), which he cites, may be compared a still more pronounced example of the same sort, the charter of Prince F. M. Mstislavsky to the same Ivan Tolochanov, whose exploits we have mentioned above. "Our bailiffs [and other officers] shall not go out [into the hamlets granted to Tolochanov] for any purpose," writes Prince Mstislavsky in this charter, "nor shall they make levies on them or judge his peasants, but Ivan himself or whom he pleases shall administer and judge, while if justice is to be done between his peasants and our peasants, our bailiffs shall judge them, and he shall judge with them, and the perquisites shall be divided into halves, except in cases of murder and theft, and robbery taken red-handed, and plough taxes; and whoever is at law with him, him I, Prince Fedor Mikhailovich, or whom I please, shall judge." The editor of this interesting document, Mr. Likhachev, justly remarks in his preface that this Prince Mstislavsky not only was not an independent landholder, but did not even occupy a conspicuous place among the servitors of the grand prince of Moscow; he was not even a boyar. It must be added that this land which he "granted . . . to his knight"[10] with these rights was not his by inheritance, but had been granted to him by Grand Prince Vasily III (1505-1533). And in all probability the latter considered delegation to a still lesser landholder of this "privilege" he had granted quite usual; not without reason did he himself and his father and his son give such charters to petty pomeshchiks. From the registers of the first half of the sixteenth century we have already cited the case of two grooms of the grand prince who were systematically wronged by their powerful neighbours, the boyar Morozov and the Princes Mikulinsky and Shuisky; in proof of their rights, however, these grooms produced an immunity granted by "Grand Prince Ivan Vasilyevich of All Rus" (it is not clear whether it was Ivan III or Ivan IV). A little further on in the same register we find an immunity bestowed on the holder of half a village in which there were altogether 30 desyatinas of arable land. Thus, in Russia as in Western Europe, not only a great lord but each independent landholder was a "sovereign on his own estate"; Mr. Sergeyevich is quite right when he says, not altogether in consonance with his original definition of votchina jurisdiction as an exceptional privilege of individuals, that "long before the binding of the peasants to the land the population was under the votchina jurisdiction of the landholders."

From the evolutionary point of view the origin of this "votchina

---

10 This word is employed for *syn boyarsky* (literally, "son of a boyar"), a Russian term having no biological significance. It should not conjure up any chivalric formalities, but rather the mediæval English "knight of the shire," who frequently was never knighted.

law" is quite analogous to the rise of votchina landholding; as the
latter arose from the fragments of pechishche landholding—the patriarchal form of landed property—so the former was a survival of
patriarchal law, which had not distinguished political authority from
the right of property. It may even be said that in this case there
was more than "survival"; when the grand prince of Moscow granted
"to his servitor (so-and-so) the village (such-and-such) with all that
pertained to that village, and with the grain of the earth (*i.e.*, with
the winter rye already sown), saving [the punishment of] murder
and robbery taken red-handed," then in quite "primitive fashion" he
was continuing to confound economy and state and was evidently
even regarding his state functions primarily from the economic point
of view, since to liken murder and robbery to "grain of the earth" was
only possible if he saw in the preservation of public security nothing
but revenue from judicial fees. There is no need to insist that this
assigning of especially important criminal cases to the exclusive jurisdiction of the prince's court is, of course, to be explained by the same
economic motives. Murder and robbery incurred the largest fines;
these were the fattest morsels of a prince's judicial revenue. But, if
generous, a prince might renounce even this lucre; Grand Princess
Sofia Vitovtovna in a charter to the Kirillo-Belozersk Monastery (1448-
1469) wrote: "my sheriffs and their bailiffs shall not meddle in murder
in any case." There is likewise no need to say that the grant was
itself merely a juridical formality like any grant of land. It only delimited the rights of the prince and of the private landholder, as far
as this was possible, for, thanks precisely to the confounding of political
authority and private ownership, these rights threatened to become hope-
lessly entangled. But the right did not always emanate from the prince's
authority as such; in disputes about jurisdiction and tribute, votchinniks
appealed, not only to a prince's grant but likewise, again and again,
to the immemorial nature of their rights—to "olden time." It was
thus that, for example, a boyar of Belozersk proved his rights in the
middle of the fifteenth century when the Kirillov Monastery "snatched"
his patrimonial hamlet "from jurisdiction and tribute." What was
true of "jurisdiction and tribute," *i.e.*, of judicial fees and direct imposts, was true also of indirect imposts. We find private toll-houses
not only in princes' votchinas, where they might be taken as a survival
of sovereign rights once belonging to the holder, but also on the domains
of ordinary pomeshchiks whom even a simple Muscovite official, a dyak,
might sometimes outrage with impunity. From a complaint of one
such pomeshchik of Ryazan, Shilovsky, who had been outraged by a
dyak, in the second half of the sixteenth century, we learn that on
his and his brothers' votchina "on their banks they load grain into

boats; they take from an *okova* [11] a denga each, and they take toll from a big boat at 4 *altyns* [12] each, but from a small boat one altyn, and of that toll half goes to the Telekhovsky Monastery." Even customs tolls might be halved with a neighbour, as judicial fees sometimes were.

A "sovereign on his own estate" could not, of course, get along without the chief attribute of "sovereignty"—military force. Even the *Russkaya Pravda* speaks of the "boyar's druzhina" as well as of the prince's druzhina. Documents of a later time usually give specific confirmation of the general evidence of the earliest code of Russian law. In the personnel of the household of a wealthy hereditary landowner of the fifteenth and sixteenth centuries we find along with cooks and butlers, huntsmen and buffoons, also armed domestics serving their lord "on horseback and in full panoply." "As to my men in full and partial bondage, and under indenture," writes V. P. Kutuzov in his will (about 1560), "all these men shall be free, and as to the clothes and gear and sabres and saddles that they have of my giving, these shall be theirs, and my stewards shall give to my man, Andryusha, a horse with saddle and bridle, and a quilted hauberk, and a helmet. . . ." Such a *druzhinnik* of an hereditary landowner by virtue of his profession certainly stood higher than a simple domestic. He could render his lord services that it was impossible to forget and could raise himself to the position of a privileged member of the household, almost of a free servitor. This Andryusha had, besides his master's, also a "horse of his own purchase" and some furnishings, and V. P. Kutuzov is very careful that his executor should not confound this property with that of the master. To just this category, in all probability, belonged those bondsmen on wages mentioned in the will of another votchinnik, Prince I. M. Glinsky. Asking his executor, Boris Godunov, "to give allotments to my men, according to the books, whatever of my paying went to them," the testator further says of these men that they are to be set free "with all that with which they served me"; but it cannot be admitted that the cook was freed with the kitchen in which he worked, or the huntsman with the pack of hounds he took care of. Such an expression might be used only of men who served their lord on horseback and in full armour; in another will (of Pleshcheyev) the reservation is frankly made, "not to give them [the bondsmen] horses." Glinsky was more liberal to his former comrades-in-arms and even bequeathed a hamlet to one of them as a votchina. But a bondsman might get such a piece of land from his master even in the latter's lifetime. According to a register of Tver of the first half of the sixteenth century, Sozon, a "man" of Prince D. I. Mikulinsky, occupied one quarter of the hamlet

---

[11] An obsolete measure of volume.
[12] An old coin equal to 3 copecks (0.03 rubles).

of Tolutino. For such a servant settled on a piece of land to become an actual noble with a small estate was but a step. In the complaint of the Spassky Monastery against Ivan Tolochanov, twice mentioned above, he is called the "man" of Prince I. F. Mstislavsky, but the latter's father in the charter calls Tolochanov his "knight," *i.e.*, a noble. Thus, imperceptibly, the higher members of the armed household passed into the lower stratum of the military-serving class; on one side of a fine line stood the bondsman, on the other the vassal.

The existence of such vassalage among Russian large landholders of the sixteenth century—the existence of free votchinniks performing military service in return for their land, on their own horses and sometimes with their own armed bondsmen, not to the grand prince of Moscow but to "private individuals"—is irrefutably proved by the same register of the county of Tver which we have more than once mentioned above. In this book (composed about 1539) are enumerated 574 votchinniks, for the most part petty ones. Of them 230 served the grand prince, 126 served private proprietors of different categories, and 150 served no one. Of the 126 "subvassals" of the Muscovite feudal aristocracy, sixty served the bishop of Tver, and thirty Prince Mikulinsky. From other sources we know that metropolitans [13] and bishops had in their service, not only simple "servants" but also actual boyars. "The boyars of the prelates," says a historian of the Russian Church cited by Pavlov-Silvansky, "in ancient times were in no way different from the boyars of the princes in respect to their origin and social position. They entered on service to prelates exactly in the same way and on the same terms as to princes, *i.e.*, with an engagement to fulfil a military obligation and to perform service at the prelate's court, in return for which they received from him land in usufruct." On these lands they might settle their own military servitors, while their own lord, in his turn, was a vassal of the grand prince. The military druzhina of the metropolitan had to take the field together with the druzhina of the grand prince; "in case of war, when I myself, the grand prince, shall mount my horse, so also [shall] the boyars and servitors of the metropolitan," says a charter of Grand Prince Vasily I (about 1400). Thus, in the service of the grand prince of Moscow was set up the same ladder of vassals as in the service of a mediæval king of France.

The character of the relationships between the individual rungs of this ladder—between the free military servitors of the various grades and their corresponding suzerains—has been studied in detail by the late N. Pavlov-Silvansky, who summarised the whole of his special la-

---

[13] The head of the Russian Church, ranking above archbishops and bishops, bore the title of "metropolitan" until 1589, when the metropolitan was elevated to the rank of patriarch.

bours in his popular little book, *Feudalism in Ancient Rus* [in Russian]. "The official contract of vassalage was validated by analogous ceremonies [in Russia] and in the West," says the author. "The ceremony of homage, which in the feudal period validated the contract of vassalage, as well as the early ceremony of commendation, of committing, consisted in the vassal, in token of his submission to the lord, kneeling before him and putting his clasped hands in the hands of his seignior; sometimes, in token of still greater submission, the vassal, kneeling, put his hands under the feet of the seignior. [In Russia] corresponding exactly to this ceremony we find the ceremony of beating the forehead; the boyar beat his forehead on the ground before the prince in token of his subjection. In later times the expression 'to beat the forehead' was used in the figurative sense of an humble request; but in the appanage period this expression denoted actual beating of the forehead, bowing to the ground, as is evident from the customary designation of entry into service by the words: 'beat the forehead into service. . . .' In the second half of the appanage period the mere ceremony of beating the forehead was already accounted insufficient for the validating of the service contract, and to this ceremony was added a church rite, the kissing of the cross. A similar church oath to bind the feudal contract, sworn on the Gospels, on relics, or on a cross, was performed in the West as a supplement to the old ceremony of commendation or homage." "Our boyars' service is so close to vassalage that in our antiquity we even find terms corresponding exactly to Western ones: *prikazatsya = avouer, otkazatsya = se désavouer.*" As an example of the former, the author cites the contemporary formula of the tidings of the submission of the military servitors of Novgorod to Ivan III: "There beat the forehead to the grand prince into service the boyars of Novgorod and all the knights and the men of substance, and having avowed themselves they went out from him." A good example of the second term (disavow) is the story in the biography of Joseph of Volokolamsk of how this abbot, having a disagreement with the local prince of Volokolamsk, transferred from him to the grand prince of Moscow: Joseph "disavowed his lord for the great lordship." A passage in the *Nikonovsky Chronicle* has preserved for us the very formula of such a disavowal. In 1391 Prince Vasily I of Moscow, son of Dmitry Donskoi, having bought the principality of Nizhny-Novgorod from the Tatars, moved on that town with his warriors in order to give effect to the "right" he had just acquired. Prince Boris of Nizhny-Novgorod, having decided to resist to the last ditch, assembled his druzhina and addressed it in these words: "My lords and brothers, boyars and others: remember the kissing of the Lord's cross, how ye have kissed it to me, and our love and fostering toward you." At first, the boyars, resenting the rude affront offered to their prince, eagerly defended his cause. "We are all unanimously for thee," declared the senior boyar, Vasily Rumyanets, "and ready to give up our heads for thee." But Moscow in alliance with the Tatars was a dread force; resistance to her threatened final destruction to those who resisted. When the first animation had subsided, the boyars of Nizhny decided that their prince's cause was lost in any case. They therefore proposed to "disavow" Prince Boris and to go over to his antagonist. The same Vasily Rumyanets, on behalf of all, announced to the unfortunate Boris the change of attitude. "Lord Prince!" he said, "rely not on us, already we are not thine, and there is none with thee, but we are against thee." In quoting these words, the historian of Russian feudalism [Silvansky] adds, "Exactly so in the West, the vassal, renouncing his lord, openly said to him: 'I will not be loyal to thee, I will not serve thee, and will not be bound by loyalty. . . .'"

The case just cited clearly illustrates the peculiarities of the régime out of which grew Muscovite Rus, and which long survived beneath the mantle of Byzantine autocracy officially adopted by the Muscovite state at the beginning of the sixteenth century. All historians have long been agreed that it is impossible to conceive of a prince of the Kievan epoch without his boyars. The case of Prince Vladimir Mstislavich is usually cited as an example. When he undertook an expedition without the consent of his boyars, they said to him: "Of thyself, Prince, hast thou devised this, but we do not go according to thy opinion, we knew nothing of this." But even the "gatherers"[14] of Muscovite Rus should not be thought of as acting alone; not without reason did Dmitry Donskoi, in taking leave of his boyars, call to mind that he had done everything jointly with them—had vanquished the pagans, had done deeds of valour with them in many lands, had made merry with them, and had sorrowed with them—"and you were called, under me, not boyars but princes of my land." Just as at the head of every feudal state in Western Europe there stood a group of persons—the sovereign, king or duke, the "suzerain," with the "curia" of his vassals—so at the head of the Russian "appanage" principality, and later of the Muscovite state as well, there likewise stood a group of persons—the prince, later grand prince and tsar, with his *duma* of boyars. And just as the Western European feudal "sovereign" in unusual and in especially important cases was not content with the counsel of his immediate vassals, but convoked the representatives of all feudal society—the "estates of the realm"—so also in Russia the prince in

---

[14] The conventional interpretation of early Russian history was that the grand principality of Kiev fell apart in the "appanage period" and that Russia was "gathered" together again by the princes of Moscow, sprung from Ivan Kalita.

early times sometimes took counsel with his druzhina, and the tsar with the *zemsky sobor* [assembly of the land]. We shall later have occasion to study both of these institutions in greater detail. Meanwhile let us note only that the roots of the one and of the other—both of the duma and of the sobor—lie deep in that feudal principle which says that from a free servitor can be demanded only that service for which he contracted, and that he can abandon this service whenever he finds it disadvantageous. Hence any important matter that might have repercussions on the fate of his servitors could not be undertaken by the feudal lord without their assent.

How stable was this "social contract" between vassal and suzerain in feudal society? Mediæval contractual relations are very easily subject to idealisation. The "rights" of free servitors are very often conceived in the form of and similar to "rights" as they exist in the modern state governed by "law." But we know that in this latter the rights of the weaker are frequently protected only on paper, while in fact "might makes right." To the feudal state this was applicable in far greater degree; the contractual relations of vassal and suzerain were really far more like the norms of present "international law," which only he who cannot does not violate. In compacts between princes it was all very well to write, "To boyars and servitors our boundaries shall be free at will"; but in practice, ever and anon, it happened that the prince "plundered those boyars and knights" who had "departed" from him "and seized their villages and their homes and took their chattels and all that remained and their cattle." And no court and no justice could be found against him except by appealing to another, still mightier, arbitrary power. In feudal society, far more even than at present, might always took precedence over right. It is easy to be carried away by a study of the complicated ceremonial of feudal relations and to think that men who had so carefully ordered what gestures were to be made in such and such a case and what words uttered would know just as carefully how to preserve the reality of their rights. But how they were to defend their rights from abuses by the feudal lord, when they were to protect them from the attempts of his lesser servitors, were sometimes matters beyond their strength. We cannot conclude our study of the juridical régime of feudal Rus better than by an illustration borrowed from the same series of court decisions from which we have repeatedly taken examples above. In 1552 the Nikolsky Monastery was engaged in a law suit with its neighbours, the Arbuzovs. "There judged us, O lord," write the elders of the monastery in their petition, "according to the lord tsar's writing, Fedor Morozov and Khomyak Chechenin." The judges upheld the monastery and found its opponents at fault.

"And behold," continue the elders, "there came, lord, upon this hamlet, the Ilyins, sons of Arbuzov . . . and the Ilyins, the men of Arbuzov . . . , beat and robbed me, Mitrofanov, O lord, and Brother Daniel and Brother Tikhon, and the dyak of the monastery, and the servitors, and the peasants, and the peasant women they beat and robbed, and the old-dwellers,[15] O lord, who were with the judges on the land, they beat. And the judge, O lord, Khomyak Chechenin, with the knights who were with us on the land went out to rescue [the injured old-dwellers], and they, O lord, beat both Khomyak Chechenin and the knights. . . . While the abbot, O lord, with the judge, with Fedor Morozov, barricading themselves, sat it out. . . ." It was not always comfortable to decide a case against the interest of a pugnacious feudal lord. Western European feudal law clothed this rough law-breaking in a rather solemn ceremony; a man dissatisfied with a judicial decision could "repudiate the decision" (*fausser le jugement*) and challenge the judge to a duel. In a law suit of the year 1531 the judge rejected the testimony of one of the litigants, who asserted that a document referred to by the judge had never been in the case. "And in place of Oblyazov [the ligitant] his man, Istoma, asked the field with Sharap [the judge] . . . and Sharap took the field with him." To challenge the judge to a duel was possible in the Muscovite state even in the time of Vasily III (1505-1533).

For this reason the contract—a juridical concept—should not be numbered among the chief distinctive features of feudalism. Feudalism is far more a system of economy than a system of law. The state here merged with the lord's economy; into one and the same centre flowed dues in kind and judicial revenues, frequently in one and the same form, rams, eggs, and cheese; from one and the same centre came both the steward—to redivide the land—and the judge—to decide a dispute about this land. When the circle of economic interests had extended beyond the limits of a single estate, the sphere of law likewise had to be geographically extended. Such extension first took place when out of the *"volosts"* [domains] of private landholders grew the volosts of towns [town-provinces]; it took place a second time when Moscow "gathered" all the private votchinniks under her own hand. In both cases quantitative brought on qualitative change: the territorial extension of authority changed the nature of that authority; the "estate" was converted into the "state." The earlier of these conversions proceeded quite rapidly; on the other hand, it was not very lasting. The later one was very slowly accomplished; but, on the other hand, the final formation of the Muscovite state, in the seventeenth century,

---

[15] Peasants who had lived on an estate for a long period; their exact status is uncertain.

was also the final liquidation of Russian feudalism in its earliest form. Yet right up to that moment feudal relationships constituted the basis on which were erected both political superstructures—the volost of the towns and the votchina of the tsars of Moscow. Both Lord Novgorod the Great and his successful rival, Grand Prince Ivan III of Moscow, ruled, as we must steadfastly bear in mind, not a colourless mass of subjects equally devoid of rights but a variegated feudal world of great and small "lordships," in each of which sat its petty sovereign, able behind the forests and swamps of northern Rus to maintain his independence no less well than could his Western comrade behind the stone walls of his castle.

CHAPTER III

THE chief economic characteristic of the "feudal" order which we have just studied was the absence of exchange. The boyar's votchina of "appanage Rus" was an economically self-sufficient unit. One can quite justly say of it, as one historian has said, not quite so justly, of the pomestye estate of the central zone of Russia in the eighteenth century, that, if all the world around it should fall away, it would continue to exist as if nothing had happened. Such a conception of ancient Rus hardly fits in, of course, with that interpretation of early Russian history which might be called the conventional one. This interpretation has already been mentioned, in connection with the views of Storch and his modern imitators. We shall remember that this school considered trade—*i.e.*, exchange—the axis around which the whole political history of the Kievan period revolved, and to which the early Russian "state" was indebted for its very existence. Such a "philosophy of Russian history" seems to stand in irreconcilable contradiction to the facts we have just examined. What significance can trade have in view of the dominance of "natural economy," uninterrupted for many centuries? This *a priori* consideration is apparently so irresistible that one of the representatives of the materialistic tendency in Russian history, N. Rozhkov, has brought himself to declare flatly and in entire contradiction to the "conventional" view that "in Kievan Rus trade was weak. Natural economy prevailed, and only foreign trade had any influence on the economic position of the upper strata of society." The simplicity and plausibility of this view has won the sympathy even of scholars far removed from the materialistic conception of history. The modern investigator of *The Princely Law of Ancient Rus* [in Russian], A. Presnyakov, justifies his radical departure from Professor Klyuchevsky's interpretation, as follows: "It [the customary interpretation] is based on an extreme exaggeration of the depth of the influence exerted by trade on the tribal life of Eastern Slavdom." In support of his view this author gives a rather long excerpt from the works of the materialistic historian just mentioned.

Nevertheless, a number of phenomena in early Kievo-Novgorodan history—the social groupings that we find in Kiev and Novgorod, the forms of authority, so unlike anything before or since, and, finally,

32

many things in the economic life of this period—all this will be quite incomprehensible if we agree that in those times trade "was weak" and stop there. Yet, whether exchange was weak or strong, if we disregard it, the existence of the town and the "town-province" of the tenth to the twelfth centuries becomes a pure enigma, whereas their existence marks the chief distinction between ancient, pre-Muscovite, Rus and Russia's Middle Ages, the Rus of Moscow.

The Scandinavian sagas even called ancient Rus Gardarik, "the land of towns" [gorod = town]. That Arab writer of the beginning of the tenth century, Ibn-Dasta, whom we have already cited, goes even further. In his words, the "Rus," whom he, like many of the Arabs, distinguishes from the Slavs, had "neither hamlets nor ploughed fields" but at the same time had "a great number of towns" and were "living in ease." This ease the "Russy" obtained by their "sole occupation"—"by trade in sable, squirrel, and other furs." Ibn-Dasta does not forget to mention that in payment for its wares Rus "received coins"; in other words, this was not barter of the kind practised by various civilised and semi-civilised peoples in their relations with savage hunters. No, this was regular trade; in quest of customers Russian merchants went as far as Baghdad itself, and it was a rare ruler of eastern lands who did not have a shuba [pelisse] stitched of Russian furs. Arab writers go into such details in regard to the furs that it is impossible to doubt the Arabs' immediate acquaintance with this merchandise and its vendors. That is to say, Ibn-Dasta's statement, so astounding at first sight, that the Russians had no hamlets at all, only towns, is not to be regarded as a pure fable easily explained away by the writer's ignorance of the question he was treating. Evidently, the "Rus" of the tenth century appeared to close observers as pre-eminently an urban people. A slight disregard of historical perspective—and imagination is ready to draw us a picture of a wealthy country, sown with great trading centres, with a numerous and relatively civilised population. But the Arabs, with the unsparing realism of steppe-hunters just converted into world-traders, are ready to correct us; the best-informed of them draws a most unsavoury picture of the manners of Russian merchants when "abroad" in the Bolgar capital. And there is every reason to think that their manners "at home" were still worse; for not only in the tenth century—when Ibn-Fadlan observed his "Russy," washing together with the same water from one and the same cup, into which, incidentally, they also spat—but even in the twelfth century, Russian merchants did not feel the need of written contracts but ratified all agreements verbally, by the testimony of witnesses. The Russkaya Pravda treats the illiterate trader as the norm;

written obligations, "tablets," do not appear before the thirteenth century.

What mediæval trade amounted to, and how we should picture the mediæval merchant, are not peculiarly Russian problems; nor is it only Russian historians who have settled them optimistically, in the spirit of Storch. Trade, like agriculture, used to be regarded in economic history as an unfailing mark of civilisation; the old German historians peopled the innumerable multitude of German towns, large and small, mentioned in mediæval charters and chronicles with a "merchantry in the modern sense of the word." For this they incurred raillery, and justly, in the opinion of Werner Sombart, a modern historian of the economic development of Germany. He acknowledges, however, that the old historians were entirely right as far as the number of persons taking part in trade is concerned. In mediæval exchange we encounter the same peculiarity as existed in the rural economy of the Middle Ages—the dominance of petty enterprises of artisan type. On this point the modern historian and economist whom we have just mentioned has collected some figures for Western European trade in the Middle Ages. The anecdotal quality of these data does not prevent them from being very significant. In 1222, near Como in Northern Italy, two merchants from Lille were robbed; their entire stock of merchandise consisted of 13½ pieces of cloth and 12 pair of breeches. A hundred and fifty years later a similar misfortune overtook a whole caravan of merchants of Basel on their way to the Frankfurt fair; their losses did not exceed 100-200 florins each.[1] This same author fixes the average capital of a German merchant trading in Novgorod in the fourteenth century at 1,000 marks silver—"less than 10,000 [German] marks at the present [1902] exchange." It is more than probable that his contemporary Russian competitor had a like amount of capital at his disposal. In order to become a member of the very oldest, largest, and most stable trading association of Novgorod, which was grouped around the Church of St. John the Baptist, one had to invest no more than 50 silver *grivnas*[2] (1,000 silver rubles in present [1910] currency). To appreciate the real significance of such a "capital," let us compare it with other data of the same period. Fifty silver grivnas were equivalent, at the very most, to 150-200 grivnas kun; while eighty grivnas kun was the highest norm for a penal fine (*vira*) in the *Russkaya Pravda*. But penal fines, worked out case by case, had in view, of course, not capitalists but representatives of the masses, peasants and artisans. Eighty grivnas was what the prince exacted for murder of a druzhinnik, the man he most needed. Let us admit

---

[1] Werner Sombart, *Der Moderne Kapitalismus* (Leipzig, 1902), Bd. I, p. 173.
[2] The *grivna* was a money of account; the *grivna kun* was the circulating medium.

that he deemed it just to punish such a crime, particularly serious in his eyes, by "confiscation" of the culprit's whole property; then 80 grivnas constitutes the average estimated value of the whole homestead of a peasant or petty burgher, with all it contained. And a man who had two and a half times this amount could become one of the first merchants of Novgorod! Not less illuminating in this connection than the scale of capital is the scale of transport. For Western Europe one figure cited by the author quoted above is very significant. The whole annual carriage across the St. Gotthard pass, even at the end of the Middle Ages, would need but two present-day freight trains. For Russia the dimensions of vessels, both river- and sea-going, are indicative. Some idea of them may be had from certain passages in Byzantine writers, Russian chronicles, and the *Russkaya Pravda.* On the average the Russian "ship" of the tenth to the twelfth centuries carried 40-60 men. According to Aristov's calculations the smallest of the types mentioned by the *Russkaya Pravda* could accommodate some 2,000 puds of merchandise; if their rating in the *Pravda* corresponds to their burthen, the largest of them could carry 6,000 puds (about 100 tons). Nowadays the little coasting steamers plying between the small ports of the Black or Baltic Seas have such a capacity; then vessels of this size carried on trading relations between world commercial centres such as Constantinople and Kiev, Lübeck and Novgorod. But there is every reason to think that Aristov's computation is exaggerated. He sets out from the assumption that vessels designated by the same term in early Russia and in modern Russia had approximately the same dimensions, that the "barge" of the *Pravda* was the same thing as the "barge" of the 1860's, when he wrote *The Industry of Ancient Rus* [in Russian]. But this is not by any means necessarily true; in fact, it is hardly credible. From the citations of Aristov himself it is evident that they put the "barge" on rollers; to put a boat of even 30-40 tons on rollers is quite impossible without mechanical devices, and there is no evidence that there were machines in early Rus. The terms used in the *Russkaya Pravda* correspond to the type, not to the dimensions of boats. Of the dimensions even of Russian "sea-going" schooners (rated in the *Pravda* at thrice the "barge") one foreign observer says that they could float in the shallowest places; in other words, they were simply big boats.[3]

The dimensions of the vessels throw light on the proportions of the Old Russian war flotillas, which at first sight seem so fantastic. If Oleg on his campaign of 907 had, according to the chronicle, some

[3] Some idea of Old-Russian vessels is also given by the "Viking ships" found preserved in burial *kurgans*. One of them, now in Oslo, is 15 metres in length and 3½ in greatest breadth; it could accommodate 60-80 men.

2,000 "ships" and, according to Byzantine data, more than 1,000, this is not fiction; we hear of "a thousand boats" in genuinely historic times. But this was precisely a thousand "boats," nothing more. And the petty scale of trade in general explains the great number of "merchants" in the pages of the chronicle. When we read that in 1216, in Pereyaslavl Zalessky alone, there were a hundred and fifty merchants of Novgorod, and in Torzhok, one of the chief transfer points of Novgorod's trade, perhaps even some 2,000 merchants, we are not in the least astonished if only we think of the Old-Russian *"gost"*[4] as a man who (like Nekrasov's Uncle Jake)[5] carried his merchandise in a single cart or, for the most part, in a hamper on his back; the present-day pedlar most resembles the typical trader of the Middle Ages, and not in Russia alone. "Everywhere is presented one and the same picture; not counting a few greater merchants, who for the most part, however, did not engage in professional trade, everywhere we meet a swarming mass of insignificant and altogether petty traders, such as are even now seen at petty country fairs or on the highways of remote provinces, with hamper on shoulders or in a cart harnessed to a single jade."[6]

But not all mediæval merchandise could be carried on the back, nor is its small scale the only peculiarity of mediæval trade. The first Russian merchants whom the Arabs were able to observe closely imported into the Bolgar capital, along with the furs of sables and black foxes, young girls, and in such numbers that from the Arab narratives this commodity might be assumed to be the chief article of the Russian export trade of the time. From a description of the miracles of Nicholas the Miracle-Worker, it is evident that in Constantinople the Russian merchant was, above all, a slave-trader, while a twelfth-century traveller met Russian slave-traders even in Alexandria. Russian sources supply a mass of indirect, and sometimes direct, confirmation of the tales of foreigners. For instance, the chronicles tell about the hundreds (if not thousands) of "concubines" of St. Vladimir (972-1015) before his baptism; a modern church historian, Golubinsky, quite justly sees in this a reference, not so much to the personal immorality and the personal harem of this prince in the pagan period of his life as to the stores of human merchandise kept by this prince, the greatest Russian merchant of his time. Likewise, that it was not a question of paganism is proved by the sermons of Bishop Serapion, a younger contemporary of the Tatar invasion (he died in 1275). Among the sins that were bringing

---

[4] A merchant trading abroad, as distinct from the ordinary merchant (*kupets*).

[5] *Cf.* Poems by Nicholas Nekrassov. Translated by Juliet M. Soskice. London, 1929, pp. 123-127.

[6] Werner Sombart, *op. cit.*, p. 174.

divers scourges on the Russian land Serapion mentions the following one: ". . . our brethren we plunder, slay, and sell into paganism." That is to say, even in the thirteenth century Russian merchants did not hesitate to sell Russian slaves in foreign markets, including both Musulman and pagan lands. Of the fact that even around 1300 men went to Rus "to buy girls" we have documentary evidence in the complaint of one such purchaser, a Rigan merchant, against the prince of Vitebsk, who had put him in prison without reason; for it is obvious that the arrest had nothing to do with the scarcely respectable purpose of this Rigan's journey into the land of Vitebsk, but was simply an ordinary manifestation of princely tyranny. This trivial case reveals the fate, not always clear from the chronicles, of those "captives" who were the inevitable sequel to the princely feuds of those times. When a prince returned home "having captured domestics," it did not, as is usually imagined, mean that he and his druzhina had acquired a certain number of new bond-servants, male and female; rather, it meant that in the conquerors' hands remained a marketable commodity, perhaps the most valuable commodity of that time. Hence the Old-Russian feudal lords coveted "domestics" far more than their peasants' offerings in kind. For the latter there was no market; for the former there existed even in those days an "international market," able to swallow up any quantity of human merchandise. The twelfth-century princes openly avowed their exploits of this nature, evidently regarding the "capture of domestics" as a perfectly normal transaction. No less a man than Vladimir Monomakh (1113-1125), he who has supplied so many sentimental pages to the official textbooks, relates how he and his allies "devastated" a Russian town, leaving in it "neither domestics nor cattle." As we see, for complete and thorough devastation of Russian provinces there was not the slightest need for a Tatar invasion. And when a distant descendant of Monomakh, Michael of Tver (1365-1399), falling on Torzhok in 1372, led captive to Tver "of men and women an innumerable multitude," he was acting not as a pupil of the Mongol conquerors, but as a perpetuator of an old and respected, genuinely Russian tradition.

The existence of such "merchandise" no doubt further emphasises the "natural" character of mediæval economy; the slave market was indispensable, precisely because there were no other workers on the market. But this involves another consideration. How could a man be made merchandise when nothing else was merchandise? From the citations just made it is clear that under the economic methods to which we are accustomed such a miracle could not have been accomplished. To extra-economic compulsion in the province of production corresponded extra-economic appropriation in the province of exchange. Not only human merchandise but also the sable furs and the precious metals that circulated on the market of that day were not obtained by way of exchange with the original proprietors, not even by exchange effected by deception, violence, or similar "abuses," such as even now occur in the colonial trade of "civilised" peoples with "uncivilised"; they were obtained directly, by open violence. The first stage of exchange was not trade by barter, as economic history was still teaching not so long ago, but purely and simply "robber trade" (*Raubhandel*—a term absolutely scientifically established by the history of economy in our time). The line which is now so carefully drawn, separating the peaceful trader, even though he be unfair, from the plunderer, did not exist for the naïve men of the early Middle Ages. Robber into merchant and merchant into robber were conversions accomplished with astonishing facility; with incomparable realism the Scandinavian sagas, for example, mention both these professions side by side in connection with one and the same person without being in the least embarrassed for their hero. "There was a man of wealth and of illustrious origin, Lodin by name; he frequently undertook trading journeys, and sometimes engaged in piracy," runs with truly epic calm a passage of the *Heimskringla* of Snorre Sturleson. How simply and naturally this transition from the province of civil law into that of criminal law was accomplished, a tale from the same saga will show, a tale which, in view of its striking details, is worth setting forth at length. The envoys of King Olaf, Karl and Gunnstein, and their travelling-companion, Thorer "the Dog," arrived in Biarmiya (the later Zavolochye of Novgorod, along the Northern Dvina) and there carried on extensive trade with the natives, exchanging fox and sable furs for goods brought from Scandinavia, and in part for money. When the trading was ended, and with it the truce which the Northmen had concluded with the local population for the precise period and purpose of trade, the travellers immediately began to seek new sources of lucre. Thorer "the Dog" asked his fellow-travellers whether they desired to obtain wealth? Upon their answer, in the affirmative naturally, Thorer explained to them that wealth was, so to speak, within their grasp; they needed but a little boldness. The natives were in the habit of burying silver articles with their dead, while the idol of their chief god, Yumala, was all covered with precious ornaments. They had but to rifle the cemetery and the sanctuary of Yumala, which stood in the centre of it, and the merchant Northmen would augment their capital considerably. We shall not relate the details—not devoid of drama and picturesqueness—of this tenth-century nocturnal expropriation. It ended perfectly successfully, though the retreating Northmen had to wage a regular battle with the worshippers of Yumala, who, being awakened, ran to the scene of pillage. Let us note only one detail. On the way home, Thorer "the Dog," despoiled his fellow-travellers also, so that

Saint Olaf received from this expedition less return than might have been expected.

Thus we see that when our old acquaintance Ibn-Dasta writes of Russian merchants that they "make raids on the Slavs, come upon them in ships, come ashore and make captive the people, whom they later despatch to Khazeran and to the Bolgars and there sell,"—he is but describing realistically what was in his day a quite common affair, and is not by any means inventing fables. But we also see that the originality of early mediæval trading must be supplemented by many features, and that very little remains of the enlightened merchants Storch depicted. The social setting which was bound to form around "robber trade" was no more like the setting of present-day capitalistic exchange than the boyar's votchina of "appanage" Rus was like a present-day rural-economic enterprise.

The mediæval trader, in setting out for merchandise, "by custom took with him a sword," as the Rigans related in their complaint about their comrade who was injured by the prince of Vitebsk. A treaty of Prince Mstislav of Smolensk with these same Rigans (1229) contains the stipulation, at first glance very strange, "that the Latin [i.e., the German] shall not go to war, either with the prince or with Rus, if he himself does not wish; likewise the Russian shall not go to war with the Latin [prince], either in Riga or on the Gothic coast [island of Gothland]; if he himself wishes, let him go." The aim of the treaty was "to order peace anew" between Rus and all the "Latin tongue, whoever visits in Rus" [i.e., carries on trade with Rus], because earlier "it was not peaceful to all merchants" trading between Smolensk on the one hand, Riga and Gothland on the other. The "Latin" and the "Rusin" of the treaty were the German and the Russian merchants, men "by old custom" girded with a sword; their co-operation in war was valuable to any prince, all the more so since the wars of the prince were often nothing less than a peculiar form of "primary accumulation" of trading capital. The merchant himself also made war very willingly. Nevertheless, however willing the trader was to fight, a compulsory military obligation might hinder his trading operations; this is why the Riga-Smolensk treaty stipulates the consent of the merchant himself as an immediate condition of his participation in a foreign campaign. On the other hand, once it became a question of the defence of their own trading community and its interests, the merchants were appealed to first, and there was no doubt of their willingness; they were a militia ever ready for war. The veche [town assembly] of Novgorod, having quarrelled with Prince Vsevolod Mstislavich and foreseeing an inevitable armed conflict, first of all confiscated the belongings of the boyars, the "friends" of the prince, "giving them to the merchants to equip themselves for war." When Lithua-

nia unexpectedly fell upon Staraya Russa, the town was defended, not
only by the hastily thronging townspeople but by the landholders of the
neighbourhood, mercenary Scandinavian soldiers, "and whoever was a
merchant, and the gosts." In Novgorod's war with Michael of Tver,
when "by the will of God there was done not a little mischief," there
fell on the field of battle, besides "men of the boyars of Novgorod,"
"many good merchants."

The trader was a military man, merchandise was military booty, and
the place for the safekeeping of merchandise was, naturally, a military
camp. This conception of merchandise is clearly revealed by the ety-
mology of the word *tovar* [merchandise] ; to the Old Russian chronicler
the primary meaning of tovar was property of any kind whatsoever.
When a villa of Prince Igor Olgovich was attacked, his enemies found
there "many supplies, including much heavy tovar of all kinds, both iron
and copper," so much that it could not be carried off on their carts;
furthermore, that portion of the belongings which was destined for
sale—tovar in the modern sense—was in no way distinguished from the
general mass. The chronicle of Novgorod relates how Prince Mstislav
Mstislavich ("the Bold") attacked Torzhok, seized the followers of
his rival, Svyatoslav, put them "in irons" and seized "the goods of
those whom his hand could reach." Prince Mstislav's reach was long,
and his rival—or rather, the latter's father, Vsevolod, since Svyatoslav
himself was a minor—felt his hand. At first he thought of attempting
reprisals, seizing the gosts of Novgorod and their wares. But when
Novgorod, in its turn, replied with the arrest of Svyatoslav and the
remnant of his retinue, Vsevolod made peace (1209) "and Mstislav let go
Svyatoslav and his men, while Vsevolod let go the gosts with their wares."
This utter unwillingness to distinguish consumption value from exchange
value is exceptionally characteristic of the period of natural economy;
but in the connection we are investigating another confusion is still
more characteristic. When St. Vladimir, setting out to war with the
Pechenegs, obtained the consent of the Pecheneg prince to decide the
quarrel by a duel between two warriors, a Russian and a Pecheneg, he
"came to the tovars, sending a herald through the tovars," asking:
Is there not a man who will take upon himself to fight with the Pecheneg?
Nowhere, perhaps, is politics, as the outward shell of economics, revealed
with such naïve simplicity. The economic content of the concept was
brought to light; of the trader girded with a sword the sword alone is
visible, but the ear detects the reason why the sword was needed, betray-
ing a hint of the days when the military camp of a Russian prince was
simply an abode of robbers, a dêpot for the stolen goods with which
they intended to trade in foreign lands.

This blending of trading dêpot and barracks persisted for a long time after armed force had ceased to be the sole condition of exchange. In this later stage, though the original acquisition of tovar still depended on violence, its further transfer, at least, was accomplished in peaceful, legal forms. A Russian historian, Nikitsky, thus describes the settlement of German merchants in Novgorod: "As places intended to serve as a safe asylum, both courtyards, the Gothic and the German, were surrounded by a high fence, the maintenance of which was one of the most constant cares of the German merchantry. Strong gates maintained communication between these foreign citadels and the rest of the population of the alien and often hostile city. . . . Every precaution was taken to secure enforcement of the laws designed to maintain order in the courtyard [*Hof*]. Special attention was paid to the external security of the courtyard. Day and night guards defended the courtyard, and whoever of the *knechts* neglected his duty paid fifteen kuns, or his master was held responsible if the neglect was attributable to him. In addition, in the evening were unleashed large, valuable dogs, which threatened to tear apart any uninvited arrival. As a storehouse, the church was the object of special solicitude. Each night two men slept in it; under no circumstances might they be brothers or companions or even servants of one and the same master, and he who brought them into the church in the evening had to lock the door behind them and deliver the keys to the alderman. Church guard was performed in rotation and extended similarly to the dwellings, both inside and outside the courtyard. Those who kept the latter guard had at meal time to remind of their impending duty those who immediately followed them. Besides the internal church guards proper, at the gates of the temple stood also, throughout the night, a third, who watched lest any of the natives slip into the vicinity of the church; fear of them was so great that it was forbidden, under penalty of scourging, to carry the key so openly that it might be seen."

It may be thought that all this was simply a matter of tradition, a survival already devoid of significance, or that such precautionary measures were necessary only in barbaric Russia, and that the enlightened West stood much higher in this respect. But let us take the first three references in the chronicle of Novgorod to the trading journeys of Novgorodans to that same West. The earliest of them recites the adversity of the elements: "Both themselves were lost, and their wares." But in the second we meet with social relationships: "In the same year . . . a Novgorodan was slaughtered beyond the sea in Denmark." And in the third these relations take a yet more palpable form: "came a Swedish prince with a bishop . . . to trade; they had come from beyond the sea in three boats; they [the Swedish prince and bishop] were beaten without any success . . . [we] took their three vessels and slew of them [the pirates] some hundred and fifty men. . . .'' This piratical bishop once more reminds us of the participation of the mediæval Church in mediæval trade, with all its peculiarities. But usually the representatives of the Church took to themselves the less active rôle—not of acquirers, but of storers of "tovars." The centre of the German trade citadel in Novgorod was the Catholic Church of St. Peter. But Orthodox churches, too, systematically fulfilled the same function. We already know that around one of them, John the Baptist, was grouped the chief of the commercial companies of Novgorod, that of the traders in wax. Others were simply warehouses. In describing Novgorod's colossal fire of 1340, the chronicler complains of the "evil men," who not only looted what their brothers had, but slew others over their wares, taking the wares to themselves, "but even [looted] in the holy churches—which any Christian, even to the abandoning of his own home, would rescue." In the Church of the Forty Martyrs "all the wares, whatever they were, they looted; icons and books they did not allow to be carried out. As soon as they themselves [the thieves] had run out of the church, everything caught fire, and they slew two guards. And at the Church of the Holy Virgin in the Market-place a priest was burned; others say that they slew him over the merchandise, that the whole church was burned, both icons and books, but that the fire did not even touch his hair; but all the merchandise they looted." For the very widespread prejudice on the score of the strength and influence of religious feeling in the Middle Ages this realistic picture of the chronicle's is most instructive. The practical Germans were right when, not relying on the "sanctity of the place," they kept around their church-warehouse good, valuable dogs and an armed guard.

Unless we keep in mind this combination of war, trade, and robbery, we shall understand nothing of the organisation of the Old Russian town. For example, the rôle of the thousand-man—the commander-in-chief of the town "warriors"—will remain a complete riddle. Even without turning to the matter of economic relationships, we can understand the position of the thousand-man as the person first after the prince. The *Russkaya Pravda*, in enumerating Monomakh's collaborators in his famous legislation for the relief of debtors, places first after Vladimir Monomakh himself, "Ratibor, thousand-man of Kiev, and Prokopy, thousand-man of Belgorod, and Stanislav, thousand-man of Pereyaslavl. . . ." "Izyaslav," relates the *Lavrentyevsky Chronicle*, "sent two men ahead of him to Kiev, to his brother Vladimir and to Lazar the thousand-man. . . ." "Yury of Rostov and the thousand-man," says the *Ipatyevsky Chronicle* under 1130, "mounted in silver the tomb of Feodosy, abbot of Pechersky. . . ." We can understand also how the court of the thousand-man in Novgorod in certain cases superseded the court of the prince. But when we come to differentiate these cases, and try to fix the competence of the thousand-man, no modern analogies will help us. We are accustomed to think of a general as an important person, but should a modern [7] Russian governor-general decide the lawsuits of business-men, it would seem very strange. Yet the chief general of Novgorod—the *"Herzog,"* as the German merchants called him—tried just such cases. The thousand-man was the president of the commercial court, and in this field he was just as independent as was the lord-archbishop in ecclesiastical cases. "And I, Grand Prince Vsevolod," says the charter of John the Baptist, "have established for Saint John three elders from the men of means, and from the common men a thousand-man, and from the merchants two elders, and they shall judge all cases pertaining to [the church of St.] John, both of trade and of the gosts and the trading court; and Miroslav, the *posadnik* [burgomaster] shall not meddle with it, nor shall other posadniks, nor shall the boyars of Novgorod; in what pertains to John they shall not meddle at all." "And with the prelate's court and with the thousand-man's, with that it is not for you to meddle . . . ," wrote the Novgorodans in a later treaty, concluded by the still free city and explaining its "antiquity and custom" to the Polish king, Casimir IV. Remembering the Rigan merchant girded with a sword who appeared in the province of Vitebsk to purchase girls, we shall understand why the head chief of all those who bore swords was also the head judge of all who traded, on exactly the same basis on which the commander-in-chief of an army is the highest judge in a military camp. But if a general was the head chief of all the merchants, then it is natural that his colonels, the "hundred-men," were his vice-chiefs, and that the Old Russian merchants were divided into "hundreds" just as modern Russian merchants formed guilds. From a fairly old supplement to the *Russkaya Pravda* we learn that these "hundreds" were named after their commanders—"David's hundred," "Ratibor's hundred," "Kondrat's hundred"—like Russian regiments in the time of Emperor Paul, and that they possessed quite definite territorial significance, for which reason the duty of cleaning the streets of Novgorod was apportioned by hundreds. It is evident that originally such a merchant settlement represented something in the nature of the German Courtyard, the whole population of which was linked by unity of discipline and command, and that later it was gradually converted into one of the quarters of the town.

Only in the light of all these facts does the rôle of the Old Russian veche become clear to us. The time has long since passed when veche organization was accounted a specific peculiarity of certain town communities, which were consequently called "veche-towns"—Novgorod,

[7] Written in 1910.

Pskov, and Vyatka. Veche communities began to represent an exception
to the general rule only when that rule had already died out; they were
the last representatives of an order of things which until the thirteenth
century had been common to all Russia. "Veches assemble in all the
provinces," says Sergeyevich. "They constitute the duma of the province. . . . Such is the evidence of a contemporary. There is not the
slightest reason to suspect its accuracy. . . ." "From about the twelfth
century we have more than fifty private attestations to the veche life of
early towns from every part of the Russia of that time." In order to
bring out in greater relief this institution's independence of the local
conditions of Novgorod, Sergeyevich intentionally omits all data relating
to the veches in the province of Novgorod. And this has by no means
deprived his picture of its vividness; quite the contrary. "It may even
seem incredible that the accounts given in our old records about the veche
practice of Novgorod and Pskov are scantier than the reports of Kievan
practice. Yet it is so. The Kievan chronicler has left us quite a complete picture of the veche of 1147; the Northerners have given us
nothing similar."

The events of 1146-47, described by the chronicle in great detail, and
in places most realistically, are actually one of the most valuable accounts of veche practice that we have. For the present we shall not
touch upon the question of the origin of veche organisation, nor of its
evolution, for it would be very imprudent to think that throughout its
history the veche remained unchanged, as it might seem from reading
the scholar just cited. The Old Russian "republics" began with an
aristocracy of birth but ended with an aristocracy of capital. But in the
interval they passed through a stage which can be called democratic; in
Kiev this stage falls just in the first half of the twelfth century. In
this period the real master of a Russian town is the people. Let us see
what this signified. Take the Kievan veche of 1146. At it the people
decide the most important of political questions—who shall be prince in
Kiev; before us is a sort of constituent assembly. The representative
of the candidate for the prince's throne—his cousin—is carrying on
negotiations with the veche as an equal with equals. The negotiations
are ended, the parties have made their statements, there remains the
concluding ceremony of the reciprocal oath; the citizens must swear that
they will bear obedience to the newly elected prince, while the latter's
representative, and later the prince himself, must swear that they will
honourably fulfil the conditions on which he, the prince, has been elected.
"Svyatoslav [brother of the newly elected prince Igor Olgovich] alighted
from his steed and on that kissed the cross to them in veche assembled;
and all the Kievans, *alighting from their steeds,* began to say, 'Thy
brother is prince and thou.' And on that all the Kievans with their *chil-*

dren kissed the cross, that they would not betray Igor and Svyatoslav.''
Let us consider first the latter of the expressions we have italicised.
What does it mean? Did they bring little children to the veche and
make them kiss the cross? No, those kissing the cross first "alighted
from their steeds"; there could, then, be no minors among them. This
means that the oath to Igor was taken, not only by the heads of families,
"the masters of the house" in modern parlance, but actually by the
whole people, *i.e.*, by all the adult males capable of bearing arms. This
is indisputably evident from the two expressions we have italicised.
The whole scene bore a purely military character; both negotiating parties sat on horseback and were, of course, armed. Prince Igor was
elected by these "warriors," whose representative, the thousand-man,
was at the same time president of the commercial court; the town militia
elected the prince. Politically it was precisely this body that represented
the town.

Let us now take the veche of 1147. Only a year had passed, but
during that eventful period a series of changes had taken place in Kiev.
Igor, to whom they had just kissed the cross, was no longer prince; he
was shut up in the monastery of St. Fedor, while a man popular among
the Kievans, Izyaslav Mstislavich, as a representative of the "stock
of Monomakh," was on the throne. But already discords had arisen
between him and the capital town, and he had gone to war against his
uncle, Yury, without the town militia; only his druzhina and volunteers
from the burghers had set out with Izyaslav. The war had gone badly;
the Olgoviches, kindred of the deposed Igor, had taken Yury's part.
Izyaslav has to settle his affairs with Kiev, and he sends envoys to the
veche. They first make sure of the support of the foremost personages in
the town—the metropolitan and the thousand-man,—and then they appeal to the people. When all the Kievans, "from small to great" (we
know now what this means), assemble "to Saint Sophia onto the courtyard" and "begin as a veche," one of the envoys addresses them in
these words: "Your prince kisses you. I declared to you, he says, that I
intended with my brother Rostislav, and with Vladimir and with Izyaslav, sons of David [these were relatives of Igor], to go upon my uncle,
Yury, and I summoned you with me. But you said to me: we cannot
raise hands against Yury, against the stock of Vladimir [Monomakh],
but against the Olgoviches [*i.e.*, against the relatives of Igor] we will
go with thee even with the children. Now I declare to you that Vladimir and Izyaslav, sons of David, and Svyatoslav, son of Vsevolod, to
whom I have done much good, kissed the cross to me; yet later secretly
they have kissed the cross to Svyatoslav Olgovich [brother of Igor] and
have sent to Yury, and have betrayed me, have wished either to slay me
for Igor's sake or to seize me, but God has preserved me and the honour-

able cross on which they swore to me. Thus behold, brother Kievans, now has come what you wished, and the time has come to fulfil your promise; go with me upon Chernigov, against the Olgoviches, from small to great, whoever has a horse, on a horse, and whoever possesses not a horse, in a boat; for they want to slay not me alone, but to exterminate you as well.'' And the Kievans said: ''We are glad that thee, our brother, God has saved from great treason; we will go with thee with the children as well, if thou wishest.'' Let us for a moment leave this fraternisation, in itself highly significant, between the prince and the veche; rarely do the two stand out so clearly as two forces quite equal in rights. But with whom did Izyaslav fraternise? To whom was it possible to address such a speech: ''Go for me, whoever has a horse, on a horse, and whoever possesses not a horse, in a boat''? Before us again is the armed town, a people's militia with the rights of a supreme constituent assembly.

Whatever veche we consider, whether it be a south Russian one or even one of later date, of Novgorod, we find the same general picture. Rarely, to be sure, will it be so clearly limned as in the case of the veche which the men of Smolensk organised in 1185 in the very heat of a campaign against the Polovtsians, when their prince had led them farther than had been stipulated. But even in Novgorod in 1359 a political dispute was decided by one of the ''ends'' [8] of Novgorod in its own favour only because its inhabitants had had the forethought to go to the veche in full armour, while their more numerous opponents, not having taken this precaution, were ''slain and half-captured.'' The continual fights at veches, which in the good old times historians naïvely attributed to the ''turbulence'' of the Novgorod ''rabble,'' are best understood if we think of the veche as a sort of soldiers' meeting—an assembly of men little accustomed to parliamentary discipline but very much accustomed to arms and not restrained in the use of that weighty argument. Remembering this peculiarity of the Old Russian democracy, we shall likewise very easily understand why, in disputes with the princes, the veche always proved the stronger, right up to the time when the military structure of early Rus changed, and the town militias yielded place to the peasant-noble army of the grand prince of Moscow. The veche was the incarnation of that material force on which the prince directly depended in a struggle with his rivals. The prince's druzhina, counted usually by hundreds, rarely rising to thousands, was, in a military sense, something midway between a detachment of body guards and a general staff. Qualitatively, from the standpoint of military preparedness, it was the best part of the army, but quantitatively it was so weak that in Novgorod, for example, the princes never even tried to

[8] The five "quarters" of Novgorod were called "ends" (*kontsy*).

rely on it against the armed veche. Without the town "warriors" it was not possible to undertake any serious campaign, and their refusal to obey the prince was in fact the end of his authority; without any "revolution" in our sense, he ceased to be prince, i.e., military leader. For, if the veche was an autocratic army, the significance of the existence of the prince was comprised in the fact that he was commander-in-chief of this army, an autocrat himself while it obeyed him, but more powerless than any village elder as soon as it failed him.

The comparison of the prince of Kievo-Novgorodan Rus to a village elder, "to whom each in the mir is obedient, but all the mir is higher than he and can replace and punish," is not ours; it belongs to K. Aksakov. With all its scientific defects, the Slavophil interpretation of Russian history, due to the peculiar angle of vision from which it regarded Old Russia, possesses great merit; as long as sixty years ago it had put an end to that modernisation of the political institutions of Old Russia which made of the prince a sovereign in the modern sense of the word. One of the first culprits in this matter of modernisation, it is true, was a very ancient person—the Kievan chronicler himself, who in the first quarter of the twelfth century compiled the "initial digest." The chronicler, a contemporary of Vladimir Monomakh, who had, in fact, come forward with a broad socio-political programme, and a pupil of the Byzantine chronographers with their Biblico-Roman conception of state authority, was ready to depict even the first Russian prince in the form and likeness of the Old Testament rulers and the emperors of Constantinople. But the Roman empire—the eastern as well as the western—though, in the opinion of the blessed Augustine, it arose from a robber band, was in historical times a stable police organisation, whereas the purpose of the calling of Rurik was acknowledged to be the establishment of internal "order." Although this purpose is set forth as though in the very words of those ninth-century Slavs in veche assembled, this literary form must not deceive us. Not a single fact of the internal arrangements, either of the time of Rurik or of his immediate successors, was the chronicler able to cite; the little that we do glean from him can be summed up, as follows: Rurik "hewed a town on the Volkhov" and repeated the operation in other places, everywhere "hewing towns" and putting Varangian garrisons in them. Again and again we come upon Oleg, Igor, and Svyatoslav, but only in the rôle of directors of military activity, and only in regard to Olga do we learn anything of the internal work performed by princely authority; yet this internal work came down merely to the establishment of "tribute and dues." Saint Vladimir, it would seem, began the struggle against robbers, and at first unsuccessfully. With his son Yaroslav the Wise tradition links the appearance of the Russkaya Pravda. But this tradition found its way into the chronicle very late; in the oldest copies of the first chronicle of Novgorod it does not appear; and from the essence of the matter it is quite clear that this collection of judicial decisions could not be the product of the creative genius of any one legislator. The most that can be done is to attribute to the "wise" prince the first of the decisions—it is unknown when and by whom inscribed—and even that must be done with all possible reservations, for the heading, "Justice of Yaroslav Vladimirovich," cannot be traced back further than the end of the thirteenth century. Between the death of Yaroslav and that time two and a half centuries had elapsed; it is easy to imagine how many legends might arise in that space of time. In the main, the chronicle gives much the same information concerning Yaroslav as about his predecessors: he "defeated Bryachislav," "all Belz," "went upon the Yatvyags," "went upon Lithuania." At the same time it is curious that the older the copy of the chronicle, the less we find in it about Yaroslav, despite the fact that certain items—the laying of the cornerstone of St. Sophia, for example—are repeated twice under different years. In a word, in order to find a prince-reformer, striving, after a fashion, to establish order in the land, we have to pass to the first half of the twelfth century, when, in the person of Vladimir Monomakh, we find what is in all probability the original of the portrait which the chronicle has copied in many variants. But Monomakh's activity, as we shall see further on, was by no means the norm even for early Rus in general. It is to be noted that even this consummator of the Kievan "democratic revolution" of the eleventh and twelfth centuries valued in himself, first and foremost, the valiant and successful general, who had accomplished eighty-three major campaigns, not counting minor ones. Of them he tells in great detail in his celebrated *Precept*, but of his domestic activity we find there only the most meagre indications. In the case of his contemporaries and descendants we do not find even that much. The most the chronicler tells us is how energetically this or that prince collected his judicial revenue from fines and fees. But too much energy along this line gave a prince a bad reputation; the population was inclined to regard any increase in the collection of penal fines as an abuse of power and to compare it with plunder. Internal order the population knew how to maintain itself; when in the land of Novgorod the court of a veche town had taken final form, the prince's initiative was removed from it altogether. But even Novgorod could not dispense with its prince, for "grievous" it was then to the town to which there remained "no prince at all," as was the case with Kiev in 1154. But why it was grievous to the town without a prince is quite definitely explained by the old friend and old enemy of Novgorod, Vsevolod "the Great" (otherwise known as "Big Nest,"

1176-1212). "In your land there is a war," he said to the Novgorodans in 1205, "while your prince, my son Svyatoslav, is little; so behold! I give you my older son, Constantine." In the thirteenth century, as in the ninth, the prince was needed, before all else, to lead the army; whence one of the gravest charges against a prince was, that he "went from his regiment before all," as did Vsevolod Mstislavich in 1136. With especial realism this "military obligation" of the prince is depicted in a rather late charter of Novgorod (1307 or 1308)—a treaty with Grand Prince Michael. In those times, it seems, Novgorod maintained, not one but several princes, but all for the same purpose. Of one of them the charter complains in such expressions as: "they gave him . . . a capital town Pskov, and he ate bread, but when war came, he departed, deserted the town. . . ." Why should they feed a prince who in war was good for nothing?

In the fourteenth century, also in Novgorod, a prince answered for his faults to the veche. Was it always and everywhere so? Were even Rurik and his immediate successors the "hired guards" of the Russian land? Was the veche in the democratic form known to us an immediate offshoot of "primitive democracy," or was democracy, then as now, the result of a long and stubborn social struggle? The chronicle's narrative of the calling of the princes makes the decision of a veche the starting point of all Russian history; to call the meeting of the Chuds, Slavs, and Kriviches, which decided to call Rurik and his brothers, anything but a veche is, of course, impossible. But just as the characterisation of any prince by the initial chronicler reflected Vladimir Monomakh, so also the characterisation of the political situation of the ninth century necessarily reflected the conditions of the twelfth century. The whole story has undoubtedly been polished, and so much so that it is almost impossible to get at its historical basis. We know that they bought off the Northmen, that the first prince whose name tradition remembered was Rurik, that he came from the north, and that he "warred everywhere." All the rest may be the imagination of the compiler, or may equally well be a tale that has strayed; it is well known that the legend of the arrival of the Anglo-Saxons in Britain is almost word for word the same as the Russian story of the calling of the princes from beyond the sea. The first documents of Russian history, such as the treaties entered into with the Greek emperors by the first two genuinely historical princes, Oleg and Igor, are very convincing; the authenticity of the documents themselves, never disputed, has long since ceased to be subject to any doubt. It is very remarkable that neither Oleg nor Igor stands out in them as sole representative of a definite state, whether called Rus or anything else. Both these princes are simply called "grand," *i.e.*, senior among the very many

Russian princes "existing under the hand" of the grand prince; these other princes are, however, independent, and so much so that they have their own special diplomatic representatives; they have special "servitors," whose names are here enumerated. The treaty appears as the expression of the will of all these princes ("by the wish of our princes"). But, evidently, this did not suffice to give it legal force in Russian eyes; to Oleg's treaty is added the phrase: "and from all existing under his [Oleg's] hand in Rus," while Igor's treaty concludes the roster of envoys with "and from all the men of the Russian land." The princes were only the representatives of a certain whole, which had no intention of alienating all its rights in their favour. The prince handles current business, but in unusual cases all "Rus," *i.e.*, all the trading urban population, comes forward; precisely this meaning of the word "Rus" is established with perfect clearness by the first of the judicial decisions inscribed in the *Russkaya Pravda*, later editions of which even found it necessary to add this meaning ("burgher") in parenthesis, as it were, to the term "Rusin," which by the thirteenth century was not generally intelligible.

The treaties of Oleg and Igor are in themselves sufficient to dispel any thought of an alleged "great power" founded by the first of these princes, only to fall apart later into a multitude of petty principalities. The "grand princedom" of Oleg was a temporary union, in the hands of a single person, of authority over many independent political units; later another such unification of Rus took place under Monomakh and his son Mstislav. But juridically neither Oleg nor Monomakh ever abolished this independence; in all probability it never entered their heads to do so, any more than it entered the head of a boyar of that time to deprive of its economic independence even a single one of the hundreds of peasant homesteads united on his estate. On the contrary, the more individual princes there were "existing under the hand of" a grand prince, the greater was the latter's importance. Like the grand prince himself, lesser princes had authority in their capital towns only in so far as the local population supported them. The "federal" and "republican" character of the Russian "state" in the very earliest known stages of its evolution is thus quite definitely established. In view of the given economic setting we could expect nothing else. Old Russian towns were by no means markets in the contemporary sense of the word, economic centres for the surrounding country. Even Novgorod did not wholly succeed in becoming such a market; this most progressive of Old Russian trading centres could have been taken out of its province without very much affecting the latter, while its predecessors, the towns of the "great waterway" of the times of Oleg and Igor, were simply abodes of merchant-robbers, far more closely connected with the foreign markets to which these merchants delivered their wares than they were with the surrounding country, in relation to which the urban population was a typical parasite. There was no soil here for a "unitary" state nor, in fact, for any state in our contemporary sense of the word. Military-trading associations, at first purely improvised, later ever more and more stable, periodically produced from their midst leaders who stood out in the eyes of neighbouring peoples in the guise of "princes" of Rus. We do not know under what conditions the profession of leader in a number of centres was monopolised by the members of a single family, the descendants of Igor; but in itself, under the given order of things, inheritance of the princely profession was just as natural as inheritance of the merchant's, and of the merchant we know from the charter of St. John the Baptist that he was hereditary. This fact leads to a further conclusion; if the authority of the prince and the profession of trade were organised on the patriarchal principle of the hereditary estate, it is natural to suppose that the same principle underlay the whole order of things in the Old Russian town, and that the Rus, mentioned in the treaties, was a combination not of individual persons but of families— something in the nature of the "pechishche" or "dvorishche" which constituted the basic social unit of rural Rus. A fact supporting the idea of the patriarchal structure of the earliest urban community is the existence of those mysterious "town elders" whom we find along with the boyars in the duma of St. Vladimir (d. 1015). But one ought not to see in them an elected "board of town elders," as certain scholars do; the elective principle in the Old Russian town did not weaken but grew stronger with the course of time. An elective institution might change its name, but there was no reason for it to die out. It is another matter if we admit that the "town elders" were the heads of the pechishches that made up the original town; then their gradual extinction, as we shall presently see, is perfectly natural.

CHAPTER IV

PATRIARCHAL life economically was closely connected with natural economy. The pechishche might persist for centuries or slowly evolve into a votchina, preserving only its character as an autonomous economic entity. The town did not offer this fundamental economic condition. A few pechishches, which had in early times fortified themselves on this or that happily selected spot and had formed the town aristocracy, very soon found themselves enveloped by a dense mass of the most diverse elements, which the old patriarchal organisation could not assimilate or swallow up, and which with difficulty it held in check for a time. Some idea of the motley crowd that accumulated in great centres along the Volga and in the Dnieper basin is given by the story of an Arab writer about Itil, the Khazar capital. "There are established seven tribunals: two for the Mohammedans, two for the Khazars, who judge on the basis of the Mosaic law, two for the Christians living here, who judge on the basis of the Gospels (!), and one for the Slavs, the Rus, and other pagans, who judge by the laws of the pagans." The population of Kiev must have presented similar diversity. The Germans whom the Polish king, Boleslaw the Fat, brought with him to the aid of Svyatopolk, on their return to their fatherland related to their bishop (Dietmar of Merseburg) that Kiev was a very large town; it had some four hundred churches and was peopled "by fugitive slaves and swift Danes," as the Germans called all Scandinavians. From the *Life of Feodosy* and the *Pechersky Paterik* we learn of still another non-native element in the composition of the population of Kiev; there were many Jews, disputes with whom about faith constituted one of the occupations of Feodosy as noted by his biographer. Reading such a precious record of manners and customs as the *Pechersky Paterik*, we get an extraordinarily vivid and clear presentation of the ethnographic motley of the Kiev of that time. Within the walls of the Pechersky Monastery we see, one after another: the Varangian prince, Simon, who had come from beyond the Baltic Sea; a prince's physician—an Armenian by birth, competing so unsuccessfully with the native physicians of Pechersky, who with a monastery cabbage cured the very strangest diseases, which had nonplussed the Armenian physician; Greek artists, who had come in search of work and who to win friendship related miracles which had befallen them, most flattering to the Pechersky cloister; Hungarians from the banks of the Danube, and Polovtsians from the neighbouring South Russian steppe—in a word whomsoever the current of trade caught up in its waves. In this motley array of raiments and persons, of tribes and dialects, there predominated, of course, men without clan, without tribe. That is, they had clan and tribe, but they had left them somewhere afar; their natal land had long since become alien to them, and for the most part they did not expect to return to it. Family law no longer protected nor hindered them; they had but one father-master—trade, and this had brought them to Kiev. The place of the family organisation, of the pechishche, is taken by the artificial military organisation, the "hundred," with which we have already come in contact. Along with the "elders of the town" appear the ten-men and hundred-men and the thousand-man, and soon the former are crowded out by the latter.

This process of the decomposition of the old patriarchal units determined the evolution of the veche of Kiev. The democratisation of the latter did not lie in the fact that the power of the people increased and the authority of the prince declined. The latter's rights were never limited juridically; while he enjoyed the confidence and support of the "burghers," he might, without hindrance, do whatever he pleased. From the *Kievo-Pechersky Paterik* we learn that a prince might seize any man, even from outside his own principality, begin to torture him, and even torture him to death, seeking after "treasure" to which the prince had as little right as did the man he tortured. In a military republic, such as was the old Russian town, inviolability of the person was quite unknown. When the prince's abuses exceeded the bounds of his subjects' patience, they simply deposed him and sometimes slew him, and that ended the matter. In this respect fifteenth-century Novgorod really differed but little from eleventh-century Kiev. There had been development, not so much of juridical concepts and political forms (some changes that may be traced in this field we shall consider at the end of this chapter) as of the social composition of the masses, politically incarnate in the autocratic popular assembly. Around the original kernel of a few merchant clans, the founders of the town, accumulated a multitude of petty men, common labourers and artisans, whose memory remains in the names of the Potters' and Carpenters' "ends" of Novgorod. As early as the days of trouble which followed on the death of Saint Vladimir (1015), these petty folk were already playing a certain rôle; the chronicle relates that Svyatopolk "the Accursed," on becoming prince of Kiev, "summoned the men and began to give to some clothing, to others money, and distributed a great deal." It was impossible to bribe the merchant aristocracy in this fashion. In

Novgorod at that time the artisan population was already playing such a rôle that Yaroslav (1019-1054), having slain the "eminent men" who had attacked his Varangian druzhina, was nevertheless able to assemble a militia of forty thousand, which his antagonists in mockery called the "carpenters." Kiev at that time was a more conservative town, and, as we learn from an exceedingly curious description of the events of the year 1068, the mass of the population was not armed and organised in military fashion. This was the year of the first great Polovtsian onslaught on Rus, when the system of defence created by Yaroslav proved inadequate. The sons of Yaroslav, having gone out to meet the steppe-dwellers on the River Alta, were completely defeated and fled with the remnants of their warriors—Izyaslav and Vsevolod to Kiev, and Svyatoslav to Chernigov. The remnant of the Kievan militia, having summoned a veche on the market-place, appealed thus to Izyaslav: "The Polovtsians have scattered over the land; let the prince give arms and horses—we shall yet fight with them." From the compressed account of the chronicler (who perhaps had not quite accurately conceived the picture—we must remember that he had a twelfth-century point of view) it is immediately obvious that the speakers were demanding arms and horses for themselves. But how could men who had lost their horses in battle flee from the Polovtsians, and why was it necessary for merchants, who themselves always went armed, to appeal to the prince's arsenal? The demand obviously was for the creation of a new army from those elements of the population which had not previously participated in campaigns and were not armed. Izyaslav had grounds for not trusting them, and he did not comply with their demands. For this he paid with his throne. The Kievans freed his rival, Vseslav of Polotsk, from captivity and pronounced him their prince, while Izyaslav and his druzhina had to flee to Poland. Unfortunately, the chronicle imparts nothing of the order of things established in Kiev after this revolution, the first in Russian history. It is evident only that in a military respect the new régime was not strong; the strata of the population accustomed to bear arms either stood aside or left with Izyaslav; when the latter returned seven months later with Polish auxiliaries, he regained authority without a battle. Deserted by their new prince, who fled to Polotsk, the Kievans became truly desperate, threatening to burn their town and abandon the site, thus inviting the immediate intervention of two other sons of Yaroslav, Svyatoslav and Vsevolod. The town was thereby saved from destruction, but none the less it had to experience a most savage repression; seventy men were executed, others blinded or "destroyed" in some other way, probably sold into slavery. It is noteworthy that the chronicler does not call those executed "eminent men," like those whom Yaroslav slaughtered in 1015, but simply "children" or "men." No less significant is a police measure taken by Izyaslav in anticipation of similar events in the future; he "drove out trading to the hill." The hill was the very oldest part of Kiev, where the town aristocracy lived. Up there, in the year 1068, stood the homestead of the thousand-man Kosnyachek, whom at the time of the uprising the crowd had sought, and not with good intentions. The transfer of trading to the aristocratic part of the town was bound to forestall the formation of a democratic meeting in the market; far from their homes and surrounded by the dependable element, the populace was less dangerous and easier to cope with.

But the triumph of the prince's authority could not prevent the decomposition of the old, patriarchal organisation. Indeed, the prince's authority, which had established its rights with the aid of an alien military force, relied on the latter more than on the old town aristocracy. Izyaslav later, in all his misfortunes (he was expelled from Kiev again in 1073, this time by his own brothers, Svyatoslav and Vsevolod), sought aid in Poland (unsuccessfully this time), from the Western emperor, and even from the pope; but there is no evidence that he had at home anything in the nature of his own party, or that he tried to create one. The decline of family law is vividly expressed, moreover, in judicial usage. To the administration of the sons of Yaroslav—it is unknown whether before or after the revolution of 1068, but in any case before the second expulsion of Izyaslav from Kiev—are credited a number of judicial decisions which put an end to blood vengeance, and, what is still more indicative, established individual responsibility for murder in place of the former family responsibility. "If an *ognishchan* be killed in a quarrel," says the first of these decisions, "the murderer shall pay 80 grivnas, while his people shall not pay." Only for robbery did the whole clan union answer as of old. In addition, one of the decisions established that an ognishchan might be slain with absolute impunity, "like a dog," if caught in the act of stealing. In such case the ognishchan group did not dare to avenge its fellow-member, so weak had the material strength of the family union become. The new custom was undoubtedly directed against the clan aristocracy; yet it compels us to suppose that, having gained a political victory over the lower social groups, the prince afterward made certain social concessions to these same groups, making peace with them at the expense of the heads of their social enemies. The scanty data in the chronicle and other records do not permit a complete restoration of the picture of the socio-economic process that was decomposing the old society. Only here and there do we succeed in seeing, now this, now that corner of it. The chronicle relates that the third of Yaroslav's sons, Vsevolod, who survived his two older brothers, in old age "began to love the ideas of the young and with them held counsel," from which, of course, it does not follow that he surrounded himself with immature youth. The chronicler immediately explains: the "youth" had crowded out from Vsevolod his "first druzhina," the high born counsellors who were wont to surround the prince. The author (in this case hardly the "initial chronicler," but rather one of his sources; he would not have related evil of Vsevolod), sympathising with those displaced, explains the people's dissatisfaction with the last of Yaroslav's sons precisely on the ground of this change. But the grievance of the people, of course, was not that the town aristocracy had lost power; the essence of the trouble lay in the economic conditions, in that strengthening of commercial and money-lending capital then taking place. A curious fact in this connection comes to us, not from the chronicle but from the *Pechersky Paterik*, in a tale about one of the miracles of St. Prokhor "Notch-weed." If we purge this story of the fabulous details about the sweet bread from notch-weed and the ashes by a blessing from Heaven converted into salt, there remains the historical fact that the Pechersky Monastery supplied the poorest classes of the Kievan population with meal (apparently not without adulteration) and salt, whereby it acquired the riches that excited the envy of Prince Svyatopolk, son of Izyaslav, who replaced Vsevolod on the throne of Kiev. Taking advantage of this envy, competitors of the monastery, the traders in salt (obtained from present-day Galicia), who apparently had been quite crowded out of the market by the monastery, applied to the prince for the prohibition of monasterial trade. The monk-author insinuates that they did this for the purpose of establishing monopoly prices on salt, since relations with Galicia had at that time been made difficult by a war, and salt was therefore dear. But, besides this, the protest of petty commercial capital against the incipient large-scale capital of the monasteries is only too clear. Svyatopolk, himself a very typical representative of "primary accumulation," took the part of the petty traders, not disinterestedly but for the quite definite purpose of compelling the monastery to divide the profits with him. Apparently it did so; the upshot of the whole story was that the prince "began to have great love for the cloisters of the Holy Virgin," and the cloisters continued to "distribute" salt freely to the people.

That capital was at work, not only in the town but also in a wide area around it, we can judge from the development of peonage (*zakup-nichestvo*)[1] among the rural population. Material was accumulating for a new explosion, this time more social than political. The signal was given by the death of Svyatopolk, the friend of the money-lenders,

[1] The *zakup* was a peasant bound by indebtedness to work another's land [*za kupu* = in return for a loan]. *Cf. infra*, p. 58.

of the grain and salt speculators. The details of this second Kievan revolution (1113) are just as obscure as those of the first. The rebellious lower groups displayed no more consciousness or organisation than before. They were at first incited against foreign representatives of capital, "going upon the Jews and plundering." But from the outset the policy of provocation was not wholly successful; the homestead of the thousand-man suffered along with the Jews; as in 1068, in the eyes of the people the thousand-man was a representative of the town aristocracy. Shrewd men among the latter foresaw that if they allowed the movement to spread the disturbance would not be confined either to the "Jews" or to the thousand-man and the hundred-men, but would extend to the boyars, to the monasteries, and to the widow of the money-lender prince, try as she might to buy off the Kievan democracy by liberal distribution of alms from the estate of the deceased Svyatopolk. But now there was no Polish army at hand, and the masses had long since become accustomed to arms; as early as 1093 a Kievan regiment had held a veche during a campaign and had compelled the princes and their aristocratic marshals to give battle against their wish. It was necessary to effect a compromise with the urban, and in part with the rural, poorer classes. It had long been felt that the rural element was also beginning to play a political rôle; in this same year 1093 the leaders of Kievan society referred to the fact in advising Svyatopolk against the campaign, remarking that "the land had been impoverished by wars and fines." How deeply contemporaries were impressed by the anxiety ruling circles felt about the peasants is attested by the curious fact that Monomakh's well-known remarks about the peasant's arable and the peasant's horse,[2] which every text-book quotes, were reported twice by the compiler of the initial digest, under 1103 and under 1111, so pleased was he with this theme. It was time to be anxious about the peasants, and in more than words. There was need of a mediator between the restless lower classes and the terrified upper classes of Kievan society, and the most available man was Vladimir Monomakh, then prince of Pereyaslavl. He was peculiarly fitted for the rôle. The upper social classes had long felt confidence in him; in 1093 he had made common cause with the leaders of the Kievan militia, insisting on cautious tactics in opposition to the opinion of the mass of the Kievan "warriors," who demanded decisive action. At the same time he knew how to touch the democratic chord of the Kievans, whom he had called in as mediators in disputes

[2] Svyatopolk had urged that spring was not the time to fight the Polovtsians, for the peasants and their ploughing would be ruined. Vladimir Monomakh replied: "I am amazed that you are so considerate of the plough horses and do not consider this: the peasant begins to plough, the Polovtsian comes, strikes the peasant with an arrow, takes his horse, comes to his village, carries off his wife and children and all his property. Do you consider his horse and not consider him himself?"

between the princes themselves; when he and Svyatopolk had proposed
to decide a quarrel "before the townsmen," Oleg Svyatoslavich had
replied roughly, calling the Kievans "*smerds*," [3] thus playing into the
hands of Monomakh's diplomacy. Of no little service to him also were
his good relations with the Church, the significance of which as an
economic force we have already seen in the case of the Pechersky Monastery. As is quite evident from the chronicle's narrative, the initiative
in inviting Monomakh came from above. But Monomakh did not leave
Pereyaslavl at once. The chronicler gives this delay and the resultant
negotiations a moral-religious tone; Monomakh, it is said, did not come
to Kiev at once because he was mourning for Svyatopolk but finally
consented in view of evidence that, if he delayed longer, the Kievans
would plunder the monasteries. The spicy propinquity of the monasteries to the Jewish money-lenders is, of course, significant; here historical
verity has laughed up its sleeve at the pious lucubrations of the chronicler. But Monomakh probably knew enough about the practical side
of monasteries to understand their dangerous position at such a moment
without special evidence from any one. And the outcome of the negotiations—the celebrated "legislation of Monomakh"—compels us to suppose that the discussions between Monomakh and the representatives
of the ruling circles of Kievan society did not centre on the monasteries.

The "statute" of Vladimir Monomakh has come down to us in a comparatively very late edition; the oldest manuscript of the *Russkaya
Pravda* in which we find this "statute" is referred to the end of the
thirteenth century, *i.e.*, at least 150 years later than the events of 1113.
In this oldest manuscript the "statute" is very brief; it comprises but
a few lines. In manuscripts of a later time it spreads to such proportions that it becomes in itself a sort of supplementary *Russkaya Pravda;*
indeed, it is sometimes called "Monomakh's Pravda." It is not, however, difficult to notice that of the articles "on the zakup," for example,
only the first constitutes anything in the way of a principle; it offers
the zakup the right of suit against his master. "If a zakup flies to the
judges to complain of injury from his master, then for that he shall
not be returned into slavery [as for any other flight], and his case must
be examined." The full significance of this innovation we shall understand if we remember that in the sixteenth century the master-creditor
was still the sole judge of his debtor: "whoever keeps a man in money,"
says a charter of Grand Prince Vasily III (1505-1533) to the men of
Smolensk, "he himself shall judge that man and my [officers] shall not
meddle in that." The further articles relating to zakups discuss various
concrete cases of litigation between a peasant and his master. But, judging from the method by which law was created in ancient Rus—by way of

3 The old and contemptuous word for peasants; *cf. infra*, p. 60.

generalisation from individual decisions, case by case,—it is hardly probable that all these concrete examples had been foreseen in advance by the legislator, Monomakh, and by his "druzhina," the thousand-men of the most important towns along the Dnieper, assembled around him at Berestov, near Kiev. Most probably they represent the application of a fundamental principle to individual cases, *i.e.*, a further development of Monomakh's legislation. The later editor, systematising in a perfectly correct juridical manner all the articles about zakups, brought them into the one chapter that we now read in the later copies of the *Russkaya Pravda*. In all probability, however, the most accurate historically is the oldest copy, with its brief but comprehensive decisions.

It is, however, time to quote the "statute" *in extenso*. "On the death of Svyatopolk, Vladimir [Monomakh] convoked at Berestov his druzhina —the thousand-men Ratibor of Kiev, Prokopy of Belgorod, Stanislav of Pereyaslavl, Nazhir, Miroslav, Ivanka Chudinovich, the boyar Olegov [Prince Oleg Svyatoslavich of Chernigov]; and at the meeting they decreed: whoever took money on condition of paying interest on two a third [*i.e.*, 50% per annum], from him such interest shall be taken for only two years, and after that the principal only shall be sought, and whoever takes such interest for three years, he shall not seek the principal. Whoever takes 10 kuns interest from the grivna by the year [*i.e.*, 20%], such interest shall be admitted in case of a long-term loan." Then, in the majority of copies, come two decisions regulating concrete cases of indebtedness, interesting because they explain who was the object of usurious money-lending; both treat of the merchant trading on another's capital. Especially curious is the first of them. In Old Russian law, as in archaic law generally, a debtor answered for non-punctual payment of a debt, not only with his property but with his person. Under natural economy, as we saw, a man was exchange value *par excellence* and consequently the most reliable security imaginable. The transition to more modern forms of credit everywhere began, as a rule, with the abolition of this barbarous method of payment. In ancient Rus this transition is marked by Monomakh's legislation or by the decrees which developed immediately from it. Sale into slavery for debt was not abolished, but it remained, so to speak, only in the law of criminal recovery. Now they did not sell every debtor into slavery, but only such as drank or gambled away, or by gross negligence lost, the merchandise taken on credit. The "unfortunate" bankrupt, the sufferer from fire or shipwreck, did not answer for the debt with his person "because this misfortune is from God, and he is not guilty in it." As the reader sees, it is not without reason that Monomakh's "statute" may be compared with Solon's debt legislation, which "shook off" indenture for debt from the shoulders of the Athenian debtor of the sixth century B.C.

Though not going so far, the "statute" developed the law in the same direction, developing it, moreover, in a revolutionary way, reversing agreements which even yesterday had been quite legal. Thus the success of the Kievan masses, who from now on hold complete sway on the political stage, was consolidated juridically. The veches of 1146-1147, which we have already studied, give a picture of "popular rule" more complete than anything in the sources for Novgorodan history.

But it was not only juridically that indenture for debt fell from the shoulders of the debtor more completely in Athens of the sixth century B.C. than in twelfth-century Kiev; geographically, too, if it may be so expressed, the reform of Solon was the broader—not only was it impossible to sell a man into slavery for debt, but "debt sums" could not be taken from land. In Kievan Rus of the twelfth century the position of the rural debtor was only somewhat lightened; he remained indentured all the same. The chronicle does not make at all clear the participation of the rural population in the events of the year 1113. That it mentions the peasants and peons serves as proof that they were not altogether outside the political arena. But did the peasant have the same rights as a member of the town democracy, as the merchant? This is very doubtful, and doubtful not only because it was naturally very difficult for the peasantry to take an active part in the town veche; that the peasant could not go to town to a meeting every day is too elementary an explanation to be satisfactory, if only because, as we know, there were analogous conditions both in ancient Greece and in mediæval Italy. Yet nowhere do we find such a sharp line dividing the townsman from the peasant, "town law" from "country law," as in ancient Rus.

The most common name for the masses of the rural population in Old Russian records is "smerds." The chronicle quite definitely regards the peasants as a distinct group of the population, standing lower even than the very lowest category of townsmen. After gaining the victory over Svyatopolk the Accursed, Yaroslav the Wise liberally rewarded his forty thousand militia, already mentioned; he gave "to the elders 10 grivnas each, and to the smerds a grivna each, and to the Novgorodans 10 each to all." It is not important to us precisely how much Yaroslav gave to any one; it is important that the chronicler rated each townsman, without distinction, ten times higher than the rustic, although in Yaroslav's militia their functions were quite identical. Under such conditions, it is evident that, in the eyes of an Old Russian, country origin by no means served as a mark of respect; when another chronicler, not a northerner from Novgorod but a southerner from Galicia, wanted to sting two of his prince's boyars, he called them "lawless men of smerds' stock." There is nothing remarkable in the fact that on the lips of the princes themselves "smerd" was pure abuse, especially obnoxious to the townsmen, apparently, as may be concluded from the negotiations we have cited above between Oleg and Monomakh. When the latter wanted to show commiseration for a poor peasant, he found for him no more flattering epithet than "lean one." But this is everyday, common parlance, so to speak. The chronicle's report of the congress of Vitichev (1100) gives us an example of the official use of the word. Meeting at Uvetichy, the princes address to Volodar and Vasilka the demand, among others: "and deliver our bondsmen and smerds." Thus, in diplomatic negotiations the peasant proves to be something in the nature of a bondsman of the prince. The special dependence of the peasants on the prince is alluded to, not only in this passage but in a whole series of chronicle texts. When one of Svyatoslav's *voevodas* [governors] found two "sorcerers" at Beloozero, before beginning to deal with them, he asked: "Whose smerds are they?" and, on learning that they were his prince's, demanded of the population their surrender. Of a Kievan or a Novgorodan, of a free man, it was not possible to ask *whose* he was, while of the peasant it was asked. With Kievans or Novgorodans a prince could not deal at will, while with peasants he could. In 1229 Prince Michael Vsevolodovich came to Novgorod from Chernigov "and kissed the cross to all the freedom of Novgorod"; such was his relation to the townsmen, while to the smerds he himself "gave freedom for five years not to pay tribute." In the one case it was the liberty of the veche, in the other, the liberty of the prince. And if there was any limit to the latter, it was certainly not set by the liberty of the peasants, but by the veche, which, in Novgorod at least, accounted itself the supreme arbiter over the rural population, too. When the Novgorodans drove out their prince Vsevolod (1136), they listed among his transgressions: "does not watch over the smerd." Finally, the *Russkaya Pravda* names a special punishment (a fine of three grivnas) "if any one torments a smerd without the prince's word"; further on it speaks about the "tormenting" (evidently, torture) of an ognishchan—but here nothing is said about the prince's word. In other words, the prince had the right to hand over a peasant to torture whenever it pleased him.

This closer dependence of the peasants on the prince's authority long ago attracted the attention of scholars, and they have depicted the smerd, now as the prince's serf, now as a "state peasant." Such modernisation of social relationships was a logical consequence of modernisation of the prince's authority; depicting the Old Russian prince as a sovereign, it was difficult to formulate the relationship of the peasants to him in any other way. On the other hand, the smerd of the *Russkaya Pravda* has all the features of a juridically free man; the concept of a "state peasant" evidently does not fit in with the setting of the twelfth century; where there was no state, it is hard to find "state property," live or dead. Hence a quite natural reaction and attempts to prove that the relationship of the peasant to the prince was the relationship of a "subject," nothing more. Literally this characterisation is quite correct; the smerd was precisely a "subject" [*pod danyi*], but in the oldest meaning of this word, which, as we saw in Chapter I, meant a man under tribute [*pod danyu*], one who is obliged to pay tribute. The smerd is a "tributary"; this is his basic characteristic. When the Yugrians wanted to get around the Novgorodans, to deceive them they said to them: "And do not ruin your smerds and your tributes"—ruin the peasants, and there will be nobody to take tribute from. This basic trait of the smerd at once discloses both the origin of the class and its enigmatic relation to the prince's authority. We know that in early Rus tribute evolved historically out of regularised plunder, if we may so express it; at first they took as much as they wished and were able, later they replaced plunder by a regular annual levy, tribute. At a later period tribute was paid to the town; of the men of Pechora, as early as 1096, the chronicle says that they are "people who give tribute to Novgorod." But from the same chronicle's narrative about Igor we know that earlier each head of an armed band collected tribute in proportion to the physical possibility of doing so; moreover, at this earlier time, the towns themselves paid tribute to such chieftains. Novgorod, for example, until the death of St. Vladimir (and perhaps even longer) apparently paid 300 grivnas to the "kunning" of Kiev "for the sake of peace." One very ancient passage from one of the later chronicle digests links the fixing of tribute with the building of towns: "This same Oleg," it says, "began to build towns and fixed tribute through all the Russian land." Before us is a very lively picture of the building of fortified points, whence the newcomers periodically despoil the local population, and whither they slip back with their booty. From time to time the prince himself "with all Rus" appears in these fortresses, reckoning up the total of the "tovar" acquired in the course of the year. Two or three centuries passed. The town, from an abode of merchant robbers, succeeded in converting itself into a great centre of population, with four hundred churches and eight markets, like Kiev. It itself no longer paid tribute to the prince, but rural Rus paid as of old. "To go for tribute" is, as of old, a specially princely profession, like commanding the militia. On occupying another's province, the prince's first business was to send through it his takers of tribute, who did not hesitate because the population had already paid tribute to the former prince. One passage from the chronicle gives occasion to suppose that the prince not only collected tribute but also disposed of it, even at Novgorod. The *Ipatyevsky Chronicle* itself, under the date of 1149, thus reports the conditions of the truce between Yury Dolgoruky, son of Monomakh, and his nephew Izyaslav. "Izyaslav ceded Kiev to Yury, while Yury returned to Izyaslav all the tributes of Novgorod." But we already know that to "rule" meant to "take tribute"; originally political dependence was expressed merely by the payment of tribute. Conversely, in early Rus, down to the close of the Muscovite period, whoever took imposts from people "governed" them in general. The status of the peasant as a tributary made him specially a prince's man.

The prince, in the town a hired guard, was master-votchinnik in the country. Kievan Rus had to resolve this political contradiction. In the question, which of the two laws, that of town or that of country, should take precedence in further development, was involved the fate of the Old Russian "republics." In the final reckoning, as we know, supremacy remained with the country. Writers have long since noted the connection between this issue and economic conditions. Prof. Klyuchevsky establishes in his *Lectures* two facts, closely interrelated: the decline in the weight of the monetary unit, the grivna, which is, in his opinion, explained "by the gradual diminution of the flow of silver into Rus in consequence of the decline of foreign trade"; and embarrassment of the foreign trade transfers of Rus "by the triumphant nomads." But the author of the *Lectures* was evidently somewhat confused by the further question involved: why did these nomads, over whom the princes had triumphed in the tenth and eleventh centuries, themselves begin to triumph in the twelfth? The decline of external power must in its turn be explained by internal causes, and our author names two: "the juridical and economic abasement of the lower classes" on the one hand, and the "princes' feuds" on the other. But, as we have seen, the position of the lower classes was not worsened but bettered in the twelfth century as compared with the eleventh; while the struggles of Vladimir and Yaropolk, the sons of Syvatoslav, in 977-980, or of Yaroslav, son of Vladimir, with his brothers in 1016-1026 deserve the name of "princes' feuds," of course, not a bit less than do the quarrels of Izyaslav with the Olgoviches or with Yury Dolgoruky in the middle of the twelfth century. With all due respect to Prof. Klyuchevsky's method, we must seek another explanation for the economic impoverishment of Kievan Rus, the fact of which he justly perceived. This explanation takes us back to the starting point of the present outline—to "robber trade," on which the prosperity of the Russian town of the eighth to the tenth centuries was founded. Extra-economic appropriation had its limits. Predatory exploitation of a country which subsisted by natural economy could be continued only as long as the exploiter could find fresh, untouched fields for operation. The "feuds" of the princes were not casual by-products of pugnacious temperaments; "captives" were the basis of trade. But whence was this chief article of exchange to be taken when half of the country was so closely bound with great urban centres which protected their lands from injury, while the other half had already been so thoroughly exploited that "neither domestics nor cattle" remained? The last "wild" tribe, which neither Vladimir nor Yaroslav had succeeded in drawing into the compass of their predatory endeavours, was that of the Vyatiches, but Monomakh made an end of them. Just as the ancient Spartan ruler had in his time sought "unapportioned lands," so the Russian princes of the twelfth century sought lands still unplundered—but sought in vain. Monomakh sent his sons and his voevodas [generals] against Dorostol on the Danube, against the Bolgars of the Volga, against the Lechs [i.e., the Poles], and against the Chudes, whence they "returned with many a captive." But the organisational resources of the Old Russian prince were too weak to support exploitation over such a vast territory; on the other hand, both the Bolgars of the Volga and the Lechs were themselves already sufficiently organised to offer resistance and on occasion to pay in the same coin. The fate of Kievan Rus presents a certain analogy to the fate of imperial Rome; both lived on what they found at hand, and when that was consumed, and they were compelled to seek out resources of their own, they had to be satisfied with very elementary forms of economic culture and consequently of every other phase of culture. Moreover, as in the Roman Empire, the "decline" was more apparent than real, for in the thirteenth century the Rus of Suzdal, on the one hand, and the Rus of Novgorod, on the other hand, passed over to methods of production and exchange which, in comparison with the preceding period, represented an undoubted economic advance.

No one has sketched a more vivid picture of the desolation of Kievan Rus than has Prof. Klyuchevsky. The facts presented by him relate in large part to the second half of the twelfth century, in part to the beginning of the thirteenth. But one of the phenomena noted by this author—the decline of the princes' interest in the Kievan provinces—can be traced somewhat further back, to the first half of the twelfth century, in fact. As early as 1142 there took place between the Olgoviches, the oldest of whom, Vsevolod, then occupied Kiev, a very curious dispute about the provinces, during which the younger brothers expressed great readiness to exchange the Kievan provinces (bad ones, it is true) given them by their older brother for those same Vyatiches whom only a quarter of a century before Vladimir Monomakh had finally mastered. This interest in the Vyatiches is, in its turn, very curious if we remember theirs was the corner of the Russian land most remote and least touched by robber exploitation. Vsevolod's younger brothers wanted to get the Vyatiches, not, of course, in order to plunder them, for this could be most conveniently done from a neighbouring province. It is evident that the former conception of a prince as first of all a conqueror, a leader of the hunt for "captives," and, naturally, the defender of his own lands against foreign huntsmen of the same order, is yielding place to another conception. This changed attitude of the prince toward his rights and duties has for some time received attention from historians. Even Solovyev wrote of the distinction in this regard between the north-eastern princes of the twelfth and thirteenth centuries and their southern fathers and grandfathers. Inasmuch as the princes seemed to him to be the sole motive force of ancient Rus, in the political field at least, for him it became in the main a matter of changed relationships between the princes themselves. The former fraternal relations between them are replaced by relations of subjection; the "fatal word subject in place of prince" was first pronounced by Andrew Bogolyubsky. The chronicle's words about Bogolyubsky's despotism he likewise interpreted in precisely this same sense. But it is not likely that the conduct of the "despot" of Suzdal in relation to his Kievan cousins differed much for the worse from the mode of action of Monomakh's son Mstislav, for example, who subjected his kinsmen of Polotsk to administrative exile. The princes liked to talk of brotherhood, but their actual relations by no means rested on such sentimentalities; a strong "brother" always dealt as he pleased with a weak one, stopping neither at murder nor at blinding. Solovyev's successors have quite rightly occupied themselves with another aspect of the "despotism" of Prince Andrew Bogolyubsky. "Prince Andrew was a stern and wilful master, who always acted in his own way, and not according to antiquity and custom," says Prof. Klyuchevsky;[4] ". . . wishing to rule without sharing, Andrew hounded his brothers and nephews and his father's 'foremost men,' i.e., his father's great boyars." This author thinks that "Bogolyubsky's political concepts and governmental practices" had in significant degree been developed by the social surroundings in which he had grown up and under which he lived. "This environment was the dependent town, Vladimir, where Andrew passed the major part of his life." Below we shall see that the political customs of Vladimir, regardless of the fact that it was a new town and perhaps owing precisely to this fact, in no way differed from the corresponding customs of Kiev or even of Novgorod, so that Andrew could not have derived any new governmental practices from this environment. But if again we must reject the explanation that Prof. Klyuchevsky gives to the fact, the fact itself he has again rightly divined; the originality of the "new" princes lies in their "domestic policy," in their methods

[4] *Cf.* **V. O.** Klyuchevsky, *op. cit.*, Vol. I, Chap. XIV.

of administering their lands, and not in their "foreign policy," not in their relations to princes of other, neighbouring lands.

The murder of Prince Andrew is usually represented as a case of court intrigue. Its proximate causes are sketched in a vein very reminiscent of the end of Emperor Paul (1796-1801). Andrew had by his cruelties stirred up against him his own domestics, his household; the execution of one of his intimates, Kuchkovich, seemed the drop that overfilled the cup; Kuchkovich's comrades and relatives took vengeance for his death. Such is the traditional, text-book treatment of the affair. Precisely such a concept of the event the chronicler undoubtedly wished to inspire in his readers, for he himself was a great admirer of Bogolyubsky, the liberal builder of churches and the inflexible protector of Orthodoxy against all heresies. But the chronicler's literary skill—or, more accurately, that of the author of the "narrative" imported into the chronicle—was scarcely adequate to depict this event in full and at the same time to avoid contradictions. In spite of himself, while relating the facts in their chronological sequence, he gives a number of details that are quite incompatible with his general picture. First of all, we learn that the conspiracy extended far beyond the limits of the prince's court; Andrew's murderers had partisans and accomplices even among the "druzhina of Vladimir." This was by no means Prince Andrew's personal druzhina; later it appears more than once in the chronicle as something connected with the town, and not with this or that prince. To judge by the numbers (1,500 men) and by the military significance ascribed to this druzhina by the chronicle (without it the town is represented as defenseless), the chronicle is giving the name "druzhina" to the town militia of Vladimir, the Vladimir "thousand." Not without reason does the chronicler call this force now "the men of Vladimir," now "the druzhina of Vladimir," without distinguishing between these concepts. Thus, to these men of Vladimir the conspirators appeal immediately after the murder, striving to convince the townsmen that they were defending not only their own but the townsmen's interests, too. The chronicler puts into the mouths of the men of Vladimir the very loyal answer: "you are unnecessary to us." But subsequently he is compelled to state a number of facts which cannot be reconciled with this loyalty. "The townsmen of Bogolyubov [the place where the prince was slain] looted the prince's house . . . gold and silver, garments and precious stuffs,—property to which there was no limit; and much evil was done throughout the provinces; they looted the houses of [his officials], and slew them and their children and [officers], and plundered the houses of the latter, not knowing that it is written: where there is law, there is also much injury. Even the peasants from the hamlets came to pilfer. The same thing happened in Vladimir; they did not cease to loot" until the clergy went through the town "with the Holy Virgin."

Thus we see that the event of June 28, 1174, bears little resemblance to what happened in St. Petersburg on March 11, 1801. The latter was an officers' conspiracy, finding support, it is true, in the public opinion of the whole nobility, but awakening no concern in the masses of the population, either in St. Petersburg itself or in Russia at large. In the former we are dealing with an actual popular revolution, just like the events of 1068 and 1113 at Kiev. Not without reason did the chronicler deem it necessary immediately after his tale of the town riot to remind his readers of non-resistance to the prince's authority; he well knew against whom the riot was directed. The murder of the prince, the supreme head of the administration, was but the signal for the overthrow of the administration in general; and there is every reason to think that Prince Andrew's menials were right when they appealed to the sympathy of the men of Vladimir. The chronicler does not deny the factual bases for the popular movement; there had been many "injuries," and the prince's sword had been misused enough, not in foreign wars, as happened in olden time, but in domestic administration. Thus Andrew's despotism had found expression other than the expulsion of the "foremost boyars," which might even have pleased the common people. The burden of his despotism had fallen upon the masses. Bogolyubsky's administration was one of the first systematic attempts to exploit these masses in a new way—not by means of bold inroads from without, but by way of the slow but sure draining of the land "by fines and fees." In its results the new method was no better than the old; the men of Vladimir, who had become acquainted with it through a twofold experience, first under Andrew, then under his kinsmen, the sons of Rostislav, accurately defined the latters' methods when they said that they dealt with their principality "just as with a foreign land." On no account did the men of Vladimir wish to recognise this new order of things. Two years after the deposition of Andrew a new revolution burst out in Vladimir, the sons of Rostislav were overthrown in their turn, and the townsmen secured from their new prince the execution of their foes with all formality; Bogolyubsky's nephews were blinded (some say merely a pretense was made, to appease the agitated people) and their ally and patron, Prince Gleb of Ryazan, was killed in prison.

However, extermination of the representatives of the new order could not remove the causes which had created it. Having laid waste by its rapacious policy the territory all around it, the Old Russian town fell, and no one could arrest its fall. Even before the death of Andrew, at the time of the celebrated siege of Kiev in 1169, the first town of the Russian land was defended by Torks and Berendeys, detachments of steppe nomads hired by Prince Mstislav. When they deserted, the town could no longer hold out, and the Kievans were overtaken by the fate they had always so feared; they themselves became captives. Thousands of captives, and in particular female captives, were dragged from the conqueror-town to the slave markets to which it itself had supplied so much human merchandise in former centuries. But with the destruction of Kiev the devastated South lost all its interest and significance; the nominal conqueror of Kiev, Prince Andrew, under whose banner had marched the army which sacked the "mother of Russian towns," had not himself gone to the South; far more attractive to him was the new system of princely administration being consolidated in the North. The peculiar forms of the military-trading republic endured in the northwest for three more centuries; in its vast colonies Novgorod found an inexhaustible source of "tovar," while its close connection with Western Europe implied possibilities of new organisational resources. In the rest of Russia the slow process of decomposition of old, predatory, urban civilisation into rural was bound to continue. Nothing further was needed but the ruin of the town, for, as we shall well remember, the town had brought nothing new into the country. The means of production remained unchanged; the only difference was that the products, which formerly the town had unceremoniously seized as far as its arm could reach, and not infrequently along with the producers, now remained at home. Novgorod and Pskov here represented an exception. In them local exchange had developed to such a point that the town was already something more than a bird of prey (though here, too, this rôle remained dominant). In the rest of Russia the town had lived an independent life, but little concerned with the rural Rus around it. The *Russkaya Pravda,* which develops in detail questions of "tovar," of money, and of interest, says extraordinarily little about land—so little, indeed, that some scholars have felt justified in asserting that the *Pravda* "does not contain regulations about the acquisition or alienation of land." As a matter of fact, the *Pravda* mentions land four times; about interest rates it contains 23 regulations (in the fullest copies); about bondsmen, 27. How much more frequently than the landholder did the slaveholder appear in the Old Russian court! The town, economically alien to the country, was, as we saw, also juridically cut off from it by an impassable wall. In the town were free men and a powerful veche, in the country tributaries without rights, whom the princes "drove" to war, like cannon-fodder it might be said, had there been cannon then. This term, "drive," is extraordinarily expressive, and by no means accidental; in the republic of Novgorod it survived till the last years of her existence. Even under the year 1430 the chronicler of Novgorod noted down: "the peasants were driven to Novgorod to build a town." Only when unpaid working hands were needed in large number did the Old Russian democracy bethink itself of its "smerds." For their part, the peasants were little concerned about the democracy and did not stir when Muscovite feudalism advanced to crush what was left of it.

Owing to the special conditions of her existence Novgorod fell before her economic rôle had been played to the end. The southern towns, and likewise those of the northeast, in so far as they were not simply overgrown princely manors, were nearer their natural death when their last hour struck. But just as scarcely any living organism dies a wholly natural death, so the natural demise of the Old Russian trading town was hastened on by a series of causes that aided the conversion of urban Rus into rural. One of these causes, the most immediate, historians have long ago indicated; it was the sum total of the struggle with the steppe, ending with the great Tatar pogrom in the thirteenth century. From the ninth century to the eleventh Rus was on the offensive against the men of the steppe; if we compare on the map the southern defensive lines of Rus under Vladimir and under Yaroslav, we readily see an advancing southward movement. The culmination of this advance was Yaroslav's victory over the Pechenegs (1034); in 1068 the sons of Yaroslav were beaten by a new horde from the steppe, the Polovtsians. From that time on the latter hardly disappear from the chronicle's field of vision for a single year; even in the middle of the thirteenth century the Galician-Volhynian chronicle-digest calls them to mind. The devastations produced by their raids were great, of course, but it is necessary to remember that in essence they were in no way to be distinguished from the feuds of the princes. For the Polovtsians, like the princes, invaded others' lands for captives. If we add that in the feuds themselves the Polovtsians took a very active part, willingly hiring themselves out in the service of the princes, and that the princes by no means hesitated to intermarry with the Polovtsians, so that in the last analysis it could not be said whose blood flowed in the veins of any descendant of Izyaslav—then there is not the slightest foundation for thinking of the Polovtsians as an alien and obscure "Asiatic" force, as a dark cloud hovering over the representatives of "European civilisation," over Kievan Rus. But in so far as Polovtsian raids increased the devastation quantitatively, they thereby hastened on the fatal end. Nevertheless, it was not they who dealt the final blow. The men of the steppe did not know how to take towns; even when they fell on Kiev unexpectedly (1096), they could not force their way into it but had to confine themselves to devastation of the environs. If fortified centres did fall into their hands from time to time, they were only petty ones. Not until 1203 did they succeed in playing the master at Kiev itself; but it was Russian princes, Rurik Rostislavich and the Olgoviches, who brought the Polovtsians thither.

A different kind of enemy were the Tatars. Steppe horsemen, moving about just as easily and freely as the Polovtsians, they had assimilated all the military technique of their time. As early as their Chinese wars they had learned to take cities surrounded by stone walls. In the words of Plano-Carpini, each Tatar was obliged to have with him an intrenching tool and ropes for the purpose of drawing siege machines. In an assault on any Russian town, they first of all "encolumned" it— fenced it around; after that they began to strike with battering-rams on the gates or on the weakest part of the wall, striving at the same time to set fire to the buildings inside the walls; for this latter purpose they used, among other things, Greek fire, which it seems they even perfected somewhat. They had recourse to mines; in some cases they even diverted rivers. In a word, in point of military skill, as a French writer has justly remarked, the Tatars in the thirteenth century were like the Prussians in the middle of the nineteenth. The very strongest Russian towns fell into their hands after a few weeks', sometimes only a few days', siege. But the taking of a town by the Tatars meant such complete and unmitigated destruction as neither the Russian princes nor even the Polovtsians had ever encompassed, and precisely because Tatar strategy set itself a more distant goal than simple acquisition of captives. To support its "world" policy the Horde[5] needed large money resources; these it extracted from conquered peoples in the form of tribute. In order to guarantee the punctual receipt of the latter, it was first of all necessary, from the military point of view, to make it impossible for the population to renew the struggle. To destroy the great centres of population, to drive out their inhabitants, in part to exterminate them or to lead them off into captivity—all this was admirably calculated to achieve this immediate aim. This is why the Tatars were such great foes of the towns, and why Baty's onslaught seemed to the townsman-chronicler the crown of all imaginable horrors. This is why, likewise, they strove to annihilate all the higher ruling elements of the population, including the clergy; "the better, well-born men never expect mercy from them," says Plano-Carpini, while the chronicles persistently name among those slain or made captive by the Tatars "monks and nuns," "priests and priests' wives." Destruction of the towns and annihilation of the upper classes alike weakened the military-political organisation of the conquered and guaranteed their submission for the future. With one blow the Tatar devastation completed a process which had become manifest long before the onslaughts of the Tatars

[5] Literally, camp; the government of the Mongol khans.

and which had been produced by economic conditions—the process of the decomposition of the urban Rus of the tenth to the twelfth centuries.

But the influence of Tatar conquest was not limited to this negative result. The Tatar Ascendancy not only contributed to the disintegration of old Rus but also contributed to the integration of a new Rus—the appanage Rus of Moscow. A few lines above the reader must have noted that the tendency of the Horde to exploit the subjugated population as tributaries perfectly corresponded to the new tendencies that we observed in the princely policy of the eleventh and twelfth centuries. But here, too, as in the matter of the conquest itself, the Tatars ploughed deeper. In the first place, not content with the former policy of collection, based partly on the appetite of the taker, partly on the strength of the resistance of the giver, the Tatars organised a regular system of assessment, which survived the Tatars themselves by many centuries. The first registers of taxable population are directly connected with the subjugation of Russia by the Horde; the first mention of "plough description"—of the direct distribution of imposts by tax units (the "plough" equals two or three workmen)—is connected with the Tatar tribute of the thirteenth century; earlier, in all probability, the whole clan paid in a lump; for penal fines we know this to be certain, and there is no reason to think that the "tribute" was paid otherwise. Nothing remained to the Muscovite government but to develop the Tatar system further, which it did. But the Tatars did not merely introduce technical improvements in Old Russian finances; in so far as it was possible for a force acting from without, they introduced marked changes in social relationships, once again in the same direction in which the latter had already begun to develop under the influence of native conditions. In the classical period of Kievan Rus only the rural population was "under tribute." The urban population did not pay permanent direct imposts; consequently princely exploitation in the town was expressed in the form of abuses in judicial penalties. The conquerors of Russia had no reason to have recourse to such circuitous ways, and in the Tatar "number" all were reckoned, townsmen and rustics indiscriminately. In the area of immediate conquest the Horde with no great effort succeeded in imposing tribute; here the urban population was so weakened that it could not think of resistance. A different picture is presented by the large centres of population still inviolate physically, which submitted to the Horde only from fear of an invasion. The chronicle of Novgorod presents in an extraordinarily vivid fashion the tax reform there; it was not easy for the free men of Novgorod to suffer conversion into unfree "tributaries." The Tatar tribute-takers appeared here for the first time in 1257. The chronicler does not record, and probably did not himself know how, but the city succeeded in ransoming itself from the "number," sending good presents to the "tsar" (as they always called the khan) and, perhaps, liberally bribing the envoys themselves. But the khan's administration inflexibly pursued its system; whatever happened, Novgorod must be taken into the "number" with all the rest of Rus; two years later the Tatar officials again appeared, and this time bribes did not suffice. "There was a token on the moon, so that it could not be seen at all," relates the chronicler. "In the same winter came Michael Pineshchinich from the Low [the land of Suzdal][6] with a false embassy and spoke thus: 'If you do not put yourselves into the number, behold, already our regiments are on the Low land.' And the Novgorodans put themselves into the number. . . ." But this was only juridically; the veche, deceived by the "false embassy," had capitulated in words only. The old order of things was in turmoil when words began to be converted into deeds, when the Tatar *baskaks* came to Novgorod and set about the collection of the tribute. They began with the provinces, and the mere rumours of what was taking place there evoked a disturbance in the town; the provinces of Novgorod were inhabited not only by peasants but also by many townsmen, artisans and merchants who had purchased land, the *svoezemtsy*. Now all without distinction had become tributaries. When the turn of Novgorod itself came, the disturbance developed into open revolt; "the rabble did not wish to give the numbers, but said: we will die honourably for Saint Sofia and for the homes of the saints!"

And men "were made in twain." The upper strata of society, knowing what fate awaited them in case of a Tatar inroad, favoured a pacific issue, submission to the demands of the Horde. The roughly apportioned method of assessment, at so much from each individual economy, was very satisfactory to the rich. The Tatar tribute-takers rode through the streets and counted the houses; each house, no matter to whom it belonged, paid one and the same amount. "And the boyars made it easy for themselves and ill for the lesser ones." Matters had apparently gone as far as a formal agreement between the "accursed" Tatar envoy, on the one hand, and the prince, Alexander Nevsky, and the Novgorod aristocracy, on the other; in case of further resistance of the "rabble" they had agreed to attack the town from two sides. It is unknown what averted a collision at the last minute; according to the chronicler, it was "Christ's might," but a modern historian looks for another explanation. The chief cause, it seems, was the solidarity of the boyars, who felt that for them this was a question of life and death, that the "savage beasts," coming from the wilderness in the form of

---

6 The Russian "mesopotamia," lying between the Upper Volga and the Oka, was downstream from Novgorod and hence was called "the Low"; similarly the lesser Novgorod is called Nizhny-Novgorod, *i.e.*, Novgorod the Low.

Tatars, would first of all "eat the flesh of the strong and drink the blood of the boyars." The masses of the population were already too dependent on commercial capital to enter upon an open struggle with all the capitalists rather than with one of their mutually hostile groups, as usually happened in such collisions. However it was, the Tatars finally secured their tribute from the free Novgorodans, and the chronicler did not know how to explain it except as chastisement from the Lord for their sins. With a sigh of regret that even this severe punishment had no effect on the impenitents, he concludes his narrative.

The history of the Novgorod "number" shows how hostile to the Tatars were the democratic elements of the veche, and the Tatars were too versed in practical politics not to understand and appreciate this hostility. A series of events in other parts of Rus clearly disclosed that the townsmen everywhere, as soon as they had recovered from the immediate effects of the devastation, were ready to imitate Novgorod's stand. In 1262 the men of the land of Rostov "willed a veche" and drove out the Tatar tribute-takers from Rostov, Vladimir, Suzdal, and Yaroslavl. In 1289 the same thing was repeated in Rostov, in which case the solidarity of Prince Dmitry of Rostov with the Tatars stands out very clearly. The alliance, which was already apparent in Novgorod in 1259, of the "better men" and the prince with the Tatars against the "rabble" was bound to become, and actually did become, a constant phenomenon. That in supporting the princes and their boyars in the struggle with the "lesser men" the Horde would in the end create the Muscovite autocracy, which would abolish the Horde itself as unnecessary—this remote prospect was beyond the Tatar politicians' field of vision, a fact for which there was some degree of justification. The Tatar Ascendancy established itself in Rus in the first half of the thirteenth century, while it was not until the second half of the following century that the princes of Moscow decided to come out openly against the "tsar." A century and a half of absolute subjection of Rus to the Horde was assured at any rate.

As we see, then, the Tatar invasion has not without some justification occupied in national tradition a place that the modern science of history has been inclined to wrest from it. And this science is right in the sense that this external shock could bring into Russian history nothing essentially new. But, as usually happens, the external crisis helped to resolve the internal crisis and in part supplied the means for its solution. In conclusion, the reservation must be made that it would be too narrow an interpretation to call the economic crisis that undermined Kievan Rus exclusively external. The reader has probably already noted the absence in our interpretation of one factor, on which, nevertheless, the ancient town was, as we have already said, intimately dependent, and with which it was more closely connected than it was with the rural Rus surrounding it. This factor was the foreign market—the consumer of the wares, animate and inanimate, of the Russian merchant. We are not here dealing with the history of European trade and therefore have no occasion to study in detail the fate of international exchange in the Middle Ages. But the connection between certain quite catastrophic events in European trade and Russian history obtruded itself on the minds of Russian bookmen even of that age. Among the few facts culled from "universal" history by the first chronicle of Novgorod, the story of the taking of Constantinople by French and Italian crusaders in 1204 occupies a quite exceptional place. Only of the Tatar invasion does the chronicle speak at greater length and in more detail; all other Russian events are much more sparingly and drily dealt with. It is as if the author had seen with his own eyes the destruction of the capital of all Orthodox Christendom—so excited is his imagination by this picture, about which, however, he had only read in Byzantine chronographies. It is significant that what might have seemed to be most interesting for him—the religious aspect, the seizure of the centre of œcumenical Orthodoxy by the Latins—does not occupy the central foreground. On the other hand, what is emphasised, and this is not less significant, is the solidarity of the Greeks and the Varangians who jointly defended the city. The Novgorodan of the thirteenth century dimly felt the objective significance of this event. It was the last link in the long chain of phenomena, which historians of the past designated by the general name of "crusades," and more recent historians prefer to call "French colonisation in the Levant." A struggle for eastern markets was in progress. In the first half of the Middle Ages they were wholly in the hands of the Arabs and Byzantines, and only through their medium did the North European Varangians have access to them. Just at this time the Dnieper and Volkhov became perhaps the most lively trading highway of Europe; Russia and Sweden were flooded with Eastern coins (all the Arab *dirgems* found in innumerable Russian and Scandinavian treasure-troves are, as is well known, not older than the end of the seventh, and not more recent than the eleventh century), and matters had gone so far that, as Russians represented it, it was impossible to travel even from Asia Minor to Rome except by way of Kiev and Novgorod. In the chronicle's well-known story about the Apostle Andrew it is said that Andrew was teaching in Sinope, whence he came to Korsun, "and, having seen that from Korsun it is not far to the mouth of the Dnieper, had a mind to go to Rome." But from the eleventh century on commercial Europe, still headed by Varangians, but this time from Western and Southern Europe, Normans and Sicilians, begins to open its own route to the East, wresting the monopoly of Eastern trade from the

Mohammedans and Byzantine Greeks. The expedition of 1203-1204, when the chief commercial centre of the Greek East was taken and plundered at the hands of French knights brought on Italian ships and guided by the "blind doge," the incarnation of Venetian trading policy, perfectly characterises the conclusion of the struggle. Now the highway from the Black Sea to Rome went, not by the Dnieper but through Venice, while the "great water route from the Varangians to the Greeks" ended to the south in a commercial blind alley. Now it was easier for the Varangians to make contact with the Greek countries by another river, the Rhine. The union of Rhenish towns, as is well known, was the embryo of the Hansa, which embraced the whole Baltic with its counting houses; on the extreme eastern periphery of this chain appeared Novgorod, of Russian trading towns the only one for which the shifting of world trade routes was more advantageous than prejudicial. All the rest of the stopping-places on the great highway of international exchange were converted into lonely trading villages on a by-road, and almost at the same time were destroyed by the Tatars. Two such blows simultaneously even an economically healthy country could not have borne without a resultant lingering decline, but such a country would have recovered sooner or later; for early urban Rus, already internally devitalised by its outworn economic forms, decline was definitive.

CHAPTER V

THE fall of Kiev is usually treated as having directly and immediately caused the centre of Russian history to shift northeastward, to "the mesopotamia of the Oka and the Volga." But the transition was not so direct and immediate, as must be apparent to any one not unduly influenced by the Muscovite point of view—Muscovite in the narrowest and most precise sense of the word. To a fifteenth-century grand prince of Moscow and his adherents it no doubt seemed possible and even probable that he had received authority from "our forefather Vladimir Monomakh" without any intervening stages. Yet, three hundred years earlier one of the ancestors of this prince, free from the fantastic ideas that made a former dependent town of Suzdal the capital of the world, looked at things more realistically. Vsevolod Big Nest saw Kiev's successor, not in Moscow nor even in Vladimir, but in Novgorod the Great. When he sent his son off to this city, he said to him: "My son Constantine! On thee God has placed the seniority among your brothers, while Novgorod the Great holds seniority among the principalities in the whole Russian land." Doubtless this story is not unmixed with legend manufactured in Novgorod itself, but it contains a kernel of truth, as Constantine himself was to find out; later the Novgorodans seated him on the grand-princely throne of Suzdal-Vladimir, for at the moment the Novgorodans were masters in north Rus, just as a hundred years earlier the Kievans had been in the South.

The causes of this relative stability of the northern trading centre as compared with its southern rival have been noted in general outline. In Novgorod trade bore the same predatory character as in the South; the same "tribute," *i.e.*, products taken from the immediate producers by force, constituted the chief article of export. But such means of acquiring "merchandise" needed an extensive field of operations. There must be ever new and untouched, or at least only partially touched, areas to feed this kind of trade. The ascendancy of Kiev was maintained by exploitation of neighbouring Russian lands and tribes, and when these had been exhausted, there was no longer anything left on which to live. But the Rus of Novgorod had a wide colonial domain, embracing the whole southern littoral of the Arctic Ocean, approximately to the Obi. Here was a practically inexhaustible store of the objects of exchange

76

most valuable at that time—first and foremost, furs. Not without reason did the fur trade first acquire a wholesale character in Novgorod. Nikitsky, the historian of Novgorod's economic life, says: "Furs circulated in trade usually in large quantities, by thousands, half-thousands, quarters, forties, dozens, tens, and fives, rarely in ones. The more valuable furs were usually sold in the smaller units, most of all in forties; the less valuable in thousands, and even in tens of thousands. Among the more valuable the sources mention especially furs of sable and beaver, marten and fox, polecat, ermine, and weasel, skins of mink or river otter and lynx. Among the less valuable appear bear, wolf, and rabbit furs, and in particular squirrel skins, which were sold in especially large quantities. The latter must be understood, it seems, whenever the sources simply mention fur goods as *Schön Werk, Russen Werk, Naugaresch Werk.*" Almost monopolistic sway on the fur market of itself guaranteed to Novgorod a stable position in the system of exchange that grew up around the Baltic Sea toward the latter half of the Middle Ages. But still more important under the conditions of the time was the fact that in the colonies of Novgorod was to be found almost the sole source of precious metals in all Rus. "Trans-Kaman," *i.e.*, Ural, silver flowed both to Western Europe and to Moscow after passing through the intermediate stage of tribute collected by Novgorod from the Yugrians and other tribes of the Urals, who had inherited the wealth of the ancient Biarmiya which had so tempted early Scandinavian heroes. As late as the end of the twelfth century it was possible to make expeditions thither that are reminiscent of the campaigns for tribute undertaken by Igor and his contemporaries. In 1193 the whole militia of Novgorod perished in the land of the Yugrians, a victim to its own avarice and to the guile of the natives, who "deceived" the Novgorodan voevoda, saying to him: "We will amass for you silver and sables and all other splendid things; do not destroy your peasants and your tribute." The voevoda believed them, whereas in fact it was warriors that the Yugrians had amassed. When all was ready, they lured him and his staff into an ambuscade in which they perished. After this it was not difficult for the Yugrians to deal with the leaderless fighting-men, who were exhausted by hunger into the bargain. Only 80 men returned home; "and there mourned in Novgorod the prince, and the bishop, and all Novgorod." But individual disasters did not alter the fact that, by and large, "trans-Kaman silver" regularly entered the treasury of Novgorod. And not without reason was Ivan Kalita, the first grand prince of Moscow, so eager to secure this particular variety of Novgorod's tribute. A great part both of his table silver and even of that of his grandsons and great-grandsons was of Novgorodan origin, marked with the names of Novgorodan prelates and posadniks. Seizure

of Novgorod's "tribute-takers" laden with trans-Kaman silver was for
Novgorod's foes as favourite a method of warfare as, for English cor-
sairs of the sixteenth century, was the seizure of Spanish galleons with
gold coming from the New World. When Ivan the Great dealt the fatal
blow to Novgorod, he first occupied the Dvina, hastening to cut off his
antagonist's eastern colonies.

But it was not silver only that came into Novgorod from the east.
We saw that the decline of Kiev, aside from its internal, local causes,
reflected also an external change—the transfer of Mediterranean trade
from the hands of the Byzantine Greeks into the hands of the Italians
and the French. This change robbed of its value the "great water
route" from the Varangians to the Greeks along the Dnieper. But
this was far from being the only artery of Eastern trade in the Middle
Ages. There remained another route, by the Volga to the Caspian Sea;
the European end of this route, too, lay at Novgorod. One Eastern ware,
silk, even constituted an important article in Novgorod's trade with the
West. Thus that traffic which had long since been choked in the Dnieper
basin continued to hold its own on the Volkhov even 200 years later.

Novgorod was still growing when in southern Rus growth had long
since given way to decay and ruin. From the example of Novgorod we
can judge what Kievan Rus might have become, had its economic resources not been drained in the twelfth century. Herein lies the interest
of the study of Novgorod's history. This interest is augmented by the
almost complete absence (not wholly complete, as certain historians in-
cautiously affirm) of another disturbing factor, the Tatar yoke. It is
of course impossible to allege, as one very renowned scholar has done,
that Novgorod "did not look the Horde's baskak in the eyes." In
analysing the events of the years 1257-1259, we saw that there was a
moment when she "experienced the immediate weight and dread of the
Tatar." But in Novgorod's history this was just for a moment, whereas
the Low land lived under this weight for centuries. In a word, on the
Volkhov we may expect certain social combinations which did not develop
on the Dnieper, although they were the logical sequel to the system of
relationships that had existed in southern Russia.

We have just discussed one example of this further development. We
know that mediæval trade, both in Russia and in the West, was small-
scale, that the mediæval trader resembled a contemporary peddler rather
than what we now call a merchant. The attentive reader has noted,
nevertheless, that this comparison is not applicable to Novgorod's fur
trade. One does not carry thousands, and still less tens of thousands,
of squirrel skins on one's back. If Kievan Rus dealt in merchandise on
a large scale, it was in the sole case of human merchandise—slaves. There
are cases where hundreds of slaves were in the hands of a single person.

One of the princes of Chernigov, for example, had, according to the chronicle, 700 menials; it is not likely that these were servants or even field bondsmen. The Novgorodans were, of course, not squeamish about menials. The Ushkuiniks, who in 1375 plundered Kostroma and Nizhny-Novgorod, sold all their "captives," predominantly women, to Moslem merchants in Bolgary. Just as in the times of Saint Vladimir! But it is noteworthy that this article of trade does not stand out in the history of Novgorod as it had earlier stood out elsewhere. On the other hand there does stand out a new phenomenon—the accumulation in a few hands of large capital in the form of money. In 1209 the veche of Novgorod rose against the posadnik Dmitry Miroshkinich and his brothers, who, in alliance with the prince of Suzdal, had been striving to oppress the free city. For this attempt they paid with confiscation of all their belongings. The veche converted all the "substance" of the Miroshkiniches into the property of the town; their villages and menials were sold; in addition, their hidden treasures were discovered and seized. Everything taken was subjected to per capita division, and to each Novgorodan fell 3 grivnas, *i.e.*, 40-60 rubles in pre-war currency. But the chronicler says that the confiscations were not without abuses; certain men "seized hidden things," whatever fell into their hands during the disturbance, and thus grew rich. In addition, besides movable and immovable property and ready cash there were also found in Dmitry's house "tablets"—bills of exchange of Novgorodan merchants; these were given to the prince, thus making the private possessions of the Miroshkiniches state property. If we take all these details into consideration, we see that in Novgorod as early as the thirteenth century there were millionaires (if we translate the money value of that time into that of the present). The mention of "tablets" clearly indicates the basis of the authority and influence of the greatest family in Novgorod at that time. But there is another curious aspect to the affair. In Novgorod Dmitry represented that new financial policy for which Prince Andrew Bogolyubsky had paid with his life thirty years before. The Miroshkiniches were accused of making innovations in the exaction of judicial penalties. In Novgorod financial exploitation must have produced a still more powerful impression than in Suzdal, accustomed to princely tyranny; and yet Dmitry Miroshkinich had succeeded in being the master for four years (1205-1209). In fact, he survived until his own ally, Prince Vsevolod Big Nest of Suzdal, surrendered him to the Novgorodans, saying to them: "Who is good to you do ye love, but the evil do ye punish." But this was done too late, as the sequel showed. Svyatoslav, son of the prince of Suzdal and himself prince of Novgorod, outlasted the posadnik Dmitry by only a year. In 1210 Mstislav the Bold of Toropets, having heard that Novgorod "suffers violence from the princes," appeared in Torzhok and was received with outstretched arms by the Novgorodans, who immediately arrested Svyatoslav "until there shall be justice with his father." Soon the latter had to acknowledge that the collapse of Suzdal's financial policy in Novgorod entailed the end of Suzdal's dominance there. Mstislav seated himself firmly on the throne of Novgorod, and Vsevolod Big Nest himself concluded a treaty with him as prince of Novgorod.

The events of 1209 in Novgorod present, as we see, a perfect analogy with those of 1174 and the following years in Suzdal. But whereas the Suzdal revolution had no further consequences, that of Novgorod was the starting point of a remarkable epoch in the history of the town—according to the estimate of some historians the most brilliant. "For Novgorod set in in such days of heroism, glory, and honour, as for Kiev under Vladimir Monomakh," Kostomarov says of this period. If we remember that in those days Novgorod set up princes, both at Kiev and at Vladimir, and that the throne of Novgorod was contested by the most influential and renowned of the existing descendants of Rurik, it is hardly possible to add anything to its outward splendour. Unfortunately, showy external events, dazzling the eyes not only of the later historian but also of the chronicler himself, have left the domestic life of Novgorod in obscurity. We sense that for approximately forty years a desperate social struggle seethed in the city, but on the pages of the chronicle are noted only the most concrete personal results of this struggle in the form of a succession (frequently effected by violence) of archbishops, posadniks, thousand-men, and other dignitaries. Only rarely and casually do the causes of the revolution and the social forces involved stand out. Only once does the chronicler quite clearly disclose the "class contradictions" in Novgorodan society, and then only at the very end of the period under consideration. At this time the throne of Novgorod was occupied by Vasily, a son of Alexander Nevsky. The Novgorodans drove him out and seated in his place his uncle Yaroslav, who had just "fled out of the Low land"; thus, although a Suzdalan, he was now the candidate of the anti-Suzdal party. On learning that the Novgorodans had expelled his son, Alexander Nevsky went to war against Novgorod. He was supported by Torzhok, a town economically more closely connected with the land of Suzdal than with its own metropolis. This gave hope to the Suzdal party in Novgorod itself; the Suzdal emigré, Yaroslav, who was enthroned there, took fright and fled. The preponderant majority of the Novgorodans, headed by the posadnik, firmly resolved not to yield to Alexander Nevsky. This majority the chronicler flatly calls the "lesser" men. "And there kissed the cross to the Holy Virgin the lesser men—to stand in everything for the good cause of Novgorod, for their fatherland, to live or die with it; while the knightly men had evil thoughts—to vanquish the lesser men and to take a prince according to their own will.'' But it is significant that the ''knightly'' men were able to act only by intrigue; they lacked the spirit to come out openly against the veche even in sight of the Suzdal regiments. And the marshal of the latter entered into negotiations directly with the democratic elements and their representative. They agreed on what we should now call a ''change of ministry''; the posadnik had to resign in favour of another. But he was not surrendered to Prince Alexander Nevsky, as the latter had demanded; and, in general, except for this change of personnel, the veche evidently conceded nothing. Yet Nevsky attached such significance to his victory that he occupied the throne of Novgorod himself, evidently thinking that his son would not possess sufficient authority. The events just related are alone sufficient to modify significantly the opinion, very widespread in the literature on the subject, that the veche communities of Pskov and Novgorod were exclusively aristocratic in structure.

In the case of Novgorod, indeed, we have a complete picture of the evolution of the veche, of which we were able to study only the first stages in the history of Kiev. The patriarchal aristocracy was replaced, not by an oligarchy of large proprietors but by a democracy of ''merchants'' and ''common people''—of petty traders and artisans, of ''plebes'' who by reason of their plebeian outlook were akin to the peasantry, in relation to which at this moment of elation they were not so much lords and masters as political leaders, the fighting and conscious vanguard of these inarticulate masses. Hence the victories of the urban democracy were accompanied by exemptions for the peasants: the former won rights; the latter took advantage of this fact to get rid of an immediate material burden. As far as rights are concerned, it was, in the main, in this period that the Novgorodan veche made its gains. The first ''constitution'' of Novgorod that has come down to us—a charter by which Prince Yaroslav, Nevsky's brother, kissed the cross ''to all Novgorod''—is assigned to the year 1265, but its content is much older. Besides indefinite allusions to ''antiquity and custom,'' to ''fathers and grandfathers,'' there is in the charter a definite reference to the father of this Prince Yaroslav, Yaroslav son of Vsevolod Big Nest.

We do not know the exact content of the charter which the earlier Yaroslav swore to observe, but it is possible to work out its basic features, in part from what the chronicle tells us, in part from later charters (of 1265, 1270, 1305, 1308, and other years). From the chronicle we learn that as early as 1218 the veche wrested from the prince his right to remove elected town authorities, except ''for fault,'' *i.e.*, by judicial process. In this year Svyatoslav of Smolensk, who then occupied the throne of Novgorod, took it into his head to replace the posadnik

Tverdislav. It is curious that it never entered the head of this prince from Smolensk to carry out the change on his own authority, without the knowledge of the veche; the Old Russian prince was too accustomed to the idea that in the town the veche was master and that without the veche it was impossible to act. It was not on this point that the dispute arose, nor does its interest lie here, but rather in the fact that what perhaps would have satisfied any southern town did not satisfy Novgorod. The veche enquired of the prince's emissary: "Of what has Tverdislav been guilty?" And, learning that the prince had no charge against him but simply found him inconvenient, the veche refused even to consider the question, simply reminding the prince of Novgorod's rule that without fault no one could be deprived of office, and that on this the prince himself had taken oath to Novgorod. Svyatoslav apparently submitted without dispute, "and there was peace." So the chronicler concludes the story of this episode, without stating the prince's reply. Probably he did not make answer, tacitly admitting that for him Novgorod's officials actually were irremovable; for him, but not for the veche, which never hesitated to expel by force, not only posadniks but the princes themselves, whenever they gave offence. In the extant treaties reproducing this stereotyped rule the details at the same time disclose the reasons for this rule. The prince could not remove Novgorod's officials, nor could he do anything without them. Without the posadnik he could neither apportion the provinces, nor judge, nor give charters. The attempt to act personally in these cases is expressly defined by one of these treaties as taking the law into his own hands: "and upon taking the law into your own hands, prince, do not meditate." In all except his special, military function the prince of Novgorod "reigned but did not govern." A "ministry" governed, a ministry—the posadnik and the thousand-man—responsible to the autocratic people, being both elected and removed by the veche.

Since the administration of the provinces lay entirely in the hands of plenipotentiaries of the town community (". . . as to all the provinces of Novgorod, them, prince, hold ye not with your own men, but hold with the men of Novgorod . . ."), and since the prince was deprived of the possibility of making himself a great force in local feudal society (neither he, his wife, nor his boyars could purchase lands in the domain of Novgorod), he had no means of interfering in the domestic life of Novgorod. To exploit his lands "as though dealing with the province of another," following the example of Andrew Bogolyubsky, was not to be thought of in Novgorod.

The norms of public law established in Novgorod about the first half of the thirteenth century betokened a complete breach with patriarchal tradition, and herein lies their significance, not only locally, for Nov-

gorod, but generally, for Russia. Patriarchal ideology recognised no
difference between the master and the sovereign, between property rights
and state authority. In Novgorod's treaties with the princes, however,
this distinction is drawn more sharply than almost anywhere else in
the whole field of Russian history. Novgorod took every measure to
prevent the prince from becoming proprietor either of an inch of Novgorod's land or of a single Novgorodan. Neither he nor his wife nor
his boyars could purchase villages in Novgorod, and any they had purchased they must return. Neither the prince himself nor any of his men
could accept *zakladniks* [debtors who pledged their person] in the land
of Novgorod, whether peasants or traders. He could trade with the
Germans, but only through the medium of Novgorodans. If any privilege
was accorded him, its limits were nicely defined. Thus, he could go to
Lake Ladoga to catch fish, but only once in three years. He could go
hunting in Rusa, but only in autumn, not in summer. He had the
exclusive right to kill wild boars, but only within sixty versts of the
town; beyond this limit any Novgorodan could hunt boars. In a word,
the prince of Novgorod had no occasion to deem himself "master" in
the land of Novgorod. To use an old Roman expression, the prince of
Novgorod was the first magistrate of the republic; this view, apparently,
was current in Novgorod. Not without reason does the chronicler put
in the mouth of Tverdislav, in his dispute with the prince, the phrase:
"And you, brothers, are free both in posadniks and in princes." Between the prince and the posadnik there was no essential difference;
both the one and the other enjoyed authority only by virtue of its
delegation by the town, and only until such time as the town deprived
them of it.

This breakdown of patriarchal ideology in itself presupposes as an
antecedent phenomenon the breakdown of the patriarchal social order.
This process, which in Kiev became evident in the first quarter of the
twelfth century, had probably begun to manifest itself even earlier in
Novgorod. By the thirteenth century the gradual disappearance of clan
aristocracy and the appearance, on ordinary occasions as well as in
moments of crisis, of petty men of no birth, find expression in a number
of incidents. In relating Novgorod's losses in this or the other battle
the chronicle calls certain of the slain by name, evidently men better
known, the loss of whom was keenly felt. Among these outstanding men
we constantly meet simple artisans—coppersmiths, shieldmakers, silver-
smiths, and other artisans, a tanner's son, a "priest's son." In 1228
two men figured prominently in the deposition of the archbishop and
the restoration of his predecessor; one the chronicle calls by given name
and patronymic, the other by given name only, and he was a master
armourer, a coppersmith. Four years earlier, when Prince Yury of Suz-

dal demanded the surrender of the leaders of the opposition in Novgorod, he deigned to name only four of them with their patronymics, the rest are designated by diminutive given names. Nevertheless, the veche refused to surrender these petty men, just as it refused to surrender the greater ones.

In view of what was for those times a tremendous development of commercial capitalism, this democracy of petty traders and petty independent producers could not be more than a transitional stage; the "common people" could but serve as a battering-ram with the aid of which the bourgeoisie of commercial capitalists crushed the aristocracy of birth; all this is fairly obvious if we recall why Novgorod survived the "mother of Russian towns" and all her other contemporaries. Artisans might remain masters in an industrial centre, such, for example, as was Florence of the thirteenth and fourteenth centuries, but such as Novgorod never was. Wholesale trade with the West and wide colonial enterprises conditioned the concentration of capital in the hands of a few; the mass of "merchants," preserving for themselves the domestic market and the transport of foreign merchandise through the rest of Russia, speedily fell into debt-bondage to those from whom they acquired their merchandise and without whose help they could not get along. They formed an intermediate class between the lower social classes and the upper crust of Novgorodan society, which now consisted, not of the "order of boyars" alone, not of the feudal aristocracy alone, but of the boyars and the bourgeoisie, the "men of substance." Thus the former grouping of social elements, as we find it in the first treaties with thirteenth-century princes, dividing "all Novgorod" into the older and the lesser, was replaced by the more complicated grouping found in fourteenth-century treaties, into boyars, men of substance, merchants, and common people. Those who two hundred years earlier had dominated the town and disposed of its destinies were now reduced to last place in the composition of the autocratic veche.

The social dominance of the propertied classes in the last two centuries of Novgorod's history found political expression in the so-called "administrative council," "council of lords," or simply "lords." Toward the last years of Novgorod's life this council even more decisively usurps the rights of the veche, first of all, of course, in questions which the "mob" ill understood. By the fourteenth century foreign relations were wholly in the hands of the "lords"; in their collisions with Novgorod the German merchants see no one else, and they have left us the most detailed information about this institution. The law of Novgorod indicates that high justice also had passed into the hands of the aristocracy. The council granted deeds to lands and waters, directed public works, participated in the election of administrative officers, and directed military operations. The last official document of free Novgorod is the edict by which the Novgorodans were bound one and all to stand against Ivan III, prince of Moscow; the edict is ratified by 58 seals of members of the council who, at this concluding moment of their activity, stood forth as the *de facto* representatives of the whole town. This was apparently one of the fullest assemblies of the "lords." Yet the German sources know of occasions when the bounds of the assembly were still further extended, and in unusually significant fashion; one document mentions 300 "golden girdles." Here was all that was wealthiest in Novgorod; the council of Novgorod represented not birth, as did the later boyar duma of the tsars of Moscow, but wealth.

How did the masses of Novgorod react to the rise of this new oligarchy? In an industrial centre such a phenomenon would probably have evoked an uprising of "socialistic" character, "socialistic" in that broad and nebulous sense in which the word was used by the bourgeois literature of the last century. Such was the *Tumulto dei Ciompi* in fourteenth-century Florence. But Novgorod was a town not of artisans but of merchants, and there the social movement took on a very peculiar character—risings of debtors against creditors. Of just such a character, apparently, were the tumults of the year 1418, those tumults which are described in detail by the chronicle, and which in modern historiography have served as a general pattern for "the turbulent veche of Novgorod"; in any case they testify to the tension reached by the hatred of the oppressed toward the oppressors even half a century before Novgorod lost her independence. The disturbance began when "a certain man"— whom the chronicle calls by the diminutive given name, "Stepanko," without patronymic, thus marking his plebeian origin—attacked a boyar, Daniel Ivanovich, on the street and began to summon a crowd, crying out: "Masters! Aid me against this malefactor!" Instead of seizing the turbulent fellow the neighbours ran up and seized the boyar, dragging him to the veche, and there "having punished him with wounds nigh to death," they threw him from the bridge into the Volkhov. The chronicler says not a word concerning the reputation of Daniel Ivanovich, but this is made sufficiently clear by the course of events. When a fisherman rescued the boyar from the Volkhov and took him into his skiff, the mob was furiously indignant; the Novgorodans rushed to the fisherman's house and looted it. The boyar, just saved from drowning, obviously could not retaliate immediately; waiting till the veche dispersed, he ordered Stepanko seized and began to "torment" him. The tumult, however, had by no means subsided as the boyar apparently thought, and the news of Stepanko's arrest added fuel to the fire. Immediately the veche was again convoked on the Court of Yaroslav; on the following day it met again; "and there assembled a multitude of people who clamoured and vociferated for many days; we shall go on that boyar and plunder his house!'' The agitation against Daniel Ivanovich little by little passed into agitation against the boyars in general, and a crowd of Stepanko's partisans, ''coming in full panoply with a banner'' into the most aristocratic quarter of Novgorod, plundered not only the house of the offending boyar but also ''many other houses.'' The unexpected popular uprising at first reduced the boyars to panic terror. The residents of the invaded section rushed to the archbishop and besought him to interfere. In proof of their submission to the veche they brought Stepanko to the prelate; the archbishop sent him off to the ''assembly of the men'' under escort of a priest and of an archbishop's boyar. The veche received both the embassy and Stepanko, but this did not put an end to the havoc. The mob not only plundered more boyars' homesteads, but also passed on to the monasteries, which served as storehouses for the boyars. That is, there took place in Novgorod what had only been dreaded in Kiev at the time of the uprising of 1113. An attack on the principal nest of the Novgorod boyars, Prusskaya Street, was, however, beaten off, for here preparations had been made for defence. From this moment a reaction set in; the rebels were pushed back to the Torgovaya Storona [the market side of the river], the more democratic quarter, which had risen *en masse* in support of Stepanko and his friends. Soon the Torgovaya Storona was on the defensive, the bridge across the Volkhov becoming the centre of combat. Here arrows whistled, arms clashed, and the slain fell ''as in war.'' But apparently the more reasonable portion of the boyars were opposed to aggravating matters further. The ''Christ-eminent people,'' the ''God-fearing men,'' persuaded the archbishop to go onto the bridge with a procession of the Cross and separate the combatants. In the prelate's wake appeared the boyar council. The prelate again despatched an embassy to the Court of Yaroslav. This time it had more success; the veche dispersed, ''and there was peace in the town.'' This outcome had undoubtedly been prepared by antecedent negotiations; this is evident from the fact that the archbishop's envoys found already on the Court of Yaroslav the posadnik and the thousand-man, who, of course, were not the leaders of the ''assembly of the people'' which had destroyed the boyars' homesteads. The archbishop's appearance on the bridge was in reality only an official ceremony. The feud was stopped by the desire of the boyars to make use of their success without risking a new skirmish which might not have ended in their favour.

This flash in the pan neither did nor could produce any change in social relationships. The merchantry of the Torgovaya Storona could not get along without the boyars' capital. But inasmuch as such outbursts could not be advantageous to the boyars, they carefully canalised the energy accumulating in the masses. The "policy of diversion" was just as well known to later, strongly capitalistic, Novgorod, as to many other lands in analogous periods. Simultaneously with the increasing political insignificance of the masses, we hear ever more and more frequently of colonial enterprises of the only type known to early Rus, plundering expeditions against border countries inhabited by aliens and sometimes against neighbouring Russian lands. In the latter case the conventions were usually observed, the affair taking on the character of a private enterprise; Novgorod, as a state, remained in the background. The chronicle carefully distinguishes between these two types of "colonial wars": one entry states that the expedition was undertaken "by order of Novgorod"; another says that the "young men" went "without the word of Novogorod." Yet in both cases the chronicle is manifestly describing a regularly organised expedition, and the names of the commanders indicate that they belonged to the aristocracy of Novgorod. But the former was directed against foreigners, the Norwegians of Murmansk; while the latter raided the Volga, thus coming into conflict with the grand prince of Moscow, and the authorities of Novgorod hoped to evade responsibility. To be sure, Grand Prince Dmitry Donskoi, disregarding the juridical correctness of Novgorod's position, "broke the peace with the Novgorodans." Twenty years later Novgorod had to pay to Moscow 8,000 rubles as compensation for a similar expedition. But, since the "young men" were finding occupation other than the destruction of boyars' homesteads, the boyars of Novgorod could not be persuaded to renounce a policy so advantageous to themselves, though even a colonial expedition on occasion became a weapon of social strife.

Novgorod's "imperialism" afforded the great bourgeoisie of Novgorod an opportunity to divert the attention of the masses, to promise the "common people" an equivalent for the political independence they were gradually losing. But at times the "common people" were so oppressed that no imperialism, no mirages of colonial conquests were of any avail, and the "younger" men began to seek a more direct means of redressing their grievances against the "older." The quarter to which they turned was inauspicious for the independence of Novgorod. In 1340 the Novgorodans quarrelled with Prince Simeon the Proud of Moscow over the tribute which the latter had begun to collect in Torzhok. As can be conjectured from the sequel, the controversy was not so much about the collection of tribute as about its apportionment, whether it was to go into the treasury of Novgorod or into the coffers of the prince of Moscow. War was in prospect. But the government of Novgorod very quickly had to lower its tone for a quite unexpected reason; in Novgorod the "rabble" did not want to go to war against Moscow. Meanwhile in Torzhok the most serious measures had already been taken;

Moscow's namestniks and collectors of tribute had been fettered and put in prison. But when the "rabble" in Torzhok learned what was being done in Novgorod, it rose against the boyars so decisively that the latter fled to Novgorod. And the namestniks of Moscow were liberated by that same "rabble."

CHAPTER VI

THE interval of time from the thirteenth century to the fifteenth is sometimes set apart as the "appanage" period of Russian history; "the dismemberment of the Russian land into appanages" thus becomes the determining characteristic of the period. It is hardly necessary to say that this presentation is based on the conception of the "unity of the Russian land" prior to the beginning of the appanage period: Rus crumbled; later it was "gathered" together again. But we already know that to speak of a "unitary" Russian state in the Kievan period is evidence of a confusion of thought. The expression "the Russian land" was known both to the chronicle and to the poetical productions of the time, but it denoted the Kiev area and more broadly, since Kiev held the hegemony of all southern Rus, all the latter as well. From Novgorod or Vladimir one went "to Rus," but Novgorod and Vladimir themselves were not Rus. Moreover, this was purely a popular term, not signifying any definite political idea. Politically, early Rus knew of a principality of Kiev, of Chernigov, or of Suzdal, but not of a Russian state. There was therefore nothing to crumble and consequently nothing to "gather."

Into the antiquated terminology, which originated with Karamzin, an attempt was made to breathe a new content, now by alleging that at the beginning of this period there was an especial disintegration of principalities, now by linking with this particular time a marked decline in the authority of the princes, a loss on their part of all "state ideals" and their conversion into simple landowners. But we do not know the minimum dimensions of an independent province in the preceding epoch, while even in the "appanage" period we see figuring prominently on the political stage princes of Tver, Moscow, Nizhny-Novgorod, and Ryazan, ruling over large provinces, no smaller than the former principalities of Chernigov, Smolensk, or Pereyaslavl. As regards state ideals, these can be found in embryo in the veche of Novgorod—which for official historiography was the negation of the state—but by no means among the old Russian princes. Not even the most outstanding of them rose beyond a certain foggy conception of "social justice," and all of them in general accounted the acquisition of thrones the chief goal of a prince's policy and armed raids on neighbouring provinces a prince's chief occupation. The only public business which from time to time united them all was the struggle with the nomads of the steppe, but such union could never in the slightest degree become stable and lasting. The military alliance of the northeastern princes, under the headship of the prince of Moscow, against the Tatars at the end of the fourteenth century, was no less stable than the unification of southern Rus against the Polovtsians in the days of Vladimir Monomakh; in this regard "appanage" Rus had no cause to envy pre-appanage, Kievan Rus. In internal administration "to rule" meant the same in the thirteenth and fourteenth centuries as in the twelfth or even the tenth century. Both earlier and later it was a matter of gathering revenues in various forms, and even contemporaries could hardly have decided who was in this sense the more energetic "gatherer," Andrew Bogolyubsky or his kinsman of three centuries later, Ivan III of Moscow.

As we follow the chain of events in the chronicles, we easily perceive two catastrophes, either of which can be made to mark a "new period of Russian history"; one is the fall of Kiev in the second half of the twelfth century, the other the conquest of Rus by the Tatars in the thirteenth. The first conditioned the shifting of the centre of the historical stage some degrees north and east, a change that fastened on historical Russia the character of a northern country of a poverty-stricken nature which it had not had in the mild climate and on the fruitful soil of the Ukraine. The second assured that decline of "urban" law and that triumph of "rural" law which for many centuries determined the political physiognomy of the future "northern monarchy." But in both cases the catastrophe was more apparent than real. Both revolutions had been prepared by profound economic causes—by a shifting of world trade routes and by exhaustion of the country through predatory methods of economy. To make either of these catastrophes a "limit of the times" would be very superficial. And from this point of view one should not speak of a special "appanage" period of Russian history. The grouping of feudal units which was destined to replace the town provinces of the eleventh and twelfth centuries, and which has received the name of grand principality and later state of Moscow, grew up slowly and imperceptibly, so that when the men of the seventeenth century became conscious of the roughly finished edifice, it was difficult for them to answer the question: who began to build it? Kotoshikhin, as is well known, was inclined to record Ivan [IV] the Terrible as the founder of the Muscovite state. Later historians pushed the critical moment ever further and further back into the recesses of time until they came upon figures so like all their contemporaries that another question arose of itself: why did they, rather than the others, become the founders of the new state? The first "gatherer" of Rus, Ivan [I] Kalita—according to the pages of the school textbooks—emerges from the pen of a modern historian as "altogether devoid of the qualities of a sovereign and statesman," so that the formation of the Muscovite state must be ascribed to a lucky chance. "Chance plays a great rôle in history," says this same scholar, V. Sergeyevich. But to appeal to chance in science is to exhibit a certificate of poverty.

This *reductio ad absurdum* of the individualist method, which charges all historical changes to the actions of individual persons and remains in perplexity when changes are obviously taking place, and yet there are no persons on the stage—this catastrophe in the domain of historical literature is nevertheless in itself a great gain for scientific history. The author we have just cited was able to name, along with "chance," another historical factor, impersonal but none the less absolutely concrete, which must be substituted for those "gatherers of Rus" whom science had found bankrupt. Mr. Sergeyevich accounts the minority of Dmitry Donskoi an especially favourable moment in the development of the grand principality of Moscow. "In this circumstance"—that the "gatherer" was nine years old—"was comprised an extraordinarily favourable condition for the progressive development of Muscovite territory. During the minority of a prince the administration was in the hands of the boyars. . . . The boyars needed rich 'feedings.'[1] The fewer the princes, the more of these 'feedings.' The boyars were, then, the natural partisans of a unificatory policy."

From this, it might seem, it would have been but a step to let the personalities of the "gatherers" rest in peace and to treat the Muscovite state of the fifteenth century as a vast association of feudal landholders which, by virtue of especially favourable conditions, swallowed up all remaining associations. But our author does not venture this step; he continues to occupy his reader with the thoughts and deeds of the Ivans, Dmitrys, and Vasilys, although he has just demonstrated their political insignificance. So strong is the tradition, far older than may be thought and inherited by our scholarly university historiography from the prehistoric period of Russian recording of events, that even the *Nikonovsky Chronicle* had the Muscovite government carrying on negotiations with the Kazan tsar, Utemish-Girei, although the chronicle itself had noted that this "political actor" was but two years old (and would hardly be carrying on negotiations except with his nurse). But what in the old Russian chronicler was symbolism noteworthy in its naïveté becomes in a contemporary historical work either artless copying or stupid superstition. The reader will not be disappointed, therefore, if on the one hand we do not pay special attention to the distinctive characteristics of "appanage Rus"—for these characteristics are found on a more ex-

[1] Lucrative posts as provincial governors; *cf. infra*, pp. 119 *et seq.*

tended scale in the Rus of Moscow—and if on the other hand we leave
to the old official textbooks the exploits of the "gatherers" and do not
discuss the question as to whether they were men politically ungifted or
politically talented—the more so since over and above everything else
the scantiness of the data regarding their personal qualities renders the
last question quite hopeless.

Among the impersonal factors which determined the "gathering" of
Rus around Moscow one of the first places was long since assigned to
economics. The original observations along this line, made by Prof.
Klyuchevsky and accessible to all in the pages of his *Lectures*, were supplemented and further developed by Zabelin in his *History of the City
of Moscow* [in Russian]. The latter author discusses the question, not in
the narrow compass of the history of "appanage Rus" and the forma
tion of the principality of Moscow, but somewhat more broadly. He
points to the rôle of the Moskva-Klyazma trade-route, which united the
industrial region of the Kriviches of Smolensk with the largest centre
in the Volga country of the tenth and eleventh centuries—the "Great
City" of the Bolgars with its fair, the forerunner of those of Makaryev
and Nizhny-Novgorod. In the immediate vicinity of Moscow two nodes
of this route may be observed—one on the River Skhodna (or Vskhodna),
the other on the Yauza. The presence of a numerous population around
the former is shown by a mass of burial-mounds (*kurgans*). The commercial significance of the Yauza and of the portage from it to the
Klyazma is still evident in the name of the village, Big Toll-house, a
reminder that a customs-house once existed here. It is significant that
the Yauza is definitely mentioned by the chronicle (under 1156) in
its report of the building of the "town" of Moscow, *i.e.*, of the earliest
Muscovite fortress. Evidently this geographical reference had practical
value for contemporaries. But on the route from western Rus to the
Volga country Moscow was only one of the nodal points; it became the
most important of them only thanks to the fact that the old highway
of eastern trade was intersected by the new route of western trade, from
Novgorod to southern and eastern Rus, to Nizhny and Ryazan. The
route by the Volga from Novgorod the Great to Novgorod the Low
describes a sharp arc, a goodly portion of which, moreover, was in the
hands of Great Novgorod's nearest neighbour and most constant antagonist, the grand prince of Tver. The route through Volok na Lame
[Portage on the Lama], which belonged to Novgorod, and then by the
Moskva and the Klyazma, was almost a chord of this arc and far less
dependent on political vicissitudes. The princes of Moscow in early
times seemed very mild and reasonable; from them Novgorod saw no
immediate danger; and in the first half of the fourteenth century there
was no more usual political combination than the alliance of Novgorod

and Moscow against Tver. In their turn the princes of Moscow found nothing dishonourable in entering the veche-town "at the will of Novgorod . . . and glad were the Novgorodans to have their wish." When the prince of Moscow, thanks to the adroitness of his policy toward the Horde, became hereditary grand prince of Vladimir, the Novgorod-Moscow alliance became an economic necessity for both parties: the Rus of Suzdal, now the Rus of Moscow, could not dispense with European wares, which, in the main, came by the Baltic route; while the Novgorod gost "in the lowlands," in the modern provinces of Moscow, Vladimir, and Nizhny-Novgorod, as of old could not dispense with the protection of the grand prince of Vladimir. "And our gost shall trade in the land of Suzdal" stipulated Novgorod's treaties with the grand princes. But, it must be noted, the necessity was not equally pressing on both sides. Whereas Novgorodan traders, in case the Rus of Suzdal was closed to them, lost their chief market and almost lost their *raison d'être*, Moscow had besides Novgorod another outlet to Western Europe. Under 1356 the chronicles mention the presence in Moscow of "gosts of Surozh," traders from the Genoese colonies in the Crimea. "But, in all probability, even earlier than this year Genoese traders were already well acquainted with the road to Moscow, inasmuch as northern trade, which until the thirteenth century had been directed along the Dnieper to Kiev, had shifted, being directed along the Don through Moscow; even before the Tatar invasion the Don had been extensively used by these same Italian traders from Genoa, who concentrated their businesses at the mouths of the Don and in the Crimean towns of Surozh and Kafa."

The mention of "gosts of Surozh" explains Moscow's rather unexpected Italian connexions, a monument of which remains to this day in the Kremlin of Moscow, with its Cathedral of the Assumption built by Aristotle Fioraventi and its Gates of the Saviour built by the "architect" Pietro-Antonio "from the town of Mediolano." And the international, as well as the local, significance of Moscow is made clear by yet another, far more important fact. Even in the fourteenth century Ivan Kalita's capital was becoming a large bourgeois centre, the population of which was beginning to conduct itself in almost Novgorodan fashion. Of the size of this population the chronicles give some indication. In 1382, when after Tokhtamysh's attack the slain Muscovites were being buried, Grand Prince Dmitry Donskoi—who had fled to the North from the Tatar havoc and who reappeared just at the time of the burial of the slain—paid a *poltina* [2] for each forty corpses, spending 300 rubles in all; that is, 24,000 men were buried. It is true that this figure would include not only the townsmen in the narrow sense but also the population of the immediate vicinity, who had sought protection from the Tatars

---

[2] 1 *poltina* = 50 copecks.

behind the walls of the town; on the other hand, not all, of course, of
the urban population had been exterminated; on the contrary, one is
led to believe that a great many survivod or were led away into captivity.
In 1390 the chronicle notes the great Moscow fire, in which were burned
down some thousands of homesteads; five years later Moscow burned
again, and again "some thousands" of homesteads were burned down.
Judging by all these data, the population of the city toward the end
of the fourteenth century may be estimated at some tens of thousands.
For the Middle Ages, when in all Europe there were hardly three towns
with a population of a hundred thousand, this is not inconsiderable; in
the Russia of that time, with the exception of Novgorod and Pskov, there
was no town larger.

The numbers of the townsmen of Moscow compel us to modify the
very widespread concept of Moscow as an overgrown prince's manor, a
concept much indebted for its popularity to the same Zabelin we have
just cited. However numerous the household of a prince of Moscow,
it fell far short of the tens of thousands of Moscow's townsmen; and
however tempting it may be to see in the Weavers', Armourers', Bakers',
and Drapers' Lanes traces of the settlements of court artisans, it is
more prudent to see in them the Muscovite doubles of the Carpenters'
or Potters' Quarters of Great Novgorod. In the fourteenth century,
whenever the townsmen of Moscow appear as a political force, they
present an aspect altogether unlike that of a prince's menials. Such a
case was Tokhtamysh's attack (August, 1382), already referred to. The
Tatars had appeared on the Russian frontiers quite unexpectedly, and
the Muscovite authorities, secular and spiritual, had lost their heads.
Grand Prince Dmitry Donskoi, so recently the victor on the field of
Kulikovo, fled first to Pereyaslavl and later, finding even this place too
unsafe, to Kostroma. He left the metropolitan in charge in the city;
but the metropolitan—Cyprian of scarcely honourable memory—was,
of course, still less inclined to military exploits than was the grand
prince himself. To Cyprian Tver seemed a safe refuge, and he decided
to flee thither. The "eminent boyars" also evidently prepared to
follow the example of the prince and the metropolitan, leaving the
townsmen to defend themselves from the foe as best they might. And
behold, relates the chronicler, "the men of the town were disturbed
and agitated as though drunk, and they convoked a veche; rioters, good-
for-nothings, rascals rang all the bells and held a veche; and not only
did they not allow those wishing to leave the city to pass, but they
plundered them . . . they stood at all the city gates, from above they
threw stones, and below on the ground they stood with boarspears and
pikes and with naked weapons allowing no one to go forth from the
city." Later, probably realising that in case of a siege the panic-

stricken metropolitan and the boyars, and especially Grand Princess Eudocia, who was also hastening to get herself out of the city, would be of no use, they let them go but confiscated all their possessions. The chronicler, whose sympathy, as is evident from this excerpt, was on the side of the propertied authorities, would have been very glad to reduce the whole affair to a drunken riot, vigorously emphasising the breaking-into of the boyars' cellars and the plundering of the "lords' meads." But undoubtedly the "men of the town" were about serious business; they were organising that very defence of the city, the possibility of which the metropolitan and "eminent boyars" had doubted, and they so organised it that the Tatars, after an unsuccessful assault, were compelled to resort to craft in order to take the town. On the walls of Moscow Tokhtamysh had perceived, along with old missile weapons, such innovations of military technique as cross-bows (arbalasts) and even cannon, which were still novelties even in Western Europe. All these engines the bourgeois of Moscow (the chronicle mentions a "clothier" named Adam, probably an Italian) handled most successfully. But against all these Western innovations the Tatars found a Russian weapon, old and tried. There were in Tokhtamysh's army two Russian princes, brothers-in-law of Dmitry Donskoi, who undertook to take oath to the men of Moscow that the Tatars would do them no injury if they surrendered the city. The townsmen, trusting the word of the princes, opened the gates; the city was plundered, and the inhabitants slain or led away into captivity. The whole narrative is a perfect portrayal of the relationship existing between the "people" and the "authorities" in appanage Rus—between the "builders" and "gatherers," selling their city to the Tatars, and the "rabble," capable of defending themselves from the Tatars far better without the "gatherers" than with them.

The events of 1382 are not isolated in Muscovite history. Through the following two centuries, to the middle of the seventeenth, the townsmen of Moscow from time to time appeared as a political force, indicating that the Russian bourgeoisie was far less inarticulate then than at times nearer our own. But if the presence of a large commercial centre with abundant money resources [3] offered a point of support for the unificatory policy of the principality of Moscow, the active rôle in this policy was not taken by the commercial city. Had it been, the result would have been the formation of a new town province like that of Kiev, not a feudal monarchy such as was the Muscovite state. A priori it can be assumed that feudal elements played a large part in the creation of this state, and that in the "gathering of Rus" the large

[3] Some idea of these resources is afforded by the levy of 200,000 rubles (some 20 million gold rubles in pre-war currency) made by Makhmet on Vasily [II] the Dark in 1446.

landholders were of determining importance. We have seen that their importance has been duly appraised by modern science, which, in the person of Prof. Sergeyevich, has recognised that the real "gatherers of Rus" were the boyars, who displayed far more alertness and understanding than did the nominal founders of the Muscovite state. There is therefore no need to labour this point. We have already surveyed in detail the political significance of large landholding in early Rus.[4] We know that at the head of each appanage principality stood not a single person, the prince, but a group of persons, the prince and the boyar duma, and that this circumstance guaranteed the continuity of appanage policies even when—as frequently happened in appanage days—the nominal wielder of state authority was not available, whether because he was a minor, or at the Horde, or in captivity. A struggle between appanage principalities should be visualised as a struggle between groups of feudatories defending their own interests at all costs. In the first episode of the struggle between Moscow and Tver, at the very beginning of the fourteenth century, the princes scarcely appear on the Russian stage; they are far away suing for thrones, for juridical title to the dignity of grand prince is obtained at the Horde from the "tsar." The actual struggle on the spot was carried on by the boyars. The boyars of Tver waged the war with Moscow, and Tver's army was headed, not by the prince but by the boyar Akinf; Moscow's army was nominally headed by Ivan (the future Kalita), a younger brother of Prince Yury, who had gone to the Horde, but he took not a step without his boyars. Some years later Dmitry of Tver led an army against Nizhny-Novgorod and Vladimir and acquired the throne of the grand princes. But all this is only the customary symbolism of the chronicle; the pretender to the grand princedom was but twelve years old, and what happened to him was literally the same as what the boyars of Moscow fifty years later did with their infant princes when, taking all three grandsons of Kalita (the oldest, Dmitry, the future Donskoi, was then not yet twelve), they went on a campaign against Moscow's rival, Prince Dmitry of Suzdal. Nor, under the grand princedom of Moscow, did the Muscovite feudatories by any means lose this habit of acting independently; on the contrary, they became all the more powerful and they were all the more numerous, the more extended and the more powerful became the patrimony of Kalita. In 1446 when Shemyaka, taking advantage of the unsuccessful war waged by Vasily [II] the Dark with the Tatars, seized Moscow and took Vasily himself captive, he was faced with the combined resistance of the Muscovite boyars, headed by the Princes Ryapolovsky. This resistance compelled Shemyaka in the following year to return the throne to the opponent he

4 Cf. supra, Chap. II.

had deposed and blinded. The conventional antithesis of "boyars" and "sovereign" as centrifugal and centripetal forces, respectively, in the young state of Moscow is one of the most unfortunate survivals of the idealistic method, which represented the "state" as some independent force acting upon society from above. In actual fact the state in appanage Rus was, as always, simply a certain form of organisation of the dominant social elements, and the princes of Moscow, for their part, did not think of denying the fact that they ruled their principality, not alone but jointly with the boyars, as "first among equals." An even more flattering characterisation of the boyars is ascribed by the chronicle to Dmitry Donskoi who, it reports, said at his death: "And you were called with me, not boyars but princes of my land." Even if this be literary fiction, the advice of his uncle, Simeon the Proud, to his successors, "hearken to the old boyars," occurs in an official document, his will. Similarly, the most practical politicians of the time, the diplomats of the Horde, unhesitatingly and frankly recognised that Moscow's course of action depended upon the personnel of the boyar duma.

Granted then that the Muscovite state was the creation of a feudal society, it was inevitable that in its construction a conspicuous rôle should be played by the Church, the greatest of the feudal organisations of appanage Russia as it was of mediæval Europe generally. It would seem impossible to exaggerate the importance of Orthodoxy in the history of Russian autocracy; yet it must be acknowledged that until the appearance of the second volume of the well-known work of Prof. Golubinsky everything that was said on this point was too weak and, what is more important, beside the mark. The emphasis was laid chiefly on the influence of ecclesiastical *propaganda* upon the growth of the *idea* of autocracy. It is true that Moscow's political ideology was, first and foremost, ecclesiastical ideology; that the tsar of Moscow was thought of by his subjects, not so much as a national sovereign, the ruler of a definite people, as a ruler of the whole world, the tsar of all Orthodox Christendom. We may see extraordinarily vivid and clear reflections of this central idea of Muscovite official publicism; but publicism does not make history. What was the rôle of the Church in the creation of the objective conditions which called Muscovite tsarism to life? What did the Church give, not in word but in deed, as a definite *organisation?* How was the policy of the state being created under its influence determined in the interests of this organisation? Here are questions, answers to which were first supplied by the material collected by the above-mentioned historian of the Russian Church, material itself entirely objective and devoid of any idealistic elaboration.

Feudalisation of the Orthodox Church had begun long before the period now under consideration. Even in the Rus of Kiev and Novgorod the monasteries were large landholders, and metropolitans and bishops exercised a large share of political authority; among other things, they were the judges over the clergy in all cases in general, and in a large number of cases over the whole population in general. But, being appointed to their sees either by the local veche or by the local prince, the Old Russian bishops were dependent on these secular political forces, and we have already seen how at Novgorod party strife was immediately reflected in a change of archbishops. The monasteries, on the other hand, frequently owed their very existence to the princes; each princely dynasty had its own monastery, in which the members of this dynasty were buried and, if anything interrupted their political careers, took the tonsure. Such a monastery, independent of petty secular authorities, constituted a sort of prince's manor, and, therefore, of course, offered no political opposition to the princes. In a word, the dependence of the Church on the state in the Rus of Kiev and Novgorod had been less than its dependence in the modern, post-Petrine period only in so far as the Church of the veche town had been a democratic organisation. The Church owed its emancipation from this dependence to an event most grievous for the rest of Russia—the conquest of Rus by the Tatars. The supreme political centre of Rus was transferred to the Horde. The bishop, except in the case of Novgorod, became just as independent of the veche of his native town as did the prince. But at the same time he ceased to be dependent on the prince, at least juridically, for juridically the legal position of the Church was now defined by the khan's *yarlyk*.[5] In these charters granted by "infidel" tsars the privileges of the Russian Church were so definitely and so broadly consolidated as they had never been under Orthodox Russian princes; not without reason were the seven yarlyks of the Horde cited even by sixteenth-century metropolitans in defending the rights of the Church from the encroachments of secular authority. The first of these yarlyks, dating from the thirteenth century, perhaps thirty, or at most forty years after the catastrophe of the Tatar conquest, granted to the Orthodox clergy not only the broadest liberty of religious profession but also a whole series of "liberties" of a purely civil character. "Priests, monks and all men of God" were exempted from all levies, including the Tatar tribute. The privilege was extended to all Church folk, *i.e.*, including laymen in the service of the Church. The khan's charters thus established for the Church the most complete immunity enjoyed anywhere in Europe in the Middle Ages; in this particular Eastern Orthodoxy had no occasion to envy Western Catholicism. The reasons for such graciousness on the part of the "infidel" (at first pagan; later, from Uzbek on, Mahometan) conquerors of Russia

---

[5] A letter from the Tatar khan granting or confirming a privilege, etc.

toward the Orthodox faith, its representatives, and even toward all in any way in its service, are quite explicitly set forth in the yarlyks. In vain does Golubinsky seek to spare the last remnants of ecclesiastical historical decency by attributing the attitude of the Tatar rulers to their customary tolerance; the whole question was far simpler. The yarlyk given to the Metropolitan Alexis (c. 1357), for example, says: "Tsar Jenghiz and the first tsars, our fathers, rewarded the Church folk *who prayed for them*. . . ." Of course, it was public, official, "prayer" that was meant, not private prayer; the latter was a matter for the conscience of the prelate and did not trouble the conscience of the Horde; its viewpoint on all matters was strictly practical. What was important to the khan was that in Russia he should be formally acknowledged sovereign by those whose voice had weight and authority in the eyes of the masses. The Tatars understood uncommonly well the elementary truth that it is possible by arms to conquer a country but impossible to hold it by the aid of arms alone. They could not fail to appreciate that the Church was putting at their disposal its influence over the faithful, and in return for this it was but natural to reward the Church with privileges. That these privileges hampered the authority of the local secular rulers could not, of course, fail to please the Horde. The alliance between the Orthodox Church and the Tatar khan was in the early days equally advantageous for both sides; that in the sequel the alliance would prove more advantageous for the Church than for the Horde, the Tatars could not foresee, precisely because, as politicians, they were too practical. Meanwhile they secured the support of the greatest political force, permitting them to substitute the spiritual for the material sword, which it was not convenient to draw from the scabbard too often. With the exception of Tver, the princes of which were not on good terms with the Church and were therefore persecuted by her, we nowhere have before the fourteenth century a great *national* uprising against the khan; and when the uprising of the princes began, under the headship of Moscow, the Church had already succeeded in making permanent all the advantages offered to her by the yarlyks.

The Church, for a time in the service of the Tatar "tsar," did not by any means immediately assume a similar relationship toward the grand prince, the future tsar, of Moscow. In Russia the question of secular *versus* spiritual supremacy could be posed as late as the seventeenth century, but in the fourteenth century no such question had arisen; Simeon the Proud, to whom the khan handed over all the Russian princes, frankly and simply recommended to his successors obedience in everything to "our father the prelate Alexis" exactly as he recommended obedience to the boyars—but to the prelate first. From this will of Prince Simeon it has been deduced that the Metropolitan Alexis was a sort of president of the boyar duma; but from later published Greek documents we know that after the death of Grand Prince Ivan II, Simeon's younger brother, Alexis was *de jure* regent of the principality of Moscow, which *de facto* he probably ruled until his own death in 1378. This circumstance must never be forgotten when we read of the "services" rendered by the Church to the princes of Moscow in their struggle with their rivals—services, as we shall presently see, not always above reproach. For example, in 1368 "Grand Prince Dmitry and his father, the Most Reverend Metropolitan Alexis, lovingly invited to Moscow Prince Michael of Tver" in order to submit his dispute with Moscow to an arbitration court; while there they "seized him and arrested the boyars who were about him," matters evidently having taken such a course that the Muscovite government, headed by Alexis, found it convenient and seemly to get rid of its opponent with the aid of this trap. As often happened in similar cases, the rôle of the eighteen-year-old Grand Prince Dmitry, who even in manhood was not distinguished for his strength of will, was purely symbolic. In collisions of this kind the dual functions of the metropolitan-regent made Moscow particularly invulnerable; if she committed a sin, she could herself remit it; what was more, she could subject her foes, in addition to secular chastisements, to ecclesiastical punishments of every kind. When the ill-starred Michael of Tver succeeded in escaping from the Muscovite trap and in raising against Moscow the inevitable Lithuania, Alexis, not strong enough to injure the prince of Tver physically, attacked him spiritually, excommunicating him and his allies. Sometimes it was possible to combine the operation of the two "swords"—the secular and the spiritual—with an effect still more striking. So it happened when the holy Sergius appeared in the capital city of Prince Boris of Nizhny-Novgorod, who had been disobedient to Moscow, and closed all the churches, *i.e.*, laid an interdict on the whole city, while under its walls soon appeared the Muscovite regiments; judging by his biography, Boris was very stubborn and put much trust in his kinship with Olgerd of Lithuania (he was his son-in-law), but at this juncture he hastened to yield.

The cases we have cited suggest two hypotheses: first, that Muscovite policy determined the direction of ecclesiastical policy; second, that the fusion of the two powers, spiritual and secular, was the result of an accidental and personal circumstance, of the position of Alexis as metropolitan and as regent of the grand principality of Moscow. But the first proposition would not always be true, and the second proposition is false. We have instances of similar fusion under Alexis' successors— more important cases, at that, in which the guiding rôle falls to the lot of the interests of the Church. Such was the history of the metropolitan's controversy with Novgorod over the "month court," the undoubted prologue to the catastrophe that put an end to Novgorod's freedom; the subjection of the diocese of Novgorod to the metropolitan of Moscow was not attained until Novgorod was politically subjected to Moscow.

But in the history of this subjection ecclesiastical matters and interests are so intertwined that it is quite impossible to imagine the "fall of Novgorod" apart from ecclesiastical policy. In this the greatest episode of the "gathering" policy of Moscow's princes it is particularly evident to what extent, and not merely in ideology, the Muscovite state was created by the Church. The ideology quite accurately reflected the real relationships, while, as is hardly necessary to say, the real essence of the matter lay, not in those ideals of which the Church officially declared herself the bearer but in the Church as a definite feudal organisation. First of all, it was on ecclesiastical soil that the severance took place between Novgorod and her younger brother, Pskov, an event exceptionally advantageous for Moscow's policy. If the metropolitan of Moscow exploited the Church of Novgorod, the archbishop of Novgorod stood in the same relation to the Church of Pskov. The development of this ecclesiastical struggle gradually led the men of Pskov to desire a separate archbishop; this desire, of course, they made known to Moscow, the ecclesiastical centre. Their request was not granted, for the history of the "month court" in Novgorod had made the Moscow authorities ill-disposed toward an increase in the number of veche churches; but they utilised the ecclesiastical antagonism between Pskov and Novgorod to make sure of an alliance with the men of Pskov in case of a war between Moscow and Novgorod. When this struggle came under Ivan III (1471), success was assured largely by the fact that, whereas the grand prince of Moscow had entirely at his disposal the forces of all his vassals, Novgorod was deprived of military assistance from her ecclesiastical lands; for the metropolitan of Moscow, by no means for the first time, openly made common cause with his prince, while the archbishop of Novgorod lacked the courage to precipitate an open schism in the Church. Ecclesiastical relationships even gave the final rupture between Moscow and Novgorod its juridical form; juridically the "worker of piety," Grand Prince Ivan III, did not march against the veche and the freedom of Novgorod; he went to re-establish Orthodoxy, which had been shaken in Novgorod owing to her alliance with the "Latins," personified by the Polish-Lithuanian King Casimir. This was a crusade, all the participants in which were guaranteed the Kingdom of Heaven and remission of all the sins inevitably connected with war. Metropolitan Philip and the whole "holy synod" solemnly blessed Ivan III when he set out on the campaign "as Samuel blessed David against Goliath." The public opinion of Moscow was thoroughly permeated with this point of view, and the spirit of a crusade is superbly sustained by the Moscow chronicle: "Infidels know not God from the beginning, but these Novgorodans were in Christianity so many years, and at the end have begun to desert to Latinism! The grand prince went upon them, not as upon Christians but as upon pagans and deserters from Orthodoxy; they have deserted not only their sovereign but also the Lord God himself. As formerly his great-grandfather Grand Prince Dmitry armed himself upon the godless Mamai, so also the Orthodox Grand Prince Ioann went upon these deserters," relates the chronicler. And all the motifs of the individual details of the struggle are reduced to the same basic level. "This Martha the Accursed," says the chronicler of the woman who headed the anti-Moscow party, "wanted to seduce the whole people, to turn them from the right way, and to join them to Latinism, because the darkness of the Latin seduction had blinded the eyes of her spirit. . . ."

The "darkness" of religious fanaticism actually so beclouds the last minutes of Great Novgorod that it is hard at first glance to discern the actual causes of the catastrophe. But they are significant, and they remind us of those two factors in the unificatory policy of Moscow which we have already noted. These were the boyars of Moscow and the bourgeoisie of Moscow, who must by no means be forgotten although, because of the scantiness of records and the unwontedness of putting their needs into literary form, they have yielded first place to the men who knew how to speak "from divinity." Nowhere, it is true, do we hear their voice; but the facts speak for them and speak no less eloquently than do the chronicles of Moscow. The first great collision between Moscow and Novgorod, under Grand Prince Vasily I, in 1397-1398, was a highly typical "struggle for markets." For the first time Moscow made bold to take away from Novgorod the Dvina and all the North Country [6] the chief source of peltry, of which Novgorod held the European monopoly. This was not simply a robber raid; it was a colonial war in the grand style, in which Moscow acted most cautiously, evidently expecting to consolidate her seizure of the land. There is extant a charter of Vasily I to the men of the Dvina; it is an extremely interesting one because it shows the direction in which internal relations were developing in Novgorodan society, and how the policy of Moscow took advantage of this development. The charter was given primarily to the boyars and at the outset shows anxiety for their immunity, moral as well as physical. On the other hand, a boyar might with impunity not only "insult" a man under his authority but even slay him in a fit of wrath. Thus we see that, if the lower classes in Novgorod were inclined to eye Moscow with hope, feudal Moscow was by no means

[6] Zavolochye, *i.e.*, the territory beyond the watershed separating the basins of the Volga and Northern Dvina.

inclined to look upon the lower classes with favour; she was striving to assimilate those elements of Novgorod society which were markedly feudal. Yet, out of the mass of "common people" the Dvina charter distinguishes one element about whose interests Moscow is no less concerned than about the interests of the boyars. This element was the merchantry of the Dvina. The charter frees the commercial class of the Dvina, not only from imposts but also from the toils of Moscow's judiciary; they were to be judged either by their own local authorities or directly by the grand prince himself. The prospects unfolded by Moscow before the landholders and merchantry of the Dvina were so alluring that a Muscovite party was formed there, which all but succeeded in effecting a union of Novgorod's wealthiest colony to the grand princedom of Moscow. But this would have been such a catastrophe for Novgorod that in the struggle over the seizure of the Dvina she strained all her forces and in the end was victorious. The Dvina and the North Country remained for the time in the hands of the Novgorodans; Moscow yielded but for a time, firmly resolving, nevertheless, that postponement should not spell loss. Twice subsequently Dvina émigrés with a Muscovite army appeared in the North Country, suddenly, without declaration of war, plundered, slew, and with their captives took refuge in the domains of the grand prince. Only strife over the throne of Moscow, in the reign of Vasily the Dark, checked this colonial war. When Ivan III set out on his crusade against Novgorod (1471), a special detachment of the Muscovite army was despatched to the Dvina, which it conquered without great difficulty; the Novgorodan chronicler frankly accuses the men of the Dvina of treason. But it was hardly worth while to be much disturbed about the seizure of one of Novgorod's colonies at the moment when the metropolis itself, with all its colonies, was about to fall prey to Moscow. And hardly had this come about than the princes of Moscow put an end to the commercial independence of Novgorod; in 1494, quibbling over an insignificant pretext, Ivan III closed the German Courtyard in Novgorod, arresting in the process forty-nine merchants and confiscating merchandise to the value of 96,000 marks silver (about half a million gold rubles in pre-war money). This did not mean that trade with the West was terminated, but merely that its centre had passed to Moscow; the bourgeoisie of Moscow took the place of the bourgeoisie of Novgorod at the same time that Novgorod definitively and irretrievably became the votchina of the prince of Moscow.

The enthusiasm of Muscovite public opinion for the "worker of piety," Grand Prince Ivan III, had, as we see, a very material basis. The townsmen of Moscow could not but sympathise with a campaign which handed over to them the commercial hegemony of Rus. But still more must the boyars of Moscow have sympathised with a deed in which they had been the immediate leaders. To the bourgeoisie of Moscow Novgorod was a trade rival, the possessor of dainty morsels which Moscow herself hankered for; similarly, to the boyars a region rich in silver was an enviable source of levies and imposts of all kinds; and it was with good reason that these levies and imposts had made the Dvina such an apple of discord. Moscow's financial exploitation of Novgorod had begun even earlier than the colonial wars. As early as 1384, after the devastation of the principality of Moscow by Tokhtamysh, Dmitry Donskoi had tried to shift to Novgorod part (perhaps the larger part) of the Tatar contribution, assessing on the Novgorodans the so-called "black levy" (a capitation tax). This time the Novgorodans succeeded in evading payment, but Moscow did not forget its pretensions and two years later, having recovered from the Tatar havoc, sent an army to Novgorod; Dmitry Donskoi succeeded in getting 8,000 (in pre-war money 800,000 gold) rubles. This contribution served as the starting point for further disputes; the Novgorodans regarded it as something extraordinary and unusual; the Muscovite government saw in it a precedent, of which it made use ever more and more frequently. Both Vasily I and Vasily II demanded the "black levy"; and toward the end Novgorod had begun to pay it, apparently without haggling, especially if Moscow "requested" the levy urbanely and civilly. But the appetite of the princes of Moscow grew with eating. During the protracted feud between Vasily II and his uncle Yury and the latter's sons, Vasily Squint-eye and Shemyaka, each of the contending princes watched his opportunity to snatch from the wealthy city something for himself, under the pretext, however, that Novgorod, while maintaining neutrality in these domestic feuds of Moscow, had harboured his rivals. It was on these grounds that Vasily II extorted from the Novgorodans a fresh contribution of 8,000 rubles just as his grandfather had done. One cannot but see that the city's resistance to these extortions became ever more and more feeble; in proportion as "the principality of Moscow" and "north-eastern Rus" became fused into one concept, Novgorod fell economically more and more into twofold dependence on the grand prince of Moscow. On the one hand, Novgorod, as of old, could not get along without grain from the Low Country; Moscow could always reduce her to obedience through starvation, and it was vain to hope for help from any of the other princes, because not one of them now dared to oppose Moscow. On the other hand, the Novgorodan merchant needed the Low Country as a market, while the Low Country was now a single realm under the headship of the prince of Moscow; in case of a quarrel with Moscow, there was no place where he could either buy or sell. Moscow understood this and pressed ever harder upon the liberties of the veche, not because she was conscious of the theoretical incompatibility of the veche with the Muscovite order of things or was even interested in this aspect of the matter, but because the veche order of things impeded the financial exploitation of the country. Vasily the Dark had succeeded in abolishing the sovereignty of Novgorod in fact when, after the campaign of 1456, which once more showed the military weakness of the bourgeoisie of Novgorod, he forced the latter to renounce its "veche charters," in other words, to acknowledge that the urban community alone could not issue laws without the sanction of the grand prince. Charters now had force only if the seal of the grand prince was appended to them. The significance of this limitation becomes quite clear when we learn that by the same treaty of 1456 the "black levy" was converted into a permanent tax, and judicial fines, "gifts" from the provinces, and all traditional imposts were secured to the grand prince. There was little in principle for Ivan III to add. It is noteworthy that after his "crusade" in 1471 he left the administration of Novgorod unchanged. In Novgorod's treaty with him after this war—the last treaty to be concluded by the still nominally free city—are preserved all the stereotyped limitations of the prince's authority: not to deal justice without the posadnik, and not to apportion the provinces without him, and to administer the provinces through men of Novgorod. All this was of slight moment to the conqueror; his chief interest was that "justice [*i.e.*, judicial revenues] be not taken from the governors," that "fines be not concealed," and that Novgorod divide with him, the grand prince, the new fines that the "code of Novgorod" introduced; and over and above this he took a contribution of 15,000 (1,500,000 pre-war) rubles. The chief pretext for future controversy—the transfer of appellate jurisdiction to Moscow, contrary to the rule of all the treaties—likewise came down to a financial question, and the Novgorodans knew what they were doing when they proposed to Ivan III, in return for restoration of the old order, a payment of 1,000 rubles every four years. But the grand prince reckoned, and he was probably right, that keeping the right to administer justice in the hands of Moscow would yield still more. The final ruin of the city, expressed in the transfer to the Lowlands of 7,000 of the men of substance—the prosperous bourgeoisie of Novgorod—in part corresponded to the interests of the Muscovite competitors of Novgorod, in part aimed at rooting out all resistance to financial exploitation. The area of the "feedings" of the boyars of Moscow, geographically doubled, now embraced the richest province of the Russia of that time, and they made such exhaustive use of the possibility opening before them, that thirty years after the subjection, Grand Prince Vasily III, son of the "worker of piety," had to limit the judicial authority of his governor in Novgorod, fearing that otherwise the land would be made an utter desert.

The coup d'état effected in Novgorod by Ivan III was one of the very clearest episodes of the "gathering" policy. With the exception of the struggle with Tver nowhere did open violence play such a rôle. But extensive application of open violence did not in itself impart an exceptional character to the "conquest of Novgorod." Ivan III did not attack Novgorod in order to abolish Novgorod's autonomy; he abolished it only because it prevented him from being as sovereign at Novgorod as at Moscow, *i.e.*, from collecting revenues in the same way. He would perhaps have left the veche—after his first victory, in 1471, he did not touch it—had there been any hope of securing from it "observance of the rights" of the grand prince of Moscow. Only recognition of the fact that the veche would always be the bulwark of anti-Muscovite sedition compelled Ivan on this point to depart from that "custom" to which he so liked to refer, not merely hypocritically, of course. Like all the descendants of Ivan Kalita he was anything but a revolutionary. The boyar council, once the ranks of the Novgorod boyars had been purged, seemed more innocuous, and it was left, though it is true, we do not know how long; however it happened, in 1481 a treaty with the Livonian Order was concluded by this very council, as had been done of old.

The conservative character of Muscovite conquest was no less clearly manifest in the subjugation of Pskov, the "younger brother" of Novgorod, in the reign of Ivan's son, Vasily III. The city had been deprived by Ivan of all financial rights over the surrounding country; these rights passed to the Muscovite sovereign. When Vasily became grand prince, the "better" men of Pskov, mainly from the ranks of the bourgeoisie (the landholding aristocracy was not as strong in Pskov as in Novgorod), were transported to central Russia, and in their place appeared three hundred merchant families from Moscow and its dependent towns. With them came to Pskov the Muscovite commercial order of things: customs duties and probably other trade imposts and dues. Pskov's former privilege of free trade, both at home and in the lands of the Livonian Order, was destroyed; and the merchants of Pskov were put on the same footing as those of Moscow.

But Vasily confined himself to the financial-economic conquest of Pskov (supplemented by the introduction of Muscovite coinage in place of the native). And after his time we find in Pskov, as also in Novgorod, elected officials. More than that: perhaps in imitation of the former veche communities, these institutions became widespread in the sixteenth century over the whole Muscovite state. In any case, it was not the newly-come Muscovites that introduced a new order of things, but the reverse; among the judicial elders of Pskov half were elected by the Muscovite merchants who had been transferred to Pskov. And in this preservation of justice in the hands of the bourgeoisie Muscovite dominance did not cut across the local order, but strengthened what had independently taken form locally; in Novgorod, as we know, the people had long since been removed from the administration of justice, and in Pskov evolution had proceeded in the same direction. To see here any conscious preservation of local peculiarities is, of course, not justifiable. But to remark this conservatism of Muscovite conquest is necessary in order not to fall into the very widespread error of imagining the "gathering of Rus" as the formation of a unitary state. The political unity of the "Great Russian people" we find only at the beginning of the seventeenth century, under the influence of economic conditions much later than the "annihilation of the last appanages." The Muscovite state of the seventeenth century was the result of the liquidation of feudal relations in their earlier form, but the princes of Moscow, down to Vasily III (d. 1533) inclusive, did not even think of such liquidation, since they themselves were typical feudal holders. Their sole anxiety was the punctual receipt of revenues, and their whole administration regarded the matter in this light. The charters of the early sixteenth century are nothing more than schedules of levies of the same type as on any feudal votchina. Compare the charter which Grand Prince Vasily granted to his "black peasants" with the charter that the Solovetsky Monastery gave its peasants, and you perceive no differences. What afterwards became the function of the police state was effected by the inhabitants themselves; "and they shall seek out a murderer, and they shall surrender him to the governors and their bailiffs"; and further, through their plenipotentiaries, "the older and the better men," they shall see that the governor and his bailiffs deal with the man arrested. The grand prince's officials for their part only saw to it that there was no "self-justice" in the provinces: "and self-justice is this: who takes a thief redhanded and lets him go, and to the governor and to his bailiff does not appear and they detect him in that . . ."; in other words, self-justice is the attempt to conceal judicial dues. The "administration" of the grand prince of Moscow, like the "administration" of his appanage forbear, was a special form of economic activity—and only that. When they came to organise on a broad scale the police of security, they imposed it "on the consciences" of the local inhabitants, dismissing the governors by reason of their complete unfitness for such business.

And the provinces themselves, gathered in such large number in the hands of Kalita's descendants, continued to preserve their former appanage physiognomy even territorially. The boundaries of these provinces likewise remained inviolate, and very frequently the same men administered them. The Obolensk principality in the middle of the sixteenth century was still entirely in the hands of the Princes Obolensky, who had long since become servitors of the prince of Moscow. The grand prince of Yaroslavl, even after the annexation of Yaroslavl by Moscow in 1463, remained as a governor of the grand prince of Moscow, and after his death his son inherited this office. "In 1493, when the Muscovite voevoda took Vyazma from Lithuania, and brought the Princes Vyazemsky to Moscow, the grand prince invested them with Vyazma as their votchina and bade them serve him." If we add to this that even in earlier times the independence of the petty appanage princes was never complete,[7] we shall understand that the mediatised prince, on ceasing to be an independent sovereign, might not perceive the fact, continuing to give charters "according to custom like his grandfather and father" even two generations after his mediatisation. Let us add that it would be hard for him to explain that he had ceased to be sovereign; sovereign he continued to be, inasmuch as every landholder was a sovereign.

[7] External, diploamtic relations, in particular with the Horde, always constituted a prerogative of the grand prince; the right to begin war and to conclude a peace independently also belonged to him alone; he also collected the Tatar tribute and what he did with it concerned him alone,

CHAPTER VII

IVAN THE TERRIBLE

1. *The Agrarian Revolution of the First Half of the Sixteenth Century*

THE earliest historian of Tsar Ivan [IV] "the Terrible" was Prince Kurbsky, who wrote while Ivan was still on the throne of Moscow. In explaining why Ivan ruined the Russian "princelings" "by whole families," Kurbsky sounds the motif: "they had great votchinas; I think probably for that he destroyed them." Ivan's literary antagonist was distinguished neither by talent as a writer nor by an especially profound understanding of what was taking place around him. In mentioning votchinas as the cause of the extermination of his kinsmen, Kurbsky hoped perhaps to attain a very limited practical goal—to terrify the Polish-Lithuanian aristocracy, who at the time the *History of the Grand Prince of Moscow* was written were thinking of seating Ivan on the Polish throne, too. But practical men, just because they lack a wide horizon, frequently perceive the proximate causes of a phenomenon better than do men who look at things through the eyes of an idealistic theory. A long time was to pass before Kurbsky's casual remarks about the causes of the "tyranny" of Ivan the Terrible were appreciated. Only in the 1870's did the late Professor Zhdanov of St. Petersburg adopt the view that the key to the whole tragedy of the *oprichnina* [1] must be sought in the quarrel over land. In the meantime how many interpretations has not Tsar Ivan's memory had to suffer! From the most sublime, which, employing Hegel's method, made the autocrat of Moscow the tool of a universal spirit in its destructive-creative labour, to the most realistic, which asserted that sixteenth-century Russia was a madhouse—let any one of them be applied to Ivan IV, and there is no tragedy at all.

To-day the agrarian background of the oprichnina may be said to be a commonplace; to-day there is no novelty in defending the views of the sixteenth-century historian [Kurbsky]. To contest them would be original. "The oprichnina was the first attempt to resolve one of the contradictions of the Muscovite state order," says Prof. Platonov, one of the most cautious of Russian historians; "it shattered the landholding of the aristocracy as it had existed from antiquity." All hypotheses about the "personality" of Ivan the Terrible lose importance before this

[1] *Cf. infra*, pp. 142 *et seq.;* see also Glossary.

simple, prosaic fact remarked by contemporaries three hundred years ago. But this simple, prosaic fact requires explanation no less than does the most complicated and romantic view of Ivan's "mental state." Why did Ivan the Terrible need his boyars' votchinas when he himself had enough such votchinas, when his father and grandfather, in putting the finishing touches to the Muscovite state, had dwelt in peace with the holders of these votchinas or at any rate had not gone so far as to ruin them "by whole families"? The oprichnina was but the culminating point of a long socio-political process, which had begun long before Ivan the Terrible, which did not end until long after his death, and which by its inexorable, elemental nature makes cogitation over "characters" and "mental states" peculiarly idle. The policy of the oprichnina runs like a red thread through the reigns of Ivan, Fedor, and Godunov alike, from the 1560's right up to the Troubles, with moments of relaxation and moments of tension, but wholly unconnected with any one's volition. Twenty years in advance (in the 1540's) the approach of the catastrophe was already so definitely felt that it proved possible for a man [2] who perhaps did not himself live to see the oprichnina with his own eyes, to outline its programme. Yet in the 'forties even the "beneficent" period of Ivan's reign, which Karamzin contrasted with the period of his "tyranny," still lay in the future. As yet Ivan had not succeeded in becoming either "good" or "evil," though it had already been prophesied to him that if he "threatens not the nation with great terror, then he will not bring law into the land." The nickname "Terrible" was hovering in the air before the commission of the deeds which were to secure him this nickname in history.

Ascending the throne in 1533, at the age of three, Ivan IV inherited from his father and grandfather the votchina of Moscow in the feudal guise which we have already characterised in detail. The grand prince of Moscow was suzerain of innumerable landholders, both large and small, who "held" their lands from him; one might be an appanage prince who had passed into the service of Moscow, another a petty vassal, a "knight" who, perhaps, had only yesterday been raised from amongst the boyars' "servitors," if not their bondsmen, into the service of Moscow. The distinction between these two strata of Moscow's vassals was quantitatively enormous, but qualitatively they both belonged to the one category; theoretically both had agreed to serve their suzerain on certain conditions, and the removal of these conditions ended their obligation to serve. This was the theory. In practice observance of the rights of a military servitor was wholly dependent on the good will, on the strength, and on the ability of him whom he served. The free servitors' celebrated "right of departure," of which one can read to one's

[2] "Peresvetov," cf. *infra*, pp. 123 *et seq*.

heart's content in old courses of Russian history, either never existed
or existed in its traditional form right down to the time of Ivan the
Terrible; the answer to this question will depend on whether or not one
considers this right apart from its connexion with "force." A powerful
prince never hesitated to execute a weak "departer." In 1379 Dmitry
Donskoi's government executed the boyar Velyaminov, who had "departed " from the service of Moscow to that of Tver; at that time the
boyars of Tver and Ryazan passed freely into the service of Moscow, for
the prince of Moscow was stronger than their former suzerains. But
on paper the right of the military servitor to elect whom he would serve
was still recognised in 1537 and even in 1553. Under the former year
the chronicle relates that Prince Andrew of Staritsa, uncle of the grand
prince, who had recently taken oath "not to call away men from the
grand prince," began to send out letters to the pomeshchiks of Novgorod, writing, "The grand prince is young, and the boyars hold the state,
and whom have you to serve? Come to serve me, and I am glad to make
grants to you." The boyars who then held the state ordered those
pomeshchiks who had been seduced to the "granting" of the prince of
Staritsa to be beaten with the knout and to be hanged "along the Novgorod highway, not together, but all the way to Novgorod." In 1553
these same boyars, during what at the time all believed to be the fatal
illness of Ivan, deliberated whether "to serve the young to the exclusion
of the old," the infant son of the grand prince to the exclusion of the
adult descendant of Ivan III, Prince Vladimir of Staritsa, son of the
man who had tempted the pomeshchiks of Novgorod to their destruction;
the boyars deemed it possible to exchange their infant suzerain for his
adult rival. But such cases were becoming more and more rare, for by
purely quantitative accumulation Ivan Kalita's patrimony had destroyed
a very essential phase of feudal relationships. The form long survived
the content. On paper the seventeenth-century pomeshchik still "contracted" with the government about the conditions of his life. "He
shall be on an ordinary horse, while with state pay he will be on a good
horse," was inscribed of this or that military servitor in the general
register. The scale of his compensation, whether in land alone or in land
and a money salary besides, determined the quality of his service. The
parties were supposedly still bargaining, but it was only the ritual of
bargaining. In actual fact a pomeshchik dared not refuse the service
that was offered him; for in the seventeenth century there was not even
for a moment any suzerain other than the tsar and grand prince of
Moscow to whom it would be possible to "depart."

Was this decay of old Russian feudalism confined to juridical relationships? Given the old economic basis such a modification of the
juridical superstructure would even at first glance seem incomprehensi-

ble. The independent position of the vassal in relation to the suzerain was the political equivalent of the economic independence of this vassal's votchina from the world about him. Sitting in his manor-house, a landholder rarely entered into immediate contact with the world—only on ceremonial occasions, so to speak. For his workaday life he had everything he needed at home. As we see, the origin of the classic pride of the mediæval knight was very prosaic. In Russia in the sixteenth century (as in the West from the twelfth to the fourteenth centuries, depending on the country) there is abundant evidence that the economic independence of the feudal votchina was not so great as it had been a century or two earlier. The most noticeable symptom of this is the feudal landholder's desire to receive his revenue in the form of money. It will be remembered that on the old Russian votchina peasant dues were usually paid in produce—grain, flax, mutton, cheese, eggs, etc. If we take the Novgorod registers, which contain data for several successive periods, we find that only dues in grain persist unchanged; by the middle of the sixteenth century money had to some extent, and by the end of the century completely replaced payment in cheese, eggs, mutton, etc. In this respect the grand prince and his governors did not differ from other votchinniks; in fact, among them we can trace this appetite for money to a considerably earlier period. The first charter translating the natural obligations of a population (Belozersk) into money payments dates from 1488. It lists both the governor's "feedings" and the judicial fines in their original form, produce, but immediately sets down their money equivalents: "for a half shoulder of meat, 2 altyns; . . . for a ram, 8 dengas," etc. The introduction of money payments was the occasion for a great number of the extant charters of the beginning of the sixteenth century. Thus the administrative cares of the Muscovite government had a very real, purely economic, basis.

Votchinniks both great and small strove to get their revenues in a form less unwieldy than produce intended for immediate consumption. But this new and more flexible form of revenue—money—would be unthinkable under the economic order within the bounds of which the feudal votchina had taken form. An appanage prince had always needed money on "ceremonial occasions": for example, when he was preparing to despatch the tribute to the Horde, or when he or his subjects bought cloth, wine, or fruits from beyond the sea. Everyday, workaday needs were satisfied out of their own domestic resources; for this purpose money was not necessary. So long as money was but rarely needed, there was no occasion for desiring to receive revenues in money form. Thus the feudal votchinnik's adoption of money economy was only the outward expression of a far greater change. This change consisted in the destruction of the feudal votchina as a self-sufficient economic unit and in the appearance in the market as both buyer and seller of the landholder, who had formerly been proud of his economic isolation.

Evidence of a votchina's connexion with the market—a connexion that was not casual but permanent, normal, so to speak—is first found in the fifteenth-century code of Pskov, which originated, it is true, in the economically most progressive region of the Russia of that time. One of the last provisions of this document deals with the obligation of an "old *izornik*" (*i.e.*, a *former* peasant) to bring horses and carts to his lord, even though at the termination of his field labours on St. Philip's Eve (November 15) he had "renounced" his master. Grain and poultry were sent to town, to the market, at the first sledging, but winter might not begin till after November 15, *i.e.*, after the formal cessation of the obligations between an "izornik" and his "lord." Then the latter might find himself in an embarrassing position, with something to sell but no one to take it to town for him. Protecting the interests of the landholder, the law of Pskov made the reservation that although the relations between lord and peasant had formally ended, the former peasant must none the less fulfil his last economic function; he must take the products of his labour to market. "Cartage" is also mentioned in sixteenth-century Muscovite documents.

Especially valuable is the evidence of the existence of petty, local markets. Large-scale exchange, even in objects of prime necessity, in grain especially, had existed even earlier in so far as there had been large trading centres, like Novgorod, with a numerous non-agricultural population. In the sixteenth century, although Novgorod preserved a good deal of her former importance, her place had been taken by Moscow, which, in the words of foreign travellers, stretched for almost nine versts along the course of the River Moscow and in the second half of the reign of Ivan the Terrible numbered more than 40,000 homesteads, *i.e.*, not less than 200,000 souls.[3] According to Fletcher, who was there in the reign of Ivan's son, Fedor, "the citie of Mosko is not much bigger than the citie of London," while there is reason to believe his assertion that Moscow was at this time suffering mightily from the Tatar raid of 1571 and, it must be added, from the general economic crisis that was desolating all the towns of central Russia. Moscow must have absorbed a vast quantity of the products of rural economy; and the 700-800 cartloads of grain that daily entered Moscow along the Yaroslavl road alone, as related by a foreign traveller, were in all probability no exaggeration. Yet this was only a quantitative change as compared

[3] *Cf.* G. Fletcher, *Of the Russe Common Wealth* (London, 1591), in Sir E. A. Bond, *Russia at the close of the sixteenth century* [Works published by the Hakluyt Society, No. XX, London, 1856], p. 17.

with the preceding period, though quantity was already effecting a qualitative change in the economy of Moscow. From the point of view of economic evolution far-more interest attaches to the petty urban centres in central and northern Russia in this same period, the reigns of Ivan the Terrible and his successor. We shall cite only a few examples. Toropets of Smolensk, once the votchina of Mstislav the Bold, in the sixteenth century "was of moderate size and not distinguished by the prosperity of its trade." None the less in 1540-1541 it consisted of 402 taxable homesteads, as well as 80 of military servitors, 79 shops, and a population of about 2,400. In Solvychegodsk, in the second half of the same century, there were about 600 taxable homesteads, *i.e.*, not less than 3,000 inhabitants, though "these places were distinguished neither by populousness nor by activity." In a no less backwoods corner, Kargopol, documents of 1560 tell of 476 taxable homesteads, *i.e.*, at the very least some 2,500 inhabitants. To the south of Moscow, in Kashira, at the end of the 1570's, there were "about 400 homesteads of townsmen and a considerable market comprising more than 100 shops." Even the destruction of Kashira by the Tatars, who burned the town to ashes, did not destroy its commercial significance. In Serpukhov as early as 1552 a fifth of the town had been deserted, yet there still remained more than 500 homesteads and 250 shops. From this we see how imprudent it would be to imagine a town of Muscovite Rus as a fortress peopled almost exclusively with military servitors. However meagre by modern standards the above figures of the trading-industrial population, for a mediæval country like Muscovite Rus of the sixteenth century one may justly speak of the bourgeoisie as a fairly distinct social class—a social force, the influence of which could not fail to tell at critical moments. This influence attained its apogee in the days of the Troubles, when the bourgeoisie proved strong enough to put forward its own tsar and to maintain him for several years. But the statesmen of the period of Ivan the Terrible were already reckoning with this force, and by that very fact compel the historian likewise to reckon with it.

One of the largest items in the growth of commercial capital was the trade in salt, which was almost monopolised by the monasteries in Muscovite, as in Kievan, Rus. The Solovetsky Monastery sold some 130,000 puds of salt annually. The Kirillo-Belozersk Monastery traded in it "on the Dvina, and in Tver, and in Torzhok, and at Uglich and at Kimr, and in Dmitrov, in Rostov, and on the Kineshma, and at Vologda, and at Beloozero with its subsidiary towns and in other places; where salt is dearer, there they sell," as the monastery's authorities naïvely admit their engrossing trade. Certain second-rate monasteries sold as much as 20,000 puds of salt a year. Along with this the monasteries carried on an extensive trade in other products: fish, butter, cattle.

Monasterial storehouses in Vologda stretched for sixty *sazhens*[4] in length and eight in breadth. When, at the end of the sixteenth century, the Kirillov Monastery transferred its market to a new site, the tsar's custom-house too had to be moved thither, to such a degre had the cloister become the commercial capital of the region.

If the monasteries in engrossing salt were almost without rivals, the rest of society did not lag behind them in engrossing other objects of prime necessity. In connexion with the monasteries is significant the commercial rôle of the clergy, of which there is abundant evidence. To that priest and cattle-dealer whom N. A. Rozhkov discovered in a sixteenth-century biography may be added Silvester, archpriest of the Cathedral of the Annunciation, a person renowned both in history and in literature, Ivan's mentor in the days of his "beneficence." Urging his son to be honourable in payments, Silvester adduces truly bourgeois arguments, to which any mediæval merchant would willingly have subscribed: "And when I purchased something of any one I entertained him kindly: payment without intriguing, and broke bread with him besides, and friendship forever; and he will sell nothing over my head. . . . And when I sold something to any one it was all in love, and not in deceit . . . good men have trusted me in everything, both local men and foreigners." This participation of a Muscovite archpriest in *foreign* trade is interesting because it indicates the circle of his relationships and acquaintances; later on we shall see that certain projects of the first half of Ivan's reign should be linked with this very circle. Foreign trade was even then not insignificant, which is not surprising if we remember that the fall of Novgorod had not meant rupture of commercial relations with oversea countries but only concentration of them in Moscow itself. In the 'sixties was added one more "window to the West," the route opened by the English along the Northern Dvina, through Archangel; but even this of course by no means wiped out the old route. Fletcher asserts that while Narva was in Russian hands (1558-1581) there sailed thence annually with flax and hemp alone not less than 100 ships, "large and small." It is said that some 50,000 puds of wax, some 100,000 puds of salt, some 100,000 hides were exported annually. The decline of exports by the reign of Fedor (by two-thirds or even three-fourths) he ascribes to the failures of Russian foreign policy; the latter's connection with commercial interests we shall consider later. On the score of Silvester it is also worth noting that besides being himself occupied with trade, he prepared others for the same activity; many of his pupils, according to his story, "work by hand at various industries, and many trade in shops; many visit for trade in divers countries for all sorts of trade." Not without reason was Tsar Ivan's

[4] 1 *sazhen* = 7 ft.

tutor the author of the moderate and accurate, truly petty-bourgeois *Domostroi* [household-order] ; he was the founder of commercial education in Russia.

Explaining the rise of grain prices in the 'eighties, Fletcher says: ". . . the fault is rather in their nobilitie that use to engrosse it, then in the countrie it selfe." [5] Actually, grain prices in the sixteenth century rose regularly and inexorably, quite independently of occasional bad harvests. That landholders were directly interested in grain prices is shown by the widespread collection of dues in "threshed grain" which we have already noted.

Dues in grain, or participation of the pomeshchik in a share of the harvest, were the very simplest means of extracting money from an estate in agricultural localities, as dues in money were in non-agricultural regions. In 1565-1568 in the coastal section of Novgorod's territory threshed grain and a share of the harvest constituted 84.1% of the whole dues, and money only 15.9% ; in the section to the northeast the pomeshchiks' revenue in grain in both forms did not exceed 25%, while money dues supplied more than 75% of their whole revenue. But the colossal rise of grain prices was bound to excite the pomeshchiks of agricultural Russia to new and more complicated forms of production. Even at that time there were men to whom the traditional, petty, peasant economy did not seem productive enough. The petty economy of the peasant had been calculated to satisfy the needs of his homestead; to the lord's homestead went the smaller part of the harvest, a quarter or a third, according to the Novgorod registers of the end of the fifteenth century. But now it was advantageous for the lord to take into his own hands everything except what was absolutely necessary for the subsistence of the workers themselves. In the preceding period the lord's arable had served only for the satisfaction of the needs of the lord's homestead and therefore was usually not very great in extent. However, Nikitsky, the investigator of Novgorodan economy at the end of the fifteenth century, has noticed quite a sharp change; "with the establishment of Muscovite overlordship," he writes, "the lord's arable increases considerably." The expanding lord's arable was worked by the lord's bondsmen. In the chapter on Russian feudalism we had occasion to note the rôle of bondsmen as military collaborators of their masters; now their economic utilisation begins. What proportions this attained is shown by the will (1545-1546) of Prince Sudtsky, a wealthy man of the time of Ivan's youth. In this will can be counted not less than 55 families of bondsmen whom the Prince bequeaths to his wife and daughters, not counting those he emancipates; among them are 30 families of field hands, who worked the Prince's arable. Ten years later,

[5] G. Fletcher, *op. cit.*, p. 9.

in the will of another wealthy pomeshchik, we find besides "field servants" (*i.e.*, bondsmen) indentured field hands, workers bound by way
of a loan. It is curious that the testator disposes of both categories alike,
and quite freely, as his own property, counting them by "heads" like
cattle. Thus one of the roots of serfdom is clearly visible even in the
1550's.

The labour of bondsmen on the arable was very common in the first
half of the century; according to the computation of N. A. Rozhkov,
on pomestye lands, in the county of Tver in 1539-1540 masters' homesteads constituted 4.5%, bondsmen's 8.8%, peasants' 86.7% of the total
number of agricultural homesteads. On individual estates bondsmen's
homesteads rose above ten per cent. But despite artificial expansion of
the contingent of "field hands" by indenturing free peasants, the lord's
arable grew more rapidly than the number of bondaged hands employed on it. Striving with feverish haste to increase the area of land
the revenue from which went wholly to him, the pomeshchik seized not
only upon individual peasant homesteads which had for some reason
become deserted but also upon whole hamlets and clearings. Individual
small landholders could still get along with the labour of bondsmen
despite the expansion of their arable; but the large proprietor in order
to organise his economy had to seek a more extensive reservoir of working hands. Very quickly he hit upon the idea of extending the natural
obligations of the free peasants dwelling on his lands. The first examples of the development of barshchina [obligatory labour] are found, as
might be expected, on Church land, in the famous charter of the Metropolitan Simon which once played such a rôle in the controversies over
the origin of the Russian landed commune.[6] But the document, which
has only recently been printed in full, has proved to have capital importance in another respect; it has irrefutably established the existence,
even at the turn of the fifteenth century, of the regularly organised
labour obligation of the free peasants. Barshchina was not burdensome
at first; for each five desyatinas of his land the peasant had to plough
one desyatina of the Church's land. This represented, however, an
augmentation of barshchina; the occasion for the charter was that the
peasants "plough the arable for themselves much, while the monastery's
arable they plough little." On this estate three-field economy had
already been introduced; its cultivation was, for those times, quite
intensive. Still more intensive economy, likewise accompanied by regulated labour obligation, is found forty years later on the court votchinas
of the grand prince; in the county of Volokolamsk the court peasants

---

6 This document cannot, however, be used as proof of the existence of the commune, for the repartition mentioned in the charter was effected, not by the peasants
but by the votchinnik.

were obligated for each six desyatinas of their land to plough a seventh for the grand prince, and at the same time the scale of seeding on this desyatina was accurately defined: "2 quarters of rye, and of oats double." The peasants had to manure the grand prince's land at their own cost; at the same time, not only the number of "piles" of manure to the desyatina but also the dimensions of each pile were exactly defined. The estates of middling and petty landholders had to wait a long time for such a rational economy. But here, too, barshchina appears quite early; even an investigator who asserts that until the end of the sixteenth century "barshchina did not exist" cites a number of references to barshchina estates in the first half of the century, and this number might be further increased. Along with economy based on indenture was bound up this other root of serfdom; with its further growth we shall acquaint ourselves when we study the economic life of Muscovite Rus of the seventeenth century. To the modern reader, accustomed to regard "bondage economy" as a synonym for retrogression, it seems strange to find the first beginnings of peasant bondage bound up with intensification of cultivation; but the feudal votchina, which knew no proletariat, could not construct a new system of economy on anything but involuntary labour in some form or other.

In the period we are now considering, the first half of the reign of Ivan the Terrible, the agrarian crisis still lay far in the future, and no one then anticipated the blighting of the incipient economic bloom. Money and money economy were new; every one hankered after money. The fact that grain became a commodity made the land that supplied the grain also a commodity. Men who desired this latter commodity were numerous, and seldom in early Rus had land mobilisation proceeded more briskly than it did in the first half of the sixteenth century. But the fact that men were purchasing land often and in quantity meant that some one was selling land, i.e., making himself landless. In Chapter II we have seen one category of those who were losing land, viz., the petty votchina landholders, the peasant-proprietors. But they were not the only ones to make themselves landless; at the opposite extreme, among the greatest boyar-votchinniks, we notice the same phenomenon. Two conditions led to the rapid liquidation of the Muscovite *latifundia* of the time. In the first place, their holders rarely possessed the ability and the desire to organise their economy in the new way. Pursuing a career at court and in the army, "the boyar of the sixteenth century rarely visited his suburban estates, and it is hardly likely that he ever beheld his distant votchinas and pomestyes." In the second place, the feudal aristocracy was "under obligations" in those times, as later; a great boyar or a mediatised appanage prince had, by tradition, to maintain an extensive "court," a swarm of parasitic menials and a retinue, sometimes, as Kurbsky testifies, of several thousand men. As long as all these people lived without expense on his peasants' grain, a boyar might not notice the economic burden of his official prestige. But when many things had to be purchased for money —money that was ever falling in value from year to year, in proportion to the growth of exchange economy—it became a grievous burden on the shoulders of the great landholder. Rozhdestvensky, the historian of military landholding in the sixteenth century, cites what might be called a touching episode, which clearly depicts this aspect of the matter. In 1547 Tsar Ivan betrothed the daughter of one of his most eminent vassals, Prince Alexander Gorbatov-Shuisky, to Prince I. F. Mstislavsky, also one of the foremost boyars of Moscow; it turned out that the bride's mother had nothing to wear to the wedding, for her husband, on setting off on the tsar's service, i.e., in mobilising his appanage army, had pawned everything he could pawn, including his wife's whole wardrobe. In this respect the petty vassal was in a far more advantageous position; not only did he not spend money on his service, but he received money for it. In the course of the sixteenth century a money wage to the petty military servitor becomes ever more customary. If we add that a small estate was far easier to organise than a large one since it was easy to "blend together" two or three hamlets or clearings and altogether impossible to carry out this operation over several tens and hundreds of hamlets, and that it was easy for a petty landholder personally to supervise the obligatory labour of his peasants and bondsmen whereas a great one had to do it through a steward who was not loath to become the real master—then we shall see that in the nascent struggle between large and middling landholders every advantage economically lay with the latter. In expropriating the wealthy boyar-votchinnik in favour of the lesser noble holding a small pomestye, the oprichnina followed the lines of natural economic evolution. Herein lay the first condition of its success.

2. Publicism and the "Reforms"

The political consequences of the fundamental economic fact of the period, the crisis in large votchina landholding, were very soon felt. Even in the first half of the sixteenth century the boyars felt the ground trembling beneath them and took measures to stabilise their shaken position. These measures and their consequences are very concisely and expressively described in a government document of the 1550's. "Formerly we rewarded our boyars and princes and knights," this document makes the tsar say, "gave them towns and provinces as *kormlenies* [feedings], and to us from the peasants came great petitions, and the importunity was ceaseless, that our governors of towns and of townships

and their [agents], exceeding our edict, inflict on them great fines
and costs; and from the governors of towns and of townships and from
their [agents] came to us importunity and many petitions, that the men
of the towns and the townships do not submit to their jurisdiction and
do not pay them the kormlenies, and beat them, and therefore between
them arise great calumnies and law-suits. . . .'' In order to understand
this text it is necessary to have a clear idea what the governors of towns
(*namestniks*) and of townships (*volostels*) were in appanage Rus. They
were not at all like the governors of the nineteenth century (*gubernators*)
or even like the governors of the seventeenth and eighteenth centuries
(*voevodas*), just as the appanage prince was not like the tsar of modern
times. For a prince his principality was, above all else, a source of
revenues, in the form of tribute, judicial dues, and such like. These
revenues, in natural form, he could not everywhere collect in person,
and sometimes it was advantageous for him in this or that locality
to farm them out to a lesser feudatory. The latter appears in the rôle
of the prince's namestnik, a *kormlenshchik* [feeder], as they called
him, because he fed himself from his office. This was in the full sense
of the word *natural* administration, corresponding exactly to all the conditions of natural economy. The boyar who farmed the prince's revenues
went to his province with his whole household. His bondsmen and
petty vassals, his ''serving men,'' became in the province judges, police,
and tax-gatherers. A kormlenie was, consequently, a sort of business
undertaking, and a very lucrative one, if we are to believe a contemporary publicist, who asserted that where ten rubles were to be taken
into the tsar's treasury a hundred slipped into the boyar's pocket. The
official document does not contradict this, painting a picture of savage
extortions, as a result of which ''in the towns many peasant homesteads, and in the townships hamlets and homesteads, were deserted.''
Of course, we must not be confused by the usual form of early Russian
documents and chronicles, which represent matters as though the tsar
gave towns and townships as kormlenies; in the 'thirties and 'forties the
throne of the universal Orthodox realm was occupied by a child, who
could not give anything to anybody. Impoverished votchinniks greed-
ily helped themselves to the kormlenies as the sole means of mending
their affairs, especially after ''tributes and dues'' had been commuted
into money, and the farmed grand-princely revenues had begun to come
in in the form most advantageous for the farmers. In the colossal abuse
of kormlenies lay those ''horrors'' of the boyar administration of which
so much is to be heard both from contemporaries and from later historians. In 1547 a popular revolt, the apparent occasion for which was
the great Moscow fire, united into one huge outburst all the petty

"resistances to the authorities" referred to in the charter we have cited. This revolt was by no means a casual disturbance among the ruins of the fire; the disturbance began on the fifth day after the fire had been extinguished, while the fact that Prince Yury Glinsky, Ivan's uncle and head of the Moscow government, and his officials were victims of the revolt emphasises quite definitely the political causes of the movement. It must be said that the movement was not local or confined to Moscow; its instigators found asylum "in other towns"; the whole Russian land sheltered them. The "enterprises" of the kormlenshchiks had aroused every one against them—both the poor, who could get no justice from them, and the rich, whom the kormlenshchiks systematically robbed. It is enough to cite an instance of the kormlenshchiks' administrative measures to make quite clear the attitude of the possessing classes toward the boyar administration. "The tsar's dignitaries in the towns and in the townships," relates the same publicist, "in their double-dealing and diabolical practices have gone so far as to exhume newly buried corpses, re-interring the empty coffins; they thrust a disinterred dead man, pierced with a boarspear or hacked with a sabre, and smeared with blood, into the house of some rich man; then they find an informer who knows not God, and having condemned the rich man by an iniquitous trial they plunder all his household and his wealth." This example makes very vivid the contradiction of interests between the kormlenshchik and the *whole* population. The former lived, above all else, on his judicial revenues; the more crimes in his district, the higher his revenue, whereas to society—and especially to the higher strata—order and security were the more necessary the more advanced it was economically, and we have already seen the tempo at which Russian society was advancing economically in the days of Ivan the Terrible. That which destroyèd the economic basis of the boyar order likewise raised up opponents to it; when after the Kazan campaign "the sovereign rewarded all the land" with kormlenies, he did so in reply to the unanimous declarations, not only of the "simple populace" that had revolted in 1547 but of all save only the boyars themselves. Some of these declarations have come down to us: the most important part of the Vaga charter of 1552, for example, is simply a transcription of the petition of the men of the Vaga themselves, including all the compliments the petitioners had addressed to their governors, whom they baldly likened to "thieves, rascals, and other evil men." That other declarations of this kind have not come down to us does not mean that there were none. Indeed, it was more than a matter of simple petitions; there was an integral, consciously worked-out plan of reform, which found both private and official expression from the pens of the first Russian publicists and in the form of the questions which Ivan addressed to the Stoglav Sobor.[7]

Both the publicism of the 'forties and 'fifties and the "tsar's questions" are especially interesting because they make it possible for us to discover the social forces behind the so-called "reforms of Ivan the Terrible." It has long since ceased to be possible to represent these "reforms" as the product of the wisdom of the tsar himself and of a close circle of his counsellors. Participation of the population in the "reforms," even its initiative in them, has likewise long been acknowledged. But analysis of this fact has usually not been carried beyond references to the "course of events" and the "force of things." Valuable in themselves as a recognition of the material factor as the driving force of history, these phrases do not, however, suggest the concrete form in which the "force of things" arrayed itself. The economic changes we noted at the beginning of this chapter inevitably produced new social classes or, at least, new social groups. Now it was the middling landholders, who had successfully adapted themselves to the conditions of the new exchange economy; now it was the bourgeoisie, strong of old in Moscow itself, and, thanks to the new economy, acquiring peculiar importance and influence far beyond the limits of the capital. We have just seen an illustration of the attitude of these two classes toward the great feudal landholders, the masters of appanage Rus. But this attitude is not revealed merely by obscure hints in the sources, as might have been supposed. It was quite accurately formulated by contemporaries, and the establishment of this fact is a great scientific discovery still insufficiently appreciated by the historians who have made a special study of the sixteenth century, although the suggestion that there had been conscious planning of the "reforms"—planning that went far beyond what was actually accomplished—was made in 1876. Although it would seem self-evident that the tsar's correspondence with Kurbsky could not have been an isolated fact, for formulation of political views on paper and defence of them with the pen could not have been a habit peculiar to two men, the existence of *publicism* in the days of Ivan the Terrible evoked especial scepticism. This scepticism was supported by the firmly rooted conviction of the general illiteracy of old Muscovite Rus, but this conviction could not remain unshaken among those who knew that even under Ivan the Terrible literacy was a prerequisite for the holding of certain offices (for example, as head of a *guba*, to be discussed below) and who knew the rôle played in those

---

[7] The "Council of the Hundred Chapters," so-called from the number of its resolutions, was held at Moscow in 1551 to give moral support and ecclesiastical sanction to the reforms of Ivan IV; it was attended by the higher clergy and high secular dignitaries.

times by the men of pen and paper, the dyaks, who frequently seemed to foreigners to control the destinies of the state. There was, of course, no "reading public" in our sense, but in any backwoods corner might be found men able to read and to recount what they had read to their neighbours. As yet printing was not worth while (a printing press was set up under Ivan the Terrible for divine-service books only), but anything that found favour circulated widely enough in manuscript to influence the minds of the upper classes at least. Thus arose a number of productions, written, as was usual at the time, in the form of a parable, an apocryphal book, or a moralising historical narrative, embodying a very practical content. It was sometimes a petition supposed to have been submitted to the tsar by some serving man; now it took the form of conversations about Russia, carried on by foreign notables of the time; now tidings of strange lands and rulers in which, nevertheless, it was not difficult to recognise Ivan IV and the state of Moscow; now revelations of holy miracle-workers. Many of the extant productions of this kind are connected with the name of Ivan Peresvetov, the "emigrant from Lithuania," undoubtedly a legendary person, though there were real men of that name. A "warrior" who had traversed the "whole world," who had in his time served "Fordynal the Czech" and "Yanusha, the king of Hungary," and "Peter, the voevoda of Wallachia," made an extraordinarily convenient screen for keen criticism of the order of things in the fatherland; on the one hand, he wrote with the authority of a semi-foreigner, who had seen Europe and who could on occasion allude to conditions there; on the other hand, as a foreigner, he was free to sin somewhat against Orthodox tradition.

Peresvetov's writings all centred around one theme: the causes of the fall of Constantinople, of the ruin of the Orthodox ruler "Constantine Ivanovich,"[8] and of the success of the infidel "Saltan Makhmet." The theme was then most popular in Russian literature, but no one had treated it from his viewpoint. Pious booklets were inclined to view it as a happy event: heresy had been put to shame, while the older piety had begun to shine like the sun, and the place of the fallen second Rome had been taken by Moscow, the third Rome. Decency demanded the shedding of a few tears over the downfall of the old capital of the Orthodox realm, but her heiress was ready, and there was really nothing to weep over. For Peresvetov the fall of Constantinople was a terrible historical example of how states perish when they are badly administered, when there is no "justice." The "Third Rome" did not interest him at all; if things were managed in the same way in Moscow as in Byzantium, Moscow, too, would meet a like fate. Moscow's future political career depended wholly on whether there was

---

[8] Constantine Palaiologus, last of the Byzantine emperors.

"justice" there. It mattered not that in Moscow "the Christian faith is good and the beauty of the Church is great"; "if there is no justice, there is nothing." And there would be no justice, so long as the appanage method of government was preserved. Peter, the voevoda of Wallachia, into whose mouth were put Peresvetov's very boldest sentiments (which needed a double pseudonym), particularly criticises Tsar Ivan for "letting loose private war in his realm": he gives the towns and the townships to magnates to hold, and the magnates grow rich from the tears and the blood of Christians. The kormlenshchiks thus appear as the prime obstacle to the realisation of "justice" in the Russian land. Sultan Makhmet had long since set an example of how to dispense with kormlenies: though an infidel, he "wrought works agreeable to God, great wisdom and law he brought into his realm," sending his loyal judges through all the realm, *"paying them salaries from the treasury."* "And judicial revenues he bade to be brought into his treasury" so that the judges should have no temptation to judge unjustly; and he gave out to them law books by which they should judge and rule.

Peresvetov's pamphlets, as can be judged from a number of indications, appeared between the years 1545-1548, while the so-called "Tsar's *Sudebnik* [Code]" of Ivan IV was published in June, 1550. This information alone suffices to show how closely the publicism of the times of Ivan the Terrible was bound up with events of the time. But Sultan Makhmet did not confine himself to centralisation of judicial revenues alone; he introduced "unity of the treasury" for all his revenues without exception: "and from the towns, and from the townships, and from the votchinas, and from the pomestyes all revenues he bade to be gathered into his tsar's treasury at every hour," while he paid his collectors salaries from the treasury. His whole military strength was organised in just the same way, on salary. The Muscovite state had long since begun to pass from natural to money economy but had not yet achieved any such wholesale change of the administrative apparatus as complete replacement of the feudal state with its vassalage by a centralised monarchy with a salaried officialdom. What "Peresvetov" dreamed of was not to be realised until the eighteenth century. Not until a still later date could another of our publicist's ideas be realised. He was a great opponent of bondage; his hero, Sultan Makhmet of Turkey, ordered all the records of bondage "burned with fire" and even permitted captives to redeem their liberty on the expiration of a seven-year term. And from the lips of a Turkish lord comes a splendid apology of the freedom of the people as an indispensable condition of national independence: "In what realm men are enslaved, in that realm men are not brave. . . ."

But Peresvetov was not only a representative of a new economic philosophy; this was not a feature peculiar to him, and on this head he could find comrades even among his most violent opponents. The boyars were not averse to taking advantage of money economy, and their plunderings as kormlenshchiks were a special form of exploitation of new sources of revenue. Peresvetov was neither a landholder-entrepreneur nor a bourgeois from the city. The merchant he regards from the point of view usual to the mediæval consumer: the merchant is a cheater; he must be strictly watched; trade must be accurately regulated; prices must be fixed by the state; and, if any one cheats, gives false weight or measure, or takes a price "more than the tsar's regulation," "such shall be executed." Nor does the wealthy landholder, whoever he be, excite Peresvetov's sympathy. Ivan's magnates are bad, not only because they grow rich "from the tears and the blood of Christians," but because in general they grow rich "and are idle." "A rich man thinks not of war, he thinks of repose; and if even a valiant champion waxes rich, even he waxes idle." It is easy to see where all Peresvetov's sympathies lie; of nothing are his heroes so solicitous as of their "warriors." Sultan Makhmet "opened his heart to his army and made his whole army glad. From year to year he gave them the tsar's pay from his treasury, whoever was worthy of anything,—and to his treasury there was no end. . . ." Peter, the voevoda of Wallachia, exhorts Ivan IV: "maintain a warrior, as one keeps a falcon—always gladden his heart and let not sorrow come nigh him. . . . Whatever warrior is terrible against the sovereign's foe to play the game of death and firmly stands for the Christian faith, for such warriors *exalt their names* and gladden their hearts, and add salaries from the sovereign's own treasury . . . *and admit them to the sovereign's person and trust them in everything,* and hear all their complaints, and love them as a father his children, *and be liberal unto them.* . . ." Constantinople had fallen because "Tsar" Constantine's "warriors" had been impoverished and reduced to beggary. Yet not all military men are equally effective; the great vassals of the grand prince of Moscow, who "are called his servitors because they go out on his service in full trappings, on horseback, and followed by their men but do not stand firmly for the Christian faith," only "impoverish" the realm of Moscow. Peresvetov's ideal is the warrior who "in humble manner" came to Augustus Cæsar, "and Augustus Cæsar for that rewarded him and kept him near him and his family." In place of sumptuous vassals Peter, voevoda of Wallachia, recommends a small, but select, mercenary army—"twenty thousand valiant warriors with firearms." The origin of the "valiant warriors" matters not: "Whoever for the tsar [Sultan Makhmet] firmly stands against the foe, plays the game of death, breaks up the regiments of the foe, faithfully serves, though he be of lesser degree, His Majesty raises him and gives him a great name. . . . And though it is not known of what father they are the sons, the tsar for their wisdom raised them to high office. . . ."

In order to understand these allusions of the first Russian publicist (Peresvetov was absolutely the first lay publicist in the Muscovite state; Kurbsky did not begin to write until twenty years later) the modern reader must remember that the definitive, juridical stabilisation of one very celebrated Muscovite usage comes just at this period. While seeking economic support in kormlenies, the declining boyar order strove to find juridical support in *mestnichestvo*. The essence of mestnichestvo was comprised in the heritability of relationships between offices; each family in Moscow's service occupied a definite position in relation to other such families, and each member of it, independently of his personal deserts, could claim a place (*mesto*) in the service hierarchy corresponding to the one his forebears had occupied. In form, of course, mestnichestvo is bound up with patriarchal concepts—with that "group principle" which we have already had occasion to mention more than once; personal services were not taken into account because neither law nor manners knew how to distinguish the individual from the family group. As long as patriarchal concepts held full sway, there was no need to support them artificially; each knew his own place and did not encroach on another's. In case of doubt they called on old men to "remember," and that sufficed. If now, to reinforce custom, men begin to refer to written *documents* (and even to fabricate them), it is a sure sign that the usage had been shaken, and that men were striving to reinforce artificially what could no longer maintain itself. Modern research has established almost beyond dispute that like the first *razryadnaya kniga* [register of service appointments of the highest grades of the court of Moscow] the *Gosudarev Rodoslovets* [register of the most eminent families, which sought to fix the composition of the aristocracy of Moscow] arose in the 1550's. What seemed an innocent, perhaps simply a stupid, remnant of "pre-state" tradition, was in reality a weapon of the class struggle, an attempt to stem the rising tide by artificial dikes. If the razryadnaya kniga was a selection, even though a very partisan one, from authentic documents, the gosudarev rodoslovets was crammed with tales frankly fantastic, which made all the Muscovite boyars "eminent foreigners." All boasted among their forebears some doubtful magnate who had emigrated to the service of the grand prince of Moscow, from the Germans, from the Lithuanians, at worst from the Horde. Extremely significant is this epidemic of genealogies just at a moment when the term "foreign" implied authority, and the "base-born" gained prestige by referring to their "foreign" origin.

But such artificial props became necessary to the "well-born" only when the "base-born" made their existence evident in other ways than by studied apocrypha and political yarns, when they had become a real force, sufficiently menacing to be feared by the Muscovite aristocracy. Though maintaining their control at the centre the feudal boyars were compelled to surrender their position in the provinces. Reform of the provincial administration was the first triumph of Peresvetov's ideas, and we may well pause over it, not only for its own sake but also because it throws most unusual and vivid light on the means by which the admirer of the Turkish Sultan Makhmet, the interlocutor of Peter, voevoda of Wallachia, expected to "bring justice into the land."

According to Peresvetov's story the police of security had been organised by Sultan Makhmet, as follows. If a theft or a robbery occurs in the army or in the towns "a royal inquest is carried on vigorously by the ten-men, by the hundred-men, and by the thousand-men"; and if any of these officers shelters an evil man he is executed. *"And for a thief or a robber under the Turkish tsar there is no prison; on the third day they execute him,* that iniquity shall not multiply; only for suspects is there prison until the royal inquest. Karamzin, who regarded Peresvetov's pamphlets as "fraud and invention," pointed out in part proof of his opinion that "this plotter" advised the tsar to "do everything great and good that was already being done." Generally speaking, this is quite unjust; we have seen that "Peresvetov's" projects were frequently in advance, not only of Ivan the Terrible but of Muscovite Rus in general. Yet in this case we really do hit upon something that calls for explanation; the police organisation described in the lines quoted above, with all its characteristics—special authorities to cope with robbery, general inquest, and responsibility of the investigators for the results of the inquest—already existed in Rus in the 1540's. Two charters are extant from as early as 1539 : one granted to the Belozersk region, the other to Kargopol; in both the grand prince "laid on the consciences" of the local population the inquest for robbers and their execution after the inquest without trial. Herein lay the root difference between the new and old methods of meting out justice; formerly all prosecutions, including those for robbery, were begun on private accusation and were decided either by the oath of the parties or by the "field," the judicial duel. In these prosecutions the local governor "looked to his lucre," first and foremost seeing to the punctual payment of judicial fees and fines. Under such circumstances, of course, repression could be only very weak, even if we ignore those cases, not rare in practice, when the kormlenshchik simply went shares with the robbers, deeming such revenue more certain that "judicial perquisites," which he might never get. In both the charters referred to above mention is made of the foundation at Moscow of a special Robbery Bureau ("our boyars to whom cases of robbery are commended. . . ."). Its local agents were not the kormlenshchiks but special "heads," elected by the local population and assisted by elders, tithing-men, and "better men." Not only Belo Ozero and Kargopol but also "other towns" had "heads"; this was an all-Russian reform on a broadly thought-out plan. The reform undoubtedly hurt the pockets of the kormlenshchiks by taking from them their chief source of revenue, and contemporaries so understood it. The chronicler of Pskov, for example, relates that the governors took violent offence at the new order of things; "there was great dislike by the governor for the Christians," "to the Christians there was joy and immunity from evil men." What the boyar-kormlenshchiks lost passed to the pomeshchiks, to the middling and small landholders; the Belozersk charter definitely indicates that the "heads," who waged the struggle against robbers, had to be taken from among the local knights, and the literate ones at that, as we have already noted. The elders and tithing-men from among the peasants were subordinate to them. The new authorities gained far more than the old lost: the kormlenshchik could initiate a prosecution only on a complaint; the "guba head" might on his own initiative put any man to torture and punish a man who confessed under it. In the whole guba [police-unit] there was no one who was not dependent on him. Moreover, the old judicial guarantees—duel and oath—were abolished for cases of robbery, and new ones not introduced; the new system was not trial but "inquest"; they hunted robbers as one hunts wild beasts in the forest and, on finding them, slew them without further formalities, quite in accordance with Peresvetov's advice "to execute the robber and the thief and the slanderer and every spoiler without any accounting." If the terror of Ivan's reign consisted in summary punishments, and not of boyars alone, then Ivan became "the Terrible" in 1539 when the "tyrant" was but nine years old. But why did the publicist of the democracy of military servitors need to knock at an open door almost nine years later? To this there can be only one answer: the basic ideas of Peresvetov's writings are considerably older than the edition in which they have come down to us; the story of Sultan Makhmet probably existed in the 1530's.

Peresvetov's pamphlets were far from reflecting all the economically progressive currents of their time. They reflected the thoughts and desires of the "needy warriors," the masses of the petty vassals of the grand prince of Moscow; but these "warriors" were not the only active element in the Muscovite social order of the time. We have seen that the military servitors were suspicious of commercial capital, but its representatives could regard the military servitors in no better light. The political views of the two groups were naturally very different, and it needed both time and quite exceptional conditions to make possible an alliance between them. In the days of Ivan's youth this was a thing of the remote future. Transfer of local police into the hands of the pomeshchiks did not at all satisfy the interests of the burghers; both then and later, in the seventeenth century, the guba "head" was, for them, more often a foe from whom they must defend themselves than a defender and protector such as Peresvetov described him. The guba reform had not prevented a revolt of the townsmen of Moscow in 1547. Something more was needed; just what this something was the townsmen expressed no less loudly than did the "base-born." It was not by chance that the Moscow rebellion brought together the tsar and the archpriest Silvester, whose intimacy with commercial-industrial circles is so definitely attested by his own words. In all probability, it was he who edited the "questions" which the tsar addressed to the Stoglav Sobor and which expressed the programme of the townsmen more concisely, but no less fully, than Peresvetov's writings expressed the programme of the petty military servitors.

As the latter programme found fulfilment in the guba "heads" and the guba inquest, so from the town programme resulted the "zemsky reform" of Ivan IV. In 1555 or a little earlier the kormlenshchiks were withdrawn from the towns and the townships and replaced by "elected heads." Of the "bourgeois" character of this reform there can be no doubt, if only because the transfer was immediately accompanied by the conversion of every sort of "feeding" into a money due, the despatch of which to Moscow constituted the first duty of the "elected heads"; such a tendency could come only from the town. If matters had ended here, there would still have been no collision of class interests. But the "elected heads" inherited from the kormlenshchiks their judicial rights; thus in some places they came to be called "elected judges." Here was manifest an evident parallelism of town and pomeshchik institutions. We have seen that the appearance of guba "heads" was a clear diminution of the authority of the kormlenshchiks. Was not the appearance of elected judges a limitation, even though only a geographical one, of the rights of the guba "heads"? In certain cases at least this was undoubtedly true. The special business of the guba authorities was the capture of robbers; but on the Vaga, for example, with the introduction of the "zemsky" elective authorities those who "go about to steal or to break in, or whoso goes about to slander, or whoso goes about to commit forgery, or bandits who go about to rob, go about to play dice, or to commit any such thing, or whoso has intercourse with evil men" were ordered to be handed over to "their elected heads," who had all the rights that in other places belonged to the guba "heads." The plenipotentiary of the townsmen was put on the same footing as the plenipotentiary of the local landholders and received even broader rights; for the guba "heads" dealt only with robbery, but the "elected" with all criminal cases without exception.　In the north of Russia, where there were hardly any pomeshchiks, or none at all, there could be no collision on this score, but everywhere else the struggle between the military servitors and the townsmen over the control of local administration was protracted far into the seventeenth century.

CHAPTER VIII

3. *The Oprichnina*

THE circumstances under which a rapprochement between the townsmen and the great feudatories took place are not specifically given in the sources. We know only the bare facts that the representative of the bourgeois element, the archpriest Silvester, was in every court conflict aligned with the representatives of the old aristocracy, and that the literary exponent of the latter's views, Prince Kurbsky, was a great admirer of the archpriest of the Cathedral of the Annunciation. But there have survived in the records certain indirect allusions. Throughout the sixteenth century the Moscow townsmen were closely connected with the boyar family of the Shuiskys, whose eminence put them in the first rank of the appanage princes "despoiled" by the descendants of Ivan Kalita. The family votchinas of the Shuiskys, in the [pre-revolutionary] province of Vladimir, were even then hives of industry; the family's last historically renowned descendant, Tsar Vasily (1606-1610), his opponents contemptuously called "*shubnik,*" an allusion to the fact that his prosperity was based on the labour of the hand-workers who supplied all Moscow with sheepskin jackets (*shubas*). The ancestors of this "shubnik" played a conspicuous political rôle during the minority of Ivan IV. In manhood the "terrible" tsar recalled with indignation how two of the Shuiskys "set themselves up" as his guardians, "and thus enthroned themselves." The rule of the Shuiskys had continued "for a great time," regardless of the fact that they evidently were a great source of irritation to the youth Ivan. When he (or rather the Shuiskys' opponents, manipulating him) desired to be rid of them, Ivan Shuisky "summoning all his men and putting them on oath, brought a host to Moscow," and a palace revolution took place. The Shuiskys' opponents were arrested and banished; and even the metropolitan was roughly handled by the mob. A squabble took place in the grand-prince's dining-room where many boyars were likewise "jostled" and "pulled about." Ivan IV was at this time in his thirteenth year, so that he could well remember these events; and despite all the special pleading of the crowned publicist the historian rarely catches him in a downright invention. Ivan was too clever for that, and, as far as the Shuiskys in particular are concerned, his stories are generally confirmed by other sources. But these stories present the spectacle, not of an ordinary palace intrigue but of a mass movement; the disorders in the palace were of course not committed by the princes themselves but by the intruding mob, the "Judas throng," which must have been composed of the burghers of Moscow. Connexions of industrial magnates with commercial-industrial circles were in themselves probable, while the fact that these two elements were very soon faced with common foes, and that in 1547 the townsmen of Moscow beat and slew the Glinskys, who had ever been the rivals of the Princes Shuisky, supplies strong factual foundation for this probability. The events of the 'thirties and 'forties, obscure in the chronicles, are most correctly to be regarded as portents of the great movement that preceded "the reforms of Ivan the Terrible." The alliance between the townsmen and the boyars may have been formed at this time, and an alliance so stable that only the oprichnina could paralyse it—and then only temporarily—and only the catastrophe of the Time of the Troubles could destroy it.

From a general political point of view there was nothing surprising in such an alliance. In foreign policy the interests of the Muscovite bourgeoisie and of the Muscovite feudatories had long coincided, as may be seen, for example, in the history of Moscow's last conflict with Novgorod; while the foreign policy of the boyars in the middle of the sixteenth century, which involved the seizure of the great Volga route by the conquest of Kazan and Astrakhan, likewise corresponded perfectly to the demands of the commercial class. In this foreign policy, for that matter, the interests of all the dominant social groups temporarily coincided; the middling landholders looked with envy on the rich black-earth of the Volga country and would gladly have exchanged for it the exhausted clay-soil of the counties round Moscow. Indeed, in one of Peresvetov's writings we find an extraordinarily curious project—the transfer of the capital to Nizhny-Novgorod; there should be "the throne of a tsar, while Moscow is the throne for a grand prince." The realm of Kazan seemed to the pomeshchik publicist almost a paradise, "a heavenly land, fit for all"; and he very cynically declares that "such a land" ought to be conquered even if it "were in friendship" with Rus. Inasmuch as the men of Kazan were in fact harassing Rus, there was an excellent pretext for settling accounts with them. Thus three hundred years ago a sixteenth-century writer ruthlessly shattered the well-known historical interpretation that makes the interests of state defence the mainspring of Moscow's whole policy; to Peresvetov this "state defence" was simply a good pretext for seizing "extremely fit" lands.

On the basis of this community of interests, apparently, was established that compromise between the feudal aristocracy, the bourgeoisie, and the petty pomeshchiks which lasted approximately until 1560 and is usually described as the "happy time" of the reign of Ivan the Terrible. The petty vassals were satisfied, in the first place, by the establishment of guba institutions and the abolition of "feedings," and further, in anticipation of allotments of "heavenly" lands, by a large-scale special distribution of land in the counties round Moscow; in 1550 a thousand of the better nobles [1] and knights from the provinces, who formed a sort of tsar's guard, were given pomestyes immediately round Moscow. The distribution was of course attributed to military considerations, but it is easy to see that there were no military reasons for placing the select part of the army round the capital itself. This was the moment of supreme tension in the Kazan wars, and from a strategical viewpoint one might have expected concentration of the best part of the Muscovite army somewhere round Nizhny. In actual fact the distribution was a sop to the upper stratum of the pomeshchik class, nor was the boyar youth cheated of its share; as is well known, among those who received pomestyes near Moscow was Prince Kurbsky, then twenty-two years old. The townsmen were satisfied with the "zemsky reform" and with the transfer to them of the collection of indirect imposts, effected about this time. Modern historiography has been inclined to represent this "credit service" as a peculiar kind of burden, supposedly very onerous for the Russian merchantry. But complaints of the burdensomeness of "credit services" are not heard until the middle of the following century when Russia had become definitely a nobles' state and the competition of the pomeshchiks in every field had become intolerable to the commercial class. In essence, the handing over of the indirect imposts "on credit" was a less burdensome form of farming the taxes; the tax-farmer assumed the same obligations as the collector "on credit," but he had to advance a large sum to the government whereas the credit "head" had the same advantages as the tax-farmer without expending a single copeck in advance. That some "credit heads" really were ruined is possible, but tax-farmers, too, were sometimes ruined; every enterprise has this reverse side. In the majority of cases, of course, concentration of enormous sums from customs and tavern levies in the hands of a few merchants immensely facilitated the concentration of merchant capital. [2]

What Kurbsky and Ivan relate, each from his own point of view, of the organisation of the supreme administration in these years suggests that the compromise extended to the political field. Into the

---

[1] The word "noble" has been adopted throughout for the Russian "dvoryanin"; it should be understood that these were not titled nobles and that the "boyars" are not included among them.

[2] One of the first cases of handing over customs revenues "on credit"—not to an individual but to a company of 22 men—dates from 1557.

personnel of the government were introduced representatives of groups which hitherto had had no place in the tsar's "curia"; along with the princes and boyars we find our old acquaintance, the archpriest Silvester, and a man sprung from the ranks of the petty military servitors, Alexis Adashev, whom Ivan, to use his own words, "had taken from the dung-hill and ranked with the magnates." Adashev's functions, so far as we know them, quite definitely indicate that he entered the ruling group as a representative of the anti-boyar opposition. He was entrusted with the receipt of "petitions from the poor and the oppressed"; at the same time he was recommended not to fear "the strong and the renowned who snatch honour for themselves, and who by their violence ruin the poor and the impotent." There is no doubt that he had an intimate share in the liquidation of "feedings" and the celebrated "reconciliation" of the kormlenshchiks with the people. To the modern eye, of course, he occupied a rather strange official position; he was *valet de chambre* to Ivan IV and washed the tsar in the bath, which supplies the occasion for speaking of him as Ivan's "favourite" and thus explaining his political significance. But we should not forget that this was in the heyday of the Middle Ages, and that even at a later period the household of the tsar could not be distinguished from the administration of the state. The degree to which everything bore a purely mediæval character is shown by the means employed by the archpriest Silvester to influence Ivan, means on which there is essentially absolute agreement in testimony from the most diverse sources, from Kurbsky and Peresvetov and Ivan himself. The latter's words about "childish bugbears" are fully supported by what his opponents say about "nightmare terrors" set in motion by the archpriest to curb the young tsar's manners. Peresvetov's constant allusions to "magic and sorcery" indicate that this practice had very soon become well known to quite wide circles. Just what Silvester frightened Ivan with we do not know. Probably it was a matter of "visions" and "apparitions"; later, in the Time of the Troubles (1598-1613), as we shall see, these began to be manufactured to order. In any case, fictitious miracles as a means of attaining the predominance of one's own political party yield nothing to Ivan Kalita's successful attempt to use the relics of the Metropolitan Peter as a means of attaining the political predominance of Moscow over Tver. In this respect no great change had taken place from the fourteenth century to the sixteenth.

Introduction into the Muscovite "curia" of new, unwonted elements was accompanied by some change in the mechanism of administration. Inasmuch as this change has left no documentary traces (except one negative one, of which we shall speak later), it is not surprising that historians have failed to notice it or have paid it little attention. At

the head of the Muscovite state, as at the head of the appanage principality of Moscow, stood the boyar duma, the council of the greatest
vassals under the presidency of the suzerain. Historians have long since
remarked that even from the first half of the sixteenth century there
appear in this council, along with members by position, so to speak (such
were all the former appanage princes and their descendants), members
by appointment, "the knights who are in the duma." It has likewise
long been remarked that in proportion to the expansion of the circle
of obligatory members of the duma, whom it was usual to invite, the
grand prince of Moscow ever more and more frequently manifests a
tendency, in matters especially affecting the grand prince's authority,
to summon not all the members of his duma but only a few. But this
has always been regarded as a manifestation of the personal will of
the sovereign. Without pausing over the question of whether such
was the case before Ivan the Terrible, we can affirm that in the days
of Ivan's youth it was not so. At the head of the administration there
stood not the whole duma but a small conference, in part members of
the duma, in part, perhaps, not members of the duma; but the members of this conference were chosen not by the tsar but by some one else.
Later, in the heat of a polemic, Ivan even affirmed that it was purposely
packed with men repugnant to him, but from his words it is clear that
they were repugnant to him by reason of their independent attitude
toward the tsar's authority, and it is possible that this very factor
determined their selection. If Kurbsky's words be taken literally, this
conference was accordingly called the "council of deputies" (or "elected
council"), deputies, of course, of the full membership of the boyar
duma though not always from this membership. Bowing to circumstances, the boyars had to admit to it men who did not belong to their
corporation, but as a preliminary they fixed the membership of this
corporation with precision. We have already mentioned that the social
struggle had compelled the Muscovite boyars just about this time to find
artificial support for mestnichestvo usages. One phrase of Ivan's suggests that in this self-defence the Muscovite aristocracy did not confine
itself to *ex post facto* compilation of razryadnya knigas and the *Rodoslovets*,[3] but that mestnichestvo was given the force of law, binding
on the sovereign himself. Ivan accuses Silvester and Adashev of taking
from the tsar the power to define the precedence of the boyars in the
duma. Sixty years later, in a mestnichestvo dispute, the boyar duma
formally declared that the sovereign can reward only "with money and
a pomestye, but not with *otechestvo* [hereditary rank]"; at that time
this sounded like an anachronism, a survival of moribund antiquity, but
in the 1550's it was evidently a living reality. Unless we assume that

3 *Cf. supra*, p. 126.

at this time mestnichestvo calculations acquired juridical force, binding even upon the state authority, and that thus the personnel of the order of boyars was guaranteed against arbitrary reshuffling from above, we shall not understand the famous codicil to the Tsar's Sudebnik, which has evoked so many learned controversies. As is well known, this codicil runs: "whatever new matters there be, not inscribed in this sudebnik, as such matters are dealt with on the tsar's presentment and with the sentence of all the boyars, these matters shall be added in this sudebnik." Prof. Sergeyevich has drawn from this the conclusion that thenceforth "the tsar was only the president of the boyar college and without its consent could not promulgate new laws." He explains this innovation by the "pretensions" of the elected council, thus evoking the legitimate perplexity of Prof. Dyakonov: why should this "elected council," *i.e.*, a comparatively narrow circle, bother about legislative rights for *all* the boyars? Inasmuch as the sudebnik's formula is frequently repeated even after the fall of the "elected council," Prof. Dyakonov concludes that it is futile for Sergeyevich to attach any special importance to it. But, as we have seen, the "elected council" represented precisely "all the boyars" or, rather, was their executive organ; the vitality of the formula only proves how lasting was the gain of the boyar order in 1550 (or perhaps a little earlier; we first meet with the formula in 1549). The oprichnina itself was an indirect recognition of this gain; the tsar would not have needed extraordinary full powers, had he not in the usual order of things been bound by the decisions of the boyar college. The expression "all the boyars" would have no meaning if the personnel of these "all" had not been defined with precision and made independent of arbitrary action from above; thus, the codicil to the sudebnik indirectly supports the deduction that about 1550 mestnichestvo calculations acquired binding juridical force.

As we see, the classic "reform" of Ivan the Terrible must be sought in the changes that had taken place in the position of the boyar order. "Reforms" always mean that the ruling class or group, at the price of more or less serious concessions in details, saves the foundation of its position. Ivan's boyars made many concessions, and capital ones; chief among them were the abolition of "feedings" and the introduction of the commercial priest Silvester and of Alexis Adashev into the "elected council." On the other hand, the boyar families became a closed corporation, the membership of which became inviolable for any one whatsoever, and without the counsel of the full membership of this corporation the tsar could not undertake what was then the most important legislative matter, a supplement to the sudebnik. The boyars displayed great political tact; by renouncing many materially advantageous privileges, they maintained in their own hands the source of them all, the sovereign authority.

The compromise could endure so long as all the "contracting parties" could deem their own interests satisfied. That only the boyars had made permanent gains could not fail to become clear, and in fact soon did become so. First, apparently, were dissipated the hopes of the middling and petty pomeshchiks who had expected great and rich favours in connection with the subjugation of Kazan. In the first place this subjugation proved to be no easy matter; six years after the fall of their capital the population of the khanate of Kazan was still offering obdurate resistance, and the Russian towns constructed in the newly subjugated province "were besieged by them" all the time. The seriousness of the rebellion is evidenced by the fact that the insurgents succeeded in annihilating a large Muscovite army headed by the boyar Boris Morozov, whom they took captive and later slew. In Kurbsky's words, so many Russian military servitors perished in the pacification "as is unlike to truth." The "heavenly land" had cost Peresvetov's comrades dear. Moreover, the first to enjoy it were not the pomeshchiks but the peasants. Long before the country had been sufficiently pacified to permit of the establishment of pomeshchik economy, long files of emigrants had trailed eastward in the wake of the Russian detachments. They perished by the tens of thousands; but freedom was so alluring, and there was so little free land left in the central provinces, that destruction of the vanguard did not check those who followed. From certain symptoms we may conclude that the ebb of population to the east began parallel with the Kazan campaigns, without waiting for their success: by 1552 the town of Serpukhov had already lost about one-fifth of its taxpayers; in the same year, the Vaga land with good reason asked and obtained the right "to bring back its old taxpayers without term and without fee." At the beginning of the 'fifties the peasant is already becoming a rare article, which men are striving to bind to their land by all possible means and to entice from their neighbours' land. The pomeshchik's best means to that end was "investment of silver" in peasants; the prospect of a fat money loan, procurable at home, without going away, was the only thing that could offset the hope of "free land." The pomeshchiks needed money capital as never before, and we have clear evidence of what this quest brought them to. The 1550's are marked in Russian history by legislation for the relief of debtors similar to that enacted in Kiev at the beginning of the twelfth century, except that it now served the interests of a different social class, the pomeshchiks.

There were two possible avenues of escape. The first had long been insisted upon by pomeshchik publicists: rather than borrow from usurers,

secure money from the treasury in the form of the "sovereign's wages."
"The tsar's liberality to his warriors is his wisdom," Ivan Peresvetov
had written: "a liberal hand never grows poor, and gathers great glory."
The other way out consisted in an exchange of one's desolated pomestye
for another in good working order. The "princelings' votchinas," the
estates of the former appanage princes, abounding in permanently established "old dwellers," where weak exploitation of the peasants and low
dues in kind gave no occasion for emigration, must long since have
attracted the greedy glances of the poorer pomeshchiks, threshing about
like fish out of water. How much land was wasted in the hands of these
"idle rich"! But the "idle rich" blocked the first avenue, too. The
"sovereign's wages" were pay for a campaign; no campaigns, no wages.
But the great boyars, who had to mobilise whole regiments at their own
expense, did not look upon war as did those for whom war meant extra
money in the pocket. The *Colloquy of the miracle-workers of Balaam,*
which represented the point of view of the boyars, preached a peaceful
foreign policy: only "infidels strive in hosts for murder, and for robbery, and for lechery, and for every impurity and iniquity with their
braveries, and of them they boast." Another publicist, akin in spirit
to the author of the *Colloquy,* rates the "tsar's great wisdom" far higher
than the "tsar's bravery." The elected council resolutely insisted that
defensive wars were to be preferred to offensive ones. The "men brave
and valiant," with whom Prince Kurbsky is much in sympathy, "coun-
selled and urged" Ivan the Terrible after Kazan to begin a great campaign against the Tatars of the Crimea, setting forth, as a moral motif,
the necessity of "freeing the numerous captives" languishing in Crimean
slavery. For the mass of military servitors this was the most uninteresting campaign imaginable—difficult, long, and very unremunerative
since it was impossible to reach the Crimea itself, and in the waste steppes
of South Russia there was nothing to be appropriated. On the other
hand, when some of the tsar's advisers, doubtless from the ranks of the
"warriors," raised the question of a campaign in Livonia, promising
easy and rapid seizure of the lands of the former Livonian Order, the
project met with stubborn resistance on the part of the "elected council."
With bitterness did Ivan IV later recall "what verbal oppression he
suffered" in those days "from the pope Selivester, and from Alexis,"
and from the boyars. "Whatever affliction comes to us, it all happens
because of the Germans"; Silvester explained even the fatal illness of
the Tsaritsa Anastasia as a punishment from on high for the Livonian
War. This "cruel oppression" of the tsar by the boyars, in favour of
a passive, and against an active, foreign policy, could not be kept secret
from wide circles among the military servitors any more than had the
same Silvester's "magic and sorcery."

The Livonian War was the first apple of discord cast into the midst of the social groups that had struck hands before the conquest of Kazan. At the same time, it disclosed how useless to the lower military servitors was the modicum of representation in the "elected council" that the boyars had been willing to concede. Stumbling into the midst of the feudal aristocracy, Alexis Adashev very quickly made a boyar of himself; in 1555 he became formally a member of the boyar college, receiving one of the higher duma grades, and quietly followed the lead of his highborn colleagues. This was very keenly felt at the time of the celebrated conflict of 1553 when Ivan the Terrible had fallen grievously ill— fatally, it was thought at the time. The boyars wanted to take advantage of his demise to impose on the throne of Moscow a purely feudal candidate, Vladimir, son of the "rebel" of the 'thirties—the appanage prince, Andrew of Staritsa. The success of this candidate would have definitely consolidated the victory gained by the boyars in 1550; a tsar elected by the boyar corporation, with no hereditary right to the throne, actually would have been only *primus inter pares*. It is significant that later Kurbsky was ashamed of Vladimir's candidacy and repudiated it; and not less significant is it that the Adashevs favoured it and only very reluctantly took oath to Ivan's son under pressure from the opposing party, which was headed by the Zakharins, the future Romanovs. This was the first instance of an open breach between the tsar and his "elected council." But this was not so important as the fact that the mass of the nobility, outside of the high-born, was bound to become convinced that its man in this council had become a boyars' man. Adashev's political career ended the very moment he formally entered the ranks of the Muscovite aristocracy.

War with the "Germans" was a decisive victory for the "warriors" and, for the first few months, evidently better corresponded to their expectations than had the conquest of Kazan. The Protestant Reformation had undermined the political power of the Order of Knights that ruled Livonia; from this point of view, therefore, the moment had been most happily chosen. The absence of almost any formal pretext for beginning military operations (one could hardly take seriously non-payment by the bishop of Dorpat of some semi-mythical tribute, which at Moscow had been forgotten for fifty years) was offset by religious considerations; the Livonian Germans, "who had deserted the Christian faith," "taking to themselves a new name, calling themselves Evangelicals," had in one of their fits of Protestant fanaticism burned, among other things, Russian icons. Thus, as in the case of the subjugation of Novgorod, the war was undertaken "for the faith." The objective of the military operations was Narva which, as we have already indicated, was then very important to Russia's export trade. In May, 1558, Narva was taken, and a week later Syrensk, where the Narova flows into Lake Chud; the road from Pskov to the sea was now entirely in Russian hands. Success encouraged the "warriors." The campaign of 1558 had yielded enormous booty; war in a wealthy, cultivated country was not at all the same as a struggle with men of alien race in far Kazan or as a chase through the steppes after elusive Tatars. The pomeshchiks were already dreaming of the permanent conquest of all Livonia and of the distribution as pomestyes of the wealthy country-seats of the German knights; in fact, this distribution had already begun. But passage of the whole southeastern Baltic littoral into the hands of Russia aroused all Eastern Europe; neither the Swedes nor the Poles could permit it. The former occupied Reval (1561). The latter went much further: at first, by the treaty of Vilna (1559), they bound themselves to defend the holdings of the Livonian Order against Moscow; later (November, 1561) they annexed Livonia altogether, guaranteeing it domestic autonomy. The motives that provoked the interference of Poland were accurately formulated by contemporaries. "Livonia is renowned for its position by the sea, for its abundance of harbours," we read in a contemporary record. "If this country shall belong to the king, then to him will belong lordship over the sea. All the aristocratic families of Poland testify to the advantage of having harbours in the realm; the prosperity of private persons has increased extraordinarily from the time when the kingdom secured control of the Prussian harbours, and now our people yields to few peoples of Europe in luxury as regards clothes and ornaments, in abundance of gold and silver; and the royal treasury grows rich by the collection of commercial taxes." But if Livonia were ceded, all this would pass to a "dangerous neighbour." What Russian commercial capital was seeking to grasp was equally coveted by Polish capital, and the latter's military resources were infinitely superior to those of the Muscovite Rus of Ivan the Terrible, whose military organisation was still purely feudal. Even before the direct intervention of the Poles, when they were merely giving their support, the master of the Livonian Order, Ketler, had proved able to hold his own against the Muscovite armaments. Russian victories in this period of the war were assured only by the colossal numerical preponderance of the armies of Ivan the Terrible; where the Order was able to put forward hundreds of soldiers, the Muscovites had tens of thousands. As soon as the Polish-Lithuanian troops appeared on the field of battle, Russian progress was retarded, even though the Polish government evidently hoped to gain its end without serious warfare, by demonstrations alone, and without breaking off negotiations with Moscow. At the beginning of 1563, by straining all the forces of Moscow, and under the personal leadership of Ivan himself, Polotsk was taken. That the Muscovite government strove to exaggerate the importance of this victory clearly indicates that it was necessary to "maintain morale" at Moscow. The tsar's envoy who went to the capital with tidings of the victory had to organise in all the towns along the road solemn prayers with ringing of the bells "that God had shown his great mercy to the tsar and grand prince, had given his patrimony, the town of Poltesk, altogether into his hands." The tsar himself returned to Moscow, as he had done after the taking of Kazan. But all this could not disguise the fact that immediately after this splendid victory a truce was concluded; evidently they did not have very much hope of further successes. When the truce was ended, it was still clearer that things were going from bad to worse. The best of Moscow's generals, Prince Kurbsky, with 15,000 men, lost a battle to 4,000 Poles, and in January of the following year (1564) a whole Muscovite army was wiped out under Orsha, and all the senior generals perished, including the commander-in-chief, Prince Peter Shuisky; the remnants of the army fled to Polotsk only "with their heads," leaving all their artillery and baggage in the hands of the foe.

The boyars had not desired the war; now the boyars were losing the war; clearly this was boyar treason. Quite inevitable was such a train of thought in the heads of the "warriors," who were now living in hope of Livonian lands, as earlier they had lived in hope of the lands of Kazan. The Terror of the oprichnina can be understood only in connexion with the misfortunes of the Livonian War, as the French Terror of 1792-1793 with the invasion of the allies. And in both cases individual instances were bound to reinforce and exaggerate the mood of suspicion. Rumours of the treason of the boyars frightened the boyars themselves; the block and the stake already haunted them; on the other hand, the war itself had been a victory for the petty vassals over the coalition of boyars and townsmen (who had very soon abandoned the war party). All this is sufficient explanation of the emigration of boyars, instances of which become frequent just at the beginning of the 'sixties. Here we encounter the very greatest names of the feudal aristocracy of Moscow: now we hear of a Prince Glinsky's attempt to "depart"; now surety is taken for Prince Ivan Belsky; now Prince Belsky himself goes bail for a Prince Vorotynsky. Naturally, the most profound impression was produced by the flight to Lithuania in April, 1564, of Prince Andrew Kurbsky, the Muscovite commander-in-chief in Livonia; in the moral preparation for the coup of the following January 3 there was perhaps no moment more decisive. Ivan might now speak of "boyar treason" with the facts in his hands, as they say.

The objective conditions were as follows: the war in the west, like the war in the east, had not satisfied the land hunger of the petty vassals, and, in general, had not justified the expectations with which it had been undertaken. Foreign policy no longer promised either lands or money; both the one and the other must be sought within the confines of the state. But the state was still ruled by the boyars. They were the government, and really held matters in their own hands; the tsar was only a symbol, an ideal magnitude, which in practice neither helped nor hurt the pomeshchiks. Boyar publicists willingly acknowledged that "by God from on high all had been given over to the anointed tsar and grand prince elected by God," but, "having given over" all authority to the tsars, the Lord "bade" them *"hold the state and have authority with the princes and with the boyars."* In this respect ecclesiastical ideology hallowed feudal practice; the Church, as an institution, needed a strong Muscovite state but by no means a strong Muscovite sovereign. On the contrary, for the *personal* restraint of the tsar's will new means were offered by the ascetic morality of the Church; one needs but to read the "correspondence" of Ivan the Terrible to see how carefully the tsar's whole household was regulated by the archpriest Silvester. Ivan IV learned by personal experience that it is pleasanter to be a simple, ordinary, secular sovereign—even though one like Sultan Makhmet of Turkey—than to be a God on earth. And when he wrote, "The Russian autocracy from the beginning ourselves do hold over all the men of the realm, and not the boyars and the magnates," he was uttering, notwithstanding the semblance of historical allusion, a great new idea,—though perhaps not one that belonged to him personally, for obscure allusions to Peresvetov are frequent in the "letters" of Ivan the Terrible, and it is still a question whether the "letters" themselves represent the product of personal or collective labour.

There is nothing more unjust than to deny that there was a principle at stake in Ivan's struggle with the boyars or to see in this struggle only political stagnation. Whether Ivan IV was himself the initiator or not—most probably he was not—yet his "oprichnina" was an attempt, a hundred and fifty years before Peter's time, to found a personal autocracy like the Petrine monarchy. The attempt was premature, and its collapse was inevitable; but he who ventured it unquestionably ranked above his contemporaries. The "warriors' " road lay over the dead body of old Muscovite feudalism, a fact which made the "warriors" progressive, whatever the motives that immediately guided them. The old votchinas within the realm were now the only source of land at the expense of which middling pomestye landholding might expand, the tsar's treasury, the only source of money capital. But to enjoy either it was necessary to take into their own hands the power that was in the hands of a hostile group, which held it not only with all the tenacity of secular tradition but also with all the force of moral authority.

Peresvetov might have the audacity to declare that politics is higher than religion, "justice" than "faith," but his rank-and-file partisans would not have countenanced such a sentiment, much less have expressed it, and still less have acted upon it. The coup of January 3, 1565, was an attempt, not to infuse a new content into old forms, but to set up new forms alongside the old and, without touching old institutions, so to act that they might serve merely as a screen for new men who did not have the right to enter these institutions as actual masters. Peter was bolder; he simply seated his officials in the boyar duma and called it the Senate, and every one made the best of it. But by Peter's time the boyars were in the eyes of all already a "riven and falling tree." A hundred and fifty years earlier the tree had, it is true, begun to lose its foliage, but its roots were still firmly fixed in the ground and were not to be torn out at the first wrench.

Denying to the "oprichnina" significance in principle, historians have, on the other hand, depicted its appearance in most dramatic form. How Ivan the Terrible, on an unusually solemn expedition, suddenly left for Alexandrovsk (they generally explain the location of this mysterious place that so unexpectedly bobs up in Russian history), how from there he began to exchange letters with the "people" of Moscow, and what effect this produced—all this, of course, you have read many times, and there is no need to repeat the story. In fact, like everything in the world, the event was much more workaday. Alexandrovsk had long been Ivan's summer residence; in the chronicle we constantly find him there in the intervals between military campaigns and his very frequent trips through the Muscovite provinces, on pilgrimage and for economic purposes. The suddenness of his departure is considerably weakened by the fact that Ivan IV took with him all his valuable movables—all the "holy things, icons and crosses, with gold and precious stones adorned," his gold and silver vessels, his whole wardrobe and his whole treasury, and mobilised his whole guard—"the nobles and knights selected from all the towns, whom the sovereign had taken to be with him." All these preparations could not have been made in one day, or in two—especially since the tsar's courtiers were ordered to "go with wives and with children." Setting forth, Ivan did not disappear somewhere for a whole month; the Muscovites knew very well that the tsar celebrated the day of Nicholas the Miracle-Worker (December 6) at Kolomensk, that on Sunday, the 17th, he was at Taininsk, and that on the 21st he arrived at Troitsa to spend Christmas. In a word, this was the customary itinerary of his trips to Alexandrovsk, except for the passing visit at Kolomensk, explained by the thaw and the overflow of the rivers, unusual in December. While the fact that matters moved so swiftly at Moscow—on the 3rd the courier arrived with the tsar's letter, on the 5th the embassy from Moscow was already at Alexandrovsk —clearly shows that the month had not been wasted, that while the tsar was travelling, his partisans had been carefully preparing the dramatic effect that so beguiles modern historians. If during this month Ivan the Terrible really grew grey and aged by twenty years, as foreigners relate, it was, of course, not because he had been quaking all this time for the success of his unexpected "prank," but because to break with the whole past was not an easy thing for a man reared and educated in a feudal environment. Peter was born in a different environment, and from childhood was accustomed to think and act without reference to custom. Ivan in his thirty-fifth year had to smash everything; that was something to grow grey over. That material strength lay in his hands, that the external, so to speak, physical success of the coup was assured for the tsar and his new counsellors,—this was so evident to all that we find not the least attempt at resistance on the part of the old counsellors. And, of course, not because in their servility they did not dare think of resistance; flight from the tsar of all the Orthodox to the service of the Catholic king of Poland-Lithuania was a leap incomparably greater than would have been an attempt to repeat what Andrew of Staritsa had done only thirty years before when he raised the pomeshchiks of Novgorod against the Moscow government. But now the boyars would have had no one to raise against their foes; the pomeshchiks were siding with Alexandrovsk, and the Moscow townsmen were now siding with the pomeshchiks, not with the boyars. The gosts, the merchants, and "all Orthodox Christendom of the city of Moscow," in answer to the gracious letter of the tsar, which was read at an assembly of the higher Muscovite merchantry, "in order that they might retain no doubt, that there was no wrath upon them and displeasure," unanimously replied that they "stand not for the sovereign's evildoers and traitors and themselves destroy them." And in the embassy despatched to Alexandrovsk, along with bishops, abbots, and boyars, we find gosts, merchants, and even simple "common people," who, it would seem, had no place at all in a matter of state. The Moscow townsmen gave up their allies of yesterday. For negotiations with them, in all probability, the future *oprichniks* had needed a whole month, and their decision definitively tipped the scales to the side of the coup. What evoked this decision is easily determined from the sequel; commercial capital itself was associated with the oprichnina, and this promised advantages that no amount of protection from the Princes Shuisky could counterbalance. Soon after the coup we find merchants and gosts acting as official agents of the Muscovite government both at Constantinople, and in Antwerp, and in England—in all the "seaboard states," toward which they yearned so much; and they were all equipped not only with all sorts of safe-conducts, but also with *"bologodet"* [subsidy] from the tsar's treasury. "Into the oprichnina fell all the chief [trade] routes, with a great part of the towns located along them," says Prof. Platonov; and here he gives a very convincing list of these towns. "Not for nothing did the English who had business with the northern provinces beg to be taken into the oprichnina; not for nothing did the Stroganovs seek to be included; commercial-industrial capital, of course, needed the support of the administration that controlled the country and, as is evident, did not fear the horrors attendant upon our conception of the oprichnina." Why should capital fear what it itself had helped to create?

Just as the "reforms" had been the work of a coalition of the bourgeoisie and the boyars, the coup of 1564 was carried out by a coalition of the townsmen and the petty vassals. This explains, in all probability, one peculiarity in the tsar's letter as read at Moscow which hitherto has not attracted great attention but possesses great interest. In form the coup was an act of self-defence on the part of the tsar against his great vassals, who "had begun to betray." But these "treasonous matters" are mentioned very obscurely and only at the end of the letter. On the other hand, the document develops three points in detail. First, the conduct of the boyars during the minority of Ivan IV—"who committed treasons and caused losses to his realm before he the sovereign reached maturity." Second, that the boyars and voevodas "seized upon the sovereign's lands" and, holding great pomestyes and votchinas, by unlawful means gathered great wealth. This motif, taken straight from Peresvetov, envisaged a quite definite fact, which had already led to a partial confiscation of votchina lands three years before the coup. On January 15, 1562, Ivan IV "decreed with the boyars [not with 'all the boyars'!]: whatever old votchinas are in the possession of the princes of Yaroslavl, Starodub, Rostov, Tver, Suzdal, Obolensk, Beloozero, Vorotynsk, Mosalsk, Trubetsk, Odoev, and *other serving princes,*[4] those princes shall not sell nor exchange their votchinas." The right of these men to dispose of their lands had been reduced to a minimum; they could bequeath estates only to their sons. If there were no sons, the votchina reverted to the sovereign, who did what was necessary—"ordered his soul," *i.e.,* dealt out lands to the Church for prayers for the soul of the deceased, allotted a portion "for life" to his widow, dowries for his daughters, etc. What is more, the sovereign confiscated, without compensation, all votchinas of this category that had been sold fifty or twenty but not less than ten years before the publication of the edict. The basis for such an extraordinary measure was that under decrees even of the times of Ivan III and of Vasily III, father of Ivan the Terrible, princes' votchinas

---

[4] Formerly independent "appanage" princes who had accepted dependence on Moscow and as boyars rendered military service to the grand prince.

might be sold only with the licence of the grand prince: a new land-holder meant a new vassal and, in accordance with widespread feudal custom, not peculiar to Russia, the suzerain must be asked for his consent. Votchina lands were simply treated as the sovereign's, and arbitrary disposal of them as embezzlement of treasury property. Finally, the third point made in the letter—it, too, occurs in Peresvetov—is the aversion of the boyars to an active foreign policy; they "did not wish to take care of all Orthodox Christendom" and did not wish to defend Christendom against the Crimea, and Lithuania, and the Germans. These were all themes popular among wide masses, and those who read or heard the proclamation did not, of course, stop to question why in his thirties the tsar had a mind to punish the boyars for sins and faults committed in the days of his youth. Had it been a palace coup organised from above, these demagogic methods would, of course, be very strange; but the point is that in December, 1564—January, 1565, as in 1547, and as in the 'thirties under the Shusikys, the masses of the people were on the stage and must be addressed in a language they could understand.

Yet the content of this proclamation, as of any other, by no means defined the current policy of those who published it. When business negotiations began between Ivan the Terrible and the Moscow deputation that had come to Alexandrovsk, the tsar put forward demands relevant to the immediate causes of the coup, demands that had nothing to do with recollections of the days of his youth. In these demands two aspects must be distinguished. In the first place, Ivan insisted on fulfilment of the promise, given freely by the merchantry of Moscow and subscribed to by the terror-stricken boyars and officials left in Moscow, namely, surrender his foes to him unconditionally. In fulfilment of this demand in February of the same year (the negotiations had taken place, we shall remember, at the beginning of January) a number of boyars of old princely families were executed, others given the tonsure, still others banished for life to Kazan with their wives and children, while the property of all of them was confiscated. Banishments and executions at once gave into Ivan's hands a supply of land probably sufficient to remunerate the immediate participants in the coup d'état. To secure them a money salary the tsar and grand prince decreed that *for his expenses* a hundred thousand rubles (about 5,000,000 rubles gold, according to the reckoning of Professor Klyuchevsky) be taken from the treasury of the land. From this aspect the coup was only the affair of a small circle, but Ivan was serving the interests of a class. Not all the pomeshchiks could be satisfied out of the proceeds of a few banishments and a small appropriation from the treasury chest. The form devised to satisfy the "warriors" was as old-fashioned as the content of the change effected was new. In the state the sovereign could not give orders without his boyars, the suzerain without his curia; but on his "domain," in his court economy, he was as absolute as was any votchinnik at home. Conversion of half the state, and the wealthiest part of it at that, into the sovereign's domain made it possible to hold sway over a vast territory without consulting the feudal aristocracy. Without violating the decrees of 1550, he might here do all that he liked, not only without the assent of "all the boyars" but without that of even a single boyar; the right of the boyar college did not, of course, extend to the sovereign's court management. And for the tsar's court, now increased to colossal proportions, a very old name was at first chosen; the tsar demanded that "from his realm be set apart an *oprichnina*." This was the name given to the estates in former times portioned out to widowed princesses "for life." Later there came into use the more accurate and newer term, *dvor* [court]. In its arrangements this "dvor" was an exact copy of an old sovereign's votchina, so exact that one modern scholar has even doubted whether the oprichnina had any institutions of its own, or whether new men were not simply seated in the old institutions along with the old "clerks," for management of "oprichnina" (select) matters. While effecting a genuine revolution, the creators of the oprichnina apparently strove to conceal all juridical traces of it, and we cannot but see in this fact a conscious purpose, issuing from the same impulses as were reflected in the tsar's proclamation that we analysed above. The people needed a scapegoat, and they were assured that the coup was directed against individual persons, however numerous, the old order remaining inviolate.

The sovereign's dvor began to expand enormously, but it never came to embrace the whole country, and the *zemshchina*, which administered all that remained outside the limits of the oprichnina, was more than merely decorative. The best study of the territorial composition of the oprichnina has been made by Professor Platonov; we shall therefore describe it in his words. "The territory of the oprichnina," says this scholar, "taking form gradually, in the 1570's comprised the towns and townships lying in the central and northern parts of the state. . . . Resting to the north on the 'great sea-ocean,' the lands of the oprichnina cut into the zemshchina like a wedge, dividing it in two. On the east were left to the zemshchina the Perm and Vyatka towns, the Low country and Ryazan; on the west the border towns 'of the German frontier' (Pskov and Novgorod), 'of the Lithuanian frontier' (Veliky Luki, Smolensk, and others), and the Seversk towns. To the south these two zones of the 'zemshchina' were connected by the frontier towns and the 'wilderness.' The Moscow North, the Littoral, and two of the Novgorod pyatinas [5] the oprichnina ruled integrally; in the central provinces its lands were interspersed with those of the zemshchina in a patchwork that is as hard to understand as to describe," but that can nevertheless be characterised in a general way. "In the oprichnina administration," says Professor Platonov in another passage, "were gathered the *old appanage lands.*" The goal toward which the law of 1562 had striven, by inches and within legal bounds, was attained three years later, all at once and by a revolutionary road; the most valuable part of the territory of the Muscovite state, together with the greatest commercial-industrial centres, became immediately an appanage of the sovereign where, unrestrained by the old boyars, the men of the "Peresvetov party" now began to hold sway. The old authority retained the worst and poorest regions; it is curious that just as Kazan had become a place of exile, so the newly-conquered lands in the west were now willingly ceded to the "men of the zemshchina." The Novgorodan "knights" from the Obonezh and Bezhets pyatinas, when these were taken into the oprichnina, received pomestyes around Polotsk, on the recently annexed and very insecure Lithuanian lands.

The tsar's edict, even in the brief résumé preserved in the official Moscow chronicle (like a great part of the official documents of this stormy time, the original edict on the oprichnina has not come down to us), states quite distinctly in whose favour and for what proximate goal all this shuffling of lands was effected. "And to give to the sovereign in the oprichnina princes and nobles and knights, of court and town, 1,000 head, *and to them to give pomestyes in those towns which he took into the oprichnina,*" says the chronicle. Modern historians have seen in this something in the nature of the establishment of a corps of gendarmes charged with the detection of domestic sedition, the protection of the tsar, and the defence of the realm. But tempting as is this analogy, one must not yield to it. Police work, and that alone, has always been the task of gendarmes; not they—there were too few of them for that—but the standing army has constituted the material support of the government. The oprichniks represented something quite different. The detachment of a thousand knights really constituted a corps of ten or twelve thousand men, inasmuch as each appeared for service with several armed bondsmen. Not a single large landholder, even among the former appanage princes, could have such a retinue; even two or three together of the very greatest probably would not have raised so many men. Besides this mounted detachment there were in the oprichnina infantry as well—"and he ordered the *streltsy* to be to him especially," says the chronicler. To cope with a "domestic foe" such a force would have been

_____
[5] Novgorod's territory was divided into five *pyatinas* [fifths] corresponding to the five *kontsy* [ends] that made up the town itself.

more than sufficient; the grand prince of Moscow was now, in his single person, the very greatest of the Muscovite feudatories. The oprichnina army was a logical corollary to the oprichnina dvor of the sovereign, and, it must be added, the very possibility of forming this dvor had been conditioned by the existence of such an army; for the novelty of this part of the edict was not the appearance close to the tsar of a "thousand heads" but the quartering of them on lands unceremoniously taken from other holders—"and the votchinniks and pomeshchiks who are not to be in the oprichnina [the sovereign] bade to be removed from these towns." A detachment of a thousand had long existed, even from 1550, and in the coup of January 3, 1565, it had played exactly the same rôle as did the Paris garrison in the coup of December 2, 1851. This tsar's guard, founded, as we shall recall, by the boyar government as a concession to the upper crust of the pomeshchik masses, had become a powerful weapon in the struggle of the pomeshchik class against the boyars themselves. Only by its closeness to the tsar is to be explained the fact that the "base-born" now standing around him dared so audaciously to raise their hands against their feudal lords of yesterday, and in the tsar's train this "picked" thousand, moving "after the tsar with men and with horses, with all service attire," was, of course, the most imposing part. In all probability, all of them, with the exception of a few individuals, were taken into the oprichnina corps, so that actually the latter represented nothing new. And as before, so also after 1565, along with its military and police significance it continued to have political significance; there entered it the "better," *i.e.*, the most influential, elements of the local bodies of nobles. As Klyuchevsky has explained in detail, they did not while in the tsar's guard lose contact with the local communities; in other words, they were the political leaders of the pomeshchik class, and distribution of oprichnina lands to them signified nothing else than that along with the old, boyar-votchina state, now more than cut in half, there arose a new, noble-pomestye state.

Clear proof that the coup meant merely the establishment of a new class régime, of which the tsar's personal authority was only a tool, and not the personal emancipation of Ivan from the boyar tutelage that had trammelled him, is the singular assembly that was held in Moscow in the summer of the following year (1566). On June 28, 1566, the Tsar and Grand Prince Ivan IV of All Rus "spoke" with Prince Vladimir of Staritsa, with his archbishops, bishops, and the whole "Holy Synod," with all the boyars and officials, with the princes, with the knights and military servitors, "and with the gosts, and with the merchants, and with all trading men." The subject of this conversation was a truce proposed by the Polish-Lithuanian government on the basis of *uti possidetis*. Thus, it was proposed that Ivan the Terrible renounce his original goal, the seizure of all Livonia. In essence, the question was put: is it worth while to keep on fighting? And it is significant that Ivan and his new government did not presume to decide this question upon their own responsibility but referred it to the judgment of all those in whose name they ruled. It would, of course, be very naïve to imagine that this "zemsky sobor of 1566," the first sobor whose existence is historically indisputable,[6] even remotely resembled modern popular representative bodies; the very worst of them, if only in theory, speaks in the name of the "people," a concept alien to feudal Europe. Mediæval assemblies, both in Russia and in the West, represented, not the people but "estates," *états, Stände*. From this point of view the important point about the sobor of 1566 was the rôle of two "estates" whose political importance had hitherto scarcely been openly recognised—the petty vassals or "nobility," and the bourgeoisie. Quantitatively the pomeshchiks even constituted a majority of this assembly. The Livonian War had been decided on by the boyars, unwillingly and under pressure from below, and now they were asking the "warriors" and the "trading folk" whether this war should be continued. Between 1557 and 1566 lay a wide gulf. The details of the debates at the sobor, assuming there were debates, have not come down to us. The one-day sobor was, of course, not summoned to learn the opinions of those assembled; the pomeshchiks and the merchants were summoned because their opinions were already known, and it was hoped that the authority of their voices would reinforce the authority of the declarations of Muscovite diplomacy. The sobor was, in essence, a ceremonial façade; the real negotiations took place, of course, before the sobor met and, apparently, by no means inspired the government with the confidence breathed by the solemn speeches at the sobor itself. The sobor decided to continue the war, come what might; but in fact *negotiations* were continued and a few years later terminated in a truce on the conditions proposed by the Poles. The suzerain Ivan needed the formal promise of his new, extensive vassalage to "die for the sovereign on horseback" in case of war, and of the trading men to give their last red cent if need be. This promise Ivan received, and on their speeches the military-serving and the trading men kissed the cross. Whether or not to make the fullest use of this promise was the business of the government, which was, of course, guided by the views of its supporters, but these views were not ascertained at the sobor.

With the 'sixties terminates, properly speaking, that intensive evolution of class relationships which fills the second third of the sixteenth century. In rebellion against their feudal lords, inferior landholders

---

[6] It was long conventional to reckon this as the second sobor, but it may now be considered unconditionally proved that the so-called "first" sobor of 1550 is a legend.

in 1537 were hanged as rebels along the highways "not together but all the way to Novgorod"; in 1566 they were masters of the situation, while yesterday's lords were now "executed and hanged" as rebels. The economic revolution, the collapse of old votchina landholding, found political expression in the accession to power of a new social class. Of further struggle within the oprichnina (that there was one, we cannot doubt) we know nothing. In studying this period of Ivan's reign the historian is faced with a difficulty similar to that presented by imperial Rome; detailed accounts are to be had only from the camp of the boyars, and it is not surprising that we find nothing there except the "horrors of the oprichnina." That the pomeshchik régime was terrorist there can, of course, be no doubt. Under the given circumstances, in the face of powerful "traitors" and of a foreign foe who was becoming more terrible every hour, and in whom the "traitors" easily found support, revolutionary governments even of more civilised times have ruled with the aid of terror. In the sixteenth century terrorism was the usual and accepted practice. Twenty years before the oprichnina the nobles' publicist depicted the way in which his hero and favourite, Sultan Makhmet, dealt with unjust judges: "the ruler did not accuse them, he only ordered them flayed alive and said: if they grow new skins, the fault shall be forgiven them. And their skins he bade to be peeled off, and bade paper to be nailed on, and bade them to be affixed in the law courts with an iron nail, and bade to be inscribed on their skins: *without such terrors justice cannot be brought into the realm.*" Such was the theory. The practice, exemplified in guba institutions, did not lag behind the theory. The guba "head" might subject any inhabitant to torture, not only on direct accusation, but simply on the basis of evil rumours about him. Simple suspicion that a given person was an "evil man" was enough to begin to pull his joints out and break his bones, to lacerate his body with the knout and burn him with fire. This was the norm of criminal law then generally accepted, and Ivan appealed to it in reply to Kurbsky's reproaches of "unheard-of cruelty," writing that if traitors be not punished, then robbers and thieves cannot be tortured—"then all realms are in disorder and all are corrupted with intestine quarrels."

4. *Economic Balance Sheet of the Sixteenth Century*

By the end of the sixteenth century, in the old counties of the Muscovite state, middling, pomestye landholding definitely prevailed. Large votchinas survived only as exceptions. Petty landholding had also been definitively swallowed up by pomestye landholding. The typical holding was from 150 to 525 desyatinas, under the three-field system, with all the characteristics of the "new" economy: lord's arable, money dues, and peasants bound to the land by unpaid debt. However strange to modern eyes, in the first half of the century this had been the economically progressive type, as we noted at the beginning of the present chapter. Its victory ought to have signified a great economic advance, the definitive triumph of a "money" over a "natural" system. In fact, we see something quite different. Natural obligations, which had been crystallised into a complicated whole known to us under the name of "serfdom," reappear in the centre of the stage and this time hold their ground tenaciously. The free wage-labourer, dreamed of by the nobles' publicist of the first half of the century and in places actually established on more advanced estates, vanishes for two centuries; Ivan Peresvetov has no successors until the nobles of the "Manchester school" in the 'forties and 'fifties of the past century. The bitter land hunger of the middle of the century, so vividly expressed in the confiscations of the oprichnina, would seem to indicate that in the centre of the realm, at least, a great part of the available lands had already been made use of. Not so, however: according to the registers of 1584-1586, in eleven subdistricts of the county of Moscow, there were only 23,974 desyatinas of arable to almost 120,000 desyatinas of waste, land neglected and abandoned, in part grown over anew with forest. Contrast this with the first half of the century when the forests had been so radically reduced that around Moscow foreign travellers found nothing but stumps and saw no "forest beasts" but rabbits, at which they were much amazed, accustomed as they were to think of Muscovy as a forested land abounding in all sorts of wild beasts. One very authoritative scholar even makes bold to assert that the retrogression was not merely quantitative, but that the technique of agriculture declined in Muscovite Rus parallel with the triumph of middling landholding. "In the majority of these [central] counties," says N. Rozhkov, "with remarkable regularity the three-field system, prevalent in the fifteen-sixties, is replaced toward the end of the century by a cruder system of fallowing; the sole exception is the county of Moscow, and that only in part." The pomeshchik, having crushed the feudal votchinnik in the name of economic progress, himself very quickly becomes an economically backward type. Such is the paradox that concludes the history of Russian national economy in the epoch of Ivan the Terrible.

Among the economic conditions which toward the end of the epoch of Ivan the Terrible hampered the development of money economy in Russia (and this general condition coloured all the details), the most palpable was the course of foreign policy. The Livonian War, it must not be forgotten, was a war for trade routes, i.e., indirectly, for markets. The future was to show that the economic evolution of Russia, in its tempo at least, was three-quarters dependent on whether or not she succeeded in establishing direct connections with the more progressive countries of the West. Contemporaries understood this and expressed it quite distinctly. The port of Narva, which remained in Russia's hands even after the first setbacks of the Livonian War, very seriously perturbed her competitors. "The Muscovite sovereign daily increases his might by obtaining the goods that are brought into Narva," the king of Poland anxiously wrote to Elizabeth of England in striving to dissuade the English from trade relations with Moscow, "for hither are brought not only merchandise but also weapons hitherto unknown to him; they bring not only productions of the arts, but thither go the artists themselves, by whose aid he obtains the means to vanquish all. Your Majesty knows not the strength of this enemy and the authority he enjoys over his subjects. Hitherto we have been able to vanquish him only because he was a stranger to education and knew not the arts. But if Narva shipping continues, what will remain unknown to him?" All this was patent to them at Moscow, and inasmuch as the harbour of Narva was only a narrow wicket to the west, they strove to obtain wide gates by mastering one of the great ports of the Baltic Sea. But the repeated attempt to seize Reval (in 1570 and 1577) only led to a war with Sweden, in which the Muscovite state lost Narva, too,—and not Narva alone but its Russian suburb, Ivangorod as well; the Baltic was now hermetically closed to the Russians. This loss of the principal stake of the war and the expulsion of the troops of Ivan IV from the Livonian towns he had occupied at the beginning of the war had great moral significance, though later historical narratives say a great deal about the campaigns of Bathory of Poland, and only a couple of words about the war with the Swedes. The appearance of a Polish army under the walls of Pskov, the greatest of the commercial centres on the western frontier still in Russian hands, only marked the close of the whole "Livonian adventure." In the last years of his life Ivan the Terrible no longer thought of conquests in the west; he was only defending himself and was glad not to lose his own. Lithuanian detachments burned down Rusa and laid waste the country round the headwaters of the Volga; it was even anticipated that Moscow itself would have to be defended from Bathory. Long before this critical moment, central Russia, and the outer town of Moscow itself, had already experienced such destruction as no one could recall since the times of Tokhtamysh. This was the raid of the Crimean Tatars in 1571, which is not sufficiently stressed in modern historiography but was fully appreciated by contemporaries. It was directly connected with the Livonian War; the khan of the Crimea had been an ally of the Poles from the very beginning. Less clear, though none the less real, is its connexion with the domestic affairs of Russia: the khan was led to Moscow by four fugitive "knights," probably acting on commission from Prince Mstislavsky. In its immediate destructiveness the Crimean raid far exceeded all the burning and plundering of the Lithuanian partisans. The whole outer town of Moscow the Tatars burned to ashes; and, as we shall remember from Fletcher's account, seventeen years later it was not yet fully restored. A number of other towns were overtaken by the same fate. According to contemporary accounts, in Moscow and its vicinity alone some 800,000 people perished, and 150,000 were led away into captivity. The general loss of population must have exceeded a million, out of a possible total of ten million inhabitants and, at that, it was the old and most cultivated regions that were subjected to desolation; not for nothing did the men of Moscow long afterwards reckon from the Tatar devastation as in the nineteenth century men long reckoned from "1812."

To the devastation wrought by the Tatars must in large measure be assigned the depopulation, almost sudden, which scholars find in the central counties, beginning at this very time. "The beginning of the 'seventies of the sixteenth century is the chronological starting point of the depopulation of a great part of the counties of the centre of Muscovy," says N. Rozhkov, the historian of the rural economy of Muscovite Rus whom we have already cited more than once. "The weak beginnings of the ebb of population to be observed in certain of these counties in the 'fifties and 'sixties are now converted into an intensive, strikingly acute, phenomenon of the flight of peasants from the central region." Perhaps the desire to get farther away from the Tatars explains the migration of the population from the centre to the infertile regions of northern Rus which is to be observed about this time. The towns along the newly opened Dvina trade route (it had been opened by the English in the 'fifties) to Archangel had begun to play a conspicuous rôle even in the preceding decade. We frequently see the tsar here on his trips to the Kirillo-Belozersk Monastery, and he evidently regards them as something more than stopping-places on his pious excursions; in Vologda he laid the foundation of a "stone town" and later made a special trip to see how it was being built. Apparently this was not merely a fortress but a tsar's palace, for the sovereign went to "inspect" not only the "town foundation" but also "all of his the tsar's buildings in Vologda." Not for nothing did the English here build themselves a house "huge as a castle." Around the newly rising urban centres the countryside came to life; it was natural that, in the wake of traders and artisans, peasants, too, trailed hither. But what displaced them from their comfortable berths? The extent of the depopulation shows that mere dread of the Tatars is insufficient as an explanation. In those subdistricts of the county of Moscow where, following the registers of 1584-1586, we have noted such a preponderance of waste over arable land, there were 2,182 deserted holdings and only 3 clearings to 673½ hamlets; deserted hamlets constituted 76% of the total, newly arisen ones only 0.1%. Even this, it seems, was an improvement; from incomplete data for the same county (for a smaller number of subdistricts) for the preceding years (1573-1578) may be counted, in one case 93%, in another as much as 96%, deserted holdings. Other central counties fared no better; in Mozhaisk, for example, on individual estates deserted hamlets constitute 86%, in Pereyaslavl-Zalessky 50% to 70%. Moreover, the depopulation affected also the more northerly counties of the centre, which were safe from the Tatars; of the Tver court hamlets of Prince Simeon Bekbulatovich (whom Ivan for sport ranked among the tsars of Moscow) half were deserted in 1580. Between Yaroslavl and Moscow even Chancellor, in the middle of the 'fifties, had found a multitude of hamlets "remarkably filled with people." Another Englishman, Randolph, who was in Russia a little later than Chancellor, also speaks of the dense population of these localities, while in the 'eighties their compatriot Fletcher was amazed by the deserted hamlets there. But the Tatars of the Crimea did not go far north of Moscow; in the raid of 1571 Ivan IV himself sought refuge from them no farther north than Rostov. Besides, dread of them must have been particularly strong in the first years after the devastation, while in the words of the author we have quoted above "the flight [of peasants from the centre] does not cease until the very end of the century, as a number of facts convincingly attest." This non-correspondence, both chronological and geographical, between the "Tatar devastation" and the area of depopulation compels us anew to seek other, more potent and less accidental, causes of the latter.

One of these the same author notes in passing. "In the sources," he says, "have been preserved curious facts, illustrating the acts of violence and the plundering of the pomeshchiks and the consequent well-nigh irreparable injury to the economic value of pomestye land." Unfortunately he cites only one such fact, but it is an extremely vivid one. "At the very end of the sixteenth century, in the village of Pogorelitsy, county of Vladimir, lived 'among the peasants' a certain Ivan Sokurov. In 1599 Pogorelitsy was granted in pomestye to the 'knight' Fedor Sobolev. The latter, in Sokurov's absence, appeared at his homestead and there wrought complete havoc: he took three bondsmen; led away his horse, cow, ox, and four sheep; took from Sokurov's wife one ruble 13 altyns in money (= 35 rubles gold); and carried off as much as he could of rye, oats, barley, flax, and 'three bees.' More, when Sokurov returned, the pomeshchik took possession of his homestead, too." The picture of such an expulsion of a peasant from his nest by a landowner is by no means peculiar to Russia; about this time we find a number of similar phenomena in Germany, where a special term has been coined for them—*Bauernlegen*. The conditional character

of pomestye tenure of course has nothing to do with the question, but
it is not hard to imagine how the peasant masses must have reacted to
the goings-on of thousands of such Sobolevs, suddenly invading lands
theretofore untouched by pomestye landholding. And this is just what
happened when the oprichnina, with its shuffling of land, caused a number of princes' votchinas, with their traditional feudal order of things,
with peasant obligations that were not burdensome and that at the
same time were handed on from generation to generation, to be simultaneously converted into pomestyes. Like ants from a disturbed ant-
hill the population ran off from these old cultivated places, seized by
the oprichnina—ran off with no thought but how to save themselves
from the new order of things so abruptly ushered in. It is no accident
that the maximum depopulation of the county of Moscow coincides with
the peak of the oprichnina.

Nor is the oprichnina in and of itself, as a "measure of state,"
involved in the present question, of course; the example we have just
cited does not relate to the oprichnina; in 1599 the oprichnina was a
thing of the past, and Sobolev probably had never served in it. It is
merely that in the 'sixties and 'seventies a phenomenon common to all
pomestye landholding was augmented to unusual proportions. Predatory exploitation of an estate, the desire to squeeze out of it in the
shortest possible time as much money as possible, are just as characteristic of Russian pomeshchiks of the sixteenth century as of any "entrepreneurs" in the early period of money economy. One contemporary
publicist, writing shortly after the Troubles, gives from his own personal
impressions an extraordinarily striking general picture of that unrestrained speculation, a petty example of which we have just cited. In
his words, at the time of the great famines under Boris Godunov many
not only put their money into circulation but capitalised all their move-
able property, including their wearing apparel, "and gathered into their
granaries all seeds of every grain," thus making a profit of thousands
per cent. To a considerable extent this speculation explained the famines
themselves; let us recall that even twenty years earlier Fletcher ascribed
the rise of grain prices to engrossing by the pomeshchiks. If our author
is to be believed, there were at the height of the famine great stores of
grain, so that afterward, when civil war had actually devastated the
country, and seeding had been much curtailed, all Russia was fed from
these old stores, which the grain speculators, in order to keep up prices,
had not let out of their hands during the famine. Judging by the
description of society in the time of Godunov as given by this publicist,
cornering grain offered great profits. In his words, even the provincial
nobility, rich in gold and silver utensils, with horses in the stable and
menials in the homestead, "resembled the first magnates and the kins-

men of the tsar"; nor was it only among the nobility "but also among the merchants were men of substance and among the cultivators." From the sumptuous attire of their wives and daughters one could not tell what they were, they wore so much gold, silver, and all other adornments; "all were boyars at this time."

Given such a state of affairs, it was evidently more profitable to plunder one's peasants, converting their property into money, than to carry on regular economy; this fact, and not any juridical norms, impelled the pomeshchiks to predatory exploitation of their estates. Regular economy demanded each year more and more outlays of money capital, for the value of money fell with amazing rapidity. According to N. Rozhkov's calculations the ruble of the beginning of the sixteenth century was approximately equal to 94 rubles gold, and the ruble of the end of this century to only 24-25 gold rubles; in less than a hundred years the value of money had fallen 75%. In Western Europe during this century it fell as much as 80%, but there was a definite external cause for this—the discovery of America with its gold and silver mines. This cause undoubtedly exerted its influence on Russia, too, a fact which shows how mistaken is the opinion that the realm of Muscovy was completely isolated from the rest of Europe. Moreover, enough facts have been cited to show how early had begun the economic "Europeanisation of Russia." The "triumph of cupidity" thus had an entirely objective basis; more was involved than the "greediness" of the pomeshchiks. Another cause, in Russia, was the rapid growth of money economy, fostered by compulsory liquidation of the large feudal estates with their "natural" order of things. Such a mass of land was thrown on the market that land values fell by almost one third. In the first half of the century a desyatina of land was worth 0.3 rubles, in the second 0.7 rubles, but when translated into gold money the first figure becomes 28 rubles, and the second only 17.

By the end of the sixteenth century predatory economy, ever tending to liquidate and convert into money as quickly as possible both stock and buildings, and even the peasants themselves, as we shall presently see, was confronted with its own inevitable consequence—a shortage of labour on the land. The peasantry, stampeded by the new order, scattered from the centre like chaff before the wind—both to the far north, where grain was cropped only three times in five years, and into the steppe, regularly visited almost every year by the Tatars of the Crimea; most of all, of course, to the Oka and the Volga, to places even then comparatively safe. One chronicle as early as the middle of the reign of Ivan the Terrible noted the ebb of population from the counties of Mozhaisk and Volokolamsk "to Ryazan, and into the Meshchera, and into the lowland towns, to Nizhny-Novgorod." In all these regions arose

new settlements even while the centre was suffering depopulation. The
crisis we have observed was, then, by no means an all-Russian one. It
was above all a crisis of pomeshchik economy just as the first half of the
century had witnessed the crisis of the old votchina economy. The old
votchinas had perished because they were not able to adapt themselves
to the conditions of the new money economy; the pomeshchiks made too
good use of it, wishing to take at once the maximum that it could offer.
The decline in the value of money drove them forward on this road;
what one could "live on decently" became insufficient in ten years' time.
It was necessary to drain more and more an economy that was already
sufficiently ruined. It was necessary to invest capital in it; but where
get the capital? It was necessary to bind to the estate the working
hands that tended irresistibly to leave it, but how was this to be done
without capital, without the "silver" with which the peasants might
be bound? This dual dilemma faced pomeshchik economy on the eve
of the Troubles. Indeed, at the root of the Troubles lay the attempts
of the pomeshchiks to get out of the blind alley created by their own
rapacity.

Money might be gained through speculation—a game of chance in
grain and in men. From as early as the 1550's there is evidence to
show that trade in peasants by no means waited for the official establishment of serfdom. In a petition of this date one pomeshchik
complains of another in the following terms: "I sent my men to effect
the disavowal of two peasants from a homestead in his hamlet, and he
. . . accepted their disavowal and took the *pozhiloe* [residence fee] ; and
I sent to have those peasants brought to me, but he did not let those
peasants leave him and is holding those peasants by force." The pozhiloe
was in form a rent for the homestead occupied by the peasant, but by
the middle of the sixteenth century this formality no longer bore any
relation to reality, for the annual rent for a homestead was equal to
one-fourth of the value of the homestead itself. Inasmuch as the residence fee was, as we have just seen, actually paid by the new master
to whom the peasants passed, payment for the homestead was essentially
masked payment for the peasant himself. This is why documents of the
time call pozhiloe a "fee" and the taking away of a peasant without
pozhiloe taking away "without fee." If the peasant had, in addition, taken the "lord's silver," the factual difference between him and
the lord's bondsman almost disappeared; "disavowal" on the part of the
peasant was then replaced by "release" on the part of the master.
Indebted peasants were, of course, more easily made the object of speculation. It must be added that the men of Moscow were by no means
such worshippers of legality as they are made out to have been by certain
modern scholars, who even perceive in the evolution of the institution

of peasant bondage certain features reminiscent of Roman law. The law of Moscow was still feudal law, *i.e.*, when it did not rest on force, it meant nothing. A pomeshchik never made any bones about whether a peasant actually owed him anything or not, and the rates of pozhiloe established by the sudebnik he observed only when he wished. Documents are extant attesting that when a lord did not want to release a peasant, he "threw him into irons" and demanded from him a pozhiloe, not of one ruble, as the law decreed (50 rubles gold, in the middle of the century), but five, and even ten rubles (250 and 500 rubles). In general, it may be regarded as the rule that without the master's consent a peasant could not "disavow."

"Lord's silver," the peasant's debt to the landholder, was in Muscovite Rus not a juridical means of indenturing peasants but a means of enticing them from other pomeshchiks or an antidote against peasant flight; the momentary advantage might tempt the less far-seeing and restrain them from attempts to seek happiness elsewhere. Hence the abolition of peasant "disavowal" must be regarded, not as the starting point of peasant bondage but as one of the aspects of the crisis of pomestye landholding. From the tangled snarl of lawsuits over peasants which clogged the courts of the time there was no escape except to forbid "disavowals" altogether, binding the peasants to those on whose lands they were settled at the given moment. Then would have ceased the pomeshchiks' destruction of each other, and the money that went into the struggle to secure labourers might have been otherwise employed. But as expenditures on the "disavowal" of peasants grew beyond the power of the pomeshchiks, they were driven to desperate means to get along without money. Most interesting in this connection is a transitional step to the abolition of peasant "disavowal" which we find in an unofficial document (the so-called "Code of Fedor"), but borrowed, of course, from current practice: "write double indentures on the peasants." Demand for double repayment of the peasants' debt must, of course, have restrained those who desired to disavow him. But the peasant had become such a "rare bird" that the wealthier landholders did not balk even at this; the mass of military servitors therefore procured a new limitation of "disavowal," which we find in the well-known edicts of 1601-1602, the first documentary evidence of peasant bondage. These edicts limited the number of "taken" peasants to not more than two, and only petty pomeshchiks could "take" from one another; competition by large landholders was excluded in advance. "Disavowal" by this time was an exception; as a rule the peasants were settled on the lands of those owners with whom the registers of 1590-1593 had found them. Rid of money expenditures on the peasants, the pomeshchik was at the same time rid of expenditures on the state; in the registers of

1592-1593 the lord's arable was excepted from assessment. All sorts of palliatives were devised to appease the money hunger of the nobility, but the crisis developed with irresistible force and the pangs of hunger became ever keener. To the pomeshchik a sop from the treasury was not enough; he needed the whole treasury. In the days of the oprichnina he had left some power to the boyars, taking for himself only the very fattest morsels. Now he did not want to leave anything to anybody; he needed all power for himself.

CHAPTER IX

1. *The Feudal Reaction; Godunov and the Nobility* [1]

THE crisis in pomestye economy, like the crisis in large-scale votchina economy at the beginning of the sixteenth century, was bound to have political consequences. In the earlier case the political result of economic revolution had been the oprichnina—the liquidation of the dominance of the feudal aristocracy in favour of the middling landholders. In the present case the result of economic reaction was bound to be the revival, even though partial and temporary, of political feudalism.

In the first place, the feudal aristocracy was not nearly so completely ruined by Ivan the Terrible as he might have wished, and as certain modern historians have assumed. "To raise from stones the seed of Abraham" proved harder in practice than on paper. The mere fact that all the frontiers of the Muscovite realm, *i.e.*, all its military defences, had to be left in the hands of the "zemshchina," that is, of the feudal boyar duma, is significant enough. Nor is it less significant that the oprichnina, as an institution, predeceased Ivan IV by several years; and we are hardly surprised when we are told that Ivan the Terrible "commended" his children—the one, Dmitry, a minor, the other, Fedor, an imbecile—to three representatives of old boyar families, Ivan Petrovich Shuisky, Ivan Fedorovich Mstislavsky, and Nikita Romanovich Yuryev. It is true that the last-mentioned was closely related to the dynasty, and that the first two belonged to the most complaisant families of the old aristocracy, the Shuiskys having gone so far as to serve in the oprichnina themselves. Yet not one of them had been created by it, and all of them, according to mestnichestvo reckoning, stood at the very apex of feudal society. This stability of the hierarchical position of the old families was but emphasised by the political misfortunes of individual members of them. The senior representatives both of the Shuiskys and of the Mstislavskys perish in exile; yet in the campaign against the Tatars of the Crimea, who in 1591 again threaten Moscow, the commander-in-chief is the son of the exiled Mstislavsky. The Shuiskys were the acknowledged mortal enemies of the Godunovs; yet at the head of the army sent by Boris Godunov against the False Dmitry we find these

---

[1] *Cf. supra*, p. 133, N. 1.

very Princes Shuisky, including the most untrustworthy of them, Vasily Ivanovich, the future tsar; and the Shuiskys are succeeded in this post by members of another old boyar family, the Princes Golitsyn. The first project of a Russian constitution, an historically famous one (the treaty with Sigismund of Poland, February 4, 1610), puts the boyar duma at the head of the administration of Russia, and after the defeat of the partisans of this constitution the old boyar family of the Romanov-Yuryevs is placed on the throne of the tsars. And under the first sovereign of this family, the boyar duma has occasion, God knows how many times, to state that as reward for service the tsar may bestow "money or a pomestye, but not *otechestvo* [rank]." The system of places (mestnichestvo), already tottering in 1555, survived juridically until 1682, and as a matter of fact even the members of Peter's *collegia* occasionally disputed over the question of precedence.

But the oprichnina not only did not kill off the old aristocracy, it created a new one. Men from the middle nobility, on becoming intimates of Tsar Ivan, very quickly familiarised themselves with their new station and became a copy of the high-born order of boyars they had displaced. A typical example of such feudatories sprung from the oprichnina was Bogdan Belsky, the "squire" of Ivan the Terrible, close to him, however, not because of this his official duty but because of other, unofficial and much less honourable functions. In the last years of Ivan's life, if we are to believe one of his contemporaries, well acquainted with the service relationships of the time, Belsky was the "first intimate and chief counsellor" although he bore no duma title; "the heart of the tsar was always burning for him." Resting on such a purely personal foundation, his position could not be a lasting one; no sooner had Ivan closed his eyes than Belsky saw himself out of employment. He made an attempt to take advantage of what was in fact an interregnum; the one tsarevich was in swaddling clothes, the other was an idiot; some one or other must rule in their names—why might not this "some one" be Belsky? In contrast to the regency of the Shuiskys in the minority of Ivan the Terrible we see no social force behind this candidate to the regency. His hope lay wholly in court connections (he was close to the Nagois, the brothers of little Dmitry's mother) and, probably, in his own armed servants, with whom later he was to appear in Moscow to support his candidacy to the very throne of the tsars. At least, otherwise it is difficult to understand how he succeeded in seizing the Kremlin, when from the chronicle's narrative it is evident that the military force (knights and streltsy) was not on his side. The intervention of this military force decided matters; seeing the artillery directed against the Kremlin, Belsky surrendered (not without a battle, however, since the chronicle mentions killed and wounded), but not unconditionally. The victorious side had to be content with his exile from Moscow, at first to the governorship of Nizhny-Novgorod; later, it appears, he resided on his votchina, living the life of a wealthy feudatory. Such lenient behaviour toward Belsky on the part of the government which dealt severely with the Mstislavskys and the Shuiskys could be motivated only by fear. The former "squire" of Ivan IV was personally, as a landholder, so strong a man, apparently, that it was no easy task to reach him on his estates, and at the same time he was not so dangerous as to warrant risking new troubles on his account. He never gave up hope of returning to power, and scarcely was Tsar Fedor (1584-1598) dead than, as we have mentioned, Belsky again appeared in Moscow "with many people," this time reaching straight for the tsar's throne. He was once more to be convinced that his "household" alone was not enough to make him a political force; he was again left at the post, and again we see him in honourable exile. But he still cherished ambitions; having failed to become tsar, he was ready to content himself with an appanage principality. On the southern frontier of the Muscovite realm, whither they had sent him to establish border fortresses against the Tatars of the Crimea, he conducted himself as absolute master; at his own expense he maintained the troops more generously than it was possible for the Moscow government to do; he built fortresses "according to his own plan"; he lived in them like a tsar and boasted that Boris Godunov was tsar at Moscow, and he, Belsky, was tsar here. Here, of course, he was more dangerous than in the interior of Russia, for now he was the nearest neighbour of the Crimean Tatars and, as we shall remember, even in the time of Ivan the Terrible, the Muscovite feudal opposition had been suspected of treasonable dealings with this foe; at the same time his antagonist held power firmly in his hands and was free to act. They seized Belsky, his "court" was dismissed, his estates confiscated, and he himself, after ignominious punishment, was "appointed" to "far places." He appears on the stage again at the time of the False Dmitry, but this time he did not play for high political stakes.

Boris Godunov had succeeded in disposing of the greatest of the new feudatories the oprichnina had created. But on a closer examination of Godunov and his career we see the same familiar traits of a great feudal *seigneur*. That this feudatory proved to have a head for politics was an individual peculiarity, which did not change his objective position. The tragedy of the fate of Boris lay in the fact that he was woven of contradictions; resolution of these contradictions terminated in catastrophe. Our historical literature has persisted in giving Godunov the reputation of a man who stood for the interests of "the plain service people, whosoever serve from petty votchinas and pomestyes"; in other words, he was a "nobles'" tsar, in contrast to the boyars' tsar, as Vasily Shuisky is usually represented to have been. But to interpret Godunov's whole policy, from beginning to end, as protection of the interests of the nobles is to make the end of his reign a complete enigma, for, as we shall presently see, it was precisely the masses of the nobility that overthrew the Godunovs. Why, then, did the nobility destroy its own instrument? For treason? But in favour of what social class can Boris be said to have played traitor—Boris who persecuted the boyars almost as much as Ivan the Terrible had done and who enserfed the peasantry? If his history unquestionably supplies a number of facts that permit us to speak of his "nobles'" policy, we have also a body of evidence from well-informed contemporary foreigners, who unanimously affirm that "under Boris the common peasant was better off than under any former sovereign," and that the peasants looked upon him "as upon God." Had we toward the end of Godunov's reign but consulted the nobles themselves, they would no doubt have declared him a peasants' tsar just as confidently as our modern historians declare him a representative of the pomeshchik class. And the boyars were not all and not always his enemies. With the Romanovs he even had some special agreement, to which, almost more than to anything else, Boris owed the tsar's throne; with the Shuiskys an open quarrel broke out, but toward the end, as we have seen, he trusted them in the matter that was most important for him and for his whole family. In view of all this, we see that "the tsar of the nobles," "continuator of the oprichnina," is perhaps a not altogether untrue, but all the same a very summary characterisation of so complex a figure as was this "slave tsar," without any "otechestvo" [hereditary rank], who had perched himself on the topmost pinnacle of Muscovite boyardom.

Boris began, let us repeat, as one of the magnates of the oprichnina— like Belsky, if you like, but in a more honourable rôle. Personal influence and family position—these formed the starting point of his career. Second in influence during the last years of Ivan's life (Belsky had stood first) and brother-in-law of the elder tsarevich, Fedor (who, though weak-minded, was "competent" and the most likely successor to Ivan IV), Boris reached by a legal path that goal toward which his rival had aspired illegally and became a kind of appanage prince, or "prince of the blood," if you like. Barely two years after the death of Ivan the Terrible, foreigners were calling him "prince" and "lieutenant of the empire." A few years later this had become his official title; Muscovite diplomatic documents style him "imperial brother-in-law and lieutenant, servant and master of the horse, commander of the guard and lord of the great states, the realms of Kazan and Astrakhan, Boris Fedorovich." To foreigners it was explained that he was "not a standard for any one," for he was above all the serving princes, tsars, and tsareviches. He treated independently with foreign governments, with the Holy Roman emperor, with the khan of the Crimea. One old document, which well preserves what was said about Godunov among the masses of the people, ascribes to Tsar Fedor the following words: " 'To you all I say, do not bother me with any petition, go on any business to petition the great boyar Boris Godunov,' thus the Sovereign Tsar and Grand Prince Fedor Ioannovich was pleased to call him great, 'for I have ordered him to set the whole realm in order, and to deal out all justice to it, and to punish for fault and to pardon, and there should be no bother to me at all,' " and Fedor himself "applied himself to sacred writings, and chanted all the night." If we take these words literally, it follows that Godunov was tsar in fact long before his election, an impression confirmed by the document we have cited, which says of Boris: "The damned fellow has not the name of tsar, but all the power is in his hands." In reality, popular fantasy, as always, exaggerated; Godunov was not quite alone on the topmost pinnacle of the feudal hierarchy. But there was something to be exaggerated; the personal position of Boris Godunov, over and above support from any social force, is such as we should strive in vain to match in the history of Moscow, always excepting the case of Metropolitan Alexis in the days of the youth of Dmitry Donskoi. No favourite nearer in time to Godunov can be compared to him; when some one speaking of Boris to a Muscovite diplomat mentioned the name of Alexis Adashev, the diplomat was absolutely right in replying: "Alexis was clever, but this man is not of Alexis' stature." Adashev held his own by force of intellect and by the support of the social class that had pushed him forward; Godunov personally had in his hands such material strength that he did not fear the fate of Adashev.[2]

If from the very beginning the policy of Boris Godunov bears a definite class impress, it is only because any and every policy is a class policy and cannot be anything else. Very tempting is the idea of exhibiting the base-born "tsar's favourite," "the slave and Tatar of yesterday," as the leader of the base-born small-pomestyed nobility in the struggle with high-born boyardom; but such a combination would be historically untrue. Godunov's opponents strove hard to injure him, after his death, because he had come "from the lesser servants," but, during his lifetime, they ascribed to this fact hardly more significance than to the fact that Boris was "not used to Godly writing," was a man uneducated theologically, another fact that the opposing party always recalled with satisfaction. In no feudal society does origin play an independent rôle, and the pride of birth of Muscovite boyardom need not be exaggerated; the "elected council" had suffered in its midst men taken "from the dung-

[2] Contemporaries put the revenues of the Godunovs from their lands at 94,000 rubles (2,500,000 in pre-war currency). From their own votchinas they could equip a whole army.

hill," and princes descended from Rurik, yes, even of the very oldest according to the *Rodoslovets*, had taken service in the oprichnina along with Vaska Gryazny [Jack the Dirty] and Malyuta Skuratov. The petty vassals were the first to support Boris in a scuffle, not with the boyar order, but with a magnate sprung from the oprichnina such as Belsky; in 1584 the crowd that collected to bombard the Moscow Kremlin was headed by the Ryazan knights, the Kikins and the Lyapunovs, the future leaders of the nobility at the time of the Troubles. And they were aiding not Godunov alone but all "the boyars," *i.e.*, in general they were for the existing government against an individual usurper. The first clear and definite case of class struggle occurs three years later, and again the struggle of the nobility against boyardom as such was not involved. We have two versions of this affair; the one is undoubtedly partisan, the other knows the externals but does not know the inner workings. But in a diplomatic document the Moscow government itself blabbed out that in 1587 "they sat in the Kremlin-fortress in siege and placed a strong watch," and that this was done "on account of the trading louts," who had organised a revolt. This is sufficient in confirmation of what the partisan account of the events has to say about the "popular assembly of a multitude of the men of Moscow," which had assembled "to slay" Godunov "and all his kin without mercy with stoning." It was an anti-Godunov revolt, organised by the townsmen of Moscow, who were supported not only by the Shuiskys and other "great boyars" but also by Dionysius, metropolitan of Moscow and of all Rus. All these circumstances show that it was by no means a matter of more or less casual street disturbances, but that a coup d'état had been prepared, for which both the juridical form and what then passed for political motivation had been thought out. The motivation was that Godunov's rule was said to threaten the very existence of the dynasty; Fedor had no children and the Tsaritsa Irene, Boris' sister, was to blame. And so the metropolitan, the "great boyars," and "the magnates of the tsar's palace and the gosts of Moscow and all the trading folk held counsel and bound themselves in writing to petition the Sovereign Tsar and Grand Prince Fedor Ivanovich of all Rus, that he the sovereign be gracious to all the lands of his realm and take a second bride, and that the Tsaritsa Irene be pleased to retire into a convent; and that he take a bride for the sake of offspring." To make this political conspiracy an episode of palace struggle within the narrow circle of the Muscovite court aristocracy is very convenient, perhaps, from the point of view of artistic interest (the reader probably remembers the scene from *Tsar Fedor Ivanovich* [3]), but historically it is quite incorrect. It would, of course, not have entered the Shuiskys' heads to risk their necks in this business, had they not felt

[3] *Cf.* the novel by Alexis Tolstoi.

behind them the "popular multitude" which half a century before had made their fathers the powerful guardians of the little Ivan IV. But this time the correlation of forces proved to be different. After the first fright the Godunov government, which had taken refuge in the Kremlin, made short work of the conspirators; Dionysius was deposed from the metropolitan throne, the Shuiskys and a number of other boyars were banished, and six gosts of Moscow were executed. There is no doubt that the affair was decided, not by the weak will of Tsar Fedor but by those same "knights" whose presence in the Kremlin is disclosed by the diplomatic document we have just mentioned. Ivan IV's old guard, his oprichnina "dvor," was now loyal to Boris Godunov, who, it may be said in passing, was its immediate commander.

The clash of 1587 was the greatest event in Moscow's social history in the interval between the death of Ivan the Terrible (1584) and the election of Godunov as tsar (1598). It marked the factual disintegration of the oprichnina, which juridically had ceased to exist some years before Ivan's death. The oprichnina had been a bloc of the urban bourgeoisie and the middling landholders; without the townsmen the coup of January 3, 1565, probably would never have occurred. Previously the bourgeoisie had been on good terms with the boyars; the pomeshchik party had made a great gain in tearing it away and transferring it to their side. Now we find again, as it were, the combination of 1550—the "merchant folk" together with the "great boyars." As it were—because now the initiative belonged rather to the "merchant folk," while the "great boyars" were acting as a group of separate families, not as a class; Godunov, you see, was himself a "great boyar" and had with him a whole boyar party, many "boyars of the tsar's palace seduced by him," together with the nobles. The significance of the event does not lie in the revival of a feudal-bourgeois opposition, but in the appearance of the bourgeoisie as an *independent* political force. The Moscow townsmen had probably been disenchanted with their aristocratic leaders even before the oprichnina; the story regarding Fedor's divorce took away the last remnants of their authority, if indeed they still had any. The bitter words of the Moscow merchants, addressed to the Shuiskys—"you have made your peace [with Godunov] at the price of our heads"—served as the epitaph of the alliance of boyars and townsmen. It is remarkable that connexions with the Shuisky family remained; economically these holders of industrial votchinas were more closely connected with bourgeois circles than with their titled brethren. When the bourgeoisie needed "its tsar," it sought him in the ranks of this family. In 1587 that critical moment was still far in the future; this first political appearance of the "merchant folk" had a more limited aim. Yet this outbreak was a political event and not a palace intrigue as was presently made evident by Boris' foreign policy. The experience of the Livonian War had made the Muscovite government very pacific; but in 1589 the Muscovite envoys, sent (and not for the first time) to negotiate with the Swedes for retrocession of the Russian towns occupied by the latter, were instructed to talk "on a big, lofty scale" and to demand "for the sovereign's part Narva, Ivangorod, Yam, Koporye, Korela without indemnity, without money." This was a challenge, and in January of the following year (1590) a Russian army moved on Narva with Tsar Fedor himself, Boris Godunov, and Fedor Nikitich Romanov at its head. The Muscovite government declared that it would not make peace without Narva, i.e., without the restoration of Russia's Baltic trade. Narva was not taken, but in general the campaign was not a failure, for three other Russian towns seized by the Swedes, Yam, Ivangorod, and Koporye, passed back into Russia's hands. This whole chain of events becomes intelligible if we remember that it was a question of foreign policy that had caused the townsmen to break with the boyars and to effect a rapprochement with the "warriors," and that the failure of the Livonian War had been the first thing to alienate the bourgeoisie from the pomeshchiks. Now Godunov was trying once more to carry on a bourgeois policy, but cautiously and not persistently; the bourgeoisie was not the chief piece on his chessboard.

If this great feudatory wanted to keep himself in power, there was no one for him to rely upon except the "warriors." It was not his personal social position that determined his policy; on the contrary, it was his policy that conditioned his social sympathies. An occasion to repay his allies very soon presented itself. In 1591, as we have already mentioned, the Tatars of the Crimea again appeared under Moscow, but this time they utterly failed to take the city. The experience of the preceding Tatar inroad had been turned to good account by the Muscovite generals; new means of coping with the horsemen of the steppe had been worked out which proved most effectual. Contemporaries ascribed special importance to the "walking town," a movable wooden fortress on wheels, said to be an invention of Prince M. I. Vorotynsky, though something very similar had been projected long before in one of "Peresvetov's" writings. As a means of defending the city, Godunov had greatly strengthened the artillery.[4] In a word, the Tatars were confronted with a picture very different from that of twenty years before, and they withdrew without even making an attempt to take the city. But to repulse them a huge army had already been called out; all the service landholders of central Russia, and even of Novgorod and

---

[4] The famous "Tsar-Cannon" has survived as a monument of the skill of Russian founders of those times.

Pskov, had been set in motion. The pomeshchiks, of course, did not do their duty for nothing; they were paid for the campaign, paid exceptionally rapidly [5] for the dawdling Muscovite exchequer, and on an augmented scale; so augmented indeed that the service men themselves, it is said, were amazed and said that in former times a high-born man had not been given for a difficult campaign and many wounds what rank-and-file knights were now given for a war that was more like a manœuvre, for only the Muscovite vanguard had got a glimpse of the Tatars, and the main forces had remained far in the rear. If we remember the significance of the sovereign's money wages to pomeshchik economy, we shall realise that Boris could have found no better way to attach the "warriors" to himself. With good reason was all grumbling against the state administration stilled for long after this campaign, a fact attested by authors not at all favourable to Boris.

Disposing of vast personal means (and presumably an enormous coterie of personal satellites); having reconciled, even though only in part, the bourgeoisie, which was now beginning to raise its head; having the full support of the petty vassals, the whole armed force of the state,—Boris stood so firmly that, it would seem, he could have wished nothing more. Tsar Fedor was not yet old and might still have children; a year later (1592) a daughter was born to him, the Tsarevna Fedosia (d. 1594). Under a son, who would have been Boris' nephew, his position as regent would, in all probability, have remained just as firm as under the father. It would be exceedingly strange if in such a position a man should begin to "strengthen" himself by means of crimes—crimes that were very clumsily committed and, as it might seem, purposely devised to compromise the reputation of Boris Godunov. However, the preponderant majority of historians accept as trustworthy the story that in these very years, with the cognisance, if not at the direct command of Godunov, the Tsarevich Dmitry, the younger son of Ivan the Terrible, was murdered—murdered with the purpose of "clearing Boris' way to the throne." If one needed a special illustration of the infantile condition of the very important discipline called "historical criticism" and of the pressure on our historical science of circumstances and interests that have nothing in common with any science, no better one could be thought out than the "affair of the murder of Tsarevich Dmitry."

The first categorical assertion that Boris was the murderer of Dmitry is found in a source, the most superficial analysis of which is sufficient to discredit its testimony. In 1606, having been seated on the throne by means of a coup d'état, over the dead body of the Pseudo Dmitry,

---

[5] Apparently contrary to custom, the distribution was begun while the troops were still in camp, without waiting for the end of the campaign.

Tsar Vasily Shuisky found it necessary to offer juridical and historical justification for his conduct, to prove that the murder of this tsar had been an act of "necessary self-defence" and that rights to the throne of Moscow had belonged to the Shuiskys from time immemorial, although—purely from modesty—they had not hitherto preferred their claims. For this purpose a whole collection of documents was circulated, of whose falsification nobody, it seems, ever had doubts, and a little historical tract, very well written, to be sure, was distributed to supply a "historical introduction," as it were, to these documents. From these documents it appeared that the "serf, notorious robber, apostate, heretic, unfrocked monk, Grishka Bogdanov, son of Otrepyev" had wanted no more no less than to slay the "boyars, and nobles, and officials, and gosts, and all the better people, and wanted to destroy the whole Muscovite state to its foundations, and to scorn the Christian faith, and to destroy the churches, and to build Roman chapels." Clearly, to murder him was not only permissible, it was obligatory. The introduction was phrased to confirm the reader in the idea that there was no one who could rightfully take the place of the murdered heretic except Prince Vasily Shuisky, "from the beginning of his forebears fearing God and holding in his heart great faith toward God and unhypocritical truth toward men." If all these qualities had not earlier gained the pious Prince the throne, the fault had lain in the oppression "from a certain slave, called Boris Godunov," who "was like unto the ancient serpent that formerly in Paradise did tempt Eve and our forefather Adam and deprived them of the enjoyment of the food of Paradise." When in the midst of a text like this one reads that Boris Godunov sent the murderers to the Tsarevich Dmitry, elementary historical fairmindedness compels one to regard the story with a high degree of incredulity. This feeling is bound to be heightened when the reader perceives that, on the one hand, our excellently informed author is not able to give a single, vivid, concrete detail of the crime but confines himself to a conventionalised picture of the "murder of an innocent lad," outside of time and space, and that, on the other hand, all the other "independent Russian writers of the seventeenth century . . . ," as Platonov writes, "speak of Boris' participation in the murdering of Tsarevich Dmitry reluctantly and very cautiously."

To this analysis of the original accusation against Boris may be added one more very interesting observation: the further from the event of 1591, the more details about it do we find in literature. The detailed story of the murder, cited by Solovyev and well-known from textbooks, is to be read in the so-called *New Chronicle,* a historical compilation on the Times of the Troubles, the definitive redaction of which is no older than 1630. Forty years after the event more was known about it than an interested and partisan author had been able to collect after fifteen years! Such a phenomenon, familiar to every historical scholar, can have only one explanation; we have here a typical case of the rise of a legend. Popular imagination supplied what history lacked, gradually, detail by detail, giving colour to the dry outline of the accusation originally thrown out without any proofs. Any one who knows the relations between Godunov and the Romanovs,[6] who occupied the throne when the history of the Troubles was first written, will not be surprised that contemporary popular imagination imparted this particular bias. But for any "independent" Russian historian of the nineteenth century, it would, in view of all these facts, seem obligatory to reject entirely the fiction put in circulation by the Shuiskys' pamphlet, even if we had no documents, contemporary with the event, that asserted the contrary. But there is such a document; the genuine brief on the murder of Dmitry—the "inquest" held on the hot trail in Uglich by a commission of the boyar duma—is extant, and in this brief by a series of depositions (among them those of the uncles of the tsarevich, the Nagois) it is established that he fell a victim to an unfortunate accident, that he injured himself while playing a game with his knife. The investigation, it is true, was conducted by that same pious Prince Vasily Shuisky, with whose publicist activity the reader is already acquainted; for a very great sceptic, it may be agreed, this offers grounds for suspecting the documentary report of the investigation. But, in the first place, Shuisky was not alone in the investigation, and, if we are to suspect official documents that Vasily Shuisky had anything to do with, what confidence does his unofficial publicism deserve?

A hundred years ago a historian, not in academic service but none the less fairminded for that, drew from all the facts enumerated above the only possible conclusion, that if we are not to adopt the viewpoint of absolute scepticism, we must credit the brief of the investigation rather than the literary records. And he wrote in his book that Tsarevich Dmitry perished in 1591 at Uglich by accident. But the public was not to read such a heresy. Academic science kept strict watch, and one of its most eminent representatives hastened to cut off the evil at the root; at his insistence the offending page of heretical history, already printed, was torn out of every copy and burned. This scholar's argument, it seems, was just as simple as it was convincing: if Dmitry was not a martyr who had innocently suffered at the hands of malefactors, how could his miracle-working relics have survived? From this we can see how sagacious Tsar Vasily Shuisky was in converting the younger son of Ivan the Terrible into a saint and miracle-worker almost on the day after he ascended the throne (Shuisky became tsar May 18, and

6 Cf. infra.

the relics of Dmitry were in Moscow on June 3). The measure he had taken proved sufficient to influence the "public opinion," not only of the beginning of the seventeenth century but also of the times of Emperor Nicholas I (1825-1855).

As for the "murderer of a saint," Boris Godunov, he, it seems, suffered not so much from pangs of conscience over an evil deed he had not committed as from *doubts*—strange enough to our view, although until lately there were still lone scholars who shared them. There are grounds for thinking that Boris doubted whether Dmitry actually was dead. If the personality of the weak-minded Fedor was in his hands a powerful means of maintaining his own power, the little tsarevich might in the hands of Godunov's opponents, if given the opportunity, be similarly used against him. And this peril became the more imminent, the clearer it became that children could not be expected of Fedor, and that Dmitry, were he alive, was the sole representative of the descendants of Ivan Kalita. Rumours that the tsarevich was alive and was somewhere abroad, perhaps in Poland, became current in Moscow even before Fedor's death. Only a month after his death a Polish frontier governor had heard of some sort of proclamation in Dmitry's name that had appeared in Smolensk. Only in this connexion can be understood those exceptional measures taken by the Muscovite government, *i.e.*, by Godunov's government, in these very days. "On the death of the tsar," writes Platonov, "the frontiers of the state were immediately closed, permitting no one to pass them either way. Not only on the high roads but also on the bypaths they placed a guard, lest any one bring tidings out of the realm of Moscow into Lithuania and to the Germans. The Polish-Lithuanian and German merchants were detained at Moscow and in the frontier cities, Smolensk, Pskov, and others, with their wares and servants, and all these people received bread and hay even from the treasury. Official couriers from neighbouring states were likewise kept under guard and as soon as possible sent back beyond the Muscovite frontier by the border governors. At Smolensk they did not even allow the courier of the Polish governor of Orsha to lead his own horse to the water-trough, and buying anything in the market was not to be thought of." Simultaneously with these police measures were taken extraordinary measures of military defence, and precisely on the western frontier. "The walls of Smolensk they hastily finished, bringing various building materials in thousands of carts; to the two generals already at Smolensk were added four more. The reinforced garrison of Smolensk not only kept watch in the fortress itself but sent out patrols in its environs. At Pskov likewise they observed the greatest precaution." All this, of course, is not to be explained by the desire of the Muscovites to hold the election of the new tsar "in secret from the

eyes of outsiders." They quite definitely were afraid of relations
between some one in Moscow and some one whom they suspected to be
beyond the western boundary of the Muscovite realm; relations, moreover, which might end in a sudden apparition of foreign troops on the
Russian frontiers. In a word, in 1598 they prepared for what actually
happened in 1604. The "pretender" was not a black speck that suddenly appeared on the cloudless horizon of Boris' reign; this dramatic
picture we must leave to Pushkin's tragedy.[7] In actual history the
figure of Dmitry was discernible in the wings the whole time, and
Godunov waited nervously until he should at last make his entry. In
this sense, perhaps, the late tsarevich disturbed his dreams, not in the
form of a "bleeding child," but rather at the head of a Polish-Lithuanian host, in the very guise in which he did appear in Rus on the eve
of Boris' death.

These fears explain the unusual circumstances that surrounded Boris
Godunov's election to the throne in the spring of 1598. This curious
episode has passed through several stages in modern historiography. At
first historians felt unconditional confidence in the very circumstantial
account of this event given in Shuisky's above-mentioned pamphlet; in
it may be found all that Russian readers have been familiar with from
childhood—the bailiffs at whose command the people began to bow and
shout, the spittle as a substitute for tears in dry eyes, and the fines
imposed on those who were unwilling to go to the Novodevichy Monastery to pray Boris to become tsar. But since there were no special
grounds for trusting Shuisky in this question, reason soon got the upper
hand, gossip ceased to be scrupulously believed, and into the centre of
the stage moved the zemsky sobor that elected Boris; it was emphasised
that in the make-up of this sobor "it is impossible to observe any traces
of electoral agitation or any packing of members." The intriguer, who
had perched himself on the tsar's throne by guile, turned out to have
been legally and regularly elected by a "representative assembly,"
which "was acknowledged as the legal mouthpiece of public interests
and opinions." There is no doubt that Boris' election was an act
juridically quite correct; we shall presently see that it was surrounded
with every juridical formality, perhaps even in superfluous profusion.
No tsar either before or since has so striven to convince his subjects of
his right to reign. But this solicitous argumentation of his rights—
we can in part trace it even in process of evolution and observe how
some arguments are replaced by others that seemed more convincing—
in itself compels us to be somewhat suspicious of what was taking place,
independently of any contemporary pamphlets whatever. No one cares

---

[7] *Cf.* A. Pushkin, *Boris Godunov.* Rendered into English verse by Alfred Hayes,
London (1918). *Cf.* also Moussorgsky's opera, *Boris Godunov.*

so much for juridical impeccability as do intelligent and experienced swindlers. Besides, we have already emerged from the stage of political development in which "electoral agitation" seems something "in the nature of packing" public opinion. We are now all very well aware from personal experience that it is impossible to conceive of any organised mass action without preliminary agitation, and if the people of Moscow on February 21, 1598, surged "in the wake of the patriarch" to the Novodevichy Monastery, it is obvious that some one had taken the lead in this affair and prepared it. The assertion that there had been preliminary agitation in favour of this manifestation is therefore no "slander" on Boris, but the insinuation that it was effected by measures of a police nature, through bailiffs, is a different matter. It is this that the lampoon put in circulation by the Shuiskys dwells on. Other authors, not at all sympathetic with Boris, say only that the latter had "assistants" (electoral agents, as we say) everywhere and "strong-talking zealots," whom we should now call agitators. Thus, there was "agitation," but there was no "packing." Nor could there be; it was quite unnecessary, for when the popular manifestations began, the decision of the zemsky sobor had already been taken and consecrated by religious authority; on February 18, in the Cathedral of the Annunciation, they had solemnly prayed the Lord God to grant to Orthodox Christendom, on its petition, the Sovereign Tsar Boris Godunov. The vassals great and small (the boyar duma, of course, attended the sobor in full force) and the Church had already recognised Boris as tsar when the people set out to beseech him. Godunov was not content with the social forces usually constituting the "body politic" of the Muscovite realm—the "estates" represented at the zemsky sobor; he needed the participation of "all multitudinous popular Christendom." As far as we know, he was the first tsar to summon to his aid the masses of the people, for the "appeals to the people" of Ivan the Terrible really were addressed to the upper strata of the merchantry of Moscow. Boris' action was unusually important for the future but is no less important in characterising his position at this moment. The unusually solemn character of the election must have barred the way in advance to any "adventurers," whom they evidently expected.

Similar anxiety permeates both the very act of election, which has come down to us in two editions, and the oath the population had to take to the new tsar—and take in an unusually solemn setting, in the churches, and during service. Boris' opponents here found new cause for complaints; on account of the noise raised by the throngs taking the oath, it was impossible even to hear the divine chanting in the Cathedral of the Annunciation, so that devout Muscovites who wanted to pray were this day left without mass. The zemsky sobor's "act of election" was placed in the shrine of the Metropolitan Peter, which on this occasion was opened to the public; this, of course, was interpreted as manifest and intolerable sacrilege. In content both these documents—the oath and the decision of the sobor—are very curious, especially the latter, which has come down to us not only in its definitive form but also in a rough draft. It is remarkable for the abundance of reasons assigned for the election of Boris; there are so many of them that they even interfere with each other, and in the definitive edition it was found advantageous to omit some of them. The mere enumeration of them is interesting; before us is revealed the series of layers of which by the end of the sixteenth century the Russian law of succession to the throne was made up. The oldest layer was appanage tradition, in virtue of which the "sovereign's votchina," like any one else's, passed by bequest, though only within the circle of the given family, not to outsiders. The document notes that Godunov is a "kinsman of the great sovereign" and alleges that even Ivan IV had appointed Boris his successor in case of Fedor's death. But the appanage of Moscow had managed to convert itself into the universal Orthodox realm; its throne could not be disposed of as private property. As a matter of common sense, it was clear that the Orthodox Church could best determine who was worthy to be tsar of all the Orthodox; the document asserts that the bishops have from the Apostles the power, "when met in synod, to establish for their fatherland a pastor and teacher and tsar." But in 1598 this stage, too, was a thing of the past, and the decisive argument is the "petition of all multitudinous popular Christendom," an argument so decisive that at the end of the document all others are forgotten on account of it. Kinship with the dynasty, the testament of Ivan the Terrible, and the decree of the Church in synod, all were forgotten by the editor of the document; he remembered only that Boris was an elected tsar, that this was an innovation, and that this innovation might be objected to in order to dispute the right of the Godunovs to the throne—the Godunovs, for, of course, the whole family was elected; the oath was taken to the whole family, including the "Tsarevna Oxinia [Boris' daughter Xenia]." In the definitive text of the "act of election" nothing is said about Tsar Ivan's testament; this bold assertion would have been too hard to prove. On the other hand, this text lays more stress on the kinship of the Godunovs with the last descendant of Ivan Kalita through Irene, sister of Boris and wife of Fedor. That there might be still other persons having hereditary or some other rights to the throne this document does not say; but the *oath* mentions one such person, and the mention is startlingly unexpected. We remember that Ivan the Terrible once, not exactly as a joke, not exactly for the sake of observing formalities, set up as special tsar over the "zemshchina" the baptised

Tatar tsarevich, Simeon Bekbulatovich. He was now a blind old man, probably himself but poorly remembering that he had sometime been "caliph for an hour." None the less, Boris found it necessary to ask his subjects whether they wanted Tsar Simeon to rule the state. One modern scholar has drawn from this the conclusion that the former tsar of the zemshchina was, as it were, a serious candidate for the throne at a certain moment of the electoral campaign. As a matter of fact this remarkable detail only shows how scrupulously careful the new tsar was and what measures he took lest perchance even the very dead should walk. Boris would probably have preferred to mention his real opponents: the children of Nikita Romanovich Yuryev, who were also kinsmen of Tsars Ivan and Fedor, and of still longer standing than the Godunovs; and the not exactly living, not exactly dead, Dmitry of Uglich. But it was impossible to mention the latter officially, for officially he was in the next world; and with the Romanovs Boris had some sort of agreement, even ratified by oath. The essence of this agreement is not known to us, but one circumstance is significant: the Romanov version of the history of the Troubles, which found its earliest expression in an author of unknown name, used by the very well-known Avraam Palitsyn for his compilation, seeks to lay the blame for violation of the agreement on Boris, at the same time carefully concealing from the reader just why Godunov banished the sons of Nikita. It is a sure enough sign that their integrity could not be proved as indisputably as this author would have liked.

Thus, as soon as he ascended the throne, Boris felt himself unsteady on it and strove to find the greatest possible supports, both juridical and material, for his power. The rule of Godunov had outlived itself; as regent he had met no serious impediments to his authority, but hardly had he become tsar when revolution boiled up under his feet. According to the generally accepted view, the boyars prepared this revolution. But just at this period we should seek in vain for a united boyar opposition; had there been one, the affair would scarcely have ended with such a strange adventure, risky and most unpleasant for the boyar order itself, as the appearance on the throne of Moscow of the Pseudo-Dmitry, brought to Moscow by pomeshchiks from the *ukraine* [frontier] in alliance with robber cossacks and Polish adventurers. In examining Boris' policy, we readily see that the rift between him and the dominant elements went much deeper than is usually supposed. If his policy down to 1598, the policy of Godunov the regent, was still a class policy in favour of the noble class (though not so much because of his close connexion with that class as because all the other classes were at the time opposed to him), the policy of Tsar Boris begins to assume a quite original character, as new and unexpected as the electoral principle advanced by Boris was new in the field of public law.

With the exception of the pamphlet circulated by Tsar Vasily, all authors, whether sympathising with Boris (they are very few) or sympathising with his opponents (they are the majority), testify with one voice to the extraordinary solicitude, unprecedented in Russia, of this sovereign for the masses of the population. The partisan of the house of the Romanovs whom we have just mentioned asserts without any reservations that Tsar Boris "thought much of the poor and the lowly and there was great mercy from him to such" and that he "was fond of building for the sake of such people." The clerk Ivan Timofeyev greatly disliked the "crafty and insidious lover of power"; yet when he comes to this aspect of Boris' rule, this bilious official, who had carefully collected the most odoriferous scandals about the brother-in-law of Tsar Fedor, pens something like a panegyric to Godunov, nor is it written without feeling, as though the author were delighted with this bright isle in the midst of the sea of filth he himself had collected in the pages of his *Annals*. The most objective of all the historians near in time to Boris, the author of the articles on the Troubles in the *Chronography* of 1617, has on his palette hardly anything but bright colours for Godunov: "made liberal gifts to all . . . many were fed to repletion from his generous hands . . . blooming like a date-tree with foliage of good works." If we pass from these general estimates to individual concrete points of Godunov's policy, we find one on which a whole series of writers, both Russian and foreign, agree: Boris sternly prosecuted extortions and venality. "None of the judges or officials dares take any gifts from suitors," wrote the French adventurer, Margeret, who had been in Godunov's service: "for if a judge is accused either by his own servants, or by the givers (who rarely report, concealing it in the hope of winning the case), or by other people, the man detected in extortion loses all his property and, having returned the gifts, is subjected to distraint, for payment of a fine set by the tsar, of 500, 1,000, or 2,000 rubles, according to his rank. But a guilty clerk, not too beloved by the sovereign, is punished with the knout, *i.e.*, flogged with the lash and not with rods, and around his neck is tied the purse of silver, the fur, pearls, even the salt fish or other object taken as a present; then they send the man punished into exile, with a warning to cease illegality for the future." "Despite all this, extortions are not exterminated," Margeret melancholically adds, again agreeing with the Russian author who informs us that though Boris strove very zealously to root out such "undesirable business" as administrative abuses, "yet it was not possible at all." We shall not fall to wondering at this; in practice, all police states have broken their necks over the insoluble task of combining "justice" with complete absence of rights on the part of their subjects. Peter the Great met with no better luck on this road than did Godunov; but for the end of the sixteenth century the very ideal of a well-ordered police state was a forward step.

Our knowledge of Boris' social and fiscal policy is too fragmentary to permit us to form a comprehensive judgment of his projects in this field. Foreigners ascribe to him a very bold design, grandiose for its time, namely, legislative regulation of the obligations of the peasants to the landholders. It is reported that he tried to shift the fiscal centre of gravity to indirect taxation; in condemning his "ill-smelling gains," his opponents give prominence to the increase in the farm of the public-houses, "and many other farms there were beyond measure." This remark is interesting, among other reasons, because it discloses the class relationships existing under Godunov. We know that there were in Muscovite Rus two means of collecting indirect imposts, by farm and "on credit," and that the latter, contrary to a widespread opinion, was more advantageous for commercial capital. The author whom we have just cited displays rare understanding of the economic relationships of his time and, judging by another work of his, was very close to the townsmen. His disapproval of Godunov's fiscal policy therefore carries much weight; the bourgeoisie was not now on Boris' side, and the Moscow townsmen did not "hold their peace in dread" when the Godunovs fell; they were simply completely indifferent to this fact. It was not their dynasty.

And it had long since ceased to be the nobles' dynasty. In regard to the pomeshchiks Boris was faced with a problem frankly insoluble. On the one hand, the ever continuing crisis demanded ever more and more pumping of silver from the treasury chest into the pockets of the middling landholder. Boris did his best; on the occasion of his election he organised a frankly fictitious campaign against the khan of the Crimea and distributed double wages for it. But this kind of thing could not be kept up; the state was living on that same roving peasant whom the pomeshchiks were unable to bind to their lands. Boris could not make up his mind to rob the town in favour of the nobles, as was to happen later, in the seventeenth century; after the events of 1587, at least, the benevolent neutrality of the bourgeoisie seemed indispensable. The only other course was to sacrifice temporarily the class interests of the nobles and to check the peasant dispersion by creating for the peasants tolerable conditions of existence in the central provinces. By actively colonising the frontiers at the same time, Godunov's government might hope to emerge from the crisis in a few years. Meanwhile the hunger of the pomeshchiks was satisfied by confiscations of the estates of Boris' opponents, by "stealing the homes and villages of the boyars and magnates"; in this particular Boris could not and probably did not wish to depart from the course bequeathed by the oprichnina. The red thread which runs through the whole second half of the sixteenth century may be traced through the reign of Godunov also; hence, upon a general survey, from a bird's-eye view, as it were, it appears to us, as it appeared to contemporaries, to be a continuation of the reign of Ivan the Terrible. But Boris' significance did not lie in the fact that he was an oprichnik. For him confiscations were not a universal means of unravelling tangled agrarian relationships; under the existing circumstances they were only a continuation of the destruction of the old votchinas. But one fine day there would be nothing more to destroy, and catastrophe would be inevitable; how long it could be warded off was the only question. Was not Boris too late with his policy of improving the condition of peasant economy? History alone could answer. Its answer was not in favour of Godunov.

The agrarian question was brought to a head by the famine of 1602-1604, itself the combined result of speculation in grain by the nobles, of the depopulation of the provinces nearest the capital, and of accidental atmospheric causes which destroyed the grain. For the pomeshchiks the immediate effect of the famine was appallingly advantageous; parallel with an enormous rise in grain prices (eighty-fold, if we are to believe the chronographer) there was an extraordinary decline in the price of working hands; men went into bondage gratuitously, for bread alone. These cheap bondsmen their masters did not even deign to feed the year round; keeping them until field labours were over, they then drove them out to the four winds, with complete confidence that the spring would find abundant workers still cheaper. The relations between lord and peasant were already such as to remind us of the eighteenth century, the classic era of serfdom, even to the bondage harems. Subsequently the famine was bound to aggravate and actually did aggravate the crisis, creating an enormous "reserve army" of roaming folk, ready material for an anti-noble movement, and driving out in all directions the last "old-dwellers." But no one thought of the morrow. Godunov's government made an attempt to feed the starving, but the undertaking proved too much for the technical resources of the administration; the sums disbursed by the government sufficed for about one-third of what a man needed at the established grain prices. Besides, famine relief was concentrated in the cities; there the needy congregated in masses, prices were further inflated, and the famine situation became still more aggravated. Boris was powerless to relieve the people's need, but in the effort he completely lost the sympathies of the pomeshchiks. Any insignificant occasion would have been sufficient to make the social isolation of Godunov's régime, long a possibility, a fact evident to all. The occasion soon presented itself nor was it an insignificant one; from Poland, the long-expected Dmitry appeared, at last.

2. The Rebellion of the Nobles

"Who was the first False Dmitry?" was once considered an important question in Russian history. That historians no longer give attention to it is a manifest proof that this science has attained greater maturity. "For our purpose there is not the slightest need to pause over the question of the first pretender's identity," writes Professor Platonov, one of the latest historians of the Troubles. "Whomsoever we consider him to have been, whether the real tsarevich, or Gregory Otrepyev, or any third person, our view of the character of the popular movement raised in his favour cannot be changed; this movement is perfectly clear in and of itself." Let us add only the comment that this author continues to call Dmitry "pretender," even though Solovyev two generations earlier had demonstrated quite conclusively that he did not of himself assume the rôle of tsarevich, but that others created the rôle for him, others called him Dmitry, and he believed it just as afterwards the masses of the people believed it; therefore the term "Alleged Dmitry," coined by Kostomarov, is so much more apt that we shall employ it. With this reservation, the opinion of the modern historian of the Troubles may be accepted as definitive, and the question, "Who was Dmitry?" may be replaced by the question, "Who put Dmitry forward?"

The earliest version of the answer to this question is to be found in that same pamphlet of Shuisky's in which Godunov, for the first time in Russian letters, figures as the murderer of the real son of Ivan the Terrible. This coincidence is in itself sufficient comment on the value of the version, but this has not prevented it from becoming the dominant one in our historical literature and from finding its way into all the textbooks. To make it more plausible, this story was worked into the fabric of the testimony of "a credible witness," the "delation" of a certain monk Varlaam, supposed to have fled over the border together with "Grishka Otrepyev" and to have long accompanied him in his wanderings. Undoubtedly he was one of Godunov's spies, sent to watch Dmitry as soon as rumours about him had reached Moscow. For his zeal in this direction he fell into a Polish prison, but he had already succeeded in collecting a good deal of information about the future pretender's Polish connexions; thus his story gives facts and details that, it seems, have misled modern scholars. In working over this "police spy's report" the editor of the pamphlet did not eliminate all that he might have; for example, he preserved a reference to the "privity" of the

Shuiskys, a fact important and useful for Godunov's government, which had ordered the monk Varlaam on reconnaissance, but superfluous, of course, for the Shuiskys themselves. Aside from a certain carelessness in finish (a carelessness easily understood since the pamphlet was intended to produce a general impression, and on a wide public which would not delve into such trifles), the Shuiskys' pamphleteer was able to give the "delation" a bias in perfect harmony with the general tone of the work in which it was inserted. Here Dmitry figures as really a "pretender"; the idea of declaring himself tsarevich is his personal idea, the product of his personal moral perversity and of the "violent heresy" into which he had fallen. His chief support and first guides are Polish *pans* [magnates], whose purpose is clear—to destroy the Muscovite state and to introduce into it the "Jesuitical faith." The "delation of the monk Varlaam" thus augmented the list of documents intended to justify Shuisky's coup d'état of May 17, 1606. The original text of the report of Godunov's spy, let us repeat, presented a different picture: it made evident Dmitry's long-standing Muscovite connexions; it made evident the absolutely exceptional position that this boy-monk (Dmitry was given the tonsure at the age of 14) occupied in the household of the patriarch of Moscow, who took him with him even into the sovereign's duma. But even if we restore the genuine "delation," removing the bias imparted to it by the pamphleteer (which is not so easy, for we do not know just what cuts he made), we still do not, of course, get an accurate and truthful story of the first steps of the future tsar of Moscow. It is therefore interesting to turn to another Russian version of the affair; this is a much later one, nor is it free from official interpretation, but it gives the story that was circulated widely in Muscovite society; this does not, of course, guarantee accuracy in details, but it does remove the one definite bias. In this version the monk Varlaam is absent altogether; absent also are the adventures supposed to have attended the joint journey of Varlaam and the "tsarevich" from Russia; and there is no "Polish intrigue." Everything is presented much more simply and plausibly. Dmitry turns to the circle most likely to interest itself in his fate, to the Russian population living under Lithuanian rule, which in those days included many outright Muscovite émigrés. Varlaam's report, in a totally different connexion, names quite a few of the latter, connecting them in strange and unexpected fashion with the "loutish townsmen of Kiev." This scrap of the original "delation," accidentally left in by the Shuiskys' pamphleteer, is fully explained in the later version; among the population of "the mother of Russian towns," among both natives and newcomers from the confines of Muscovy, the cause of the Tsarevich Dmitry found its first proselytes. Soon Kiev becomes a centre whither flows all outlaw

Rus; Dmitry is visited by agents from the Zaporozhian cossack brother-hood and by a deputation from the cossacks of the Don; finally, but only when he already has a following, the Polish government begins to take an interest in him. The Poles were not so naïve as to be taken in by a high-sounding name; but when they sensed real strength behind the bearer of this name, this strength entered into the calculations of Polish diplomacy. Likewise it was no accident that Dmitry's party was formed on the Russian-Lithuanian border; we have direct evidence that this region had long been the scene of agitation in his favour, that rumours of a tsarevich had been circulating here since 1601. Delving into Dmitry's Muscovite past, so far as it is accessible, scholars invariably find that every agitation originates with the Romanov family, the Muscovite family second only to the Godunovs, connected with them by a certain "vow of testamentary union," but ultimately ruined by Tsar Boris. No one now considers the accusation and banishment of the Romanovs to have been utterly unwarranted; there can apparently be no doubt that a serious conspiracy lay at the root of the matter. And some modern historians are inclined to link this conspiracy with the appearance of the Tsarevich Dmitry. Evidently, Godunov's police did not succeed in arresting (or did not bother to arrest) all the participants in the affair; some, perhaps considered unimportant and secondary, remained at large. Tsar Boris was content to punish the most influential and popular of the conspirators, calculating, as an administration often does in like cases, on terrorising the rest. And, as almost always happens, the calculation went astray. The revolutionary elements were so numerous and multiplied so rapidly that the remnants of the conspiracy easily fused into a new organisation, which Godunov did not succeed in arresting. When its subterranean activities came out into the open, military measures had to replace police measures. But this put the odds in favour of the revolution.

The movement against Godunov immediately assumed the character of a military rebellion, a fact not to be lost sight of for a minute in appraising its successes. The Romanov pamphleteer, whom we have cited more than once, is far more intelligent and perspicacious than the "mercenary pen" of the Shuiskys; he gives a very clear and able description of the social elements that the Alleged Dmitry, advancing on Moscow from Kiev, was most likely to meet. The Russian ukraines [southern frontier provinces], through which he must pass, were the military boundary of the Muscovite realm; here it was not unusual to see one-half of the population reaping or mowing, the other half under arms, guarding the farmer from a sudden raid by the Tatars of the Crimea, an event hardly more uncommon in these areas than is a good thunder-storm in summer or a good snowstorm in winter. Pomeshchiks from central Russia regarded appointment to these posts as exile and came hither with extreme reluctance. In order to colonise these areas the government had to resort to the services of real exiles; as early as the reign of Ivan IV it had become the custom to commute punishments for crime, even capital punishment, into exile to these frontier provinces. Here they strove to utilise every newcomer, especially as a military element; a man sent from Moscow under arrest was immediately taken into the sovereign's service, received an arquebus or a horse, and became a strelets or a cossack. Under Godunov political exiles were added to this criminal element; they began to send to the ukraine "unreliable" men not dangerous enough to be executed and not famous enough to merit confinement in a monastery. This political contingent increased with extraordinary rapidity; the ruin of boyar families, first of the Mstislavskys and Shuiskys, later of the Romanovs, Belsky, and others, sent to the ukraine wave after wave of fresh involuntary colonists. All who were in any way connected with the fallen families, their whole "clientele," fell into the category of "unreliables," especially their "courts," *i.e.*, their military retainers. The author we have mentioned fixes the number of such exiles (of course, purely offhand, with no pretension to statistical accuracy) at twenty thousand souls. In any case, a whole army might be mustered from them alone, all the more so since, of course, they remained armed. Those who were taken directly into the sovereign's service represented the most untrustworthy of Boris' subjects; those who did not happen to be taken into the service joined that mass of men swaying from side to side of the border, who served the Moscow government when they found it advantageous and instantly converted themselves into "foreigners" as soon as this advantage vanished. The term "cossackdom" is usually applied by historians to this very mass, which was, however, not by any means amorphous or absolutely unorganised; military organisation is just what it did have and its elected *atamans* were able to maintain discipline over their followers as well as could any Muscovite general. This, too, was a ready military force, not a whit inferior to the forcibly recruited garrisons of the ukraine fortresses. To draw a line of demarcation between these men and others in these areas would be an impossible task; yesterday's "free" cossack to-day becomes a cossack in the sovereign's service, and to-morrow is "free" again. Just as difficult would it be to make a social distinction between these petty military servitors, who frequently secured small pomestyes, and genuine pomeshchiks, who in these areas never held large pomestyes. Among the cossacks there were, of course, wholly democratic elements, fugitive bondsmen, but their influence should not be exaggerated as is sometimes done. It was not they who worked out the ideology of the mass of cossacks. When this mass became a political force, it did not raise the slogan of freedom for the serfs, but a demand for estates, which would, of course, be worked by these serfs. The cossack was, as a rule, a petty pomeshchik in embryo, while the petty pomeshchik, of course, had no higher dream than to become a great one. Hence the cossacks and the mass of military servitors, Peresvetov's "needy warriors," understood one another so well and in the political outbreaks of the Troubles so often made common cause. Both the First and the Second Dmitrys were simultaneously the tsars of the cossacks and of the nobles. And it was only when it had definitely become clear that there were not enough estates for all, and that the new military servitors who had come with the "tsareviches" could become landholders only at the expense of the old ones, that the "nobles and knights" finally began to offer serious resistance to the "cossacks." When these rivals had again been crowded back to the ukraine, there arose anew that unstable equilibrium from which the Troubles had begun—and which was to become more stable only in proportion as the nobility consolidated its grip on Russia.

The appearance of the cossack armaments under Dmitry's banners was, therefore, the beginning of the rebellion of the nobles, and it was no accident that from the very first the pretender made promises "to give the military orders landed estates and to heap riches upon them." The decline of Boris' popularity among the nobles, then, was evidently no secret to the Russian émigrés in Lithuania; on the contrary, this was the very thing they had been speculating on when they revived the Romanov conspiracy. Had Tsar Boris been on the same terms with the pomeshchiks as in the year of his accession, it would have been ridiculous folly to raise a revolt against him. But now Godunov's army had to be driven into the field, and it was ready to take advantage of any convenient opportunity to decline battle. If the campaign of the alleged tsarevich was not wholly a triumphal procession, the explanation lies, on the one hand, in the mistakes of the immediate leaders, on the other, in the fact that Boris' military forces were not made up of his vassals alone. The Muscovite émigrés were not free from infatuation with the West (Dmitry's own Catholic sympathies are only one aspect of this phenomenon); they rated too low the military qualities of the force that rallied to them unsolicited, the military servitors of the border and the cossacks, and expected too much of the Polish detachments they had hired. As a matter of fact the latter cut no great figure, whereas the former saved the cause; surrender without a battle, in the course of the first weeks of the campaign, of a whole series of ukrainian fortresses—Chernigov, Putivl, Rylsk, Sevsk, Kursk, Belgorod, Tsarev-Borisov—put in the hands of the "tsarevich" a number of bases from which Boris' generals could not dislodge him even in what were for Dmitry the darkest days of the war. In substance, the splendid defence of Kromy by the Don ataman Korela decided the campaign; here the Muscovite army was definitely convinced that Godunov was not competent to cope with the "pretender," whence it was but a step to the conclusion that it was more advantageous to serve the Alleged Dmitry than to serve Tsar Boris. On closer examination of the military operations, beginning with the fall of 1604, we see that every time Dmitry meets serious resistance (as under Novgorod-Seversk, for example), the field is not held by the feudal army, but by the streltsy of Moscow (later the Guard) and foreign mercenaries, the rudiments of a regular military force. This fact was soon appreciated by Dmitry himself; he made haste to take Boris' *landsknechts* into his service and strove in every way, and with some success, to win the sympathy of the strelets army. But for these elements, new to the Muscovite army, the death agony of Boris' reign would have been of still shorter duration.

Yet there was nothing left but the agony. From the moment the "tsarevich" appeared in the open, Godunov's government lost its head and knew not what to do. Its military measures were most irresolute and stupid; it did not concentrate its armies where they were needed; it sent smaller armies than were needed; and it put at their head marshals manifestly untrustworthy, Mstislavskys and Shuiskys and Golitsyns. At the same time it vigorously strove to prove to all (and especially, it seems, to itself) that the "Tsarevich Dmitry" was none other than Grishka Otrepyev, as though calling the leader of the anti-Godunov revolution by his real name were enough to put an end to the revolution. This confusion on the part of their superiors was fully appreciated by the lower ranks, and the government army had begun to disperse even before Boris' death. At the moment of his death (April 13, 1605) it comprised, aside from the small regular detachments, hardly any but the most untrustworthy regiments, the local military servitors of the northern ukraine, who had not yet had time to go over to the pretender.

Under such circumstances there was no difficulty in forming a new conspiracy. There is such definite documentary evidence as to the elements that composed it as to leave no room for dispute; those who rose against Godunov were the middling pomeshchiks, who had been his chief support in the days when he was struggling with his rivals for power. The cossack movement was now passed on to the upper strata of the "warriors." Indeed, the chronicle even gives the names of those who were "in council" against Boris and his son; they were knights of Ryazan, Tula, Kashira, and Alexin, and foremost among them was "Prokopy Lyapunov with his brother and with his counsellors." Other sources name the knights of Novgorod as well as the "towns beyond the Oka." But the decisive fact, of course, was that the conspiracy was joined by the pomeshchiks of the provinces geographically nearest to the theatre of war. Half the Muscovite realm was actually in Dmitry's hands. If the other half had stood as resolutely for the reigning dynasty, there would have ensued civil war on a grand scale. That this was objectively possible the reign of Shuisky was to show. But the other half of the Muscovite realm, where land tenure conditioned on military service did not prevail, was made up of towns and a "black-plough" (unbondaged) peasantry, economically and socially linked to the bourgeoisie, and the bourgeoisie was not at all disposed to sacrifice itself for the Godunovs. Its relations with Boris had always remained a "bad peace," which was, of course, better than a "good quarrel," such as that in 1587, but which was very far removed from devoted loyalty. The "tsarevich" had good reason to count on the support of the townsmen, explaining in his letters that, under Boris, the gosts and trading folk had not had freedom in trade and customs, and that a third of their chattels had been taken by Godunov's government. In this respect both of Boris' policies—both the "noble" one of the first years and the "democratic" one of the later years—came to the same thing; whatever the tsar's treasury set about, whether gifts to the pomeshchiks or "feeding of the hungry," it had to be replenished at the expense of commercial capital. To save such a régime the townsmen gave not a single mite nor a single warrior. The collision between the noble conspirators headed by Lyapunov, and the detachments still loyal to Boris of the army besieging Kromy was the last act of the campaign of 1605. The correlation of forces was such, and so great was the confusion of the troops still left to the government, that the knights of Ryazan in alliance with the cossacks scattered them, almost without resort to arms. The Alleged Dmitry, who had continued to "sit it out" in Putivl, much to his own surprise received tidings (at the beginning of May, 1605) that there was no longer any one for him to fight. The boyars who nominally were commanding the now vanished armies and administering the country had no other recourse than to acknowledge the pretender. Their political rôle at this moment was as piteous as at the height of the oprichnina; again the rebellious nobility was the actual master of the state, and the boyars, no longer as a class, but simply as a throng of classic "courtiers," could utilise the moment merely to avenge on Boris' family what they had suffered in their time from the "slave tsar," who had raised the base-born above the well-born. Vengeance was so sweet that one of the best-born, Prince V. V. Golitsyn, did not refuse the function of executioner; under his eyes and under his guidance Godunov's widow and son were strangled. But even here the boyars were merely carrying out the designs of others, for the overthrow of the Godunovs was organised by agents of the "tsarevich" who had come from the army, and its accomplishment was possible only thanks to the neutrality of the Moscow townsmen, who not only did not lift a finger in defence of the "lawful government" but took an active part in the plunder of Godunov's "chattels," remembering how the late tsar had taken "a third of the chattels" from the townsmen.

The similarity between the order of things established at Moscow in the summer of 1605 and the oprichnina of Ivan the Terrible was not confined to the depressed position of the boyars. Like their fathers just forty years before, the pomeshchiks who had brought Dmitry to Moscow made extensive use of their victory; such an orgy of land distributions and money compensations had not been seen at Moscow for a long time, not even, indeed, in the days when Godunov was paying special court to the nobility. According to Tsar Dmitry's secretary, Buchinsky, the alleged son of Ivan the Terrible distributed in the first six months of his short reign seven and a half million rubles (at least a hundred million in modern rubles). Part of this money went into the pockets of the cossacks and the Polish mercenaries, but by far the greater part melted away in the form of wages to the Russian military servitors, whose money salaries without exception were exactly doubled: "who had 10 rubles pay, to him he bade be given 20 rubles, while whoso had a thousand, to him two were given." They evidently distributed all it was possible to distribute; the Russian chroniclers well remembered that "in this reign of the abominable Unfrocked Monk the abundant tsar's treasures of the Muscovite realm, gathered over many years, were exhausted." The author cited ascribes this, in the main, to the greed of the Polish and Lithuanian men of war; but another contemporary historian does not conceal the fact that the bounties of the "Unfrocked Monk" were not poured out on foreigners alone. Of the extraordinary distributions of land, paralleling the doubled pay, in 1605-1606, such a mass of documentary evidence has been preserved that we do not need to depend upon the chronicles; what is significant in the latter is the identification of "all the towns" (*i.e.*, the knights, the pomeshchiks, of all the towns) with "all the land"; as in the days of the oprichnina, the pomeshchiks were "all the land," because all the land was held by them. The enormous estates of the Godunovs might at first satisfy the new masters' greed for land; but there were in prospect measures of a more general character. They had already begun to confiscate portions of Church land, turning at the same time to the wealth of the monasteries to fill the rapidly emptying treasury chests; this circumstance should be constantly borne in mind when we hear of the "heresies" of the Alleged Dmitry. And confiscations of boyar estates threatened to extend beyond those of the kinsmen of the deposed dynasty; the fall of Vasily Shuisky, who in the first days of the new dynasty was condemned and banished, whether for an actual conspiracy or simply for malicious rumours about the new tsar. was another ominous reminder of the oprichnina.

Tsar Dmitry certainly recalled to men's minds his alleged father, and if there was no boyar conspiracy in the first weeks of his reign, when Shuisky was banished, one was bound to be formed very soon from the sheer instinct of self-preservation. All the more so since the position of the boyars was now less hopeless than it had been forty years before. Then they could demand justice from Ivan the Terrible only with the aid of Lithuania, a course imperiling their own orthodoxy; now the Orthodox Church itself was quite ready to co-operate with the boyars against the "Latinising" tsar. In Ivan's time—and this was most important—the military servitors had been supported by the Moscow townsmen, and the boyars, taken both in front and in rear, had no place of retreat; now the townsmen were very soon convinced that they had no more to expect from Dmitry than from Godunov, and ferment among the Moscow townsmen became more perceptible from day to day. Scattering references in the chronicles and other documents throw some light on the spread of this ferment among the various strata of the bourgeoisie of Moscow. The small traders, the shopkeepers, and artisans were not among the malcontents. The silver that found its way into the pockets of the nobles and of the cossacks was quickly converted into consumption values, and in the Moscow bazaars trade was brisk. Here, then, to the great chagrin of pious writers like our old friend the Romanov pamphleteer, very little attention was paid to the "heresies" of the "pretender." Here men were not disturbed until on the occasion of the tsar's marriage the unwonted influx of Poles (counting the household, armed and unarmed, there were some 6,000 of them), taken together with absurd rumours circulated by conspirators, roused downright fear for their skins; then the bazaars ceased to sell the newcomers powder and lead. Uneasiness must have developed much earlier amongst the large capitalists. Among those who had brought the Alleged Dmitry to Moscow had been the most democratic elements of the "warriors," the pettiest pomeshchiks of the Russian South and even those who, like the cossacks, were only candidates for that status. Even under Ivan the Terrible the petty military servitors had been in the clutches of money capital, and the Tsar's Sudebnik of 1550 had had to limit their right to sell themselves into bondage by restricting its exercise to those "whom the tsar released from service." The indenturing of military servitors had continued under Godunov; at this period very many wealthy men, beginning with the tsar himself, "took to themselves many men to serve in bondage," and among these bondsmen were "chosen swordbearers, strong with weapons in warfare," and at the same time holding "villages and vineyards." The spread of indentured bondage was, then, a fact to which the military-serving masses were by no means indifferent, and which for the lower ranks was wholly undesirable. A decree of Dmitry's boyar duma (January 7, 1606), considerably restricting indenture by making it purely personal (so that on the death of the master the bondsman became free), was therefore in harmony with the policy of the new tsar in favour of the nobles, merely reminding us that he had behind him, not only wealthy pomeshchiks like the Lyapunovs, but also petty military servitors. With good reason did the pettiest of the petty, the cossacks, now walk the streets of Moscow, where in their time more than one of them had experienced bondage, with shining faces extolling their "blessed sun," Tsar Dmitry. But this turn of the government's policy could not be pleasing to those who made a business of money-lending, and the Romanov pamphleteer, who was close to upper bourgeois circles, severely condemns both the "robber cossacks" and the fickle Muscovites who hearkened to them.

This new policy manifestly served the interests of the lower strata of the military-serving masses rather than of the whole class; sometimes perhaps it was not without prejudice to the interests of the upper strata and thereby affected Dmitry's security; the fact that the coup against him met with hardly any resistance at Moscow itself was not at all unconnected with the fact that the nobility of the vicinity of the capital had received fewest of the tsar's favours. The alleged son of Ivan the Terrible was not merely the tsar of the nobility but, more immediately, the tsar of a very definite group of the nobility, of the knights of the ukraine and from beyond the Oka, as another boyar decree (February 1, 1606) makes apparent. This decree deprived pomeshchiks of the right of seeking and demanding back those peasants who had left them during the years of the famine; "he was not able to feed his peasant in the famine years, and now he shall not seize him." But Muscovite emigration had been from north to south and from the centre to the frontiers; it was at the expense of the depopulated regions round Moscow that the ever multiplying estates of pomeshchiks were growing up like mushrooms in the black-soil of the southern steppe where there was a shortage of labour. It was not surprising that Dmitry's name was so popular in the south, popular long after its bearer had been slain and burned, and his ashes scattered to the winds.

To depose the armed Dmitry seemed far more difficult than to overcome the Godunovs deserted by their army. The Alleged Dmitry was genuinely tsar of the military men, and his military suite did not for a minute forsake him. Through the city he always "went with many military, before and behind him they walked in armour with partisans and halberds and many other weapons," so that it was "dreadful for all to see the multitude of gleaming weapons"; in these excursions the boyars and magnates had no part. And the military men loved Dmitry; when conspiracy penetrated the Strelets Quarter, the streltsy slew the traitors with their own hands; and on the day of the catastrophe they were the last to quit the tsar.

But there was a reverse side to the picture. A military man by nature, Dmitry could not sit still. The interests of the southern pomeshchiks, who suffered chronically from the Tatars of the Crimea, also urged him to a campaign—and in the south; the men of Moscow, terrified in the past by Tatar raids, said, not without terror and not without reproach to the tsar, that Dmitry was "teasing" the khan of the Crimea, sending him, it was said, a pigskin coat. In the central and northern provinces men did not feel toward a distant campaign in the steppe as did men in the south. Meanwhile, such a campaign was daily becoming more inevitable; Dmitry was actively mobilising his army and organising enormous magazines at Yelets; thither he ordered the greater part of the Muscovite artillery, thereby adding to the terror of the Muscovites, who felt that the tsar "had emptied Moscow and other cities for that fortress." All these fears were played on by conspirators, who systematically circulated rumours that the tsar was "stirring up the race of the Hagarenes" for no good purpose, and for no good purpose was stripping the centre of the realm of its military forces; all this was being done to "betray the Christian race" and to facilitate the seizure of unarmed Moscow by the Poles. These rumours found favourable soil even in the ranks of the military-serving class; a campaign against the Crimea alienated the sympathies of the northern pomeshchiks from the Alleged Dmitry. The knights of Belozersk or Novgorod were not at all pleased with the prospect of going a thousand versts to fight for the interests of their confreres beyond the Oka. At the same time, in moving the troops in the direction of the steppe, it was the northern regiments that were gathered around Moscow, while the southern ones were waiting for the tsar on the steppe frontier. Three thousand Novgorod knights turned out to be the military force of the conspiracy, in conjunction with the "courts" of the boyar conspirators [8] and the townsmen, whom the boyars provided with arms; these were sufficient to cope with Dmitry's German guard and even to make the Moscow streltsy waver. In any case, they sufficed for a surprise attack, on which the Shuiskys and their companions were counting.

Their calculations were strengthened by the self-confidence of Dmi-

[8] There is information that on this occasion the Shuiskys in particular mustered their full strength from their hereditary estates.

try, who believed that he "held all in his hands, like an egg, and was utterly loved by many." This self-confidence had certain objective bases; the tsar's calculations were not merely evidence of his light-headedness, they were the result of false political courses, a political mistake. The history of his accession must have given him a false notion of the specific gravity of the Muscovite boyars; he had not forgotten their humble and passive rôle on that occasion or the absence of solidarity among them that had been so manifest in the case of Shuisky, deserted by every one as soon as the tsar's ban overtook him. To Dmitry it seemed that there was nothing to be feared from the boyars at all; at the same time recollections of his childhood and early youth must have given him an equally false notion of the correlation of forces within boyar circles. Brought up by the Romanovs, Dmitry had easily become accustomed to the idea that they stood at the head of the Muscovite aristocracy, and that, with them on his side, there was nothing to be feared from the others. With the Romanovs he had striven to remain on good terms: Fedor Romanov, banished and given the tonsure by Godunov, became the Metropolitan Filaret; Ivan, the only other surviving brother, became a boyar. The indubitable participation of the Romanovs in the conspiracy against Dmitry constitutes one of the most obscure aspects of this affair. It offers some notion of the hostile temper in Moscow itself toward the end of his reign; even those whom Tsar Dmitry cherished did not venture to support him. That even in the mantle of a metropolitan Fedor Romanov remained a boyar and had no reason to feel particular sympathy for the tsar of the nobility, who had manifest "Latin" inclinations at that, may also have played a rôle. However that may be, those on whose "love" Dmitry had some reason to reckon actually stood in the ranks of his opponents. For this blow from behind he was utterly unprepared, and he cannot be blamed for that.

The decisive factor was the downright tactlessness of Dmitry's Polish partisans, who throughout his brief history brought him far more trouble than profit. The mercenaries brought by the Polish guests who gathered for the wedding of the tsar and his Polish bride conducted themselves very disreputably, and, as we have seen, they were so numerous that the rumours of Polish usurpation began to seem justified. In connexion with all that had gone before, this brought the Moscow mob to such a nervous pitch that the conspirators began to fear a premature outburst. It is possible that they had previously intended to make an end of the tsar during the campaign; now they had to risk the bolder stroke of reaching Dmitry in his own palace. The confidence the Alleged Dmitry placed in his intimate servants undoubtedly facilitated matters. It is noteworthy that the boyar conspirators, in sounding the tocsin in the bazaars, did not venture to move the townsmen against the Kremlin but directed them against the Poles; for the immediate purpose of murdering the "Unfrocked Monk" they despatched a small detachment, 200 strong and specially selected, which was readily admitted to the very sleeping-quarters of the tsar because it was headed by the foremost boyars of Moscow. The chronicles agree in naming Prince Vasily Shuisky, who had recently been allowed by the "Unfrocked Monk" to return from exile, and his brother Prince Dmitry; but they were accompanied by "many other boyars and magnates." Later we find Mstislavsky, the Golitsyns, and Ivan Romanov active on the streets of Moscow. According to later narratives Vasily Shuisky had a most direct part in the murder; in defending him from Tsar Dmitry, "many boyars and nobles" are said to have thrown themselves on the tsar. But the Shuiskys' pamphlet, as well as the Romanovs' pamphleteer, alike skim over the details of this tragic night; evidently these recollections brought satisfaction neither to the one nor to the other.

One would think that in going about this business, which must inevitably result in leaving the throne of Moscow vacant, the conspirators must beforehand have thought over how this vacancy was to be filled. As a matter of fact, however, they had not done so; for two whole days and nights Moscow was without a tsar. In boyar circles they had been silent about a candidate, an indication how burning was the question. They might quarrel over it, they feared, on the eve of the event and thus break up the whole conspiracy. This in itself should dispel the idea, so widespread in modern literature, of an "aristocratic camarilla," a "boyar cabal." A camarilla would have been able to agree to work in harmony, but here we perceive no accord of opinions or actions. If any of the conspirators had a definite plan of action, it was Vasily Shuisky alone, and he hastened to make use of his advantage. While the rest of the boyars were confusedly talking about the need of "holding a council . . . and by common counsel electing a tsar over the Muscovite realm," of the need of sending out letters about a zemsky sobor, as had been done in 1598,—talking, evidently, with the sole purpose of protracting matters—the Moscow townsmen acclaimed Vasily Shuisky tsar. That his accession was a sort of conspiracy within a conspiracy, a complete surprise for the majority of the members of the fancied "camarilla," is equally attested by Russian and by foreign sources. The semi-official chronicle of the Troubles, which we have just cited, after relating the boyars' perplexed talk of a zemsky sobor, continues: "but certain of the magnates and of the. people made haste and without common counsel elected a tsar from the magnates—the boyar Prince Vasily Shuisky . . .; not all had a share in his election, either in the provinces, or even at Moscow itself." The author of the Romanov pamphlet gives a consonant version: "by certain small men of the tsar's palaces Vasily Shuisky was chosen to be tsar . . . by none of the magnates disputed, by the rest of the people not entreated." The latter author is undoubtedly biased on this point, for in 1606 the Romanovs were rivals of the Shuiskys, as they had been of the Godunovs in 1598; but his bias is expressed in the fact that he denies the people's participation in the election of Shuisky, and not in the fact that he denies the boyars' participation. Shuisky "raised himself up without the will of all the land" inasmuch as not all the estates and not all the provinces of the Muscovite realm had shared in making him tsar. But the "people" had been involved, and the meaning of this term is made quite plain by a foreigner who witnessed the election. "The crown was offered him," Conrad Bussow says, "by the inhabitants of Moscow only, loyal fellow-participants in the murder of Dmitry, merchants, bootmakers, pastry-cooks, and a few boyars." Shuisky was the townsmen's tsar, as the Alleged Dmitry had been the tsar of the nobles. Herein was the novelty of his position. There had been more than one tsar of the nobles; such had been Ivan the Terrible in the second half of his reign, and Godunov in the first half of his. But not once had a representative of the bourgeoisie sat on the throne of Moscow; it remained a question whether he could keep it when quiet had been restored in Moscow, and life had resumed its normal course.

The "self-enthronement" of Vasily Shuisky for the moment absolutely stupefied boyar circles, all the more so since, apart from the new tsar's relatives, the "few boyars" initiated into the second conspiracy apparently meant none but the Romanovs. Filaret [Romanov], it seems, was to be patriarch, while Shuisky was to be tsar. Why the agreement was not kept, and why Filaret had to go to Tushino for his patriarchate are not questions of great historical interest. Whether in consequence of the breach between the Shuiskys and the Romanovs or from some other cause, the confusion of the boyars soon began to pass off; once there was no question of sharing the Cap of Monomakh, the boyars again formed the same friendly wall as when they had gone to slay the "Unfrocked Monk." Since they had not succeeded in setting up their own tsar, they must insure themselves against the other fellow's, and it seemed likely that Shuisky, relying on the merchants, would offer less resistance than had Dmitry, surrounded by the "warriors." During the coronation ceremony, in the church, was enacted a strange scene, at first sight utterly unintelligible. The tsar-designate suddenly began to talk about wanting to take an oath that he would not take vengeance on any one for what he had suffered in Boris' reign, and that in general he "would wreak" nothing on any one "without common counsel." The boyars and others began to tell him not to do so and not to take oath

on it: "for never had such been done, and he should do nothing new."
But Shuisky did not listen and took the oath.

If we accept the customary view of Shuisky as the boyars' tsar, none
of this can be understood. The boyars had long wished to limit the
tsar's power, to protect themselves against tyranny from above; the
new tsar undertakes to swear he will not be tyrannical, and the boyars
attempt to dissuade him. But if we read Shuisky's words attentively,
we shall understand what a loophole this astute diplomat had left himself. "Common counsel," both in the general language of that time and
in the particular narrative of Shuisky's election in the *New Chronicle,*
which we are citing, is a synonym for "zemsky sobor." The boyars had
just been appealing to this institution against Shuisky; now he is appealing to the sobor against the boyars, declaring that he is prepared
to limit his authority, but only by "common counsel," not by the boyar
duma. Thereupon the boyars very naïvely give themselves away, dis-
closing that they themselves had not been talking seriously about the
zemsky sobor, but merely for the sake of delay. But Tsar Vasily himself wished only to frighten the boyars; in actual fact, of course, it was
no part of his plan to summon the vassals of the Muscovite realm, the
majority of whom were undoubtedly on the side of the murdered Dmitry.

In this very first skirmish it was shown that the boyars were the
stronger; in the official copy of the oath circulated in the provinces the
tsar promised "not to hand over any man to death, without judging him
by true judgment with his boyars." Contrary to the opinion of certain
modern historians, this was a colossal gain for the boyars. Even if
Shuisky's oath merely ratified traditional Muscovite usage, it would
have no less significance than had ratification of mestnichestvo usages
under Ivan the Terrible. But we have no assurance at all that since the
time of the oprichnina political trials had been handled in conjunction
with the boyar duma, "by true judgment"; on the contrary, there is
every reason to believe that they were dealt with by inquisitional (not
judicial) methods, on the model set by guba institutions. The boyars
who had "harassed and chided" the Romanovs at their prosecution
under Godunov were not judges but prosecutors appointed by Boris.
Shuisky's oath restored judicial process where since the time of the
oprichnina an administrative tribunal had prevailed.

But the oath went further; it contained limitation of judicial reprisal.
Hitherto the latter had been collective; the ban fell upon the whole family, and all the hereditary estates of the banned family were subjected
to confiscation. Herein, as we saw, had lain the economic significance
of oprichnina policy; hereditary lands had passed *en masse* into the
hands of the "warriors." Now there was to be an end to these mass

confiscations: "hereditary estates, and homesteads, and chattels shall not be taken from their [the condemneds'] brothers, and wives, and children, be they not with them in thought." This substitution of individual for group responsibility is extraordinarily important from the sociological viewpoint; but for the present we shall not discuss this aspect of the matter. Let us merely note that it lends special emphasis to the boyar character of Shuisky's "constitution"; it was only the boyars who suffered from confiscation of the hereditary estates of relatives. The authors of the document felt this themselves, and inasmuch as the new government really rested on the support, not of the boyars but of the Moscow townsmen, the "boyar" articles of the constitution received a no less curious supplement: "likewise in the case of gosts and trading folk, though by trial and by inquest it be a capital offense, their homesteads and shops and chattels shall not be taken from their wives and children, be they not guilty with them in that offence. . . ."

The Russian "charter of liberties" thus protected the interests of the boyars on the one hand and the gosts and trading folk on the other. The nobility, however, it did not affect, and in the struggle with the rebellion of the nobles that immediately broke out afresh, executions and exile by administrative process were employed at every step. This was limitation of the tsar's authority, not in favour of "all the land" but in favour of only two classes, which after all had at the moment no positive interests in common. They did have a common foe, the middling and petty military servitors, who through the medium of the tsar's treasury had exploited the trading folk and through the medium of the tsar's authority had expropriated the boyars. So long as this common foe remained unconquered, they managed in some way to maintain an alliance. But when this foe gave way and the allies had to build anew, it soon developed that their interests were incompatible. Economic kinship proved stronger than a temporary political combination, and in the end the two economically new classes, the townsmen and the pomeshchiks, made common cause against the representatives of economic reaction, the boyars. Shuisky's four-year reign was a sort of *mariage de convenance* between commercial capital and boyar hereditary landholding, in which both parties hated and suspected each other but could not make up their minds to break off the union until an external impetus compelled it.

The boyars could not break the alliance, if only for the reason that without the aid of commercial capital they simply could not rule. The murdered Dmitry had prepared a grievous lot for his foes; upon his accession the new tsar was confronted with empty treasure chests. "The tsar who lacks great treasure and valiant friends is like unto an eagle without plumes and without beak or talons; poverty and straitness have come to all the men of war," and the men of war did not follow Tsar Vasily. The extraordinary measures to which he was driven in order to give even minimum pay to the military servitors who did support him showed to what "straitness" he was reduced. The zealot for Orthodoxy, who had just vanquished the "unclean heretic," had to follow in the latter's footsteps; laying hands on the monasteries' treasuries and even on the monasteries' sacristies, he melted down the church utensils offered up "for the soul" by former tsars. But all this did not suffice, and if Shuisky's government held out for four years, it was due only to the "trading folk"; without the aid of the littoral and lowland towns, both in men and in money, it would not have survived the first rebellion.

This rebellion, it may be said, inevitably ensued from Dmitry's murder. The brief reaction under Boris (after the pretender's first accidental failure) had cost the frontiersmen who had brought the Alleged Dmitry to Moscow so dear that they dared not wait for a reckoning from the Muscovites, who had now vanquished the "Unfrocked Monk." In the words of a contemporary, the frontiersmen were confident that the new tsar was preparing for them the fate that Novgorod had experienced under Ivan the Terrible. "One may be astonished," writes Professor Platonov, "how quickly and heartily the southern [fortress] towns rose against Tsar Vasily Shuisky. As soon as news of the pretender's death reached the [frontier provinces], Putivl, Livny, and Yelets immediately fell away from Moscow, and were soon followed by the whole ukraine, as far as Kromy. A little later rose the country beyond the Oka around Ryazan. The movement spread eastward from Ryazan to the province of the Mordvins. It even crossed the Volga to Vyatka and Kama into the Perm region. Remote Astrakhan rose. From the other direction, interference took place on the western frontiers of the realm, in the districts of Tver, Pskov, and Novgorod." In October, 1606, less than six months after Vasily's accession, the southern insurgents were already under Moscow itself. The author we have just cited quite correctly says that "in the ukraine in 1606 those who rose against Shuisky's government were the same men who had earlier been active against the Godunovs." But there were new elements also, and here he characterises the southern movement of this year as a "revolt of bondsmen and peasants against their lords." This is precisely the title of the chapter dedicated to the subject in the *New Chronicle*. The compiler of the latter was, apparently, particularly close to the patriarch's court, and the light he gives on the southern revolt is undoubtedly borrowed from the patriarch's letters of the period; these letters of the Patriarch Hermogen have come down to us in the original (or, what for our purposes amounts to the same thing, the official) version. In them it is actually said that the "knaves" (in Muscovite official language this term corresponded to "malefactors" in modern police documents) in their "cursed sheets" (proclamations) "bid the boyars' bondsmen slay their lords, and promise them their wives and their estates, and they bid the despicable and unspeakable knaves to slay the gosts and all the trading folk and to plunder their chattels, and they summon their knaves to them and want to give them the rank of boyars and voevodas and other high officials." But this text makes evident the imprudence of the assertion that the "knaves" posited "as the goal of the popular movement not only a political but also a social revolution." What kind of a social revolution would it be to transfer the estates of Shuisky's partisans to those of their bondsmen who had joined the movement? The estates would have changed hands, but their internal organisation would, of course, have remained intact. This stability of the old order is particularly clear in the other promise of the "knaves," namely, to make the bondsmen boyars and voevodas and other high officials; that is, the whole Muscovite hierarchy was to be taken over, and when the "knaves" had firmly established themselves near Moscow, it was reproduced at Tushino, the "knaves' " capital.

There is no doubt that we are here dealing with twofold demagogy. In the first place, in raising against the boyars the enserfed population of the boyars' hereditary estates, the leaders of the rebellion against Shuisky did not hesitate to make promises, not expecting that they would have to redeem them and trusting that in case of need the armed pomeshchiks could easily cope with a peasant revolt if it got beyond useful bounds. In the second place, in inciting against the "knaves" the urban bourgeoisie and such of the landholders of northern and central Russia as were still wavering, the patriarch laid emphasis on just those aspects of the "knaves' " programme that were bound to be particularly odious to these classes. The result was a picture of something very like social revolution, a picture somewhat premature. The chief fighting force of the insurgents' army was again made up of those same nobles and knights of Ryazan, headed by the Lyapunovs and the Sumbulovs, who had tipped the scales in favour of the Alleged Dmitry in May, 1605. When Shuisky succeeded (in November, 1606), by way of what were doubtless grievous sacrifices, in winning over this portion of the rebels, he was at once able to take the offensive. Along with them, of course, we find the cossacks; one of the deserters who followed Lyapunov and Sumbulov was the "cossack ataman Istomka Pashkov," who, with a retinue of four hundred men, "beat his forehead" into the service of Tsar Vasily, evidently calculating that this rather than revolt was the easiest way for him and his comrades to become pomeshchiks. Istomka Pashkov himself, moreover, was a typical example of that intermediate class that wavered constantly between the "free cossack" and the "liege

knight''; a ''cossack ataman'' in the chronicle, in official documents he
is noted as a military servitor, and not even as one with a very small
pomestye. The social side of the movement is represented by the former bondsman Ivan Bolotnikov, after whom the whole rebellion is frequently called ''Bolotnikov's revolt.'' But how little this meant as yet
is evident from the fact that his former master, Prince Telyatevsky,
was one of the leaders of the same ''knave'' army. The social movement was beginning to rise—but only later was it to reach flood-tide.

The immediate outcome for Prokopy Lyapunov serves as a good example of the motives behind the movement and of the means Shuisky
employed to cope with it. After his betrayal of the insurgents' cause
Lyapunov became a member of the sovereign's duma and together with
his comrade, Sumbulov, was appointed voevoda at Ryazan; in other
words, Shuisky surrendered Ryazan to the nobles' party, which had
supported the Alleged Dmitry, both before and after his death. Having become masters in their own house, the men of Ryazan agreed to
suffer Shuisky at Moscow, and henceforth we see them among the loyal
subjects of Tsar Vasily. Only relatively, as we see, can this be called a
''victory'' for Shuisky, even if we overlook the circumstance that he
never recovered the lost ukraine. One more example of the government
publicism of those days, constituting a good parallel to the pamphlet
we are already acquainted with, may serve as evidence of his critical
position in the first year of his reign. That pamphlet, as we shall remember, was issued in the summer of 1606 and confined itself to falsification of natural, mundane events. In the autumn, heavenly forces were
brought into play; a certain archpriest, Terenty (whose literary talent
had previously served the Alleged Dmitry, and who later entered the
service of the Polish King Sigismund), disclosed to the Moscow public
the visions that had appeared to ''a certain cleric,'' who wished to remain unknown. In the night the holy man, half asleep, half awake,
found himself in the Moscow Cathedral of the Annunciation, and there
he saw an awful scene: Christ Himself, in the presence of the Virgin
Mary, John the Baptist, and all the apostles and saints, who had point
for point the same appearance as when depicted on icons, was meting
out justice to Moscow, its tsar, patriarch, and people. The sentence
was severe, and the people of Moscow, the ''new Israel,'' would for
their numerous sins have been condemned to perdition but for the intervention of the Virgin Mary, who prayed the Saviour to give the Muscovites time to repent. At the tsar's command the ''vision'' was read
in the cathedral, and there can, of course, be not the slightest doubt
that the dexterous and pliant pen of the Moscow archpriest was working,
here as always, in strict conformity with official instructions. Moscow's
position in these days (mid-October, 1606) was really such that there

seemed to be no possibility of getting out of it except in a supernatural way. "The accursed ones," writes Shuisky's official publicist, "plotted to beset the city round about and to close all the roads, that no one might go out of the city or into the city, that no one might bring aid to the city from anywhere; and thus they did. In the city of Moscow on all men was great fear and alarm; from the beginning of the city never was there such woe." The "vision," testifying that the Virgin Mary herself was protecting the city with her prayers, was bound to raise the spirit of the unfortunate Muscovites, who might now in their turn expect what the frontiersmen had expected from Moscow on Shuisky's accession. To save themselves from such a calamity it was permissible to seat more than one of the "knave" voevodas in the duma.

Even after the militia of the southern pomeshchiks and cossacks had been dissipated by desertions, and the first army from the north (the streltsy from the towns along the northern Dvina) had come to the aid of Tsar Vasily, the tsar's armies were for long unable to crush the remnants of Bolotnikov's militia. Shuisky's generals were beaten off from Kaluga; Tula, where Bolotnikov later established himself, was taken by treachery after a long and difficult siege and even then not unconditionally; the last soldiers of the "knave" army, having surrendered their leaders, took oath to Tsar Vasily. Yesterday's political offenders to-day again became military servitors of the tsar and grand prince. It was quite evident that at the first pretext things would begin all over again. By the time that Tula surrendered, the occasion was already at hand; the capitulation took place on October 10, while since the end of August the "miraculously saved" Dmitry had been at Starodub-Seversk with a military force far more terrible as such for the bourgeois tsar than Bolotnikov's bands had been—with approximately ten thousand regular Polish cavalry and infantry, headed by the most experienced and talented Polish condottieri, Rozynski and Lisowski. The march to Moscow with the first Dmitry had for men of this type served as a reconnaissance. Now they "knew the road" and saw that the Muscovite government was as weak as ever; it would have been strange not to make use of this knowledge. In the spring of 1608 the Second Dmitry (whose identity has interested absolutely no one, not even in his own time) routed the Muscovite armament sent south against him, and in the summer of this year Moscow was again in the same position as at the height of Bolotnikov's revolt. For the capital to be in a state of siege (external not internal) was becoming the normal condition of this reign.

CHAPTER X

THE TROUBLES (*Continued*)

3. The "Better" Men and the "Lesser" Men

AT first sight the last two years of Shuisky's reign (from the summer of 1608 to July 15, 1610) seem a repetition of the events of 1605-1607, a new outburst, in the old form and under the old slogans, of the same civil war. On the stage again appears a Dmitry, juridically identical with the one who in the autumn of 1604 had entered the field against Godunov. Again he is supported by the cossacks, loyal to the end, and by the mass of the petty military servitors, the nobles and knights of the provinces. The social soil that nourished "pretenderism" was absolutely independent of local conditions; everywhere and always, with the most diverse personal motives and under the most diverse pretexts, the petty vassals followed Dmitry. The petty pomeshchiks around Moscow joined the men of Tushino, who were besieging the Troitsa Monastery, lest their estates be plundered; in Vyatka the commandant of the town and the streltsy "drank a cup in the tavern to Tsar Dmitry" because they did not want the fighting men to be taken from their region to Moscow. Even where they were acting as "government troops" against the "knaves," the provincial pomeshchiks soon made common cause with the latter. The knights of Kostroma and Galich arrived under Yaroslavl to fight Lisowski's detachments, then wanted to carry off the tsar's artillery for the men of Tushino, and a little later we see them with Lisowski's men destroying Kostroma.

The townsmen, on the other hand, always showed themselves loyal servants of Shuisky; when, toward the spring of 1609, victory seemed to be inclining to Tsar Vasily's side, he himself ascribed this gain to the men of Vologda, Belozersk, Kostroma, Galich, Vyatka, and "the elders and townsmen of divers other towns." They did indeed stand up for him "without sparing their chattels"; Ustyug Veliki alone up to the spring of 1609 had sent five "hosts" to the aid of the Moscow government, *i.e.*, it had raised recruits five times and, failing to recruit a sixth "host" only because there were no men left to take, had fallen to hiring "free cossack volunteers" for the service of the sovereign. Of special importance to Shuisky in those years was Vologda, which temporarily replaced besieged Moscow as the centre of foreign trade. There "all the better men gathered, the gosts of Moscow with valuable wares and their treasury, and the tsar's great treasury, sables from Siberia and foxes, and all kinds of furs," and in addition, "English Germans" also gathered there with "expensive wares" and with "fine drink" (imported wines). Even more clearly than in the case of the military servitors who supported Dmitry, social motives definitely superseded local interests; not only the local people, the men of Vologda and the Moscow merchants who had come to Vologda, but also the foreign gosts aided Moscow. The English merchantry, too, was on the side of Shuisky.

Least of all on the side of this "tsar of the boyars" (as the textbooks have it) were the boyars themselves. By the end of his rule it was hardly possible to find among Vasily's partisans, aside from his personal relatives and kinsmen, a single representative of the feudal aristocracy. The Romanovs and their circle were the first to leave him, and it was they who took the most extreme steps. Ivan Nikitich Romanov, sent with an army against the Second Dmitry, became involved in a regular conspiracy, designed to repeat what had happened under Kromy in May, 1605. The conspiracy failed, and the Romanovs' nearest relatives were banished for it. From exile they soon passed into the camp of Tushino, where gradually assembled the whole Romanov clan, headed by its senior member, the Metropolitan Filaret. In Tushino Filaret became patriarch, an episode which was afterward deemed so compromising that it was not mentioned in his official biography; but contemporaries refer to it so frequently and with such unanimity that there can be no doubt about the fact itself, even though loyal and pious men, from perfectly intelligible motives, have striven to explain it in a light favourable to Filaret Nikitich. The Golitsyns, next in rank to the Romanovs and the Shuiskys, followed a different course, but they, too, were numbered among the open ill-wishers of Tsar Vasily; their most eminent representative, Prince V. V. Golitsyn, later headed the rebellion that deposed the Shuiskys. The lesser "princelings," without presuming, like the Golitsyns, to essay an independent political rôle, did not eschew the "knave's" court since the Romanovs by their presence there had given it a certain respectability. A Prince Shakhovskoi was "servant" to the "knave," a Prince Zvenigorodsky was steward; the Princes Trubetskoi, Zasekin, and Baryatinsky sat as boyars in his duma. A Polish spy's report from Moscow at the end of Shuisky's reign said that only a few clerks "act uprightly" toward the tsar, and hardly any of the boyars.

With a duma so constituted, and with a Romanov as patriarch, Tushino seemingly differed but little from the capital of the First Dmitry. Nevertheless, on closer examination of the army that followed the second "pretender," we perceive marked differences from that host of nobles which, in 1605, had brought the First Dmitry to Moscow. The first of these differences, and the earliest to strike both contemporaries and later historians, consists in the predominant rôle the Poles played at Tushino. The Romanov pamphleteer, apparently writing at the end of 1609, while Shuisky was still tsar (that is, before Sigismund's attempt to seize the throne of Moscow, and therefore before the struggle assumed a nationalist complexion), none the less discusses this fact at length and with great pathos. In his words, the Poles, though in the minority, dealt with the Russian "traitors" as with their own subjects and, sending them first into battle, took the best part of the booty for themselves. We must not, we repeat, see a nationalistic tendency in this; there was as yet no room for that. Our author's characterisation of the Poles is in general rather sympathetic; in contrast to the Russians of Tushino they are depicted as men not devoid of a certain chivalry: for example, they did not kill their prisoners and did not permit their Russian comrades to kill them when they acted together in battle; whereas, when acting alone, the Russian "knaves" committed the greatest excesses.

And yet, in the description of these "knaves" is revealed another, and much more curious, feature of the Tushino movement; it presents a social physiognomy other than what we should expect from a rebellion of military servitors against a boyar who had been made tsar by the bourgeoisie. The Tushino detachments are particularly fond of ruining the wealthy and taking away their possessions. Where the possessions were too numerous to be carried off, they destroyed them, chopped them up, threw them into the water; "they smashed all the entrances and barriers, so that no one might dwell there." Here we have a picture strikingly similar to the familiar scene of the destruction of a landlord's mansion in Russia of the early twentieth century. When the author passes to acts of personal violence, we find "many bondsmen abusing their lords" and slaying them. We shall not torment the reader with a description of the furies of servile vengeance, but noteworthy in the highest degree is the author's admission that there were grounds for vengeance, that the lords had deserved the ferocious hatred of their slaves. The picture of how the wealthy "live by filthy usury" and take trouble with the taverns "in order to tempt all the world," and with the money acquired by extortions and depredations "found churches of God," and hear not the voices of the poor, "bid them be beaten on the face and on the breast, and with rods, which are wickeder than wicked, they break their bones, and to fetters and to dungeons . . . they condemn them"—this is one of the most vivid pictures, not only in this pamphlet but in all the literature of the Troubles. But if the excesses of Tushino could be explained only by bringing to mind all the social evil that had accumulated in Muscovite Rus by the beginning of the seventeenth century, it is evident that our author was not concerned with the mere rancour, "more malignant than devils," of the Russians who had taken the part of the "tsarlet" of Tushino. The rebellion of the lower social classes against the higher, which it would have been premature to trace in the cossack movements or in Bolotnikov's revolt, now really begins to manifest itself under the protection of the Tushino detachments.

Here the national composition of the latter was not irrelevant; pomeshchiks in revolt still remained pomeshchiks, and as regards peasant flights and peasant bondage Shuisky's foe was at one with Shuisky's partisan. Gathering under Moscow with the cossacks at the most critical moment—the summer of 1611—the knights do not for a minute forget that fugitive peasants and bondsmen must be "given back on inquest to the old pomeshchiks." Had the army of Tushino been composed only of *Russian* landlords, the Romanov pamphleteer would have had no occasion to describe the scenes we have presented above. The Polish mercenary detachments were in a different position; though nobles themselves, they were not bound by community of interests with the local pomeshchiks since they did not intend to remain in the country. The dual difficulty of coping with a social movement indirectly supported by foreign detachments who were parasites in the country could not but be clear to men observing matters at close range and in such detail as is no longer possible to us, especially when these men were directly interested in the matter. The patriotism of the Russian pomeshchiks, which blazed up so brightly in 1611-1612, was not without foundation. It was, like all patriotism, a special form of class self-preservation.

We shall presently see what special causes after the fall of Shuisky intensified this feeling and compelled the pomeshchiks to forget all their differences and to move in serried ranks against the foreigners who had taken root in the country. But we shall likewise see that this movement, which was purely the affair of the nobles, was predestined to failure, whereas the pomeshchik rising of 1612, which relied on commercial capital, was to triumph. What interest did capital have in the struggle against the Polish-Tushino army? Thus far we have accepted as a fact that the townsmen were on Shuisky's side; but this requires more explanation than the mere fact that the bourgeoisie of Moscow had seated Tsar Vasily on the throne. Long before 1610 the bourgeoisie had evidence enough that its chosen sovereign was "unlucky," and that on his account "Christian blood flows ceaselessly."

It is time to analyse this concept of "bourgeoisie," which we have hitherto employed as self-explanatory. Fortunately our sources supply sufficient material for the purpose. In standing for Tsar Vasily and later against Tsar Vladislav, the towns, frequently cut off from their organisational centre at Moscow, were bound to elaborate their own organisation, and to this end they maintained active relations among themselves. A number of documents relating to their correspondence with each other are extant; the earliest are the "answers" of the men of Ustyug to the men of Solvychegodsk at the end of November, 1608. The starting point for the correspondence between Ustyug and Solvychegodsk was the tidings of the taking of Rostov and Vologda by the men of Tushino (temporarily even these great towns had submitted to the "knave"); the men of Ustyug regarded this event as a manifestation of God's "just wrath upon all the land of Rus" and only trusted that the distance was perhaps too great for the wrath of God to reach them. But since an agent of Tushino, Nikita Pushkin, had already arrived, geographical arguments did not seem particularly consoling even to them themselves, and they had to console themselves with the hope that it was still uncertain who would win ("it is not to be guessed how it will turn out") and encourage themselves with rumours, quite absurd even then, that Prince M. V. Skopin-Shuisky had "destroyed Tushino." However that might be, the necessity of taking oath to the "knave" seemed imminent, a necessity extremely unpleasant in view of the consequences that had usually accompanied the event in other towns. In Yaroslavl, when "the rabble with Prince Fedor Baryatinsky kissed the cross to the Tsarevich Dmitry," "the better men, abandoning their homes, fled away." And here, in Ustyug, we find the "better men" at the head of the anti-Tushino movement; Mikhalko, a farmer of the liquor monopoly, assumed the rôle of chief orator at the meeting, the decision of which is reported in the first of the "answers." And the bourgeoisie of Ustyug appealed to their social compeers in Solvychegodsk, the "better men of the town and township," recommending to them in their turn that they talk it over "with the Stroganovs."

The most complete picture of this intra-urban social struggle, which presents a perfect parallel to the rural movement described by the author of the Romanov pamphlet, is supplied by the chronicler of Pskov. Next to Moscow (after the ruin of Novgorod by Ivan IV) Pskov was probably the greatest economic centre of Russia at that time. Class relationships, as they then existed, were there highly developed, and the succession of classes in power therefore stands out in the chronicle in peculiarly sharp relief. The antagonism between the "better" men and the "lesser" men was here very soon perceptible, and precisely in connection with the recognition or non-recognition of Shuisky's government. Even in the days of Bolotnikov's revolt Shuisky had asked financial aid of Pskov as well as of other towns. The municipal government, the gosts, were ready to give the money, not their own, of course, but money levied on all Pskov. The "common people" submitted to the payment very reluctantly and sent to Moscow their own

deputies, whom the gosts denounced as seditious; at Moscow these
deputies established very close relations with the streltsy from Pskov,
who were very soon to desert Shuisky. The voevoda of Pskov, the
boyar Sheremetev, who, like almost all the boyars of the time, was
hostile to Tsar Vasily, played a double rôle. Officially he was on the
side of the "lawful authority," of the representatives of the commercial
class, the gosts, who ruled Pskov; *sub rosa* he was aiding the agents of
Tushino. But as long as the "lesser" men were unarmed, they did not
go beyond "seditious speeches." Matters were brought to a head by
the appearance at Pskov of the streltsy, who had deserted the Moscow
government, and of Tushino detachments in the environs of the town.
The petty military servitors, with whom Pskov's subordinate towns
(the border fortresses) were filled, took oath to Dmitry. In the city
itself the "people," now mustering courage, "seized the better men and
the gosts and threw them into the dungeon." This was in August,
1608. The voevoda who had played a double rôle followed the gosts to
prison. The "lesser" men, with the streltsy, were masters of the city.
But the democracy of Pskov lacked confidence in its complete victory;
it seemed to it that even in prison the "better men" were organising
conspiracies against it, and on the first of September were enacted in
Pskov scenes vividly recalling the "September massacres" of the great
French Revolution. When it was rumoured through the city that "Germans" were coming from Novgorod, hired, it was said, by Shuisky, a
crowd of men of Pskov threw themselves "on the municipal authorities
and on the eminent men of the city and slaughtered those who had
been put in the dungeon": some they seated on stakes, others they
beheaded, still others they subjected to corporal punishment, and they
confiscated the property of all; the former voevoda, Sheremetev, was
strangled in prison. All this chastisement was carried out in the name
of Tsar Dmitry. But confiscation did not stop with the property of
those executed; the democratic leaders appropriated for the city the
treasure of the bishop and of the monasteries and subjected the gosts
to just such a compulsory levy in favour of the Tushino government
as the "common people" had formerly been subjected to in favour of
Tsar Vasily.

   Nor did the democratic Terror stop with the September massacres.
A great fire soon occurred in Pskov, during which the Kremlin was
destroyed by the explosion of a powder cellar. "The men of Pskov,
the common people and the streltsy, rushed up crying: 'The boyars
and gosts are burning the city,' and began to drive them into the very
fire with stones as they ran out of the city; and, gathering in the
morning, they began to drag along the eminent nobles and gosts, to
torture and to punish them, and to put them in the dungeon." But

the petty military servitors soon proved to be poor allies of the petty bourgeoisie of the town, a fact which the "aristocrats" of Pskov were able to use to excite the common people against the streltsy. The latter were driven from the city, and the popular party was deprived of its armed force; as a result, for a short time the city passed again into the hands of the gosts. A savage reaction set in; some of the "leaders of the assembly" were "given over to execution," others simply "slain." But the triumph of the wealthy merchantry was ephemeral. In the first place, they too quickly displayed their true political physiognomy by proposing to take the oath to Shuisky. Furthermore, those leaders of the democracy of Pskov who had escaped execution found support in the mass of rustics, the "smerds" of Pskov, whom we have already met in the pages of this history. Crowds of peasants appeared on the streets of Pskov, and with their co-operation the reactionary government was overthrown. More than two hundred representatives of the aristocracy of Pskov, "nobles and gosts," together with "monks and priests," were again in prison, and their property confiscated. The host sent by Shuisky to the aid of the "whites" of Pskov came too late; the streltsy and the Tushino cossack detachments were in the city once more, and the tsar's voevoda, Prince V. Dolgoruky, after besieging the city for a time, retired. The men of Pskov, preparing for further warfare, hired Polish detachments; "Lisowchiks" appeared in Pskov. Nevertheless, the democracy of Pskov is not on this account to be accused of lack of patriotism; Shuisky's party had summoned the Swedes to its aid, though to no avail. First Lisowski, then the "false tsar and knave Matyushka"[1] and his cossacks, defended the city until 1613. It was only the victory of the "better men" throughout Russia that tipped the scales to their side at Pskov, too. The leaders of the popular party were again arrested and this time despatched to Moscow, where "order" had finally triumphed.

Within Tushino itself there proved to be a class contradiction, which threatened the cause of the Second Dmitry with inevitable ruin. The rising initiated by the middling landholders was in fact assuming the physiognomy of a "servile revolt." Hence, in contrast to the First Dmitry, who in the main had relied on the military-serving masses, the Second Dmitry was, toward the end, supported almost exclusively by Polish mercenaries and by the cossacks. But the cossacks were always ready to take the side of the pomeshchiks, if only they, too, were furnished with land and given a share in the "sovereign's wages." The higher military servitors among the Tushino masses were bound

[1] After the First Dmitry the cossacks fell to turning out "tsareviches" by factory methods, so to speak; there were tsareviches named "Augustus," Lavrenty, two Peters, Fedor, Clementy, Savely, Simeon, Vasily, Yeroshka, Gavrilka, Martynka, etc.

soon to understand that the Poles represented the chief danger, though at the same time they represented the chief fighting force of Tushino. The Patriarch Filaret and the other titled men of Tushino, on the one hand, and those pomeshchiks and knights who adhered to the Second Dmitry, on the other hand, were thus confronted with the question of how to render the Poles harmless without losing their aid, which in a military sense was invaluable. In such a situation it was quite natural to appeal from the "knights" who were the masters in Russia to their government in Poland. It is true, there were among the Polish soldiers of Tushino not a few émigrés, outlaws even from the Polish point of view, the celebrated Lisowski, for example. It was, of course, impossible to make them obey the Polish authorities, but it was possible to attract them to the side of "order" by the hope of legitimation. The others, who had not broken their ties with the fatherland, the Polish king could simply order to abandon the "bondsmen" and to aid the pomeshchiks. Only one thing was clear: King Sigismund would not interfere in Moscow's troubles for nothing; it was necessary to interest him in some way, necessary to make the cause of the Russian pomeshchiks his cause. Under such circumstances there emerged in the camp of Tushino at the beginning of 1609 the candidacy of the king's son Vladislav for the throne of Moscow. In becoming the father of the tsar of Moscow, Sigismund, of course, would receive the strongest inducement to restore order in the Muscovite state.

The idea of a Polish candidate for the throne of Moscow was by no means a new idea. Even in the days of the First Dmitry, before Shuisky and the Moscow townsmen carried off the prize, the tsar the boyars desired was this very Vladislav; their agent at Cracow had been carrying on negotiations along this line, negotiations which were interrupted without result by the coup of May 17, 1606. In 1608, when Shuisky's instability on the throne had finally become clear, the question bobbed up again, and again the boyars conspired. It is sufficient to remember the position of the "ruler" in the Polish-Lithuanian state to understand why the sympathies of the boyars turned in this direction. Not for nothing were Filaret and his circle the first at Tushino to remember the Polish candidate. But in these days the boyars were already so weak politically that alone they could not possibly seat their own candidate on the throne. Reaction of the mass of the pomeshchiks against the Tushino "tsarlet," who, without his will and assent, but in virtue of the inexorable course of events, was becoming the tsar of bondsmen, lent them unexpected support; the nobility likewise needed a new tsar and had no candidate of their own. The desire, identical in both the controlling groups at Tushino (the boyar opposition to Shuisky and the provincial nobility), to render the Polish "knights" harmless very soon brought about a reconciliation of these two old opponents, who, it seemed, now had nothing to divide them. In January, 1610, an embassy representing both groups appeared before Sigismund and put the question of Vladislav on an absolutely business basis; the superior elements of the Tushino army renounced their questionable tsar and bound themselves to make every effort to seat the Polish king's son on the throne of Moscow.

The Polish king had at this time a special reason for interfering in Muscovite affairs, and in particular for interfering against Shuisky, *i.e.*, for Tushino, though of course not for the "knave." The Polish regular cavalry in the latter's service had compelled Tsar Vasily, who had, moreover, been deprived of the support of the majority of his military servitors, to seek elsewhere an equivalent force to oppose to it. There was no one for him to turn to except the Swedes. On February 28, 1609, a treaty of offensive-defensive alliance between King Charles IX and Tsar Vasily was signed in Vyborg; the inevitable consequence of this treaty was a war between Moscow and Poland since the latter was then at war with Sweden. From the point of view of Shuisky's government this was perfectly reasonable; the Poles were supporting Tushino anyway, war was being waged unofficially, and the royal army was little more to be feared than were such partisans as Rozynski and Lisowski. And so it turned out; even by the autumn of this year (1609) King Sigismund had succeeded in collecting no more than 5,000 foot and 12,000 horse, and the latter were inferior to the Tushino bands. With these forces the king advanced to Smolensk, which, as a great commercial centre (its inhabitants were reckoned at 70,000), of course supported Shuisky's party. Under Smolensk, the siege of which was conducted very indolently and unsuccessfully, the envoys of Tushino met with Sigismund.

The treaty they concluded with Sigismund (it was signed, as a private agreement, under Smolensk, February 4, 1610, and on August 17 of the same year, being accepted by the boyars who were ruling Moscow, it became an official document) enjoys high renown in Russian historical literature as the first "project of a Russian constitution." Properly speaking, the first document comprising a limitation of the tsar's power was Shuisky's oath; but it had included only negative provisions; it had defined what the tsar must not do, whereas the treaty of 1610 tried to define how the tsar must rule. On closer inspection, however, this document does not at all justify its high reputation. First of all, there is no "project" here; on the contrary, the authors take every precaution to avoid the appearance of proposing anything new. Everything must be done "as formerly"; the reservation is specifically made that "the former customs and ranks, which were in the realm of Moscow, are not to be altered." Under such circumstances the whole treaty appears, not a programme for the future but a retrospective survey of Muscovite political usage, with a manifest attempt to restore in all inviolability not only what had existed before the Troubles but also what had existed before the oprichnina. As in the days of the "elected council," it was proposed to concentrate all power in the hands of the boyars; the tsar must do nothing without consulting them. "And all that," concludes the treaty, "shall be done by the sovereign with the advice and consent of the boyars and all men of the duma; without the duma and without its consent such business shall not be accomplished." Reproducing the substance of Shuisky's oath, the treaty lays special emphasis on the participation of the boyars in the administration of justice ("whoever is guilty . . . shall be punished for his fault, having first been condemned by the boyars and by the men of the duma . . ."). From our point of view, of special importance is the control of the budget by the boyars: "the sovereign's revenues . . . over and above former customs, shall not be augmented without consulting the boyars." But here too, of course, there was nothing new; earlier, too, taxation had been within the competence of the boyar duma.

The sole innovation in this treaty, an innovation not very bold but very remarkable, is the mention of the zemsky sobor as an indispensable participant in legislation: "at Moscow and in the provinces judicial decisions shall be made and shall be executed according to former usage, according to the Sudebnik of the Russian realm; and if there shall be desire to supplement it for the strengthening of the courts, the Sovereign shall consult with the duma of boyars and of all the land, that all shall be just." Prior to the oprichnina legislative power had been exercised by the tsar and the boyars; now they shared this power with the nobles, who made up the preponderant majority of the "council of all the land." Thus did the treaty of 1610 discount the political changes that had taken place during the sixty years since the publication of the Tsar's Sudebnik—a hard bargain, if we remember that during this interval the nobility had seated two tsars upon the throne of Moscow, and now were about to unseat a third, principally because the pomeshchiks "do not love" him "and do not want to serve him." When the Muscovite boyars wielded the pen, the political usage of the Muscovite state made concessions to the "spirit of the times" only in the most homeopathic doses. This is particularly clear if we take into account that the initiative in the summoning of the zemsky sobor remained entirely in the hands of the boyars (the "desire" refers only to those who judge, i.e., to the boyars), and that they were striving to make the personnel of this omnicompetent college more permanent than it had been made in the fifteen-fifties. "Muscovite princeling and boyar families shall not be depressed and abased in rank and honour by foreign newcomers," said the final text of the treaty. In the original edition this promise was mitigated by the addition: "men of lesser station" shall be raised in accordance with personal deserts. As has often been remarked it is particularly significant that this reservation was omitted in the official text; that which had been proclaimed by the oprichniks of Ivan the Terrible, namely, that the sovereign "like God makes the little great," the Muscovite boyars refused to acknowledge even thirty years after Ivan's death. To this juridical inviolability of "great stations" corresponded, of course, guarantee of their economic basis; Vladislav pledged himself "not to take relatives' hereditary estates from any one." On this point the restrictive provisions of Shuisky's charter were extended to the new sovereign.

The "boyar rule" for which historians have sought in vain in the reign of Tsar Vasily was now to begin; nothing offers such convincing proof of the perplexity of the pomeshchik masses when faced by the rebellion of their rural inferiors as does the political portion of the treaty of 1610. Peresvetov's great-grandsons now agreed to hand over all power to the "idle rich," merely to maintain their own social position. This was guaranteed by the treaty on both sides, so to speak, both from above and from below. From above the pomeshchik obtained the money capital on which his economy existed; from below he strove to attach working hands to this economy. The boyars, on becoming the government of Moscow, formally promised in the name of Tsar Vladislav "to bid that pay be given . . . according to former custom." Thus, only the traditional rate of pay was guaranteed, presumably without taking into account the decline in the value of money. Alteration of the rate was admitted, but the initiative rested with the boyars: "and be anything added to any one . . . not according to their desert, or . . . diminished without fault . . . about this the sovereign shall consult with the boyars and with the men of the duma." The boyars did not want the sovereign to make pay a means of increasing his popularity, as it had been under Godunov and the Alleged Dmitry.

With respect to working hands special measures of precaution had to be taken; now the landholders of neighbouring Lithuania might be drawn into competition. Hence the treaty laid it down: "trading and plough peasants shall not go to Lithuania from Rus or from Lithuania to Rus." "Likewise within Rus peasants shall not go away," and serfs shall not be given freedom, added the original text of the unofficial agreement. Very curious is this fear of an emancipatory policy on the part of the new tsar; the pomeshchiks as it were remembered that Godunov had once meditated something of the kind. But again the very prohibition of "going away" merely copied Shuisky's legislation; by an edict of March 9, 1607, it had been provided: "whatever peasants fifteen years ago were recorded in the registers of the year 101 [1593] shall remain under whomsoever they were enrolled." At the time, however, this measure had been directed primarily against the pomeshchiks of the Ukraine, who "did not want to serve" Shuisky; in the famine years they had attracted a mass of peasants whose former masters were now authorised to seek them out and take them back. In the treaty this reservation, directed especially against those elements of the nobility that had been politically hostile to Tsar Vasily, naturally lapsed, and there remained only the general rule of his edict: "take not another's."

If the treaty slighted the interests of the middling landholders, it practically ignored the interests of the bourgeoisie; it was deemed unnecessary to make any reservations except for free trade with Poland and Lithuania on the old basis. And this was but natural; the position of the pomeshchiks was difficult, but the position of the townsmen of Moscow, by which men judged the bourgeoisie in general, was frankly hopeless. In the course of 1609 the Tushino detachments closed the road to Ryazan, and Moscow was without grain; Tsar Vasily's attempt to fix a maximum price for grain led nowhere; it was merely taken advantage of by speculators, and the "rabble," agitated by the "dearness of bread," expressed itself very definitely in favour of the Tushino "tsarlet." So definitely that the Polish government had to reckon with these sympathies of the Moscow "rabble"; it would have been very glad to remove altogether the now extremely inconvenient figure of the Second Dmitry, but it could not bring itself to kill him lest his murder raise the mass of the Moscow populace against the Poles. Any day the scenes at Pskov might be re-enacted at Moscow, and it was not for the "better men" of the capital to be over-fastidious in the choice of allies or to impose any conditions on them.

There is reason to suppose that in concluding the treaty with Sigismund, the boyars and military servitors thought to get rid of both tsars at once—both the one at Moscow, whom the Moscow townsmen were now indolently supporting, and the one under Moscow, whom the superior elements of his host were now renouncing. But they had to put up a while longer with both the one and the other. The "knave" succeeded in penetrating the designs of his counsellors and fled from Tushino (in the early part of January); in itself this would not have mattered, but all the cossack detachments left with him. If the treaty neglected the military servitors and ignored the townsmen, it dealt most strangely with the cossacks. Their very existence was made dependent on the permission of the "boyars and men of the duma"; the latter were to decide whether in future cossacks were "necessary" or not. This was, it is true, entirely in accord with the "antiquity and custom" which the agreement of February 4 preserved; "according to custom" there was no place for the cossacks in the Muscovite social order. But here the obsolescence of the boyars' views was promptly punished, and in a most painful way. Cheated by the Polish-boyar agreement, the cossacks were all the more bound to value the symbol of the tsar's authority that remained in their hands, and they resolved to support the "knave" with all their strength. Only the Polish detachments fell away from him, and from a military point of view he still remained a magnitude not to be ignored. Shuisky unexpectedly became a similar magnitude. In the latter part of February his deposition was just on the point of being effected at Moscow; the nobles, headed by the ever disloyal men of Ryazan and with the active support of Prince V. V. Golitsyn, gathered an "assembly" against Tsar Vasily and almost seized the Kremlin. But the Moscow townsmen saw no great difference between Vasily and these foes of his, and in reply to their summons they did not stir. After creating some disturbance, the disappointed nobles went off to Tushino. In this affair, according to the chronicle, Shuisky displayed great firmness, which was, of course, influenced by the neutrality of the Moscow townsmen, but still more by the fact that the Treaty of Vyborg had at last begun to bear fruit. Mercenary Swedish detachments, under the command of the tsar's nephew, M. V. Skopin-Shuisky, had cleared the northern roads to Moscow of the men of Tushino and had by this time reached Alexandrovsk. On March 12 Skopin was already in the city, while a few days earlier Rozynski had burned the Tushino camp and retired to the northwest with his Poles, drawing closer to the royal troops operating under Smolensk. For the first time since the surrender of Bolotnikov at Tula, and after an interval of two years replete with failures, Tsar Vasily was again victor on the field of battle.

Given the existing state of affairs this could be nothing more than a respite. The Swedish army, like every European army of the period, was a mercenary one, recruited from adventurers of all countries, who served only so long as their wages were paid regularly. But this condition was the very one that Shuisky had the most difficulty in meeting. The bourgeoisie of the seaboard contributed as long as the Tushino danger—and with it the danger of a democratic rebellion—was imminent. In proportion as Skopin cleared the north, its liberality diminished, and by the summer of 1610 Tsar Vasily again resembled a "plumeless eagle." In the first battle with King Sigismund's troops, under Klushino, June 24, Shuisky's "Germans," who had not received their pay, went over to the enemy without further ado, and Tsar Vasily's war with Poland, and likewise his reign, were at an end. Contemporaries of course ascribed this turn of affairs, so unexpected after his recent victory, to personal changes, to the fact that the Muscovite army was no longer headed by the popular Skopin [2] but by Tsar Vasily's brother Dmitry, whom no one liked. That the ungifted Muscovite commander had to deal with one of the most talented Polish generals, the hetman Zolkiewski, could not but be reflected to a certain extent in the course of the battle. But once there was no money, no ability could have warded off the desertion of the "Germans"; had the Muscovites won this battle, they could not have offered another and would only have secured a new respite, measured in weeks not in months.

From the strategical point of view there was restored after the battle of Klushino the same correlation of forces as before the fall of Tushino. Under Moscow stood the Poles, an organised military force; opposed to them stood Shuisky, weaker than ever, deprived of Swedish assistance and of the support of all the military servitors inasmuch as Lyapunov and the men of Ryazan were now against him. Now the men of Moscow could still less afford to delay, for the "knave," too, was in the field, and his presence continued to agitate the "common people" of Moscow. The Polish troops were the only guarantee of "order," if they would but agree to assume that function; but they agreed only under the very definite condition that the Muscovites recognise the treaty of February 4. The broadsheets of Hetman Zolkiewski constantly impressed this on the public of Moscow; the significance these broadsheets had in the deposition of Shuisky is evident from the fact that their argument (on account of Tsar Vasily "Christian blood flows ceaselessly") was reproduced word for word by the official announcement of Vasily's deposition from the throne. The ruling circles, dreading an alliance between the Moscow populace and the troops of the Second Dmitry, for a time enacted a comedy, officially representing the Poles as foes for a week or two even after Shuisky had been "brought down" and given the tonsure; let Zolkiewski close in on Moscow and confront the population with the dilemma—either fight the Poles (for which there were neither means nor forces) or admit them to the city. At the same time the election of Vladislav must be properly prepared, inasmuch as the Tushino envoys had not officially been vested with plenipotentiary powers to treat of the destinies of the throne of Moscow. In the light of modern research it can hardly be doubted that Vladislav's election was to have been staged with as much solemnity as later marked the election of Michael Romanov and earlier had marked that of Godunov; they had intended to summon all the "estates" of the Muscovite realm and to ratify the deed by the decision of a zemsky

[2] He had died two months before, supposedly "despatched" by Shuisky, but probably from typhus, and very opportunely for his military glory.

sobor, but time did not allow. They had to be content with an assembly of representatives of the estates of Moscow only: for that matter, such an abridged edition was not unusual in those times and was not accounted illegal even for the election of a tsar; Peter and Ivan, sons of Alexis, were later acknowledged by just such an abridged sobor (1682). In these cases the oath of the other towns served as tacit recognition of Moscow's decision, and in 1610 this condition was observed: "so in all the Russian land," says the chronicler, "they kissed the cross of the Lord that they would serve Vladislav, son of Sigismund, in everything." The traditional description of the following period as an "interregnum" is a pious deceit; in actual fact, from August 17, 1610, Vladislav was tsar at Moscow with no less right than his predecessor, Vasily Shuisky, had possessed.

Tsar Vladislav was in even greater degree than certain of his predecessors a mere symbol of the tsar's power. A minor, he did not come to Moscow; but this circumstance did not prevent the Moscow government from acting in his name with hardly any opposition—hardly any, because, as might have been expected, difficulties were immediately made by the Church. The position of the Church at that moment is especially curious to us, who usually think that the men of Moscow were exceptionally devoted to Orthodoxy, and that for them religion was of supreme importance. In actual fact, in the Muscovite state the Church was very closely bound up with the fate of other feudal forces. Regardless of the antagonism between the large landholders and the monasteries, the Church was closest to the boyar order, and the ruin of the latter by Ivan the Terrible very perceptibly diminished the independent importance of the Church. The patriarchs of the late sixteenth and early seventeenth centuries were political tools in the hands of the secular authority and changed with the tsars. Godunov's patriarch, Iov, gave way to the Greek Ignatius when the Alleged Dmitry seized power; when the latter was slain by Shuisky, Hermogen became patriarch. The rôle of Hermogen, a man whom contemporaries call shallow and weak, easily subject to others' influence, was under Shuisky quite pitiable. The clergy did not love him, on account of his rudeness and cruelty to subordinates, while laymen cherished no respect for a patriarch who was always the humble servant of Shuisky and was ready to cover all Tsar Vasily's deeds with the authority of the Church. The nobles, when they organised an "assembly" against Tsar Vasily in Shrovetide, 1610, as Hermogen came out to exhort them, "abused him every way"; they kicked him from behind, threw dirt in his face, took him by the neck and shoulders and shook him. It was quite natural that in drawing up the treaty with Sigismund, Hermogen's wishes were not consulted; probably they deemed the Church sufficiently represented in the person of the Tushino patriarch, Filaret Romanov. But when the treaty entered the official stage, the patriarch of Moscow could not fail to express himself on it, and he expressed himself adversely. It is very probable that Hermogen was on this occasion only a screen for a few great boyars of Moscow, like Prince V. V. Golitsyn, who himself was not averse to sitting on the tsar's throne, and for whom, presumably, Vladislav was only a melancholy necessity. A pretext for putting a spoke in the wheel of the candidacy the Romanovs had initiated was immediately found. The tsar of all Orthodox Christendom must, of course, be Orthodox, but Vladislav had been born a Catholic and had been baptised in the Catholic rite. It is, we repeat, exceptionally noteworthy that the Tushino envoys who carried on the negotiations with Sigismund had not faltered on account of this circumstance; Peresvetov's aphorism, "justice transcends faith," politics must go before religion, had evidently become a current truth in Muscovite military-serving circles of the beginning of the seventeenth century. In the treaty they were content with the promise that the new tsar would not "in anything destroy and dishonour the Christian Orthodox faith of the Greek law" and with his pledge to "introduce no other faiths." But whether he himself would, openly and solemnly, join the Orthodox Church, for which, according to the concepts of the time, a second baptism in the Orthodox rite would be indispensable—on this point the text of the treaty was silent, while Hetman Zolkiewski, when the question was put to him, gave the evasive answer that on this score he had "no instruction" from the king. With our notions of Old Russian Orthodoxy it is hard to imagine how the Orthodox took oath to a sovereign who himself was not yet Orthodox; but this undoubtedly took place in 1610, and it alone is a sufficient answer to those who would like to make religious motives dominate the conduct of the men of those times. The patriarch's protest did not prevent the election; its only consequence was the decision to despatch another solemn embassy to Sigismund with the petition that he permit his son to be baptised in the rite of the Orthodox Church.

Hetman Zolkiewski, who was not only a good general but a clever diplomat, was able to make splendid use of this circumstance in favour of Polish policy. On an embassy charged with such important business it was, of course, necessary to appoint the most respected men in the realm; and so, as "grand envoys" were despatched to Smolensk the heads of the most influential boyar families, Filaret Nikitich Romanov, converted from patriarch to metropolitan again, and Prince V. V. Golitsyn. The latter was invited to organise the embassy, which was of course made up of men devoted to him; thus the only really serious rival of Vladislav led his whole party out of Moscow. As for Filaret, the hetman himself later acknowledged in his memoirs that they wanted to have him "as a sort of pledge," as the father of another possible pretender; the candidacy of Filaret's son, Michael Romanov, was even then in the air. The trip of these influential men to the Polish camp was exceptionally advantageous for Sigismund; from the point of view of Russian interests, it was an idle expenditure of time, even apart from the fact that the Muscovite realm could expect no great advantages from Vladislav's baptism. For in the council of the Polish king it had long since (in February) been decided to regard the candidacy of the king's son as merely an intermediate stage; once it was accomplished, it was time to strive without delay for the final and really serious goal of the whole campaign, the union of the Muscovite state and the Polish Republic on the same conditions as those on which forty years before Lithuania had been united to Poland. Then all Eastern Europe would be converted into one enormous power with Poland at its head and, of course, under one sceptre; Sigismund was to become tsar of Moscow just as he was king of Poland and grand prince of Lithuania. In despatching the "grand envoys," Zolkiewski had been perfectly well aware of this plan; we may imagine how he laughed in spirit at the Muscovites fussing over the Orthodoxy of a Polish boy, who could make no difference to Moscow, anyhow.

The contemporary historiography of the Troubles, especially the works that came from the Romanov camp, fearfully exaggerated the importance of the "grand embassy." It would almost seem that the whole destiny of the Muscovite state depended on the "firmness" of the envoys; what efforts did not Sigismund and his councillors employ to shake the "grand envoys"—and all in vain! But one of the members of the embassy, Avraam Palitsyn, the cellarer of Troitsa, despite his Orthodoxy and despite his exaggerated loyalty, could not but admit that the embassy had done nothing. There had been nothing for it to do except to sit in Poland in honourable captivity; juridically Vladislav had long since been recognised by the Russians as tsar, and all had taken oath to him; in fact half of his realm was soon in a state of open rebellion against the new tsar for reasons that had nothing to do with the Orthodox faith. Vladislav's candidacy had been accepted by the ruling circles of Russian society under one condition and with one hope—that the Polish troops would restore "order" in the Muscovite realm by stifling the social revolt, thus making it possible for the pomeshchik to receive the tsar's pay punctually and to carry on economy on his estate, and for the merchant to trade peacefully as in the days of Boris Godunov, whom in his own day they had failed to appreciate. The stability of a Polish tsar on the throne of Moscow depended entirely on whether this condition was fulfilled. And it was very soon manifest not only that Sigismund's government could not satisfy this fundamental demand of the possessing classes of Muscovite society, but also that it and its agents at Moscow were a new ferment of decomposition. Never yet had anarchy attained such proportions as in the first months of Vladislav's reign; moreover the forms this anarchy took were particularly dangerous, as well for the bourgeoisie as for the middling landholders.

First of all, at Moscow they had deceived themselves with the hope that Sigismund would have but to give a command, and the Tushino "tsarlet," who had exercised such a bad influence on the "common people" of Moscow and on the bondsmen, would vanish like smoke. Tushino had vanished, yet the Second Dmitry remained. He had established himself in Kaluga with his cossacks, who plundered and devastated all the more as their hope of becoming pomeshchiks waned. As was to be expected, even the disappearance of the "knave" did not put an end to this state of affairs. The Second Dmitry was killed, whether accidentally or not (for history this has very little importance); but Marinka, the widow of the First Dmitry, who was officially the wife of the Second also, produced a son, and the cossacks began to make every one within reach of the "knave's" detachments, take oath to him. Patriarch Hermogen vigorously instilled into his flock that "Marinka's son" was "anathematised of the holy synod and of me"; but the patriarch's words had of course even less influence on the cossacks than on the merchants and pomeshchiks. Tushino, materially destroyed, threatened to become immortal as a symbol in the Russian land. Nor were the Polish partisans troubled by the fact that the Polish king's son now nominally occupied the throne of Moscow; the "Lisowchiks" continued to plunder just as before, merely transferring the theatre of their operations farther from Moscow so as to avoid the unpleasantness of meeting their fellow-countrymen on the field of battle.

What consequences such a state of affairs led to in the field of exchange, for example, can be seen from a single instance: in June, 1611, the men of Kazan complained to the men of Perm that they in Kazan "took in no money" because "neither from upstream nor from downstream did big salt vessels or any other vessels come from any towns." All Volga trade had ceased even in an object of such prime necessity as salt, and, of course, a Polish general occupying the Kremlin with a small detachment could not succour the distress of the men of the Volga. But matters were no better at Moscow itself. Chronic peril of a pro-Tushino riot kept Moscow in a chronic state of siege. Some of the Kremlin gates were closed; at the others an armed guard was constantly on duty, vigilantly inspecting every one who entered. Polish patrols constantly traversed the streets; they even removed some of the police barriers lest they impede the operations of the Polish troops in case of need. By night all movement was stopped. Moreover, however conscientiously the Polish officers tried to maintain discipline in their detachments, the discipline of a mercenary force of those times could not be strict. The Polish soldiers took anything they fancied in the bazaars, and if they paid, they paid not what the merchant asked but what seemed "just" to the soldiers themselves; at the slightest objection the sword leapt from the scabbard, thus ending the dispute. The result was that two months after the entry of the Poles into Moscow "the gosts in the market and the trading folk in the bazaars did not sit behind their counters [for fear] of the men of Lithuania"; if we take this police report literally, we might suppose that trade had at that time ceased altogether in Moscow. In reality the masters probably merely bolted their shops as quickly as possible and crept out into God's world whenever one of the "knights" was visible in the neighbourhood. But it was enough to make them remember with regret the times, not of Godunov even, but of Shuisky.

The worst sufferers from Polish dominance were its initiators, the pomeshchiks and the boyars. It is impossible to imagine the bitter disappointment that the authors of the treaty of 1610 must have experienced, they who had been so diligent to secure the inviolability of old customs. Boyar government did not really last for more than two months. At the end of this period the duma, which nominally held everything in its hands, was in reality converted into something like an advisory council under the Polish commandant of Moscow. The fact that the latter, Alexander Gonsevski, himself became a boyar by the favour of the new tsar, was, of course, little consolation to the old boyars. "To the boyars in the duma thou didst come," these latter described his conduct to his face, "only, having come, thou didst sit down, and around thee didst seat thy councillors, Michael Saltykov, Prince Vasily Masalsky, Fedka Andronov, Ivan Gramatin, and their comrades, and it was not for us to hear how thou with thy councillors didst speak and speak again: and what thou badest be done on any petition, thus they do, and thy councillors sign the petitions. . . ." High-born men were bound to resent especially the duma rôle of Fedor Andronov, a wealthy gost of Moscow, who had become a noble of the duma in Tushino, and under Vladislav was made one of the first men in the duma. Even his nearest comrades in military-serving circles could not endure the exclusive confidence that King Sigismund reposed in this "trading lout." "From Mstislavsky and his comrades and from us affairs have been taken away," Michael Saltykov (who had in 1610 headed the embassy that concluded the Treaty of Smolensk) complained to the Polish chancellor Sapieha, "and on such a one the government has reposed its faith." Even his confreres, the townsmen, hated Andronov as a renegade to his class, who was serving the tsar of the nobles against the tsar of the merchants. And the author of a pamphlet of the time, who was of the townsmen's circle or at least was addressing himself to it, finds no words in the Russian tongue to express his contempt for Tsar Vladislav's treasurer; he takes refuge in Greek. "For our innumerable sins how does not the Lord abase us, and what punishments does He not send us, and whom does He not bid to rule over us!" he exclaims. "You yourselves see who he is, be he a man and it is unknown who: not of the tsars' kin, nor of boyar estate, nor of the chosen heads of the host; they say, he is of stinking slaves." And while this "it is unknown who" held sway, genealogically senior members of the duma, Prince Golitsyn (brother of the "grand envoy") and Prince Vorotynsky, were under household arrest as suspects. Such "former custom" had not been seen since the days of the oprichnina!

But the oprichnina had had a definite social basis; it had rested on the alliance of the bourgeoisie and the pomeshchiks. We have already seen how the former felt toward Tsar Vladislav's government. What the Polish régime meant for the latter is well told by members of the government itself. "It must be prevented, gracious lord," Fedor Andronov wrote to Sapieha, "that they distribute pomestyes without sense; his grace the lord hetman, and Ivan Saltykov likewise, are giving writs to pomestyes; while formerly they were given only by him to whom the tsar gave orders." Michael Saltykov, in complaining of this same Andronov, wrote: "the men of Moscow are extremely afflicted that the king's favour and pay have failed, and many men are injured by divers oppressions and ruin." He also alluded to the senseless distribution of pomestyes and found that there had been no such shuffling of land even in the days of the oprichnina: "Tsar Ivan [IV] was a born tsar, and he did not so," wrote Saltykov, insinuating that the new tsar might well be more cautious than the born tsar. With good reason, when the rebelling military servitors assemble under Moscow, do they demand, before all else, that distribution of pomestyes be carried out according to former custom as had been done "under former Russian, born sovereigns," and that any pomestyes given in the name of the king or of the king's son, be taken away just like those which the boyars established in Moscow "had divided among themselves." The pomeshchiks petitioned that, over and above a share of land, pay should be issued punctually by the treasury; but in fact it turned out that they could not even count the land-grant their own, for it might be taken away at any minute by a royal charter issued a thousand versts away.

By the late fall of 1610 it was quite certain that Tsar Vladislav's councillors would soon be overtaken by the fate the Godunovs had experienced in 1605, that they would find themselves socially isolated, with not a single social class willing to support them. A handful of Polish soldiers in Moscow was all they could count on. Shuisky, struggling with his first revolts, had been far stronger; Moscow had supported him, and so had all the towns along the Northern Dvina and along the Volga. All things considered, Vladislav's government was bound to be far shorter-lived than Tsar Vasily's government. But it does not follow that its existence had no influence on the course of events in those days. On the contrary, negatively it played an enormous rôle. Threatening the interests of all the ruling classes and not even supported by the masses of the people, on which Godunov had been fain to rely, it gave cause for the reconciliation of those elements which had been at enmity throughout the Troubles. Its heterodox and foreign origin created the basis for a national-religious ideology, under cover of which an opposition movement could be organised as never before. Class self-preservation became national self-preservation; herein lies the meaning of the events of 1611-1612.

One of the earliest and most interesting examples of this ideology is the proclamation that appeared at Moscow at the end of November or the beginning of December, 1610. From a literary point of view it stands very high, strongly resembling the work of that publicist, sympathetic to the Romanovs, of whom Avraam Palitsyn made use in his *History for the Memory of Future Generations* [in Russian], and whom we have cited more than once. Indeed, it is quite possible that this publicist and the author of our proclamation (to which some one later gave the clumsy heading, *A New Narration on the Illustrious Russian Realm*, though there is no "narration" in it) are one and the same person; both were close to the bourgeoisie; both, despite their very great piety, never have recourse to supernatural motifs in their explanation of events, a practice so common in the literature of the Troubles. There is also an external resemblance between them; neither one avoids the rhythmic rhymed prose so well suited to the style of the proclamation of the time, which could not be read by individual passers-by (too few of them were literate) but must be read aloud to a whole crowd by some literate person. If we should succeed in proving the identity of the two authors, we should have an extraordinarily curious coincidence; the first summons to rebellion against Vladislav would then come from Romanov circles, whence was to come Vladislav's successor. The fact that there was no mention of the Romanovs in the proclamation itself is no evidence to the contrary; we must not forget that in these days Filaret Romanov, one of the "grand envoys," was "as a sort of pledge" to the Poles, and any such allusion might cost him dear. However that may have been, in issuing a summons to rebellion against the Polish king's son, the author let slip not a word on the score of who ought to be seated in his place, though this question was of course implied.

The central figure in his presentation is Hermogen, and the pamphlet is all the more interesting as one of the first examples of "the legend of Hermogen." The author recognised that a direct summons to rebellion could not be expected from the patriarch. But in his exposition he let it be understood that Hermogen was the soul of resistance to the Poles; "he stands alone against them all . . . like a giant without arms and without an armament of war." When this did not produce a sufficient impression, a further step had to be taken; letters of Hermogen appeared, which, however, as the distributors themselves admitted, did not issue directly from him since the patriarch had "no one to write, all the clerks and copyists and all the men of the household had been arrested." Thus was gradually created the legendary figure that adorns the pages of modern narratives of the Troubles and, it seems, has little in common with the real Hermogen.

The movement of the "better" men needed a symbol such as "Dmitry Ivanovich" had long since become for the "lesser" men; to contrast the patriarch, the strict guardian of Orthodoxy, with the tsar who "does not want to be baptised," was undoubtedly to make a very powerful appeal to wide masses. But it is noteworthy that the Moscow bourgeoisie, from which the author had probably sprung, and to which, in any case, he addressed himself, could rise above such plebeian appeals. Some pages of the *New Narration* suggest the patriotism of classic antiquity. The author praises the men of Smolensk, who had continued to resist Sigismund, because they "want to die gloriously, rather than live dishonourably and bitterly." The threatened devastation of "such a great realm" undoubtedly touches him more than the anticipated corruption of the Orthodox faith, and in the slogan he throws out for the masses of the townsmen only one-third is allowed to this faith: "let us stand together for the Orthodox faith . . . and for our fatherland and for the inheritance that the Lord has given us." And in repeating this slogan, he puts "realm" even before "faith." For him, indeed, the motif of the rebellion is not so much that Vladislav is not Orthodox as that, in general, nothing is to be expected of Vladislav; the essence of the proclamation is the disclosure to the Moscow public of the secret of the Polish conspiracy—annexation of the Muscovite realm. The author very skilfully uses as an argument the incapacity of the Poles to restore order in the country. If Sigismund had actually reserved the realm for his son, would he have permitted such havoc? "Not only does he not reserve it for his son, but he himself does not wish to live here," and the Muscovites will be ruled by such men as Fedor Andronov.

The bourgeois author was somewhat premature in summoning the Muscovites to rebellion; the sequel was to show that the movement of the towns could not be concentrated in Moscow, the only town in which purely military preponderance was unconditionally on the side of the Poles. The Moscow "barricades" of March 17, 1611, ended in complete failure; the Poles burned the city almost to ashes and compelled the surviving population to take oath anew to Vladislav. Nizhny-Novgorod came to be at the head of the movement, not only because the Volga traders were more interested than any one else in the restoration of order, but also for the simple reason that there were no Polish troops on the Volga, and no one to hinder the movement in its initial stages. The surprising thing is not that under such conditions the movement of the townsmen and nobles finally got the better of the Poles (for a handful of soldiers in the Kremlin could no more stifle an all-Russian rebellion than it could maintain order in all Russia), but that this movement needed so much time, almost a year and a half, to get under way. It is hardly possible to account for this by the purely technical peculiarities of the time, by the absence not only of railroads but also of any decent roads at all except water-ways. It is true, events of this kind were then not measured in weeks, as now, but in months; yet the first army of the insurgents, the Lyapunov armament, arrived under Moscow in April, 1611, whereas the first summons to rebellion had been distributed in December of the preceding year. The causes of the delay must be sought elsewhere, where contemporaries saw them; the author of the *New Narration* saw the "worst of all" in the fact that "division had taken place in our land." The two halves of the "better" men, urban and rural, the townsmen and the pomeshchiks, had for the last four years been waging a desperate struggle against one another, and it was not now easy for them to combine for common action. When such common action was effected in Shuisky's reign, men talked of it as a rarity and were proud of it. And when the rebellion of the nobility began under the leadership of the men of Ryazan, Prokopy Lyapunov and his comrades expected to find allies among the cossacks and even among the most democratic elements of the Tushino army rather than among the burghers. "And let bondsmen come without any doubt and fear," wrote Lyapunov at Kazan as late as June, 1611, "they will all have freedom and pay like other cossacks."

The "zigzag" described by the rebellion against Vladislav, the temporary failure of this rebellion and the temporary disintegration of the insurrectionary army in July, 1611, is mainly attributable to this cause. The original rebels, as listed in Lyapunov's February letter to Nizhny, were the men of Ryazan "and of Kaluga, and of Tula, and of Mikhailov, and all the men of all the towns" of the frontier provinces.

Such an armament had, in 1606, failed to take Moscow even when defended by Shuisky with hardly more than the streltsy of the Dvina, and now the Kremlin was held by regular European troops. The towns "sympathised" with Lyapunov but for the time being gave him no assistance. The cossacks were a technically necessary ally, and inability to appreciate this fact ruined Lyapunov. The cossacks were not consciously class foes of the pomeshchiks, as they had many times proved during the Troubles. But they wanted to be regarded as equals, whereas the Ryazan voevoda and his comrades were wholly unwilling to recognise the cossacks as the equals of the nobles. Though addressing demagogic appeals to the cossacks and even to the bondsmen,[3] when it came to fixing the status of the masses in rebellion against Vladislav, the pomeshchiks took almost the same viewpoint as had the boyars in the treaty of 1610. In the celebrated "decree" of the Lyapunov armament under Moscow (June 30, 1611) the nobles were willing to guarantee payment in land and wages in money, not to all the cossacks but only to those who had long been serving the Muscovite state. Admission to administrative office was flatly denied to these younger brothers of the military servitors: "from commissionerships from the towns, and from the court villages and from the peasant townships the atamans and cossacks shall be dismissed," the decree provided, "and to the towns and into the townships shall be sent for kormlenies good nobles, and with them, to do errands, knights and cossacks and streltsy." For Lyapunov's pomeshchiks the cossack was of old a "suitable" servitor, who was of most use as an orderly to a "good noble." With the lowest elements of the Tushino army, whom Lyapunov had decoyed, the decree dealt still more simply: "peasants and bondsmen," it prescribed, "are on inquest to be given back to the old pomeshchiks."

This decree so sharply emphasised class interests that it cost the leader of the nobles' armament his life. When they saw themselves being edged out of the picture, the cossacks "conspired" and were met with strict disciplinary measures, including "seating in the water"; an explosion occurred, and Lyapunov was killed at a meeting of the cossacks. After this the movement of the nobles for the time being lost its centre, and Vladislav's government was able to hold out for another year. But the defeat of the pomeshchiks was in a way advantageous to them; the townsmen finally ceased to fear them, and the towns now began to hire the knights into their service, thus taking the place of the First and Second Dmitrys.

Contemporaries have described the state of affairs as it took shape

---

[3] It may be supposed that this was not the first time Lyapunov had done so, and that Bolotnikov's "sheets" were not distributed without the privity of the noble leaders of the armament that marched against Tsar Vasily.

under Moscow immediately after Lyapunov's death, as follows: "The old authors of great evil, atamans and cossacks, who had in Tushino served the false-named tsar . . . slew Prokofy Lyapunov and began to commit all evil according to their cossack wont." Here the reader, accustomed to the traditional presentation of the cossacks, expects descriptions of attempts on Muscovite "statehood"; but the author of the letters, a military servitor (none other than the celebrated Prince Pozharsky), knew nothing of cossack anarchism. For him the "all evil" was comprised in the first place, in the fact, that the cossacks "dealt mortal infamy to the nobles and knights" and, in the second place, and principally, in the fact that "the chieftain" of the cossacks, ataman Zarutsky, "took to himself many towns and court villages, and peasant townships, and monasteries' estates, and distributed them to his councillors, nobles and knights, and atamans, and cossacks." The anarchism of the cossacks was expressed in the fact that they themselves took what the nobles' armament had refused them and arbitrarily made themselves pomeshchiks. To this development the towns were indifferent; but should the cossacks become masters of the situation, they would become dangerous to the upper strata of the townsmen, too, as soon as their victory over the nobility began to have political consequences. The cossack leader, Zarutsky, had his own candidate for tsar, and the son of the Tushino "tsarlet" was a terror to all the "better men" in the last years of his existence. The cossacks were not particularly dangerous as long as they were encamped under Moscow, but a cossacks' tsar, successor of the Tushino bondsmen's tsar, was an immediate menace. Dread of this eventuality had compelled the bourgeoisie to support Shuisky with treasure and men; dread of it now compelled the towns to assemble their own army, since after the seizure of lands and treasury by the cossack atamans the military servitors were left without pay and with the prospect of being deprived of their estates. As soon as tidings of the catastrophe to Lyapunov had reached the Volga towns, they immediately resolved "all to be united in counsel"; "if the cossacks undertake to elect over the realm of Moscow a sovereign at their own pleasure, alone, without consulting with all the land, we do not want that sovereign over the realm." The material basis of this union of the Volga towns, to which the Dvina towns also soon adhered, was the treasure collected in Nizhny-Novgorod, not, of course, at the individual initiative of Minin, but simply because without a military force the union of the towns was an empty phrase, and a military force was not to be had without money. Contemporary letters, and the chronicler as well, describe this hiring of the nobles by the bourgeoisie with the greatest realism, and see nothing amazing in this simple prosaic fact. In Pozharsky's letter to the men of Solvychegodsk the activity of the men of Nizhny is thus described: "In Nizhny-Novgorod the gosts and all the zemsky townsmen, zealous for God, for the Orthodox Christian faith, not sparing their possessions, have thought the nobles and knights of Smolensk and of many other towns to be worthy of a liberal money wage. . . . Whatever money, masters, was collected at Nizhny has been distributed to the nobles and the knights and to all the men of war; and now from all the towns . . . come all men, and petition all the land for a money wage, and there is nothing to give them. And it is for you, masters, whatever revenues there are at Solvychegodsk to send to us at Yaroslavl, for wages for the men of war." "Everywhere hither hurries the assembly," relates the "New Chronicler," "and from many towns men of war begin to gather; the first comers were those of Kolomna, and the men of Ryazan, after them from the towns of the ukraine many men, and cossacks, and streltsy, those who sat in Moscow under Tsar Vasily, and to all pay is given; and there was calm there then among all men." The men of war offered their hands, the townsmen purchased them with the money they had collected; "patriotic fervour" cannot be better translated into the language of materialistic history than it was by these simple and naïve Russian men of the beginning of the seventeenth century.

Description of the military operations which in the late fall of 1612 led the pomeshchik army, assembled by the townsmen, into the Kremlin of Moscow is no part of our task. There is no doubt that the successful issue of the second campaign was decided chiefly by its solid financial basis. Having undertaken to pay all the men of war, the bourgeoisie acted handsomely; to the men of Smolensk, for example, they gave "to the first category 50 rubles each, to the second 45 rubles each, to the third 40 rubles each, and to none less than 30 rubles." For purposes of comparison it is worth noting that the provincial knights of Godunov's times had received not more than 6 rubles, and even the "select" ones (the guardsmen) not more than 15 rubles pay; in former years only guard officers had received what was now given to military servitors of the rank-and-file. But it must not be thought that the towns collected the needed sums exclusively from voluntary contributions. The great bourgeoisie that ruled the towns filled the treasury of the armament they had assembled in the same way as Shuisky had once filled his—by compulsory levy. In the case of wealthy capitalists this was usually a forced loan; in this way, for example, the men of Nizhny got money from the Stroganovs and their agents. On the petty townsfolk they simply imposed new taxes, exacting them, as usual, without indulgence, "with the aid of God putting fear on the idle." A delinquent might be indentured, be given over into service on a "life writing," the money for his service being paid in advance, not to him but to the town treasury. And this, as a modern historian of the Troubles justly remarks, is no proof of the personal severity of Kuzma Minin and his comrades. It was a peculiarity of the social order, the victory of which brought the Troubles to an end.

CHAPTER XI

1. *The Liquidation of the Agrarian Crisis*

THE official close of "The Time of the Troubles" does not by any means mark the real cessation of the Troubles. Michael Fedorovich Romanov had been on the throne for a long time, but the civil war and its offspring, the foreign war, still continued. As one modern scholar, Gautier, has observed, the maximum of destruction was reached in those very years "when the national and political crisis of the Time of the Troubles was at an end" and when a "lawful government" had been installed at Moscow for some time. This observer sees the "devastation" at its height in 1616, if not, indeed, in 1620; only after the latter date is it at all possible to speak of perceptible and lasting improvement. Almost fifteen years of civil war could not fail to have their effect on a country, even if its economy had previously been in an entirely satisfactory condition.

The Troubles, it seems, were bound to bring to "complete annihilation" the Muscovite Rus that had been undermined by the agrarian crisis of the sixteenth century. If at the end of the preceding century the central provinces had been considerably depopulated, in the 'tens and 'twenties of the seventeenth century "recorders" and "reporters" sent "to inspect" the land found in places almost a complete desert. In Gautier's words, on the estates of the Troitsa Monastery, scattered in twenty counties beyond the River Moscow (and therefore more or less characteristic of the general condition of the country), "the extent of the arable is in the year 1616 one-twentieth what it was in the years 1592-1594; the number of peasants settled on the Troitsa estates decreases to less than one-seventh." Even as late as the close of the 1620's, on those estates in the counties of Moscow, Zubtsov and Klin, the history of which we can trace, the waste, that is, the land given up and abandoned, constituted not less than 80%, rising sometimes to 95%; but the land remaining under cultivation did not exceed 18.7% of the whole area, sometimes falling to 5.2%. To the south, in the modern province of Kaluga, for example, things were no better: on an estate on which in 1592-1593 there had been 161 peasant homesteads, in 1614 there remained only ten. In the county of Moscow the decrease of the arable can be estimated at, on the average, one-third the amount under cultivation at the height of the crisis that had preceded the Troubles.

Upon examining the details of this ruin of the countryside, we are, however, soon in a position to be discriminating in our ideas about the economic results of the Troubles. Every one was ruined, more or less; but some more, others less. Thanks to the Troubles and their consequences, the independent peasantry was bound finally to disappear wherever there were pomeshchiks. The first phenomenon that strikes one in studying the Russian countryside of the second and third decades of the seventeenth century is the enormous growth of cottar homesteads at the expense of peasant homesteads. If we. take the estates of the Troitsa Monastery as an example—a very good example, as we saw—we obtain the following figures: in the county of Dmitrov, according to the registers of the end of the sixteenth century, there were on the Troitsa estates forty cottar homesteads to 917 of peasants; the registers of the 1620's give 207 homesteads of cottars to 220 homesteads occupied by peasants. In the first case the cottar homesteads constitute 4.1%; in the second, 48.4%. For the county of Uglich the corresponding figures would be 2.6% and 56.6%. What then were these cottars? On the ground that the cottar homestead paid only half the tax exacted from the peasant, Belyaev defined them as peasants settled on half a *vyt*[1] [virgate]. Gautier has proved that in the majority of cases the cottars had no arable at all. For example, he gives an excerpt from the inventories in 1612 of the estates of the Troitsa Monastery. "The village of Kochyugovo . . . the cottar homestead of Vaska Antipyev, he had been a peasant, and had been made poor by war and taxes; they said he did not plough any arable, it lay neglected, but he had had three *chets*[2] of arable." Of other cottars living in the monastery's hamlets it is reported that "they became impoverished through the Lithuanian destruction, they go around the community and are fed in the name of Christ." "Idle cottars," "lame roving cottars"—are epithets met with in the registers at every turn. A cottar, as a rule, was not a proletarian in our sense of the word; he was a proletarian in the ancient sense of the word—not a worker deprived of the tools of his labour but a peasant deprived of land because he had nothing left with which to cultivate it. A man maimed in war, or a man whose last horse had been taken by the military, or whose homestead they had burned down with all his possessions—all alike fell into this category.

But, on the other hand, the peasant deprived of land could easily

---

[1] A variable land measure, reckoned as 6 desyatinas of good land, 7 of medium land, or 8 of poor land.

[2] 1 *chet* = ½ desyatina.

be enserfed. In Russia serfdom rapidly grew up out of the ruin wrought by the Troubles just as in Germany it grew up out of the ruin wrought by the Thirty Years' War. We have more than once noted that the progress of serfdom signified in Russia not so much the loss of rights by the peasant—in feudal society he was always more the object than the subject of rights—as the cessation of that gambling in peasants, so ruinous for the landholders, which had been so characteristic of the preceding period. In that period the peasant had not infrequently been an object that could be sold, bought, or bartered as they had bartered, bought, and sold bondsmen. Both at the end of the sixteenth century and in the middle of the seventeenth the peasant, already bound to his landlord [3] in one way or another, was the latter's property.

Only two changes may be remarked. In the first place, the methods of binding were changed; in conjunction with the economic results of the Troubles it is here interesting to note that the loan, which formerly had been a very widespread means of attaching the peasant to an estate, now acquires paramount importance. "In official language after the middle of the seventeenth century," writes Dyakonov, "the term 'loan contract' completely supplants the old nomenclature of the peasant 'contract.' " Formerly the loan had been an economic necessity to any well-ordered economy. Thus, in 1598 the authorities of the Blagoveshchensk Monastery in Nizhny-Novgorod complained to the Patriarch Iov that the monastery was impoverished and had not the means to erect buildings, or to pay wages, or to give loans to new peasants. Now the loan becomes a juridical necessity for any peasant settling on the land; without a loan it is impossible to become a peasant. The *Ulozhenie* of 1649 recognises that peasants give "loan and guarantee contract." Numerous new articles in this code speak only of loan contracts with peasants. The old term "contract" becomes a provincialism, clung to, paradoxically enough, in the economically most progressive localities; in the Pskov peasant registers it may be found even at the very end of the seventeenth century. Everywhere else after the Troubles, the peasant actually could not set up his economy without a loan; those not needing a loan were the exception, and the law of Moscow did not reckon with this exception.

In the second place, and this is incomparably more important and no less noteworthy, the peasant ever more and more manifests the tendency to be converted from movable into immovable property. We can ob-

[3] For the convenience of the reader the word *pomeshchik* is here translated as "landlord," the meaning of the term in modern Russian; where the original connotation of the word is still involved, the Russian word will be retained. See Glossary.

serve this interesting process from two angles,—the private and the official, if we may so call them. In the first place, not only the loan but also the obligation to live "immobile" under the given landlord, "steadfastly and without the right to go away," is an unfailing condition of the new type of peasant contract. The peasant's "right to go away," for the abolition of which the landlords had made so many demands during the Troubles, both on Shuisky and on Vladislav, had proved very tenacious and had to be undermined now by private agreements which forced the peasants to renounce their right to leave (*i.e.,* to be taken away by another landlord) just as they were forced to accept the loan. But this did not mean, of course, that the official agitation ceased. The civil war was not yet over, and the "lawful government" had scarcely had time to establish itself at Moscow when the Troitsa Monastery began to search throughout the country for any who had run away from its estates during the whole period of the Troubles. By reason of the extent of the monastery's estates the operation assumed such proportions that it required the sanction of a boyar decree (March 10, 1615), which acknowledged the right of the Troitsa authorities to bring their peasants back within eleven years of their flight; the decree strove to protect the interests of other landlords only if the monastery's fugitives had been living on their lands "twenty years and more." An eleven-year limit, it would seem, was sufficient; a limitation of more than fifteen years was unknown to the law of that time, and later a ten-year one was deemed satisfactory. But the landholders were striving to make peasants more immobile than the land itself, and the first half of the seventeenth century is therefore filled with petitions of nobles and knights agitating for permission to seek out their peasants beyond the statutory limitation, if not without any statute of limitations at all. In 1641 the ten-year limitation on actions for the recovery of fugitive peasants, which formerly had constituted the privilege of a few landholders, such as the Troitsa Monastery and the sovereign's court, was extended to all landlords; in 1649 the Ulozhenie of Tsar Alexis provided that "fugitive peasants and cottars be surrendered, according to the registers, to men of all ranks without a time limit." It is interesting that even after this law, which would seem to be quite clear, the landlords continued to exact from peasants making new contracts the *personal* promise "not to go off with any one else." The peasant who did not give such a promise was not accounted, and did not account himself, bound. In 1690, almost fifty years after the Ulozhenie, one peasant settling on a Troitsa estate relates how a landlord with whom he had dwelt "about three years" began to demand of him "written bonds, that he might dwell as his peasant, and not having given bonds he left the village."

Thus a free peasant was not juridically impossible in Russia even at the beginning of Peter's reign; but actually he was so rare an exception that Muscovite law, crude and summary, registering facts in the mass, did not take account of this phenomenon, just as it did not admit that the peasant was capable of carrying on his economy without a loan from his lord. The "free" peasant, who survived in places, was not in the least bothered by the fact that the law ignored him, and under Tsar Alexis he continued to "contract" with his lord just as he had done under Ivan the Terrible. Only two years before the Ulozhenie a Novgorod landlord, Ivan F. Panov, offered to his peasant Ivashka Petrov, the following contract: "I shall not evict him, Ivashka, and shall not sell or barter him to any one, and shall not put him in pawn, and shall not inflict any evil on him, and shall keep him as my, Ivan's, peasant as other nobles keep their peasants." In case Panov failed to observe these conditions, "he, Ivashka, shall be free to depart whither he will." A piece of property that bargains with its proprietor about the conditions under which it permits him to hold it is, of course, something contrary to all juridical logic; but the men of Moscow had no idea of altering their methods in the interests of any logic and consulted their convenience in each individual case.

Immobilisation of the peasantry, usually defined as "the definite legalisation of serfdom" (although we have just seen that the legal aspect of the matter was the least complete), was one of the most sweeping innovations in Russia's economic life in the period after the Troubles and well exemplifies the nature of their influence. The Troubles did not introduce, nor could they introduce, any economic change. The first step toward the binding of the peasant on a given estate and to a given landlord had been taken, if we overlook the "pozhiloe" of the time of the Sudebniks, in the famous law of November 24, 1597, which had established a five-year limitation on suits for the recovery of fugitive peasants. Its basis had been the agrarian crisis and the depopulation of central Russia. The Troubles had merely carried these two phenomena to the utmost possible limits—and thus furnished the occasion for making them responsible for all possible consequences.

With the cessation of the destruction, however, the influence of this cause was bound to diminish progressively. To use a current expression, the Muscovite state "righted itself" from the Troubles rather quickly. At the lowest point of the decline (1614-1616), on the above-mentioned Troitsa estates, in the counties beyond the River Moscow, the arable constituted 1.8% of the whole area and the waste 98.2%. But according to the registers of the third and fourth decades of this century the first figure rises to 22.7%, and the second falls to 77.3%. In an estate record of the 'twenties "is a reference to the colonising activity of the landholders: the great boyar, Prince Suleshov, who had bought an extensive estate in the county of Pereyaslavl, introduces on it a new economy—'founds a new' homestead of the proprietors and five whole clearings at once.'' There were landholders who prepared homesteads beforehand for future peasant colonists: on an estate in the county of Dmitrov, belonging to S. Larionov, a government official, there stood at the end of the 'twenties three empty homesteads ''established anew.'' By the 'forties this ''internal colonisation'' had made great progress: in the county of Pereyaslavl, for example, in 1646 ''appeared a whole series of new settlements which formerly (in the time of the census of the 'twenties) had not been in existence.'' These settlements included, besides the homesteads of landlords of various categories and of non-taxable dependent cultivators of the soil, 143 homesteads of tax-paying peasants with a male population of 439 and 301 homesteads of cottars with a population of 709 men; about 2,300 desyatinas of land had been ploughed up anew. In Gautier's words, ''the brief economic crisis evoked by the Troubles passed as quickly as it had arisen.''

But the phenomenon we have noted, the immobilisation of the peasantry, by no means disappeared; on the contrary, it was consolidated throughout the seventeenth century. Evidently the Troubles merely helped to disclose something the roots of which lay deeper than a stratum that civil war could wash away. The tension of the agrarian crisis passed simultaneously with the civil war. Yet the economic prosperity of the early years of Ivan the Terrible was not to be repeated. There remained a chronic depression to which pomeshchik economy gradually adjusted itself and from which recovery set in anew, but not until much later, not before the end of the seventeenth century. In this respect the first three-quarters of this century bear the clear imprint of a reaction or, if you like, of a restoration. The latter term is more apt, for in essence there was a restoration, a revival of the old, a resuscitation and a reinforcement of those economic features that a century earlier had seemed lifeless or at least enfeebled.

The peasants of the seventeenth century, bound to the estates, have probably reminded the reader of the ''old-dwellers'' of the old boyar votchinas who dwelt in one and the same hamlet from generation to generation until scattered by the oprichnina. But there are other points of resemblance. Payment of dues in kind, which a hundred years earlier had seemed to be dying out, was exceedingly common in the middle of the seventeenth century. The boyar N. I. Romanov received annually from his hereditary estates a ram, a half carcass of pork, a certain quantity of poultry, and thirty *funts*[4] of cow's butter for each vyt.

4 1 *funt* = 0.9 lb. avoirdupois.

The boyar Lopukhin also collected his revenue from his estate near Moscow in rams and fowls. The peasants of the court villages of the county of Pereyaslavl likewise discharged their obligations with rams, lambs' wool, sheepskins, cheeses, and butter. The tenacity with which obligations in kind persisted on court estates is of special interest; it will be recalled that in the sixteenth century the first experiments with rational economy, *i.e.*, with extensive and regular seigniorial ploughing, were met with on these same court lands. In the seventeenth century the seigniorial ploughing on such estates was gradually curtailed. In the court village of Klushino, as late as the 1630's, there were 250 desyatinas of the "sovereign's arable," but in the 'seventies we find them added to the taxable peasant lots. In the county of Pereyaslavl on one court estate the sovereign's arable diminished in the space of forty years from 546 desyatinas to 249 desyatinas—to a little less than half; on another the whole of it had been given over to the peasants in return for dues. Ultimately, seigniorial ploughing was continued only on court estates near Moscow, where it was less a business enterprise than a means of serving the immediate requirements of the tsar's numerous court. Elsewhere it was replaced by dues, not in kind, however, but in money or in "threshed grain." We shall see the significance of this fact presently; meanwhile let us note that the phenomenon referred to was not peculiar to court estates but was common to all large estates of the time. Even if this absence of rural-economic enterprise had been characteristic only of large landholding, we should have an example of great economic inertia, the survival into the seventeenth century of an agrarian type well known in the first half of the sixteenth. But it seems that even the middle-sized economies, which in the days of Ivan the Terrible had switched over to a new track with such bewildering rapidity, a hundred years later had not only not advanced but had even gone backward. At least, in the only case known to us, and relating to the county of Kostroma, the seigniorial arable had declined from a little over 90% in the 1620's to 16% by 1684-1686.

Different relationships existed in the south, where the pomeshchik reserved a great part of the plough land for himself; but this was a very special kind of pomeshchik controlling on the average one peasant's and one cottar's homestead (in the counties of Belgorod and Putivl), at best three such homesteads (in the county of Voronezh), and sometimes not even one (in the county of Oskol). Throughout the enormous extent of these four counties [5] Gautier found, excluding the monasteries, only one pomeshchik, using the term in its modern sense

---

[5] They embraced the eastern part of the province of Chernigov, the whole southern part of Kursk, almost all of Voronezh and the southeastern part of Tambov, almost all of Kharkov, and the northeastern part of Poltava.

of landlord; he had three homesteads of retainers, 11 of peasants, and 5 of cottars, with about 750 desyatinas of land. Moreover, the number of peasants and cottars on estates in south Russia was not increasing in the seventeenth century, but decreasing. In one of the districts of the county of Belgorod there were 146 homesteads of peasants and cottars in 1626, 130 in 1646, and in 1678 there remained but 21. For another district of this county, in the same years, we have the following figures: 255, 141, and 60. "In actual fact," writes Miklashevsky, "the number of cottar homesteads of private landholders had decreased in far greater degree inasmuch as in very many new settlements of the county the cottars lived on the lord's land." If we are not hypnotised by the division of Muscovites into "military servitors" and "taxpayers"—a division purely political and bearing no relation to economics—nothing will prevent us from identifying, from the economic point of view, the pomeshchiks of Moscow's southern frontier with peasants. This is virtually what the scholar we have cited says when he asserts that here "the dominant type was a petty economy, suggesting modern peasant economy, with only this essential difference, that the petty landholder of the seventeenth century was assured of land in abundance, at least in the first half of the century." It must be noted that the Moscow government did not allow itself to be hypnotised by this division. In 1648 a document was sent to the village of Bel-Kolodez and the crossroads and hamlets pertaining to it, bidding the peasants refuse in future service under the pomeshchiks; they were to serve as dragoons and at the same time were freed from payment of various imposts. Each was now obliged to have an arquebus, a pike, and an axe, but their land holdings were left unchanged. Thus by a single stroke of the pen taxpayers were converted into military servitors while their economic organisation remained inviolate.

It remains for us to make general application of the observation to which we were led by the microscopic "pomeshchiks" of the frontier counties. Throughout Russia petty landholding of the peasant type was "dominant," i.e., economically dominant in the seventeenth century, surviving the crisis that ruined the pomeshchik-entrepreneur. When the lord abandoned his arable, it was not left to lie idle; it was leased by the peasant. We have seen this in the case of court estates; the monasteries and the private landholders adopted the same practice. The peasant allotment grew with inexorable regularity, while the lord's arable at best stood still. At the end of the sixteenth century, at the height of the crisis, peasant arable in central Russia did not exceed 2.6 desyatinas to the homestead; in the first half of the seventeenth century it had already reached 6 desyatinas to the homestead, and in the second half a little more than 9 in some places. Gautier, from whom we have taken these figures, sees an offset to this phenomenon in the fact that the amount of arable per male soul did not increase during this time but, with the exception of court estates, even diminished slightly. He perceives in this "a fresh depression of peasant economy"; but he leaves out of sight the fact that on two and a half desyatinas it is impossible to maintain any economy at all, while on six, and all the more on nine, it is possible. The growth of the peasant homestead, which it would be very shortsighted to explain by financial influences alone (from 1630 taxes were levied not on the amount of land under cultivation but on the number of homesteads), is part of the general picture of economic restoration in the seventeenth century. The "big household" of appanage times, the direct descendant of the "pechishche" of the earliest period, is resurrected, significantly enough, concurrently with the decline of the pomestye [service-estate] and, as we shall presently see, with the resurrection of the votchina [hereditary estate]. It was now necessary, because it was the most stable economic organisation under a régime of natural economy, and Muscovite Russia was now nearer such a régime than it had been during the preceding hundred years.

This great stability of course did not lead to a "depression of the level of peasant economy." On the contrary, the best index of the way matters were tending is the gradual disappearance of cottar homesteads along with the amazing increase, in some localities, of the number of peasant homesteads. Gautier has gathered from the registers such data as the following: in the county of Bezhetsk in the 1620's there were computed to be (on the five estates traced by the author) 155 peasant homesteads inhabited by 158 male souls; according to the registers of the 'eighties, there were 175 [6] homesteads inhabited by 5,797 souls; while in the first case there were 218 cottar homesteads, in the second only 75, and the number of cottars in them had declined during these sixty years from 227 to 197. On 18 estates in the county of Dmitrov in the same period the number of peasants' homesteads rose from 125 to 611, and the number of cottars' decreased from 83 to 17. In general, on all the 115 estates investigated by our author, the number of peasant homesteads increased two and a half times, but their population increased almost five times; formerly there were less than two souls to the homestead, now there were almost three and a half. The number of cottars' homesteads decreased by one-half, and their population remained unchanged.

[6] This figure is evidently an error for 1,7... All these figures are taken from a table in Gautier, *The region beyond the Moscow* [in Russian], p. 259; another table in the same work (p. 511), based on the same *pistsovye knigi* [registers] gives the figures in slightly variant form. Addition of the latter figures gives 154, 157, 1731, and 5726, respectively.

Another symptom of the way matters were tending is the ratio of arable to waste as given in the registers of the 'eighties. In contrast to what we have seen at the beginning of the seventeenth century, or even at the end of the preceding one when the crisis was at its height, the arable now decidedly predominated. Our author cites a number of estates in the counties of Shuya, Yurev Polski, and Kostroma where either all the land was under cultivation, with the exception of meadow-land, and there was no waste at all, or the waste was reduced to the insignificant proportion of 6-7% of the whole area. On the average the arable is to waste in the ratio of 2:1, while in the 'twenties the ratio had been 1:5. Not only had the wounds dealt by the Troubles been healed, but the crisis in pomestye landholding may be said to have been liquidated by this time; and the element that profited by the liquidation was not the element that had lost a hundred years before. The predatory forms of pomestye money economy, which had destroyed both pomeshchik and peasant, disappeared for some time; they were destined to be seen anew, though in a totally different economic setting, during "the Age of Catherine." On the other hand, the peasant, enslaved as in the appanage period, to a certain degree recovered his appanage prosperity—the prosperity of a well-fed slave, it is true. That he was, however, not too discontented with his position is shown by the rapidity with which the population of central Russia, which had diminished so considerably in Fedor's reign, grew in the seventeenth century. From the 'twenties to the 'forties it increased, in various districts, from 2.3 to 6.3 times; in certain places there was by the 'eighties 7.5 times the population of the years immediately after the Troubles.

It remains for us to trace one more aspect of this retrogression, this time not economic but socio-juridical. The triumph of the pomeshchiks in 1612 was, it would seem, bound to complete the process begun by the oprichnina and to consolidate its results—to convert all the land under cultivation into pomestyes. At first sight it was so. No sooner had the cannonading under the Kremlin of Moscow ceased, than court and "black" (free peasant) lands began to be handed over wholesale to the nobles, so that by the spring of 1613 not less than 45,000 desyatinas of court land and some 14,000 desyatinas of "black" land had been distributed, principally to the leaders of the pomeshchik host, to its generals and officers. Somewhat later came the turn of the rank and file; about 1627 there took place a distribution of pomestyes to the young nobles who were old enough for service but who were still without land allotments and consequently were living at the expense of older relatives. The sources for this great distribution and for many other petty ones that took place at intervals were once again the court and black lands and, in part, lands confiscated from other landholders; but now they confiscated not "princelings' " votchinas (there were hardly any of these left) but rather those lands which had been granted by the political opponents, now beaten, of those who had triumphed in 1612, *i.e.*, granted by the Tushino "knave" and in particular by the "king and king's son"—the Polish-boyar government of 1610-1611. It is particularly noteworthy that the "knave's gifts" were not revoked with such regularity as were those of the "king." Tsar Michael's government could not forget that Tushino had once been the "nobles' nest," which had fledged the Romanovs. The total amount of land thus distributed in small lots far exceeded, of course, what the "early birds" had seized in large morsels immediately after their victory. Whole townships were distributed, sometimes 300 pomestye portions at once; in one famous case the amount of arable distributed in one place amounted to 4,500 desyatinas, in another even to 7,500. We can hardly estimate the exact total; we do not know every case of distribution; but the total sum would have to be reckoned in hundreds of thousands, if not in millions, of desyatinas.

This, however, was an obvious consequence of the victory won by the nobility. What is more interesting is that these lands, distributed as pomestyes were, a generation later, held, not as pomestyes, but as votchinas. This phenomenon is perceptible enough even in the 'twenties. At this time in one of the districts of the county of Dmitrov it was possible to count 6 old votchinas and 10 acquired ones, granted as a result of the two sieges of Moscow, the one under Tsar Vasily and the other under Michael, "at the coming of the king's son," when the king's son Vladislav encamped under Moscow. In individual districts of the counties of Zvenigorod, Kolomna, and Rostov a similar ratio held between "old" (*i.e.*, inherited) votchinas and votchinas gained through service. In the county of Uglich out of 114 votchinas 59, again a majority, had appeared in the first quarter of the seventeenth century. In the county of Moscow votchina lands constituted almost two-thirds of all estates, pomestye lands little more than one-third. In one county (Luga) votchina landholding makes its first appearance in this period. Moreover, the tendency was for the best pomestye lands to be converted into votchinas. Even in these same 'twenties, *i.e.*, long before the recovery at the end of the century, the ratio of arable to waste on votchina lands was far more satisfactory than on pomestye lands; sometimes on votchinas there was ten times more arable under cultivation than on the pomestyes of the same county.

But this of course does not mean, as the author from whom we have borrowed these statistics thinks, that votchina economy was more stable than pomestye; economically the two types, when of similar size, did not differ in any respect. Even juridically the distinction was not so great as we have become accustomed to think through following the lead of the historians of Russian law, who have very facilely transferred to feudal Rus the norms of modern bourgeois relationships. Pomestyes almost always passed by inheritance and were transferred from one hand to another even in defiance of special prohibitions. For example, the government strove hard to isolate the pomestye portions given to foreigners in its service (their number steadily increased in the seventeenth century); nevertheless the documents disclose a number of men, indubitably Russian, but holding foreigners' pomestyes. All that it had any success in attaining was that "lands should not go out of service." The holder of a pomestye, like every Orthodox Christian, desired to "order his soul," to make sure that the Church would pray for him after his death, and, like every landholder, he attained this end by sacrificing a part of his lands to some monastery or other. This practice had been common in the sixteenth century; in the seventeenth century it became an every-day phenomenon, regardless of a series of formal prohibitions; and thus a number of pomestye allotments were fused with monasteries' votchinas. To teach a Muscovite the difference between "ownership" and "tenure" was no easy task, especially when the right of property was violated at every step, not only by the supreme authority, as in the case of every banishment in the times of Ivan the Terrible or of Godunov, but by any powerful feudatory. "What I hold is mine until they take it from me"; this juridically incorrect but psychologically quite intelligible notion was lodged in the brain of every early Russian landholder, whether he held by votchina or pomestye tenure.

We shall most readily understand the difference between votchina and pomestye if we consider, not the obligations to the state incident to one or the other type of landholding but the economic interests of the holders. Then we shall readily understand why the favourite type in the second half of the sixteenth century was the pomestye, and in the following century the votchina. In the period of feverish, predatory exploitation of the land they had seized, men had striven to make a profit out of it as quickly as possible; then they had abandoned it and set about exploiting new land. When relationships had again assumed mediæval stability, it was natural that there should be a tendency to secure to oneself and one's family the land occupied; and not less natural was it that this tendency should be first displayed in respect to the more valuable estates. As pomestye they now took only what they would not regret abandoning. Little by little, however, to secure an estate to oneself became just as much a habit of the landholder as to bind the peasant on this estate, and then the "pomestye element" in Muscovite landholding, especially near Moscow, "came very close to extinction." In the county of Borovsk, for example, in 1629-1630, pomestye lands constituted two-fifths of all the land, and votchinas three-fifths, while in 1678 the former were only one-fourth of all the estates, and the latter three-fourths. In the county of Moscow in 1624-5 pomestye lands still constituted 35.4%, but in 1646 only 4.4%.

This juridical restoration would be quite a riddle to us if we did not appreciate the economic soil that had nourished it. To the resurrection of the old type of economy, with dues in kind and weakly developed seigniorial arable, corresponded the resurrecton of the old landed right. It was natural that the old type of tenure should be resurrected. The "old-fashioned" boyar votchinas of the sixteenth century as a rule had been latifundia; the pomestyes that replaced them had been an example of middling landholding. In the eighteenth century once more we find latifundia; their revival falls entirely within the first reigns of the new dynasty. The very day after the Troubles there began a regular orgy of great distributions of land, a sort of restoration of what the oprichnina had upon a time annihilated. In 1619-1620 was distributed the whole county of Galich, i.e., all of its "black" lands, occupied by a peasantry still free. Only in rare cases was this pomestye distribution by small lots; far more frequently we find a whole township handed over to a single person with a more or less "historic" name. Here we find the boyar Shein (the commandant of Smolensk at the time of its siege by Sigismund), and the boyar Sheremetev, and Ivan Nikitich Romanov, and the Princes Mstislavsky, Buinosov-Rostovsky, and Romodanovsky. The county of Galich, of course, is only one example: we find a mass of such cases in other places, both before 1620 and after; the greater part, almost 60,000 desyatinas, distributed in the first months of Michael's reign, passed into large votchinas, and in the 'twenties and 'thirties it is possible to find a number of cases when by the tsar's granting there fell into one person's hands at the same time 300 homesteads of peasants and 1,500 desyatinas of land. As a result, by the end of the seventeenth century there remained no "black" lands at all in the region beyond the River Moscow, and from one and a half to two million desyatinas of court lands had been distributed among a few persons.

The closer we are to the end of this period, the more grandiose becomes the sweep of the process. Even under Tsar Fedor II (1676-1682) a good half of all the lands granted in his short reign constitute large distributions. From 1682 to 1700 there were distributed as votchinas "16,120 homesteads and more than 167,000 desyatinas of plough land, without counting meadows and woods, which were sometimes given in enormous amounts to favoured holders of votchinas."

Among the grantees first place is taken by the tsar's kin: Apraxsins, Miloslavskys, Saltykovs, Naryshkins, Lopukhins. Sometimes at a single stroke there fell into the same hands, as in the case of the Naryshkins in 1683-4, some 2,500 homesteads and 14,000 desyatinas of land. But this was nothing in comparison with the latifundia that began to arise under Peter when Menshikov alone acquired more than three townships, with 20,000 desyatinas. During only eleven years of Peter's reign (1700-1711), of court lands alone about 340,000 desyatinas of arable land and 27,500 homesteads of peasants were distributed, as against 167,000 desyatinas and 16,000 homesteads converted into latifundia in the course of the preceding eighteen-year period. Thus, the nobles definitely seated themselves in the place of the boyars; and out of their midst arose a new feudal aristocracy that made possible the flowering of the "new feudalism" of the eighteenth century.

2. Political Restoration

Regeneration of the old economic forms was bound to be accompanied by revival of the old political régime. All the text-books are filled with descriptions of the "abuses" of Muscovite administration in the seventeenth century. These are usually represented as the product of the free "evil will" of the officials of the time. Sometimes phrases are added about the "lack of culture" of Tsar Alexis' contemporaries, and the historian deems explanation exhausted if he reminds his reader of the decline of the "zemsky [autonomous] principle" in local government and its replacement by the "prikaz [bureaucratic] principle." Not so long ago "bureaucracy" was, in the eyes of the average Russian intellectual, so universal an explanation of every social evil that to dig deeper into the "causes of things" seemed a luxury absolutely superfluous.

To simplify the question it is desirable from the outset to give up our preconceived ideas about the "prikaz principle." If we understand the triumph of the latter to mean replacement of local self-government by a tyrannous bureaucracy, we find no historical facts to support such an explanation. All those organs of local self-government which were the product of the sixteenth century remained under the same names during the seventeenth century right down to the time of Peter, and in slight disguise till a much later date. No great change, the reader will agree, could result from the fact that the "zemsky starosta" began to be called "burgomistr," the "zemsky tselovalnik" "ratman," and the "zemskaya izba" "magistrat." The guba authorities likewise survived until Peter, and the fact that in his reign we find a "landrat" or commissar in place of the *"gubnoy golova,"* marks no change in the essence of things.

If the evolution of the prikaz principle be taken to mean the formation of a group of professional officials (in the seventeenth century concerned almost exclusively with finance or diplomacy, jurists being added much later), this differentiation was effected at the cost of the feudal régime, not at the cost of "autonomy." Feudal Russia, like feudal Europe, had known but one division of governmental functions—the division into spiritual and temporal. Representatives of the one and of the other, each in their own sphere, performed all those functions now executed by the most diverse professional officials,—the administration of justice, the collection of taxes, the carrying on of diplomatic negotiations, and the command of the troops.[7] The growing complexity of governmental machinery, which paralleled economic development, caused the first three functions to be assigned to separate specialists, in part of bourgeois origin; only the military command was left exclusively to the feudal aristocracy. This was the "formation of a bureaucracy," in Russia as in the West, a fact which can be regretted only by representatives of historical romanticism, who sigh for the lost "harmony" of mediæval life. The contemporary reader, bourgeois or non-bourgeois, has not the slightest reason for joining in these sighs. The correlation of social forces could not be changed because the method of operation of these forces became more complicated; the character of the régime was determined by its class physiognomy, and not by whether it was effected by "civilians" or by military men.

But the rise of the "prikaz order of things," in this second and only correct sense of the word, does not constitute a feature characteristic of the realm of the first Romanovs. The enormous influence of the professional officials, the dyaks, had been remarked by the contemporaries of Ivan [IV] the Terrible. In the following reign two dyaks, the brothers Shchelkalov, had sometimes seemed to foreigners the very embodiment of the Muscovite government; in the words of one Russian contemporary, Boris Godunov was more than a little indebted for his rise to one of the Shchelkalovs, a view shared by modern historians. In the Time of the Troubles, as we have seen, a former dyak of merchant origin, Fedor Andronov, had for a time ruled the Muscovite state. The seventeenth century offers more numerous examples of a similar character, though not a single one so vivid. The dyaks of Tsars Michael and Alexis were somewhat more unassuming

---

[7] The representatives of the spiritual power in Russia usually exercised this last function indirectly, through the medium of their boyars; duties as military commanders sometimes fell to the lot of the heads of a few monasteries (Troitsa or Solovetsky).

than these wielders of the destinies of the realm of Moscow. The circumstance, which is usually commented on, that under these tsars the nobles, who had formerly disdained "lean grade," did not look askance at a dyakship (the best known noble family to make its career in official posts was that of the Lopukhins) can also be observed in earlier times; even in 1610 Moscow nobles had petitioned Sigismund to appoint them dyaks. The examples cited by Kotoshikhin of the power of bureaucratic institutions, such as the Bureau of Secret Affairs, in part mark the first steps in a further development with which we must acquaint ourselves in more detail when we study the so-called "Petrine reform," in part are simply an exaggeration of the authority of the dyaks,—an exaggeration natural to the pen of a *podyak* [assistant dyak] author. In general, the central administration of the Muscovite state makes no perceptible progress in this direction until the very beginning of the following century when suddenly, within a few years, the whole system of the old central administration is destroyed, both duma and prikazes [bureaux]. The chief reform in the field of local administration, the establishment of the voevoda's authority, has all the characteristics of a typical feudal institution; the voevoda commands the troops, administers justice, and collects the taxes. The loss of this last function is, again, one of the signs of further progress at the very end of the period we are studying.

We must, then, renounce the simple and easy method of explaining the "abuses" by reference to the "evil will" of the "bureaucracy"; and on the question of "culture" serving as an antidote to "abuses," the United States and France of the present day offer such brilliant answers that it remains but to apply to the Muscovite state the method we should apply to them and seek not abuses but illustrations of a class régime. Setting out on this road, we shall see, first of all, that there was no inherent antagonism between "autonomy" and "abuses"; that, on the contrary, the former, as it then existed, was a very favourable breeding ground for the latter.

The Dvina and Volga regions were the classic land of "zemsky" institutions in the seventeenth century as they had been in the sixteenth. The northern and Lowland towns were centres of the Muscovite bourgeoisie, in contrast to the southern towns, which were military-agrarian centres, behind the walls of which the local agricultural population took refuge from the foe, and whence the commanding elements of this population "ruled" the surrounding country. In the north it was otherwise; in consequence of the weak development of large landholding on the infertile soil, unfit for rural-economic enterprise, until the eighteenth century there here survived in large measure a juridically free peasantry, economically enserfed, not by pomeshchiks but by urban capitalists. Here arose real bourgeois landholding, with which the nobles' government of the seventeenth century did not know what to do, accustomed as it was to see the land exclusively in the hands of military men; at one moment it took from the "gosts" and traders and all other ranks the hamlets "purchased and mortgaged," at another moment it gave them back.

The extent of differentiation within the town population in the seventeenth century may be shown by two or three examples. In Usolye, in the second quarter of the century, are found merchants whose homesteads were valued at from 500 to 1,000 rubles (in modern money from 5,000 to 10,000 rubles); but we must take into account that, in the then forested north, building materials were literally not worth a red cent, so that the value of buildings as compared with movables was not what it is to-day. Not 1,000, but 300 rubles constituted a real capital, and a large one at that, for the merchant of those times; in Tobolsk, the chief town of Siberia, no one then had a larger capital. A man whose house with all its furnishings was worth about 1,000 rubles corresponded to the man worth a hundred thousand rubles at the beginning of the twentieth century; and God knows Usolye was no great centre. Ustyuzhna Zhelezopolskaya was still smaller, and there for the misdemeanour of a "young" man they took only one ruble and for a misdemeanour of a "trader" five rubles; the higher members of urban society were just five times greater than the lower ones. In Nizhny-Novgorod were four categories of the town population, the highest of which were the "better men," the wholesale traders and boat-owners, and the lowest the "base men," who, however, had homesteads of their own; homeless cottars were not included at all.

We have seen what a notable page in the history of the Troubles the struggle between these "better" and "lesser" men of the town of the time had constituted. The Troubles had ended with the victory of the "better" men, and the organs of zemsky autonomy, both in the town and in the county attached to it, had passed into their hands. The most modest of them took advantage of this only for the purpose of not "bearing *tyaglo*" [taille] along with the mass of the town population, in other words, of unloading on the latter the principal burden of state taxation. Thus, at Solvychegodsk in the 1620's there was a zemsky tselovalnik (in later language, a member of the county board) who, together with a few others, was not included in the general town assessment and was not responsible for the town poor. Not, of course, because he and his comrades were poor men; on the contrary, they were local bigwigs, who not only held homesteads but also possessed salt-boileries, shops, and warehouses in the town, and in the county had "little fields" and "meadows." Another zemsky tselovalnik, in the county of Totma, displayed still more aggressiveness; together with other "strong men" he seized a number of waste plots and vacant peasant lots but paid no taxes on them, leaving this for the peasants to do under the mutual guarantee. When the peasants took it into their heads to complain of him, he reminded them that the very collection of taxes was in his hands; he began to put the complainants to distraint "in excessive taxes and mir levies" "and beat them without mercy." The "prikaz" official sent from Totma to examine into the complaints proved to be on the side of the "strong men," and so openly and shamelessly that a commissioner from Moscow had to put him in prison; whether the commissioner himself did anything, we do not know; in any case, after his departure matters probably went on as before. There could, of course, be no question of any control exercised by the "lesser" men over the "better" men. At Vologda not only the "lesser" men but even the "middling" men could not obtain permission to "examine" the zemsky starostas [elders]; the "better" men preferred to settle everything within their own circle, and friendly and amicable apportionment of the revenues evidently took the place of control. At Khlynov matters were still simpler; there the starosta and tselovalniks simply "assigned" among themselves the monies collected from the mir [community], continuing to exact them promptly from the taxpayers. In this way many both in town and country "were impoverished and indebted greatly with debts and, abandoning their homesteads, were scattered asunder." The growth of indebtedness was fostered by the starosta and tselovalniks, who, among other things, engaged in usury. The depopulation of Khlynov attracted attention at Moscow, and the townsmen were permitted to elect examiners for the purpose of effecting a reform of the zemsky administration of Khlynov; it remained a question, however, who, under the conditions existing at Khlynov, might be examiners, and what practical results such a reform would yield.

The state of affairs that had existed before the Troubles and that during them had evoked a series of urban outbursts and had made the Tushino "knave" tsar of all the oppressed and injured—this state of affairs continued to prevail in Russian towns after the termination of the "Time of the Troubles." Naturally the social struggle of the Time of the Troubles was bound to break out, now here, now there, and the fact that it did not assume the same acute form as it had when all Russia was in the throes of civil strife does not detract either from its social meaning or from its interest. In the 1670's the county of Ustyug was completely in the grip of the urban capitalists of Great Ustyug; in a petition the men of the county very graphically describe the state of affairs at the time. "The peasants were in everything enslaved to them, the townsmen, and by their wealth the zemsky starostas of the town have in their pride oppressed the peasants, and treated them as slaves, and by their might and great goods have purchased from our brothers, from the poor peasants, the best hamlets in the county of Ustyug and have begun in many townships to be the proprietors, and thence we, the peasants, have grown poor under their violence, and because of this poverty the peasants work on their [the townsmen's] hamlets instead of slaves. . . ." But here, too, there finally came a moment when the "strong men" split, and apparently more seriously than anywhere else in a similar case. The starosta of the customs, himself a large trader, of course, utilising the quite unique pretext of the passage of a Dutch envoy (we shall not forget that in those days the Northern Dvina was the highway to Western Europe), assembled a meeting and at it effected a sort of municipal revolution. The assembled peasants elected their own separate "zemsky starosta of the whole county," "and set up a special, paid, new-fangled *volost izba* beside the old general *zemsky izba* of the townsmen." [8] A remarkable peculiarity of the Ustyug conflict was the fact that the local voevoda took the part of the "rebels." We do not know his reasons, but at Moscow the day was won by the deputies of the countrymen only because they did not begrudge money, in a single day distributing a hundred rubles each to the Moscow podyaks; this fact, far more than the voevoda's leadership of the insurrection, which in itself might have been an accident, proves that the Ustyug peasantry was backed by an opposition among the local capitalists; purchasing the support of Moscow with the assistance of this merchant opposition, the men of the county of Ustyug even subjected the townsmen and acquired the right to fine the "better men" if they were unwilling to "pay along with the peasants," *i.e.*, if they did not include themselves in the general assessment.

It must, moreover, be noted that the sympathies of the Moscow authorities for the "lesser" men in town and country was not always occasioned by the personal greed of these or those "authorities." In the days of the Troubles the great bourgeoisie of the towns and the pomeshchiks had been allies, it is true. But hardly had those days passed and the common menace—the danger of a revolt of the "lesser" men, supported by Tushino—subsided, than the old antagonism swiftly revived, and the basic contradiction of interests of these two elements with respect to the state treasury, of the pomeshchik as payee, of the bourgeois as payer, was bound to be felt ever more and more keenly.

But *guba*, and not *zemsky*, institutions were the chief battleground

---

[8] That is, the peasants of the township (*volost*) set up their own autonomous organs of administration, independent of the county government controlled by the bourgeoisie.

of the two dominant classes of Muscovite society. We know that this form of "autonomy" had borne a class character from the very beginning, that the guba head or starosta was always a noble or knight. But, in the first place, though elected from one definite class, he was elected by all classes of society except the bondaged peasantry. In the second place, he did not act alone, but with tselovalniks, who were always non-nobles; the guba head, a noble, was only the president of this commission, which was really composed of all classes. His rights were, as we saw, very broad, but he could not alone pronounce final decision, and if he unduly offended the interests of the non-nobles, he exposed himself to the resistance of his democratic colleagues. In central Russia—a pomeshchik country from time immemorial—these restrictions on the power of the guba starosta might be, and probably were, an empty formality. But in the north, where the bourgeoisie was powerful and strong, it sometimes succeeded, even in the seventeenth century, in deposing unpopular guba heads and replacing them with its own candidates. In Ustyuzhna Zhelezopolskaya in the 1640's, the nobles' candidate for guba starosta twice had to give way to the townsmen's candidate, though he, too, of course, was taken from the military servitors. Twice the nobles and knights regained the upper hand, but the third time the conflict was ended by the townsmen gaining the right to elect a separate starosta, who was to administer the town alone, without the county.

Under such conditions the fact that election by the nobles and knights alone was ever more and more frequently deemed sufficient, and the opinion of the townsmen not consulted, acquires special significance; though sometimes the townsmen participated in the elections, yet their votes did not count, since a pretext could always be found for declaring their candidate "unfit" to hold guba office. Still more curious is the evolution of the guba college. The tselovalnik, in the sixteenth century a colleague of the guba starosta, in the seventeenth is only his subordinate; the starosta administers the oath and makes known to him the orders that come from Moscow. In 1669 the tselovalniks were abolished altogether or, rather, they were converted into prison guards, for prison tselovalniks, who guarded men under arrest, were retained until the end of the century. But this office had long since ceased to interest any one, and in places even in the 'twenties the townsmen "did not give prison money and did not attend to the prison at all."

This very much surprised the nobles, who felt that, though guba matters were their business, the taxpayers were bound to bear the expenses of them as of the nobles' state in general. But for the taxpayers the guba starosta had long been, not an "organ of autonomy" but a weapon of class oppression, and naturally their concern was not whether guba institutions were well served (who cares about the good quality of the chain with which he is fettered?), but rather how to get rid of them. Gradually they came to think that a prikaz man would be better, for at least he would not be directly elected by their foes, the local pomeshchiks. Each outburst of desperation on the part of the townsmen was utilised by the central nobles' government to deprive them of the last shreds of their autonomy; a local voevoda received instructions to see to it that "the guba starosta does not accuse [the townsmen and the peasants of the county] on an oral report and that he does not for the sake of his greed commit oppression and inflict fines; if an oral report be made against the townsmen and the peasants of the county the voevoda and the dyak are bidden to inquire into it directly and justly and to execute the law by the sovereign's edict and by the Ulozhenie, but if it is an important matter, or one not written in the Ulozhenie, to write to the sovereign at Moscow."

The naïveté of the townsmen's hopes concerning the impartiality of the "prikaz" men from Moscow is quite apparent. In the 'sixties the men of one town who had exchanged their guba heads for voevodas thus characterised one of the latter, one evidently no worse than his predecessors: the voevoda "beats us . . . without inquest and without fault, and puts us in prison for his avarice; and taking out of prison, beats with cudgels half to death without cause and without fault. And in the past year 172 he, the voevoda, shutting himself up in his homestead, beat the tselovalnik of the customs chest, Volodka Selivanov, half to death and made great loss to the customs revenue. Many traders who came to deal in salt and fish he injured and ruined, and put in prison; and many traders who had come he drove out and scattered the market, and thy customs revenue, Great Sovereign, he stopped; and us, thy orphans, elected men, in the end he has ruined with his great oppression, and taxation, and fining, and murder. . . ." This example, which could be reproduced as often as one liked, is in itself interesting because in it stands out very distinctly the social class that suffered from the voevodas' acts of violence. These are not the petty folk who petitioned against their "zemsky" authorities; these are the authorities themselves, the zemsky starostas and wealthy merchants, dealers in fish and salt. The whole bourgeoisie suffered from the nobles' administration; the higher elements, as in the days of the youth of Ivan the Terrible, suffered even more than the lower, since they had more to lose.

In enriching themselves, in using their power to make immediate material profits, lay the essence of the whole business for the voevodas and other prikaz men. When we see a prikaz man beginning his administrative activity by taking "entry" from those he administers, and then, just like the kormlenshchik of the good old times—the times not of Ivan the Terrible even, but of Ivan III—beginning to drag out of these people under his administration all sorts of kormlenies in kind—rye, barley, wheat, calves, rams, butter, eggs, fish, sheep, hay— at any or all of these things we are not at all surprised. The reader has long since become acquainted with the familiar picture of a korm-lenshchik's administration. The essence of the administrative restora-tion, of which the above cases of guba and voevoda tyranny were indi-vidual manifestations, was the revival of kormlenies.

After the keen criticism of kormlenies that we read in Peresvetov, after what we know of Godunov's administration, which tried to realise in practice the ideal of a police state, the feudal order of things in the seventeenth century cannot be regarded as a simple survival. The new "kormlenies" were too universal a phenomenon for that. What "social conscience," in the person of the nobles' publicist of the times of Ivan the Terrible, had sharply condemned, the nobles of the seven-teenth century regarded with the utmost complaisance, as an absolutely normal affair. Offices of an "elective" character (guba offices, for example) they considered, not as abuses but as offices just like any others. The guba starosta was, as we know, to prosecute thieves and robbers, and worthy historians of Russian law have been seriously con-vinced that the Moscow government had lost its head over how it should deal with robbers. With sublime tranquillity it appointed to guba office a blind man precisely because he was blind. And this was the general rule. In 1601 it was forbidden to appoint as voevodas and prikaz men nobles and knights who were not injured, not maimed but healthy; a kormlenie, you see, was a reward for service, somewhat in the nature of a pension; why give it to a healthy man, a man still fit for "regimental service"? At the very beginning of the period under consideration, immediately after the Troubles, Moscow had sometimes bethought itself, as it were, of the Godunov traditions; in the voevodas' instructions of the 'twenties the voevodas were strictly enjoined "not to cause any injuries or levy taxes on any one out of avarice and to plough and thresh grain for themselves, and harvest hay, and not to take feed for horses, and to distil spirits, and not to bid firewood to be cut and any obligatory labour to be done, and from the town and the county not to take food and drink and money for food and drink, that there be no injuries upon them and no petitioners to the sovereign for any acts of violence." In the 'seventies, however, on abolishing a prikaz office, the government unceremoniously imposed on the in-habitants a due for "voevoda's revenues," as it might have done in the first half of the sixteenth century for the "namestnik's feeding." The famous case related by Tatishchev, in which Tsar Alexis was trying to find for a favourite noble a town with a "revenue" of six hundred rubles and found one of only four hundred, is not merely an anecdote. And probably the story of the same Tatishchev that all the towns had a fixed tariff, and that whoever paid the price got the town, is also more than an anecdote.

If we add to all this that on his estates every landholder was the judge over his peasants in all except guba (chiefly, robbery) cases, and that in all cases, guba ones included, he had the right of preliminary investigation as it was then understood (*i.e.*, including torture), our picture of the "dominance of private law" will need but one final touch. In the seventeenth century, as in the preceding one, immunities continued to exist; that is, there was special jurisdiction for special categories of persons and institutions. We have already seen how easily the least of these privileges—emancipation from the jurisdiction of the nearest local court—was obtained. It was not impossible to gain a great one—subjection in judicial matters to the central institutions exclusively. Such a privilege was enjoyed by the posterity of Kuzma Minin, but it was also given to persons altogether unrenowned. In 1654, for example, Ivan Kikin and Afanasy Strunnikov, townsmen of the town of Gorokhovets, received a perpetual and hereditary immunity; using appanage terminology, "the grand prince or whom he orders" was to judge them. A similar immunity was enjoyed by all the gosts and men of the gost hundred; only the tsar or the tsar's treasurer judged them. Strange as it may seem, a privilege might in a certain sense be a progressive feature, as we shall see later; such was the special jurisdiction for foreigners, who were tried in the *Posolsky Prikaz* [Bureau of Foreign Affairs]. The widest immunities, of course, were obtained by ecclesiastical institutions. The archpriest of the Moscow Cathedral of the Annunciation tried Church people and peasants belonging to the cathedral in all cases, not excepting guba cases, and was obliged to report to the sovereign only if he himself could not decide the case. It was a rare monastery that did not know how to obtain the same privilege; in 1667 it was made general by a Church council, which provided that according to the rules of the holy fathers Church people, including the numerous peasantry dwelling on Church lands, were subject only to the jurisdiction of the Church.

The organs of the central government were less affected by the class struggle than were the provincial institutions, for in respect to class the central administration was far more homogeneous. The bourgeoisie very rarely penetrated into the central institutions, and then only by losing its immediate class physiognomy. Kuzma Minin, like Fedor Andronov before him, had to convert himself into a military servitor in order to take his seat in the tsar's council; from a bourgeois zemsky starosta he became a "noble of the duma." But the number of such *anoblis* was insignificant in the Muscovite state of the seventeenth century, far more insignificant than, for example, in France of the same period. The democracy of the Muscovite sovereign's duma was made up of "base born" pomeshchiks and dyaks, two elements which, as we have seen, then displayed a strong tendency toward fusion. During the Petrine recovery a wave of this democracy washed away the last remnants of the old aristocracy; in the boyar lists of the last years of the duma appeared a variety of names of men scarcely bearing duma ranks, like the celebrated Romodanovsky, and even of "men" like the no less celebrated Alexis Kurbatov, a former bondsman of Sheremetev.

The "great destruction" of the Muscovite state at the beginning of the century had prepared this result long in advance, but it came tardily rather than prematurely. Mestnichestvo survived until 1682, and under the first two tsars of the new dynasty the personnel of the central institutions bore a more archaic character than might have been expected. The political influence of the old boyar order, as a social group, was already insignificant in 1610; yet as late as 1668 it supplied almost half of the entire personnel of the duma (28 out of 62), simply because, as Kotoshikhin testifies, precedence was still given to "high birth" rather than "learnedness" and personal deserts. The durability of old prejudices is, perhaps, still better expressed in what Kotoshikhin says on the score of the hierarchical position of the tsar's relatives. "And whatever boyars are relatives of the tsar through the tsaritsa, they do not sit in the duma and at the tsar's table, because it is a disgrace to them to sit below other boyars, and they are not able [to sit] above [them], because by birth they are not high." Neither the favour of the tsar nor even kinship with the tsar could add "otechestvo" to a man; on the other hand, not only the tsar's favour but just simple physical propinquity to the source of power gave him a real influence on affairs. The antinomy of feudal society, where the king could not seat a marquis below a count, but where both count and marquis alike bowed low to the king's valet-de-chambre, was integrally reproduced by Moscow's court society of the times of Tsar Alexis. According to Kotoshikhin's story, highest in the hierarchy of Muscovite grades, highest in fact and not merely for purposes of display, stood the *postelniks* [chamberlains] and *spalniks* [gentlemen of the bedchamber]. The former made the tsar's bed and slept in the same room with him, and at the same time kept the seal for the tsar's "hasty and secret" affairs, *i.e.*, they stood closest of all to that extra-duma legislation, "edicts of the sovereign," which was destined to crowd out the obsolescent mechanism of the boyar duma. The spalniks clothed and booted the tsar in the morning, undressed and unbooted him in the evening, and in consequence found themselves in the very first ranks of the tsar's men of the duma. Made boyars or *okolniches*[9] (according to their "otechestvo"—this was strictly observed!), they bore the title of *"blizhny* [privy]" or *"komnatny* [chamber]" boyars and okolniches; they had the immense privilege of unannounced entry into the tsar's cabinet [*komnata*], whither the other members of the duma could enter only when summoned, and they could stage a sitting of the duma whenever the tsar needed its sanction but did not wish to share his thoughts with all of its members. "When the tsar chooses to think of anything secretly," writes Kotoshikhin, "in that duma are those boyars and okolniches and *blizhnys* who have been recruited from gentlemen of the bedchamber or who have been ordered to come; while the other boyars and okolniches and men of the duma do not come into that sitting of the duma for any business."

The central institutions, as was natural under this feudal régime, were likewise of feudal character. We have not yet had occasion to discuss the mechanism of the central administration of Muscovy, and for the reason that the administration of the "votchina" of Ivan Kalita's descendants did not differ in any essential way from that of other votchinas, except for the difference that the unusual size of this "estate" might introduce. It is no accident that *"prikaz"* [bureau], the appellation given to a Muscovite ministry, comes from the same root as the modern *"prikazchik"* [steward or overseer]; in point of the origin and character of their authority the ministers of the tsar of Moscow did not differ from the overseers of any private votchina. Nor is this the sole example of the descriptiveness of Muscovite administrative terminology. At the end of the sixteenth century the departments of the *Bolshoi Prikhod,* the ministry of finance of the time, were, quite characteristically, named for the dyaks who had charge of them. Later these departments were given geographical names, but the character of a personal "prikaz" [command] was retained by their further subdivisions until the end of the seventeenth century. Moreover, the towns and counties were distributed among them in the most fantastic disorder; not one of these ministries or departments had charge of a definite, continuous territory. On the other hand, there was not one of them that had no territory at all to administer; even the *Posolsky Prikaz* [ministry of foreign affairs] controlled several towns, and not frontier ones, either.

In the list of Muscovite bureaux of the time of Tsar Alexis, and even later, institutions of a public character and the different sections of the tsar's private economy are interlocked in great confusion while

[9] The *okolnich* ranked next below the boyar in the duma.

very often functions of both types are fulfilled by one and the same institution. There was the bureau of the *Bolshaya Kazna* [Great Treasury], which around 1680 drew together about one-half of all the state revenues—a real ministry of finance; but it is not to be confused with the *Kazenny* [Treasury] Bureau, which had charge of the tsar's wardrobe and at the same time controlled a few traders of the towns. The Bureau of "Gold and Silver Work" was, properly, occupied with the tsar's gold and silver service, but even under Peter there entered its competence certain cavalry regiments "of foreign order"—dragoons, cuirassiers, and lancers. Sometimes this combination of diverse functions in one and the same institution confronts the historian of public law with a genuine enigma. Why, for example, was the Stable Bureau charged with the tax on baths? There can be only one answer: at some time or other both these functions had been entrusted to one and the same steward; perhaps he was a clever man, who could handle much at once, or perhaps they wanted to increase the revenues of the tsar's master of the horse—a very important person in the Muscovite realm, like his counterpart the "constable" in the mediæval kingdom of France.

In connexion with the political restoration that we are considering, it is significant that this feature—the blending of the sovereign's own economy and the ádministration of the realm—is peculiar both to the old bureaux inherited by the Romanovs from the times before the Troubles and to the new central institutions that arose in the seventeenth century. It is customary to cite as the typical example of the nascent bureaucratic organisation the "Bureau of Secret Affairs," which arose under Tsar Alexis. Properly, the "secret" of this bureau lay in the fact that hither "the boyars and men of the duma did not enter and did not handle affairs." But, on the other hand, the bureau itself had charge of the men of the duma; the officials who sat in it, the "podyaks," were sent with men of the duma when the latter were appointed as ambassadors, as voevodas of regiments, etc. "And those podyaks keep watch over the envoys and over the voevodas and on their return tell the tsar; and whatever envoys or voevodas commit negligence in their affairs, they suffer the tsar's displeasure; and they make presents to those podyaks and respect them above measure, so that they, being near the tsar, shall praise up their envoys and not report evil. That bureau was set up in the time of the present tsar [Alexis] that his tsar's thought and deeds be fulfilled, all according to his liking, and that the boyars and men of the duma should not handle anything at all." We have already said that in all probability Kotoshikhin exaggerated the power of the podyaks of the secret bureau; nevertheless the very idea of putting the men of the duma under the control of men not of the duma was indubitably a new idea; but this did not prevent the new bureau from administering, among other things, the tsar's falconry. Yet the most typical survival of feudal administration in the seventeenth century was the bureau of the *Bolshoi Dvorets* [Big Court; in modern terminology, the Department of the Tsar's Household]. To the very end of the century it remained the greatest financial institution of the realm next to the *Bolshaya Kazna* and collected a number of purely public imposts, both direct and indirect—customs and liquor duties, the streltsy tax, the post and prisoner taxes—and along with these it collected the dues from the court villages and townships.

Among the "survivals" of feudalism with which the Muscovite state of the seventeenth century is filled, it is impossible to overlook one that sums up all the rest. We refer to an institution that has acquired a famous, and not altogether deserved, though quite comprehensible reputation in modern times, the zemsky sobor. The bitterness that down to the revolution of 1905 marked the controversy over the zemsky sobor of early Rus has since evaporated. Nowadays hardly any one wants to argue as to whether it was something like the constitutional assemblies of Western Europe or a remote prototype of the official commissions of the days of Alexander III, whether it was a house of national representatives or a "consultation of the government with its own agents." Probably neither the one nor the other modernisation of the Muscovite "council of all the land" would now find protagonists. Historians have correctly surmised that it was something unique, not to be comprehended in the conventions of modern, bourgeois public law; but in vain they have seen in the zemsky sobors a national peculiarity. It was a peculiarity not native to any one country, but to all countries at a certain period.

The local peculiarity of Russian assemblies of this sort was, perhaps, the fact that in Russia they survived, in their crudest and most rudimentary form at that, up to a stage of social evolution at which in Western Europe either we do not find them at all, or they there assume a more up-to-date guise. Every mediæval sovereign constantly acted on the advice of the council of his great vassals, spiritual and temporal, and in more important cases with the council of all his vassals, all of whom, of course, were not invited, but only the most influential and authoritative among them. In the grand principality of Moscow we know of at least one such assembly, which preceded the campaign of Ivan III against Novgorod in 1471; Ivan had at that time consulted, not only with the bishops, princes, boyars, and voevodas, but with "all the warriors." Under the latter, as historians quite justly surmise, can be understood none other than the petty vassals, the "knights." The only innovation that distinguished the first zemsky sobor in the true sense (the sobor of 1566) from this assembly was the participation in it of representatives of the bourgeoisie—gosts and merchants.

It is self-evident that the norms of "representation of the people" and equally the terms "consultative" or "deciding voice" were absolutely inapplicable to any such "duma" [thinking] of the sovereign with his vassals. The vassals were not the people even in the restricted sense that the words "people" and "representatives of the people" have in countries where there is no universal suffrage. The sobor was really an "instrument" of the sovereign, *i.e.*, something without which he could not act; here we cannot speak of a "deciding" or a "non-deciding" voice. A present-day public authority is physically perfectly well able to act without the consent of the representatives of the people; in such case all its actions cease to be in accordance with law, but their material effect is then even more forcible than normally, for they usually strive to supplement the lack of law with force. The mediæval sovereign was not at all bound to listen to his vassals; juridically his declaration of will was quite enough to legalise the step he had taken. But he lacked the physical possibility of undertaking anything his vassals did not wish to execute. Any man "has the right" to bind his feet, but having bound his feet, he cannot move, wherefore not a single man in his sane mind will try to practise this his incontestable right.

The reader must have already guessed when the end of the mediæval "estates of the realm" had to come; it had to come the moment the suzerain ceased to be dependent on the natural obligations of his vassals, *i.e.*, when he got into his hands a force that permitted him to purchase services instead of begging them. This is why the definitive triumph of money economy has always been the critical moment for the "rights and liberties" of the feudal nobility. Real power then passes into the hands that have the money, into the hands of the commercial bourgeoisie, which did not need and was not at all interested in the mediæval estates, in which the landed nobility were predominant. Only where landholding became bourgeois, or where the bourgeoisie was of no importance, were mediæval institutions preserved, though in altered form; the former was the case in England, the latter in Poland. In Russia and in France matters took another course, a more normal one, it might be said; in both countries the growth of commercial capital and its influence on affairs coincides with the growth of absolute monarchy and the decline of those forms of "political liberty" that were closely connected with natural economy.

The quickening of the zemsky sobor in the first half of the seventeenth century was, then, very closely connected with the economic and political restoration which marked this epoch. Whereas the preceding century knows only two, at the very most four [10] sobors, in the course of half a century, in the forty years from 1612 to 1653 we know of ten sobors (and there would be nothing surprising if still others become known to contemporaries); for nine years, from 1613 to 1622, the sobor functioned annually. But this material invigoration of the institution was not accompanied by its evolution from primitive forms to more modern ones. The representatives were not consolidated into class groups like the separate "Estates" of Western Europe in the Middle Ages. In the sobor of 1642 (better known to us than any other) the military servitors other than the boyars, *i.e.*, the nobles, knights, and officers of the streltsy, voted in seven separate groups, based mainly on geography. It was the same with the "third estate," the gosts consulting and voting apart from the headmen of the lesser townspeople. The representation of the "fourth estate," the peasantry, was distinguished by a still more accidental character. The peasantry was not fused with the "third estate" as in France, and was not separated out into a special corporation as in the Scandinavian realms. Yet it was not systematically put aside as in the Polish diet. The peasants (of course not the serfs, for whom their masters answered, but the "black," or court, peasants) appear at the sobors, though only very sporadically. At the sobor of 1682 there were deputies from court villages, never met with earlier. Deputies of the "black peasantry" must have participated in the sobor of 1613, a fact which was long disputed and is sometimes disputed to this day, but of which there is documentary evidence. There has been preserved a charter inviting the men of Uglich to send "ten peasants of the county," that they, together with the deputies of the townsmen, should "be free in place of all and every man of Uglich to speak about state and about local business without any dread." There are, however, no signatures of peasant plenipotentiaries on Michael's election charter; it is hard to say whether this means that the peasant deputies for some reason did not get to the sobor, or whether they were without exception illiterate.[11]

Just as undefined was the competence of the sobor, if we approach it from our point of view. On the one hand, all the Russian tsars from Boris Godunov (and perhaps from Fedor I) to Peter were elected, and elected by a sobor. Recognition of the tsar "by all the land" was deemed the prime condition of the legality of the tsar's authority from the point of view of Russian public law of the seventeenth century.

[10] If we accept the existence of the sobor of 1549 and count as a sobor what took place at Moscow at the accession of Fedor I in 1584.

[11] The signatures of nobles, abbots, and archpriests frequently appear in the charter "in the place of all the men of the county."

The rebellions against Shuisky were made under the slogan that he was "made tsar" "without the consent of all the land." The impossibility of organising elections throughout the land was from the very beginning a great handicap in the candidacy of Vladislav. It would seem that "supreme constituent power" was in the hands of the zemsky sobor. Nevertheless, on the one hand, the seventeenth-century Muscovites attached little value to this prerogative of theirs. In 1636 the voevoda of Galich exhausted himself in organising elections to the zemsky sobor in the county of Galich but, try as he would, he could not raise more than twenty pomeshchiks, and the deputies of these twenty had to be sent on behalf of the whole county. Toward the personnel of the "supreme constituent assembly" (it is true, in 1636 there was no tsar to be elected) the population bore itself with, it may be said, outrageous indifference; the majority of the nobles and knights of Galich, writes the voevoda, "do not vote, holding their peace." On the other hand, the Moscow government made no bones about ignoring the demands of the "people's representatives." To the sobor of 1648-1649, which established the "Ulozhenie," the deputies brought many petitions. Some of them were respected; others the boyars who ruled the country declared "capricious," and no one thought of taking them into consideration.

But both the apathy of the electorate and the indifference of the government become quite comprehensible if we remember that the suzerain was not obliged to consult his vassals on all occasions. Where his demands did not go beyond the customary circle, he could present them categorically, and it was not possible to disobey them; having once recognised a sovereign, his vassals by that very fact obligated themselves once for all to execute all his normal commands. The assent of the vassals came into question only where the demands exceeded the norm, i.e., when they bore an exceptional character. Here it was not a matter of demanding, but of asking and sometimes imploring. When in 1634 Tsar Michael's exhausted treasury needed resources for the struggle with Poland, and commercial capital was subjected to an extraordinary levy ("fifth money," a 20% tax), and the pomeshchiks had to agree to something in the nature of a compulsory loan, the tsar's speech at the sobor was expressed as follows: "This your present direct donation will be pleasant to God the Maker Himself. The Sovereign Tsar and Grand Prince Michaelo Feodorovich of All Rus will bear this your aid ever in memory and never forget, and in future will see that his sovereign wage is paid in full measure." The zemsky sobor was ever the synonym for an extraordinary request; given such a character, it was hard for it to make itself popular.

CHAPTER XII

1. Commercial Capitalism in the Seventeenth Century *

In the seventeenth century the domestic and in part even the foreign trade of Muscovite Rus still bore a handicraft character, almost unchanged since the days of Kievan Rus. In industry small-scale, handicraft production prevailed exclusively. Europeans, who in the second half of the seventeenth century were no less acquainted with Russia than we now are with China, knew and valued Russian handicraft; at that time it filled approximately the place now held by the exhibits of various "Oriental" bazaars. And in part the round of merchandise was the same; Kilburger enumerates cartridge belts and divers articles for the road—chests, knapsacks, bags, silk scarfs, cowls of camel wool, etc. Very frequently even the methods of manufacture were borrowed from the East. A Polish author, who had witnessed the Troubles, wrote of contemporary Russian hand-workers: "All the Russian artisans are excellent, very skilful and so intelligent that a thing they have never made or even seen before they understand at the first glance and execute as well as though they were accustomed to it from infancy, especially Turkish things—horse-cloths, harness, saddles, swords with gold damascening. None of these things are inferior to the Turkish." Later they imitated Western models just as successfully. The renowned Olearius, who was in Moscow a quarter of a century later, confirms what has been said about the manual skill of Russian artisans and their ability to imitate, citing as an example that their edged and sharp articles were "no worse and even better than the very best of those that are made in Germany." "Foreigners who want to keep the secret of their art for themselves should not practise it in the presence of Muscovites," he adds, and he goes on to relate how quickly the Russians had penetrated all the secrets of the iron-founders' art regardless of the fact that the foreign iron-founders invited by the Moscow government had taken every precaution to conceal them from the natives.

Some products of Russian handicraft not only were not inferior to those imported from abroad but even themselves found a market abroad; such were, in particular, all kinds of leather work. As early as the 'thirties Olearius speaks of "Russian hides" as an article of export,

* For an explanation of the use of this term *cf*. Glossary.

mainly from Novgorod. An exceptional reputation was enjoyed by "Russian leather," which the realm of Moscow seems to have supplied to all Europe. In de Rodes' time (the 1650's) it occupied the first place among Russian exports, and there were sent abroad annually some 75,000 rolls, amounting to 335,000 rubles (not less than five million rubles gold), while the total exports slightly exceeded one million rubles. Leather mittens were another object of wholesale foreign trade; they were produced in Moscow by hundreds and sent to Sweden in large quantities. It must, however, be noted that in the Muscovite realm stock-raising was then in bad condition, and the hides of Russian cattle were unfit for use. "The finest and largest hides are collected and bought up by the Russians everywhere," says de Rodes. "They make use of the sledging-season, when the engrossers of hides and preparers of leather set out for Poland, for Podolia and the Ukraine in particular, and there buy up whatever they can lay their hands on." Then they soaked the hides till spring, at which season began the ardent, feverish work of preparing them for despatch by the spring flood from Vologda, by the Sukhona and Dvina, to the Archangel fair.

This example shows very clearly that it was only in the field of foreign trade that commercial capitalism had mastered Russian handicraft. Within the country the Russian artisan, like the Russian trader, held to the mediæval viewpoint. Foreigners relate with amazement the cheapness of the products of Russian handiwork: according to Kilburger, silver buttons were sold at Moscow for as many copecks of silver as the buttons themselves weighed, a phenomenon which he could explain only by the fact that the silver used by Russian jewellers was of very low assay; but it must be said that the silver copeck of the time was also made of very poor silver. Olearius came nearer to a correct understanding of the matter when he explained the cheapness of Russian products by the cheapness of foodstuffs in Russia; the artisan did not value his labour and demanded only that his work should feed him, for which purpose the most insignificant profit was sufficient. If we add that handicraft was frequently a subsidiary occupation (the streltsy, for example, were largely engaged in it as well as in petty trade), the cheapness of Russian handicraft production becomes perfectly clear. But once Western Europe showed interest in any aspect of this handicraft, large capital entered the field, and the situation changed abruptly.

Commercial capitalism came to Russia from the West; to Western Europe Russia was then a sort of colony. An extraordinarily interesting illustration of this "colonial" status is afforded by the attempt of the Dutch, in the first half of the seventeenth century, to make Russia their "granary." Until recent years very little attention has been paid to this attempt; the extremely interesting negotiations on this score between the government of the Netherlands and Tsar Michael Romanov did not become known in all their details until the beginning of the present century.

The ancestor of Russian-Dutch trade was the Reverend Trifon, founder of the Pechenga Monastery, the most northerly of the monasteries of Russia. This monastery carried on an extensive industrial economy, marketing its products—fish, cod-liver oil, etc.—to the Norwegians in near-by Vardö. A Dutch merchant who chanced thither proved to be a more profitable customer, and since the Norwegians, jealous of their monopoly, prevented him from trading in Vardö, he was invited by the monks to visit them at Pechenga. In the very next year (the incident occurred just about the time that Ivan the Terrible was creating his oprichnina) a regular company was formed by merchants of the Netherlands, which procured from Philip II of Spain, who still ruled all the Netherlands, a monopoly of trade with the Russian north. The matter proved more complicated than the parties had thought. On the Murman coast there still survived the traditions of "robber trade" of Viking times, and the first trading caravan from the Netherlands was plundered by Russians, and its crew slain.

But this did not interrupt relations. Ships from the Netherlands continued to visit Murmansk regularly, from year to year, and the cloister of the Reverend Trifon became a great commercial centre. In the year of the monks' first acquaintance with the Dutch the monastery numbered only 20 monks and 30 lay-brothers; only five years later there were 50 of the former and some 200 of the latter, including workers. To Pechenga came traders from Kholmogory and Kargopol, while the monastery's fishing-boats pushed even into Norwegian waters, so that the Muscovite authorities had to intervene to curb the spirit of industrial enterprise of the anchorites of Pechenga. But what the latter managed to catch in Russian waters was sufficient to supply a very wide market; not content with their original correspondents, the above-mentioned Antwerp company, the Pechenga brotherhood concluded another treaty, this time with a commercial house of Amsterdam. This may, however, have been the result of a certain northward movement of trade-centres in the Netherlands, for, with the emancipation of the northern Netherlands from the Spanish yoke, this trade became ever more and more Dutch in the narrow sense of the word. At the same time, the ships from the Netherlands ceased to confine themselves to Pechenga alone and, gradually pushing to the south, reached first Kola (where in the year of the first coming of the Dutch there were only three houses, while seventeen years later there was a regular little city, with its own voevoda and fortress) and later Archangel.

It was to the Dutch, as modern historians have disclosed, that the latter town owed its origin. The Norwegians had continued to look askance at these competitors, while the Norwegian sovereign, who was also king of Denmark, had special reasons for not encouraging Russian-Dutch trade on the White Sea; such trade would mean the "circumvention" of his customs duties, an abundant tribute hitherto levied on all ships going to and from Rus by way of the Baltic Sea, through the Sound. Accordingly, he declared the sea between the coasts of Norway and of Iceland a "Sound," a "strait," and demanded that ships passing around Norway through this "strait" must pay customs duties to the Danes. Since the Dutch refused to acknowledge that the Danes owned half of the Atlantic Ocean, they were declared smugglers; Danish cruisers began to look for "contraband" as far as the Russian coast itself, for the Muscovite state had no fleet and could only argue with the Danes on paper. Seeking safety from the Danes, one Dutch captain ascended the Dvina as far as Cape Pur-Navolok, where then stood only the Monastery of Michael the Archangel. It was this accidentally discovered harbour that proved far more convenient than the former English landing-place in the Bay of St. Nicholas, where large sea-going vessels could not enter; soon in the wake of the Dutch the whole foreign trade of Moscow passed to the "New Town" of Archangel.

But first place was firmly held by those to whom belonged the honour of opening the new port. In 1603 an English author wrote: "We [the English] have in the course of seventy years carried on a considerable trade with Russia and fourteen years ago still sent thither a great number of ships; yet three years ago we sent to Russia four ships, and last year only two or three. The Dutch are sending thither 30-40 ships, each of which is twice as large as ours." The importance the Dutch themselves attached to trade with Russia is evident from a project submitted to the States General at the end of the sixteenth century. "The wealth of our Netherlands is based on trade and navigation," says the author of this project, "if we do not engage in them, not only can we not get the means for waging the war [with Spain], but our whole people will be impoverished, and disorders may break out. Nevertheless, there is no doubt that God Almighty will not permit this and will not abandon us, inasmuch as He shows us a new path, which is just as lucrative as sailing to Spain, and this is the path to Moscow." But, for the Dutch, trade with Spain meant trade with the New World, with Mexico and Peru, which in the eyes of the Europeans of the time were fabulously wealthy: this was the trade that was now to be supplanted by "Muscovy." Admitting that, like any proposer of such a project, the Dutch author was somewhat carried away, nevertheless it can hardly be supposed that the States General was paying serious attention to the mere extravagant phantasy of a leisured dreamer. When he said that "neither Germany nor our Netherlands can get along without the trade with Russia," and that this trade "is a matter of the greatest importance for our country and its inhabitants," he was evidently saying things that to many seemed quite reasonable. A quarter of a century later, not individual promoters but the Netherlands government itself made such a radical attempt to divert all Dutch trade in Eastern Europe through "Muscovy" that the "greatest importance" of the new market for the Netherlands is incontestable. There remained only the question whether the other party, "Muscovy" itself, acknowledged these relations to be of the "greatest importance."

In order to understand the origin of this first attempt of European commercial capitalism to "conquer Russia," we must have in mind the condition of commercial relations in what was for Moscow the Far West. By the seventeenth century foodstuffs had been added to commodities of international exchange; an international grain market was already beginning to take form. The price of rye in Danzig determined the cost of living in Madrid or Lisbon. Enormous quantities of corn were carried annually from the agricultural countries of Eastern Europe, Prussia and Poland chiefly, to France, Spain, and Italy. The intermediaries in this exchange were the Dutch, whose participation in the grain trade was measured by thousands of ships, so that for the prosperity of the Dutch merchant marine this trade was hardly less important than was the far better-known trade with the colonies. "The sea-borne grain trade is almost exclusively in the hands of our nation," the envoys of the Netherlands said at Moscow in 1631.

But it was not only the Dutch marine that was concerned; the Dutch themselves, who had very largely given up the raising of grain for the cultivation of vegetables, could no longer feed themselves on their own grain. But the usual source of grain supply for the new republic had two drawbacks. In the first place, Prussia and Poland and the countries along the Baltic coast had already developed their own manufacturing industry; hence by the end of the sixteenth century the products of Dutch workshops were finding a very poor market there. At least, the author of the Dutch project we have cited very definitely asserts that "every ship to Russia or from Russia to the Netherlands brings in more than seven, eight, or even ten ships coming from Danzig, for example, because the ships bound for Muscovy are laden with valuable merchandise and not with ballast like those going to Danzig, Riga, or France." Trade with Riga or Danzig then meant an "unfavourable balance of trade" for the Dutch. This disadvantage was aggravated by a second condition of Baltic trade, already familiar to us,—the "Sound tolls" which the king of Denmark levied on every ship entering or leaving the Baltic Sea. These tolls might have been tolerated for the sake of the

cheapness of Polish or Livonian grain; but the price of grain mounted
with extraordinary rapidity in proportion to the increase of its international importance. "At the beginning of 1606 a *last* [1] of rye cost
only 16 guldens at Danzig; in the decade 1610-1620 the price fluctuated
from 45 to 65 guldens; in September of the following year it rose to 80
guldens, and in 1622 to 120 guldens." In 1628 a *last* of rye in Amsterdam had soared to 250 guldens, "and subsequently the price did not
fall but attained an unheard-of height." Here the Dutch bethought
themselves that "the Russian land is great and rich in grain" and that
in Rus "on monastery and other lands constantly lie great stores of corn
and they frequently even rot," as the representative of Maurice of
Orange, the famous Isaac Massa, explained at Moscow.

Massa did not succeed in putting his business through, apparently because he was too much concerned about his own personal commercial
interests, thus evoking the strong displeasure of all the other Dutch
merchants doing business at Moscow. His plenipotentiary powers were
taken from him, but the negotiations with the Muscovite government
touching the trade in grain were not halted, since they were not a personal caprice. The whole commercial community of Holland was interested in the matter; there appeared projects promising unusual
profits from the new enterprise and counter-projects showing that transfer of the Dutch trade from the Baltic to the White Sea would ruin the
Dutch fleet. Finally, in 1636 a formal embassy from the States General
appeared in Russia to conclude a commercial treaty. This embassy's
report gives us an idea of the grandiose character of the designs of the
Netherlands. It was proposed to exploit the Russian grain market on
the colonial principles usual at the time: the Dutch were to receive a
monopoly of the export of grain from Russia. What was more, grain
plantations were to appear in the Muscovite realm; Dutch entrepreneurs
were to receive the right to go to Russia and there cultivate "new
lands," *i.e.*, lands lying idle, which, the Dutch thought, were extraordinarily abundant in the Muscovite realm. Incidentally, it was proposed
to apply the same principles in utilising another valuable raw material
to be found in Russia—the magnificent forests of mast-timber growing
in abundance along the banks of the Dvina and its tributaries. The
advantages to the Muscovite state would, according to the Dutch
projects, be expressed chiefly in tolls on the raw materials exported;
again and again they tempted the Muscovite diplomats with grandiose
figures of exports, showing, for example, that the Netherlands needed
not less than 200,000 chetverts of grain alone.

But at Moscow they evidently had a better understanding of trade
conditions than the Dutch credited them with; they were not averse to

[1] 1 *last* = 120 puds.

making the grain trade a monopoly, but a monopoly of the tsar's. There was a good precedent for the immediate participation of Eastern European sovereigns in the grain trade: the king of Sweden was the chief competitor of the Dutch in the Baltic. Moscow was not averse to following this precedent. But why should the tsar bind himself to trade with the Dutch alone? "To our grand sovereign and his father, the grand sovereign the most holy patriarch," the boyars and dyaks replied to the Dutch ambassadors, "the great Christian sovereigns—King Charles of England, King Christian of Denmark, King Gustavus Adolphus of Sweden, and other sovereigns—do send their ambassadors and envoys, and they write in their letters that in their realms there is scarcity of grain, and that for the sustenance of their subjects there is insufficient corn." Under such conditions why should the Dutch alone be permitted to export grain?

Subsequently it was revealed that at Moscow they had some understanding of grain prices in Western Europe; for a first test consignment of 23,000 chetverts, the Muscovite commercial agent, the gost Nadya Sveteshnikov, fixed such a price that Dutch hopes of cheap Russian grain immediately faded. The envoys declared that at that price they could get grain at home. Then Sveteshnikov yielded, but very little; it was quite clear that of the kegs of gold the Dutch promoter had dreamed of, the Muscovite sovereign intended to keep half, if not all, in his own treasury. It goes without saying that in calculating on keeping the Muscovite grain market in its own hands the government of Tsar Michael could not agree to Dutch "grain plantations" in Russia. Dutch traders and others, it replied to the ambassadors, "cannot be admitted to the Muscovite realm for agriculture, because, if Dutch traders are permitted to engage in agriculture in the realm of Moscow, it will be grievous to Russians; it will evoke disputes about the land and will work loss to their grain trade." It could hardly have been more clearly conveyed that it was proposed to keep the profits from the grain trade for the "Russian men," *i.e.*, for Nadya Sveteshnikov and his colleagues.

Thus Western European commercial capitalism gave rise to the commercial capitalism of Russia. Like any novice in a similar case, it proved itself too greedy, and it miscalculated on the grain trade proper; its refusal of the Dutch proposals of 1630-1631 brought it no luck at all, and until the second half of the following century the export of grain from Russia remained an occasional, sporadic phenomenon. Yet it must not be supposed that Russian commercial capital expired in such slight travail; in a number of other cases it actually succeeded in establishing, in its own favour, monopolies which were regarded with envy in Western Europe.

In the first place, though attempts to establish a regular grain trade with foreign countries met with no success, yet such occasional trade as there was became a tsar's monopoly. One of the foreigners we have cited above gives precise information about this, while another of later date confirms his story. Up to 1653 the tsar's agents bought up annually some 200,000 chetverts; a chetvert of rye, including the cost of transportation to Archangel, came to no more than one ruble, yet it was sold for not less than 2½-2¾ thalers; since a thaler recoined at the Moscow mint yielded 64 silver copecks, the net profit to the tsar's treasury on the grain sold constituted from 60 to 75 per cent. To await high prices, grain was sometimes kept in storehouses for several years, as was Moscow's common practice with all her wares. In a short period, it is said, the monopoly yielded more than a million thalers, or 640,000 rubles (9,000,000-10,000,000 gold rubles). Yet it was abandoned before Kilburger's time; "all the grain now remains in the country, since the distilleries consume it in large quantities," writes this author. As a result of the rapid growth of population in the second half of the seventeenth century the customary supply of whiskey was insufficient, and purchase abroad (in the Ukraine and in Livonia) was necessary to enable the tsar's taverns to meet the demand; under such conditions it proved more profitable to distil the grain into whiskey than to trade in it.

The treasury's revenue from the state liquor-shops was enormous. Olearius informs us that there were more than a thousand of these "privileged" institutions, nor were they small shops: three Novgorod taverns were farmed for 12,000 thalers (more than 100,000 gold rubles). And this was in the middle of the reign of that very Tsar Michael who, when Russia was emerging from the Troubles, was so concerned about popular sobriety. Collins, court physician to Tsar Alexis, avers that there were certain taverns, each of which was farmed for ten or even twenty thousand rubles (some 300,000 gold). Therefore the figures for tavern revenues given by Kotoshikhin (100,000 rubles a year) seem very low, to be explained by the fact that Kotoshikhin, as he himself remarks, took into account only that portion of the spirit monopoly handled by one bureau, whereas probably many other bureaux had a hand in this levy. In 1680 the customs and tavern revenues together amounted to 650,000 rubles (some 10,000,000 gold). Unfortunately, it is not possible to separate out the customs revenue from the spirit-monopoly revenue.

But whiskey was far from being the only commodity of trade subject to monopoly by the tsar's treasury. The first tsars of the House of Romanov monopolised the sale of practically all the most valuable articles. "The tsar is the first merchant in his realm," says Collins, who had lived long in Russia. Enumeration of the tsar's monopolies gives us an interesting picture of the concentration of Russian exports that laid the foundation for native commercial capitalism, which, in the person of Nadya Sveteshnikov, so disheartened the Dutch when they thought to profit from Muscovite backwardness. Modern readers, persuaded that Russian food products did not begin to penetrate the West until our own day, simultaneously with Russian literature, are not a little surprised at the exact information given by Kilburger and de Rodes in regard to the outstanding commercial significance then possessed by the trade in caviar. In this the Dutch secured what they had unsuccessfully sought in the case of grain; the export of caviar was at an early date concentrated in the hands of a single commercial company, at first of a Dutch-Italian one, and later, apparently, of a purely Dutch one, though the chief consumers of Russian caviar were Italy and Catholic countries in general, which needed food for fast days. In the 1650's the export of caviar had already reached 20,000 puds a year; by the 1670's, when Kilburger wrote, this figure remained almost unchanged. The tsar's agents delivered caviar at Archangel at a price stipulated over quite a long period of time; with the Dutch, for instance, they had a ten-year contract. In the 1650's the company paid 1½ rubles, and twenty years later 3 reichsthalers (almost two rubles) a pud; the total value of the exports thus amounted in the first case to about 30,000 rubles, in the second case to about 40,000 (450,000 and 600,000 rubles gold). They exported pressed caviar only, since they did not know how to preserve the soft caviar; for that matter, they did not prepare the pressed caviar very well, and it often spoiled; in that case the gosts who served as the tsar's commercial agents were obligated to take it themselves, at one ruble for ten puds. This they sold within Russia, disposing of it in large quantities to "poor people"; "not for nothing," as one of the foreigners commenting on this operation adds, lest any one suspect that the tsar's treasury would give even spoiled goods to any one for nothing. Along with caviar the tsar's monopoly included isinglass, the sale of which amounted to 300 puds at a price of from 7 to 15 rubles a pud, and salmon, the annual catch of which was more than 200 lasts (some 25,000 puds); two Dutch ships came specially for this every year. The fisheries on the lower Volga were the business of the treasury to such an extent that the fishermen refused to sell fish to Olearius and his fellow-travellers, asserting that severe punishment would overtake them for it; "for that matter," adds Olearius, "they later very gladly netted us a fish for a few hookers of whiskey."

The most popular of all the tsar's monopolies was that in furs; the most valuable kinds of furs, sables for example, could be found only in the tsar's treasury, just as in the case of pressed caviar. De Rodes gives, from the Archangel customs records, quite detailed information about Russia's fur exports. Their total value he fixes at approximately 100,000 rubles, three-fifths of which is for sables (1,500,000 rubles gold). Yet furs, that ancient Russian product on which the commercial capitalism of Novgorod had thriven, were already beginning to lose their past importance, for valuable fur-bearing animals could now be found only in Siberia; at the same time we begin to pick up information about the importation of fur goods into Russia, e.g., from France fox furs were brought to Archangel. Still more did wax and honey, another ancient branch of Novgorod's trade, lose importance. These were now consumed almost entirely at home—wax because large quantities went into church candles, honey because it was consumed in such quantities by the tsar's spirit monopoly. Therefore these traditional categories of Russian exports evaded attempts to establish monopolies, attempts which embraced even "fish teeth" (walrus tusks, which found a very good market as a substitute for ivory) and oil (which then had not even a thousandth part of its present commercial importance, but which could be secured at Moscow only through the tsar's treasury). On the other hand, the monopolisation of wares coming, as of old, through Russia from the East assumed tremendous importance; among them first place was held by the silk monopoly.

"The trade in silk is without doubt the most important of all those carried on in Europe," Olearius reminds his readers, as he enters on his narrative about the trip of the Holstein embassy to Muscovy and Persia. The trip itself was occasioned by the desire of Frederick, duke of Schleswig-Holstein and Oldenburg—he did not then suspect that he would be one of the ancestors of the Russian ruling house—to monopolise this most precious commodity in Western Europe just as the Russian tsar had done in Eastern Europe. Duke Frederick was not the first and not the last to make this attempt; no princess in a fairy tale ever had more suitors than the boyars of Moscow had foreigners suing for leave to pass through the realm of Muscovy to Persia, then the chief export market for raw silk.

In 1614 had come to Russia the English factor, John Merrick, the well-known intermediary in the peace negotiations of Moscow with Sweden which led to the Peace of Stolbovo (1617). From the outset he expressed the desire of the English crown that English merchants be permitted to pass freely along the Volga. Merrick was a useful man, and English aid was never more necessary; the Russians tried courteously to dissuade the English, suggesting to them that "it would be dreadful at the present time for English merchants to go into Persia and other eastern realms," that on the Volga "many robbers rob," and many Russian traders had been despoiled, and "now our traders do not go to

Persia." Merrick did not give up, and after the conclusion of the Peace of Stolbovo he renewed the conversation more insistently. This time they answered him more openly. "Our Russian traders had become impoverished," they told him; "now they buy from the English at Archangel certain commodities, cloths for example; these they carry to Astrakhan and sell them there to the Kizil-Bashi [Persians], exchanging them for their commodities, from which they derive profit, and the treasury likewise; but if the English should go direct to Persia, then they will not sell their commodities to the Russians at Archangel; they will carry them direct to Persia, and the Kizil-Bashi will cease to come with their wares to Astrakhan; they will trade with the English at home."

In 1629 came a French ambassador, des Hayes Courmenin; he, too, asked, among other things, that "the tsar's majesty should permit the French to go to Persia through his realm." The boyars replied that the French might buy Persian wares from Russian merchants. In 1630 appeared our old friends the Dutch; they likewise did not confine themselves to the grain trade—the Dutch monopoly was to extend to Persian wares. With their customary preconception of the cheapness of things Muscovite, they proposed 15,000 rubles a year for the Persian monopoly. The boyars replied that it was impossible; they had refused the king of England (and what a friend he was!) at the petition of the traders of the Muscovite realm. A little later came Danish envoys, who likewise carried on negotiations for Danish merchants to be given a road to Persia. The boyars replied quite laconically that they had not commanded that any one be given a road to the land of the shah.

The Holsteiners came nearest to having any luck; they promised to pay for the Persian monopoly, for ten years, 600,000 yefimoks [2] (some 5,000,000 rubles gold) a year. Evidently Olearius' opinion that there was no trade more important for Europe than the silk trade was fully shared by his countrymen. At Moscow the figure proposed seemed imposing, and consent was unanimous. But it immediately became apparent that in Holstein theory was stronger than practice, and that they could reckon better than they could pay. When it came to the question of payment, it proved that the Holsteiners did not have the necessary capital, and the grandiose enterprise ended most regrettably in a diplomatic quarrel between the government of Tsar Michael and Duke Frederick.

Thanks to the almost continuous water route from Persia to Archangel —by the Caspian Sea, the Volga, Sukhona, and Northern Dvina—the transport of silk through Russia offered enormous advantages in comparison with its carriage overland. Whereas every bale carried from

[2] The yefimok was the German thaler reissued by the Muscovite mint.

Gilan to Ormuz on the back of a camel cost not less than 35-40 rubles
gold, the same bale by sea to Astrakhan cost no more than one ruble, *i.e.*,
15 rubles gold. It is not surprising that merchants of the time, influenced
by such figures, should conceive projects no less grandiose than the
Dutch plan of converting seventeenth-century Russia into the "granary
of Europe," a position she was to occupy in the middle of the nineteenth
century. Aside from the cost of freight there might be uncertainty as to
the political relations between the Persian shah and the Turkish sultan,
whereas the realm of Moscow assiduously maintained the very best relations with Persia. With all this in mind, de Rodes proposed to the
boyar Miloslavsky, father-in-law of Tsar Alexis, the organisation of a
company of the greatest European merchants, which, using the Russian
route, should take into its own hands all the trade with Persia (not
merely the trade in raw silk) and incidentally a good share of the trade
with India and China. Three hundred years before the building of the
Siberian railway and the projecting of the Iranian railway, a Riga
merchant attempted to minimise the results of Vasco da Gama's discovery by making the Volga and Dvina competitors of the great ocean
route to the Far East. Unfortunately for him, de Rodes had only dreams
and no capital, while Miloslavsky, like all the members of the Moscow
government, was not the man to release a bird in the hand for the sake of
two in the bush.

At Moscow they followed the lines of least resistance and did the very
simplest thing that could have been done in the given case. They did
not admit Persians beyond Astrakhan and did not deliver the silk to
Europeans further inland than Archangel, while they observed two
rules: first, they always asked the highest possible price, both for Russian
wares offered in exchange for silk at Astrakhan and for the silk itself
offered in exchange for European manufactures, or still better for ready
cash, at Archangel; second, they never reduced a price once received.
Among the wares sent to Persia were Russian linen, copper, and especially sables and other valuable furs. Copper actually cost, including
carriage to Persia, 120 thalers a *berkovets*,[3] but in Astrakhan the tsar's
gosts,[4] who alone were permitted to trade in it with the Persians, did
not supply it for less than 180 thalers a berkovets. For linen 4-5 thalers
a piece was a good price; they sold it to the Persian traders for 8-10
rubles; even against payment in ducats they artificially inflated the rate
of exchange, which was 12 per cent. higher than the customary European
rate. All of this they could do because at Astrakhan trade with the
Persians was strictly forbidden to every one except the agents of the

[3] 1 *berkovets* = 10 puds.
[4] The greatest wholesale traders, who were granted special privileges by the tsar
and were, in reality, his commercial agents.

government monopoly, the gosts. The Persians had only the alternatives, either not to take at all goods they needed or to pay the price set by the Moscow gosts. Under such conditions a pud of raw silk, delivered at Archangel, cost no more than 30 rubles, but it was sold for 45 rubles; thus the profit to the tsar's monopoly was 50 per cent. The trade turnover, however, was extremely slow; the silk caravan came to Archangel only once in three years. Its burthen usually amounted to some 9,000 puds at a total value of 405,000 rubles (more than 6,000,000 rubles gold); here they brought only the raw silk, so highly valued in the West at the time that in France, for example, there was scarcely a place where they did not attempt to rear the silk-worm; even the king occupied himself with it at Fontainebleau. The trade in silk fabrics, also brought from Persia, and to some extent from the still more remote East, was free, and prior to the 1670's a number of Persian and even Indian traders lived at Moscow. Though it did not supplant the world route discovered by the Portuguese, yet the tsar's trade with Persia was undoubtedly the greatest commercial enterprise of Muscovite Russia. The Persian caravan which the Holstein embassy overtook between Saratov and Tsaritsyn consisted of 16 large and 6 small vessels. The very largest Volga "barges" of the seventeenth century went as high as 1,000 lasts (*i.e.*, 2,000 tons) burthen, and had crews of some 400 men (properly speaking, tow-men, who hauled the vessel with a hawser when there was no wind). In the matter of dimensions modern Volga barges probably have not made much advance over their predecessors of the pre-Petrine period. It must be noted that for the most part the large vessels on the Volga were in the service of the tsar's monopoly; two other huge barges that Olearius met belonged, one to the tsar, the other to the patriarch; both were carrying caviar.

We have not yet exhausted all the tsar's monopolies mentioned by contemporaries; the trade in rhubarb, for example, was also concentrated in the treasury; but the essence of the matter must already have become clear to the reader. In handicraft Russia, which hitherto had known only small-scale trade, as well as small-scale production, the concentration of hundreds of thousands of rubles (millions in gold rubles) gave rise to commercial capital. But we should be very much mistaken if we supposed that all this capital was in the hands of the tsar. Actually it was controlled by the gosts, who in the tsar's name carried on the trade both with the East and with the West. "The gosts are the tsar's commercial advisers and factors; they hold unlimited sway over trade throughout the realm. This selfish and pernicious group, which is fairly numerous, has a head and elder, and they are all merchants; among them are several Germans. . . . They are scattered throughout the realm, and in all places, according to their calling; they enjoy the privilege of buying first, even though they may not be acting on the tsar's account. Inasmuch as they alone, however, are not in condition to cope with such a widely extended trade, they have in all the large towns subordinates in the person of two or three of the most eminent merchants dwelling there, who in the capacity of factors of the tsar enjoy the privileges of the gosts, although they do not bear the name, and on account of their private greed everywhere cause divers restraints of trade. The ordinary merchants observe this and know it very well; they speak ill of the gosts, and it may be feared that, in case of an uprising, the rabble will wring the necks of all the gosts. They [the gosts] handle the appraisal of goods in the tsar's treasury at Moscow; they control the catching of sables and the collection of the sable tithe in Siberia, just as they control the Archangel caravan; and they give the tsar advice and schemes in the matter of establishing tsar's monopolies. Day and night they strive completely to stifle trade on the Baltic Sea and nowhere to permit free trade, in order that their dominance may be the more stable, and that they may the more easily fill their own money-bags."

The foregoing characterisation of the gosts by Kilburger, which well represents, if not the actual facts, at least the impression that these facts produced upon a very attentive and very well-informed observer, is splendidly illustrated by the well-known Pskov episode. At Pskov, under the pretext that the petty traders were tools in the hands of foreign capitalists, who by lending them money actually converted them into their commissioners, the gosts monopolised all foreign trade without exception, thus converting all the second-rate merchantry into their, the gosts', commissioners. Not one of the local merchants of the second order had the right any longer to trade on his own account; they were all assigned to the great capitalists of Pskov and, receiving loans for their operations from the *zemskaya izba* [town hall], had to deliver there "to the better men, to whom they had been assigned," all the goods they purchased. For convenience of control all trade with foreigners was limited chronologically to two fairs (January 9 and May 9) and topographically to three bazaars, two for foreign and one for Russian wares; goods could be exchanged only at these times and at these places. As a measure of "protection" to native commercial capital in its struggle with foreign capital, the Pskov decree of 1665 was, for its time, an exceptionally bold step, testifying to the great class consciousness of its authors; it is no accident that it was connected with the name of Ordin-Nashchokin, the father of Russian mercantilism. But it also shows the reverse side of the picture; we see how hard it was for Russian capitalism to hold its own in the struggles with the West without artificial support.

The very methods of capitalistic exchange spelled disaster for trade of handicraft type, as, taken by and large, Russian trade of the seventeenth century remained. "And the Germans living in Moscow and in the towns go through Novgorod and Pskov to their own land five, six, and ten times a year with news of what is being done in the realm of Moscow, what prices are being paid for wares," bewailed the Moscow traders in their petition of 1646, "and whatever wares sell dear in Moscow, these they begin to prepare, and they all act according to their private information and according to letters, agreeing in concert." Outraged by such an invention of the devil as a postal system, the Russians go on to cite an exceptionally striking instance of their helplessness before the wily foreigners. Relying on the high price of raw silk in past years, the Russian traders had bought up the whole supply of silk from the tsar's treasury in the expectation of selling it to the "Germans" at a profit. But on the European market at the time the price of silk had fallen, and the "Germans" not only did not buy a single bale at the price which seemed "just" to the Russians but even laughed at them. "Gracious sovereign," implored the outraged Russian merchants, "have mercy upon us, thy bondsmen and orphans, the traders of all the realm; look upon us, miserable ones, and do not permit us, thy majesty's born bondsmen and orphans, to be in eternal poverty and destitution at the hands of these unbelievers; forbid our trades, ours from the beginning, to be snatched from us, miserable ones."

The commercial rôle that the postal system was already playing at that time is evident from the arguments and projects of de Rodes, who wrote less than ten years later than the petition we have just cited. He ascribes the successful competition of the Dutch with the Swedes mainly to the circumstance that the Dutch correspondence through Riga reached Moscow more quickly than the Swedish through Narva. He therefore advises absolute prohibition of the despatch of letters direct from Riga to Moscow through Pskov and the making of Narva the central post-office for the whole Baltic littoral; then all correspondence coming to Moscow from the West by way of the Baltic would be under uniform conditions. But Russian government circles and the business-men close to them were in this matter good enough Europeans not to grant the Swedes the postal monopoly. In 1663 the Muscovite state established its own foreign post, handing it over for exploitation to a private entrepreneur, John of Sweden. The post was despatched regularly every Tuesday to Novgorod, Pskov, and Riga, and was received at Moscow every Thursday. The Narva route, on the contrary, was completely abandoned; here the Swedes suffered a complete defeat. A letter from Moscow to Riga took not less than 9-10 days, and postage was, to modern eyes, incredibly high; to send one *zolotnik* [5] to Novgorod cost six copecks, to Pskov eight, and to Riga ten (0.9, 1.2, and 1.5 rubles, respectively, in gold). Another foreign route went to Vilna and Königsberg; letters to Germany, if sent by this route, took two days. A letter reached Berlin in 21 days and cost 25 copecks (3.75 rubles gold) per zolotnik. Letters coming from abroad were first delivered to the Foreign Office; no secret was made of the fact that there they were opened and read by the clerks in order that the government might be the first to know the foreign news. The concept of the "secrecy of private correspondence" was then absolutely foreign not only to the Muscovites but also to their foreign teachers; at least, Kilburger writes of this obligatory perlustration as of a perfectly normal fact.

For the mass of the people, on the other hand, the very existence of the post long continued to be a highly abnormal phenomenon. "And they came and cut a hole from our realm into all their lands, that they might see clearly all our state and business affairs," complained Pososhkov as late as *c.* 1701. "The hole is this: they set up a postal system, and whether there is profit in it for the great sovereign, God alone knows; but how much ruin has been wrought by that post throughout the realm it is impossible to calculate. And whatsoever is done in our realm is peddled about in every land; foreigners alone grow rich from this, while the Russians grow poor. And on account of the post foreigners, laughing at us, carry on trade, while the Russians strain all their strength to make a living." Naturally Pososhkov's advice was to "close that hole up firmly," "if possible altogether abandon" the post, and even forbid private persons to carry letters with them. Granting the backwardness of Pososhkov's views (on the point in question it is interesting to contrast him with another promoter of the Petrine period, Fedor Saltykov, whose advice was to establish, along with the out-of-town post, a city post, at the very cheapest rates), his sentiments cannot be explained by backwardness alone. Like every weapon of commercial competition, the post still further strengthened the strong and weakened the weak; since foreign capital was always far stronger than Russian, the advantages from improved means of intercourse accrued to the former. In the 1670's Kilburger could communicate to his reader the astounding fact that all the trade of Archangel was in the hands of a few men from Holland, Hamburg, and Bremen, who maintained permanent stewards and factors at Moscow; the Russians did not go to Archangel. Here he enumerates a number of German merchants who specialised in the trade between Archangel and Moscow and never went abroad themselves. What was more, foreigners had, in his words, penetrated into the college of gosts, and not only in the capacity of tsar's agents abroad, like Klink

[5] 1 *zolotnik* = 1/96 funt = 2.4 drams.

Bernhard and Fageler at Amsterdam, but, like Thomas Kellerman, even at Moscow itself.

For the characterisation of foreign trade it remains to add that imports as well as exports had, by the seventeenth century, already assumed mass proportions. The time had long passed when only articles of luxury were imported into Russia from abroad, as had been the case in the time of Ivan the Terrible and in part even at the beginning of the seventeenth century, when we find on the list of imported wares gilded halberds, apothecaries' supplies, organs, clavichords, and other musical instruments, carmines, threads, pearls, travelling utensils, mirrors, lustres, etc. Lists of wares imported in the 1670's furnish the following figures, for example: in 1671 they imported through Archangel 2,477 tons of herring, in 1672 1,251 tons; in the former year 683,000 needles, in the second year 545,000; 5 tons of dyestuffs of every kind and, besides this, 809 kegs of indigo; 28,454 reams of paper. Especially significant of the development of Russia's industry is the importation of iron and iron wares, bearing in mind that, as we shall see further on, the Muscovite realm had at that time its own iron-works, with a very great output. None the less, without counting iron wares, there were imported through Archangel in 1671 1,957 bars of Swedish iron, so great was the demand for this material in Russian workshops twenty years before Peter.

The commercial capitalism of the seventeenth century had an enormous influence both on the foreign and on the domestic policies of the Moscow government. Until the conquest of the Ukraine (1667), and in part even until Peter, foreign policy was chiefly interested in the south; colonisation of the southern frontier, which had now fallen completely into the hands of Moscow, furnished the immediate occasion both for Prince V. V. Golitsyn's expeditions to the Crimea (1687-1689) and for Peter's expeditions against Azov (1695-1696). The changed orientation of this policy in connection with the Northern War (1700-1721) was due mainly to the interests of Russia's foreign trade. De Rodes had already shown, in the 1650's, that the traditional route through Archangel was cutting the profits of the capitalists in half at least, since owing to climatic conditions commercial capital could be turned over only once on the White Sea (this turnover was accomplished in five months), but on the Baltic two or even three times (if we reckon the shipping season of Riga or Libau at nine months, and the turnover with maximum rapidity at three months). Formally de Rodes was working in favour of Sweden, but as a matter of fact rather in favour of his native city, Riga, whose trade was growing very markedly in the second half of the seventeenth century. From 1669 to 1686 the exportation of flax doubled (from 67,570 to 137,550 puds); exports of hemp more than trebled (from 187,260 to 654,510 puds, reaching 816,440 puds in 1699);

everything else increased in proportion. The territories that fed the trade of Riga were: first, Lithuania; second, the neighbouring provinces of the Muscovite realm. Economically the city was apparently more closely connected with these territories than with its juridical "fatherland," Sweden, to which it then belonged; Reval, the second Baltic port after Riga, was in a similar position.

The Swedish government, one of the best bureaucratic governments of Europe at the time, was perfectly conscious of this fact, as is evidenced by an interesting decree of Queen Christina (June 3, 1648). By this decree trade in Reval was given exceptionally favourable conditions, and every effort was made to attract thither as many foreign merchants as possible by making it quite simple for them to become citizens of Riga, and consequently for them to enjoy the commercial privileges given in such abundance to the local population as against the foreigners. Soon after the Peace of Kardis (1661) the Swedish government secured "free trade" between Russian and Swedish subjects. A little earlier, when the Russians, under the influence of the Dutch, deprived the English of their trade privilege and closed the English factory at Archangel, Sweden had attempted to transfer English trade to her own port of Narva. But all these efforts had accrued to the advantage of Sweden as a political unit rather than to her Baltic subjects. Liberally granting to foreigners the privileges enjoyed by burghers of the Baltic towns, the Swedish kings were very illiberal in granting the privileges enjoyed by Swedish merchants proper. We have noted the rôle played in the trade of the time by the "Sound" tolls collected by Denmark from all ships entering or leaving the Baltic. The Swedes had secured their abolition, but for themselves alone; the men of Riga and Reval continued to pay them. In the second half of the seventeenth century Livonian grain exports had begun to increase rapidly (from 2,380 *lofs* in 1669 to 6,991 in 1686 and 14,939 in 1695). But Charles XI had hastened to impose high export duties on it in order to create preference for Sweden, which then needed imported grain. The Baltic ports were as naturally attracted to the east as they were repelled by their Scandinavian suzerain. When Peter began the Great Northern War with a campaign against Narva, he appeared, as a matter of fact, as the emancipator of Baltic commercial capital, held captive by Swedish violence. Riga was bound to become a Russian port, since Russian trade had already outgrown Archangel; on the other hand, Riga needed to free herself from Swedish shackles, for otherwise Königsberg, year by year enticing away Riga's clients, would kill her, taking advantage of the fact that the Königsberg tolls were somewhat lower than the Swedish. Peter was thrown back to St. Petersburg, after he had failed to master Narva, while his allies, the Saxons, suffered a great defeat under Riga; the immediately manifest strategical advantages of an advanced post on the Neva were bound to secure it primacy even later, when matters were going more successfully. But from a commercial standpoint, for long afterwards St. Petersburg could not compete with the natural route through Riga or even through Archangel; it was necessary to create a whole list of restrictions on both of these ports—to prohibit the importation into Riga and Archangel of certain wares, the trade in which St. Petersburg was to monopolise.

On the other hand, the Russian government strove in every way to facilitate Riga's competition with Königsberg, whereas we learn from one document that the Swedes, who had been so concerned about "free trade," had in 1690 farmed Riga's whole trade in manufactured goods to four men, while the rest of the merchantry could trade in manufactured goods only during the fair (from June 20 to August 10). The famous "reduction," or confiscation from the Livonian nobility of the crown estates they had seized in past years is usually assigned as the cause of the transfer of the Baltic provinces, but by no means occupies first place among the causes that brought on the war. As far as Russia's conquest of the east coast of the Baltic is concerned, the "reduction" played no rôle at all. The Baltic nobility looked, not to the east but to the south, desiring union not with the Muscovite realm but with Poland. Patkul, the leader of the nobles' opposition, was much dismayed when he saw the front of the Russian advance turning toward the west, toward Narva; he would have preferred to see Peter in Finland. On the other side, the burghers of Riga evidently did not feel the least desire to pass from Swedish rule to Polish, and in 1700 it was not so much the small Swedish garrison that defended Riga from the troops of King Augustus as the armed citizens, whereas the Livonian nobility, in the treaty with the same Polish king, proposed to deprive the Rigan burghers of their immemorial privileges and to hand over the administration of the city to the landlords of the environs. The alliance of the Baltic barons with the Russian government dates from a much later period, when the nobles' reaction, which in Peter's time temporarily gave way before the alliance between commercial capital and the new feudal aristocracy, had gained the upper hand.

Commercial interests on the Baltic Sea determined the combination of powers at the outbreak of the Great Northern War, a combination which endured, with interruptions, throughout the war. On such a basis the alliance between Russia and Poland was just as natural as was the attraction of Riga toward the Muscovite realm; both powers needed for their exports a "free" Baltic Sea, i.e., annihilation of the Swedish monopoly. On this point Denmark was at one with them, though primarily in the name of the Sound tolls, which she could not compel the Swedes to pay, to say nothing of the traditional competition on the Baltic of the two Scandinavian powers.

On the other hand, the Dutch who, precisely on account of these Sound tolls, had fled to the White Sea, were bound to be very unsympathetic toward the Russian-Polish enterprise. The mutual relations between Peter and the Dutch republic during and on account of the Northern War may serve as the very best illustration of how all "cultural" influences bow before economic influences in case of conflict. What, would it seem, could have been stronger than Dutch influence on the "carpenter of Saardam," who even in his signature slavishly copied the country that was in his eyes the embodiment of European civilisation? Yet in beginning the war he knew that his friends regarded it more than coldly. Even the promise to halve the customs duties, as against those at Archangel, did not thaw the ice. "Your present war with the Swedes is very displeasing to the States," Matveyev, Peter's representative at The Hague, wrote to the tsar, "and it is quite worthless to all Holland, because it is your intention to take a port on the Baltic Sea from the Swede." When the news of the defeat of the Russians at Narva reached The Hague, it produced "untold joy" there. Peter's friends, together with the English, did not hesitate even to break up Peter's alliance with Poland by fixing up a separate peace between King Augustus and Charles XII. On Denmark, too, pressure was exerted in the same direction. At the same time, all Peter's tempting promises on the score of the commercial advantages that Baltic trade held out as compared to that on the White Sea, owing to the more rapid turnover of capital (de Rodes' old argument), had absolutely no effect on the English. The Dutch formally declared to the Russian representative that they were "bound by old treaties to aid Sweden in everything." It needed the victory of Poltava on the one hand, the manifest consolidation of the Russian's grip on the shores of the Gulf of Finland on the other, to effect some change in the attitude of London and The Hague toward Peter's foreign policy.

2. *Mercantilism*

Peter's foreign policy, then, was based on mercantilism. Mercantilism, however, is a name given to any economic policy which, setting out from the identification of wealth with money or with the precious metals in general, sees in trade, which brings precious metals into the country, the source of a nation's wealth. The first beginnings of mercantilism in Western Europe are traced back to the end of the Middle Ages (the thirteenth to the fifteenth centuries), and its full bloom to the epoch of Louis XIV. Its theory, however, did not remain unchanged; whereas early mercantilism had rested entirely on trade in valuable raw materials, especially from the colonies, in the seventeenth century men had begun to be conscious of the advantages in the sale of manufactured goods, especially when the manufactures were worked up from raw materials of which other nations had little or none. This second stage of mercantilism, connected with the name of Colbert (and therefore sometimes called Colbertism) and characterised by protection of native manufacturing industry, has, as every one knows, survived to our own time, constituting an integral part of state wisdom as preached by all conservative parties.

To the Russia of Peter the Great both these stages were familiar. The first had found juridical expression as early as 1667, in the celebrated *Novotorgovy Ustav* [New Commercial Statute], published at the instance of Ordin-Nashchokin. The *Ustav* begins with a characteristically mercantilist declaration: "In all the surrounding realms free and lucrative markets are accounted among the first matters of state; they watch the markets with great caution and in liberty they keep them for the collection of tolls and goods from all the world." The phrases about "freedom" and "liberty" must not confuse us; there is here no question of "free trade" in the eighteenth-century sense of the term, but rather of abolition of all feudal impediments and levies of a narrowly fiscal character, which had impeded trade for the sake of an immediate penny profit to the tsar's (earlier the grand-prince's) treasury. A multitude of petty levies, left-overs from appanage times, were abolished by the *Novotorgovy Ustav* and replaced by a uniform customs duty, which aimed less at immediate profit to the treasury than at creation of a favourable balance of trade; thus, the duty on foreign spirits was increased, while precious metals might be imported without any duty. The importation of luxury articles, "objects of adornment," was prohibited except by special licence.

In reality the tendencies of the *Novotorgovy Ustav* represent nothing new. In France as early as the end of the thirteenth century, lest "men of no estate should be impoverished," persons having less than 6,000 livres annual income were forbidden to acquire gold and silver utensils, to order more than four suits of clothes a year, etc.; in Germany only knights could wear velvet; gold ornaments on the hat also constituted a privilege of the nobility; and as late as 1699 a servant girl who made bold to don a dress with a train or one worked with lace risked banishment from the ball to the police-station.

In Russian letters the exponent of the views of this early mercantilism is Pososhkov, who, though he wrote in Peter's time, partly indeed at the end of his reign, is essentially characteristic of the second half of the seventeenth century. In Pososhkov's opinion "it would not be bad if every rank had its own designation: the townsmen, all the merchantry, should wear their special clothes, so that they should not be like the military or the official. Now by the clothes it can in no way be told of what rank a man is, whether townsman, or official, or noble, or bondsman, and that not only with the military men but also with the tsar's court there is no distinction.'' Further on comes a project for uniforming all the categories of the town population, in which provision is made not only for the material of which the clothing is to be made, but also for its cut and colour. Parallel is the advice to forbid the importation of silk wearing-apparel and foreign spirits. Pososhkov was much disturbed because foreigners presumed to fix a rate of exchange for Russian money instead of accepting it at the value stamped on it by the tsar.

As it happened, three-quarters of a century before he wrote his book, *On Poverty and Wealth* [in Russian], an attempt to reduce his currency theory to practice had been made at Moscow. Relatively successful debasement of the currency during the simultaneous wars with Sweden and Poland had inspired the government with the idea of coining copper rubles in place of silver. But the attempt to circulate this fiat money had disastrous consequences: prices soared; private persons began to bring prodigious quantities of the baser metal to the mint for coinage; the copper ruble declined to one-seventeenth the value of the silver ruble. The economic crisis provoked a serious revolt, which was energetically suppressed; according to Kotoshikhin, more than 7,000 were executed and more than 15,000 banished.

The ''copper ruble'' was the most striking episode in the early period of Russian mercantilism, aiming as it did to gather into the treasury chests as much gold and silver as possible. But Europe was too near, and European influences too powerful. Such typical Muscovites as Pososhkov had already begun to understand that mere ''firmness'' in dealing with foreigners did not enrich a country; Pososhkov understood that a rich treasury is possible only in a rich country. ''All the wealth that is in the nation is the tsar's wealth; likewise the national impoverishment is the tsar's impoverishment,'' he wrote in one passage, though, it is true, he was thinking only of a confiscated sable coat that had rotted in the tsar's treasury. That the wealth of a nation is not drawn from commercial profits alone was also quite clear to him; in Pososhkov we find the quite definite transition to industrial mercantilism of the Colbertist type. He would have been glad to have everything made at home—''children's toys'' and spectacles included—without buying anything of the kind from foreigners, ''not even at half price,'' and was confident that once they set smartly about a business like glassware, for example, ''we can fill all their realms.'' The measures he proposes for the improvement of Russian industry—detailed control over

the good quality of each individual article, fining of "negligent" craftsmen, etc.—are purely mediæval. But when he urges the erection of
cloth mills in Russia on the ground that then "those monies will be
ours in Russia," he is at one with contemporary European mercantilists;
perhaps he was even borrowing something from them, passed on by
Russians who had been abroad.

Russian official circles were acquainted with more modern economic
tendencies at first hand from the projects of the Holsteiner, Luberas,
who was vice-president of the Collegium of Mines and Manufactures
under Peter. In one of the memoranda he presented to Peter, this
cultured German official begins with what is really a severe criticism
of the Muscovite order of things, but without naming the Muscovite
realm. "It is well known," he says, "that in certain countries, despite
the fact that a great trade is carried on, the subjects get little benefit
from it. This happens when the inhabitants sell their products in the
raw state; in this case the subjects of other countries work up the raw
material and derive a great profit, while the former owners earn a
scant subsistence. . . . Or when the sovereign either carries on a certain trade for his own account or permits other men a trade monopoly
for an annual payment; it may seem that thus, at the beginning, the
treasury may gain a little, but in reality the manager of the enterprise
extracts the most profit; general trade, which flourishes only when it is
carried on freely by private entrepreneurs with the aid of their own
credit and their own individual efforts, experiences great injury to its
regular course. . . ." "Acquaintance with the past and with the
present makes it indisputable and clear as day that after the blessing
of God there exist two chief ways, the neglect of which, or attention
to which, conditions alike either the enslavement and ruin of countries
or their prosperity and growth; these are shipping and industry. . . ."
As an example, Luberas refers the Russian tsar to his [the tsar's] own
country, "the excellent and indispensable products of which to this day
depend on foreign exportation and are balanced in exchange against
foreign merchandise, in part not necessary at all, since Your Majesty
possesses the possibility of carrying on the like manufactures of his
own."

Luberas could not show just what manufactures it was necessary to
establish in Russia since, as he said, the native specialties of the Russian realm were unknown to him. Another promoter set about this
task, this time a native Russian whom Peter had sent to England to
build ships, where during his lifetime he was almost arrested by the
English creditors of the Russian government and after his death was
sought for arrest on the tsar's order; this much-suffering man was
named Fedor Saltykov, a grandson of the Michael Saltykov famed in

the history of the Troubles and a kinsman of the tsar's family through the Tsaritsa Praskovia, wife of Peter's brother, the weak-minded Ivan V. In his "declarations beneficial to the realm," written in 1714, along with a string of the most diverse projects (on the annexation of Livonia to Russia, on the writing of the history of Peter the Great, on the education of orphans of both sexes, on a municipal post-office, etc.), Saltykov sketches a complete plan for creating "workshops" in Russia for the production of silk brocades, cloth, paper, glass, needles, pins, white iron, and tar.

Pavlov-Silvansky, the scholar who first published Saltykov's projects, calls his readers' attention to the fact that by 1714 the government could draw little that was actually new from the "propositions and declarations." "Peter had begun to look to the production of silk stuffs, glass, and writing-paper from 1709-1710 on," he writes. "In 1709 Peter handed over to an Englishman, William Leid, the glass works existing at Moscow, with the obligation to extend production and to teach Russian craftsmen the perfected method of glass production. In 1712, at the order of the government, supplies for the glass business were sent in from abroad. One young man, a certain Korotkin, Peter despatched to Holland to study the writing-paper craft, and on his return to Russia in 1710 he received an order to build near Moscow a paper mill and manufactory in the 'Dutch manner,' and several young men were handed over to him as pupils; immediately afterward Count Apraxin, on Peter's order (1712), constructed a paper mill at Krasnoe Selo. The first silk factory was erected in 1714, prior to Saltykov's projects."

We may add that all these "beginnings" of Peter's represented in themselves nothing new at all. Glass works had existed in the Muscovite realm in the third quarter of the seventeenth century. The first paper mill was built almost as far back as the reign of Ivan the Terrible; construction of another had been begun at the command of the Patriarch Nikon (1652-1666), but it had not been completed; while by the 'seventies of the same century there were in operation two paper mills, one the tsar's, the other private, belonging to our acquaintance, John of Sweden, the farmer of the foreign post. The latter mill was working in the "Dutch manner"; its products have been preserved, with watermarks in imitation of the foolscap, the then celebrated foreign mark. The first cloth factory had been founded by the same John of Sweden in 1650; the first iron-works had appeared even somewhat earlier; and if the first needle manufactory in Russia did not arise until three years after Saltykov's presentation of his projects, that fact does not, of course, mean that without the advice of this promoter it would never have appeared.

The theory of Colbertism, in Russia as elsewhere, arose on the basis of practice; the theory was an attempt to systematise the practice. We have seen that Moscow's export trade at the end of the seventeenth century presented a system of quite regularly and stably organised monopolies. Now large-scale industry was striving to adopt the same system.

At the beginning of the century industrial production in the Muscovite realm had, like trade, borne a handicraft character. The tsar's trade had been the first to take on the character of large-scale commercial enterprise; the tsar's (or court) industrial institutions were among the first examples of large-scale industry in Russia. Next to the tsar in the business of creating commercial capitalism in the Muscovite realm came foreigners; after the tsar they are the first mill-owners and manufacturers in Russia. Moreover, like the foreign merchants, native industrial entrepreneurs operated constantly under the protection of the tsar's authority and in close alliance with him. From two examples we can very well see how the tsar's manufactories evolved from branches of the court economy.

In the court village of Izmailovo, near Moscow, glass production for the domestic needs of the court had long existed. As the tsar's court grew, more glassware was needed; as early as 1668 we find at Izmailovo a glass works with Russian craftsmen. But court tastes became finer and were no longer satisfied with the rough work of their own craftsmen; only two years later Venetians were assigned to the plant, one of whom, a certain Mignot, proved to be especially deserving of his reputation, and the craftsmanship of the Izmailovo works was acknowledged even by foreigners to be "exquisite enough." The plant continued as before to serve court requirements; in the expense books of the Izmailovo palace for 1677, for example, it is noted that on June 14 there were delivered to the Tsaritsa Natalia 25 tall glasses and 25 flat and divers other glassware. Yet foreigners speak of the Izmailovo glass works simply as a manufactory belonging to the tsar, along with another similar manufactory belonging to a certain Kojet, who in 1634 had received from the tsar a privilege for 15 years. The difference was only in the fact that Kojet's plant produced rough glass, for windows and bottles.

In 1632 the Dutchman, Vinius, received from the tsar a privilege for the construction of an iron-works, with a guarantee of treasury orders for cannon, shot, and other iron products, and with the right to export any surplus abroad; this was, then, a formal agreement between a foreign entrepreneur and the Russian government. Vinius failed, but this did not mean the collapse of his enterprise; it merely passed into other hands. The new proprietor, the Dane, Marselis, still controlled the plant "as full hereditary property" when Kilburger wrote; he had only just become the sole proprietor, having bought out three-fourths of the enterprise from his son-in-law, Thomas Kellerman; for these three-fourths Marselis had paid 20,000 rubles (300,000 gold)—*i.e.*, the whole enterprise was valued at 400,000 modern rubles. They used water power; the ore was very good and was so easily secured that they did not take the trouble to pump the water out of the shaft; when too much water had collected they simply began to dig in another spot. Accustomed as we are to think of the first Russian plants as devoted exclusively to the supply of "state" demands, we expect to find cannon, shot, swords, cuirasses, etc., their only product. But a contemporary, specially interested in Russian industry, asserts that Marselis' cannon were very poor, though an attempt was made to export them to Holland (we shall remember that this had been anticipated by the contract); when they were tested, they all burst. This information is borne out by the complaints of the Moscow government to its agent; in the words of the Muscovite diplomats, who before the Dutch Estates accused the foreign entrepreneurs of divers deficiencies, the Tula plant supplied to the treasury cannon "much worse than German work." As for small arms, both Marselis' and the tsar's armoury made only "sumptuous" ones; real ones, as of old, were ordered from Holland, where the Moscow government ordered some 20,000-30,000 musket barrels. Even Peter's infantry was in 1700 armed with Liege and Maestricht weapons. Of sword blades "they made [in 1673] few, and they were altogether bad." As for cuirasses we learn an eloquent detail from a lawsuit between the mill-owners, Vinius on the one side, Marselis and Akema on the other; the former accused the latter, among other things, of not making armour at all at their plants (contrary to the contract about the delivery of weapons); they replied that they had kept an armourer for several years, "but since the tsar's majesty had no work for him, they had let him go back abroad." It must be added that at Akema's plant no weapons at all were made; this was a wholly "civilian" plant.

What then was produced by these plants, which, as we have been assured, were founded for the satisfaction of "state" requirements? The same things as modern factories, *i.e.*, they served the domestic market. Marselis' plant prepared bar and plate iron, iron doors and shutters, moulded cast-iron plates for thresholds, and similar articles which found an ever greater and greater market, thanks to the ever-growing use of brick construction. Akema's plant, beside this, prepared ship anchors (indirect evidence of the wide extension of river shipping) and was especially renowned for its bar iron, "splendid, supple, and elastic, so that every bar could easily be bent in a circle." The tsar's iron-works near Klin prepared absolutely the same kind of wares. In 1677 were credited to income, including a remainder from the preceding year, 1,664 puds of joint-iron (*i.e.*, iron joints for brick construction), 633 puds of bar iron, 3 barrels of "white" iron, 2,480 hammered nails, 400,100 two-inch nails, etc. Eight years later there were in the stores 1,901 puds of joint-iron and 1,447 puds, 35 funts of bar iron.

There were instances in which the tsar appeared as entrepreneur pure and simple with no relation to the court economy. Collins tells of the huge rope manufactory built by Tsar Alexis for the purpose of giving employment to the needy, who, it is said, were brought together there "from the whole empire"; the needy, working in the tsar's enterprise, earned their keep so that they cost the tsar nothing. Encouraged by this experience, which so vividly recalls Michael's anxiety about national sobriety, Tsar Alexis began "each day to organise ever new and new manufactures" with workers of the same type, whose scanty pay was given in kind, while the monies "which the taverns afford him are in this way preserved."

3. *Peter's Industrial Policy*

Thus in the Russia of the end of the seventeenth century there were present all the conditions requisite for the development of large-scale production: there was capital (though in part foreign); there was a domestic market; there were working hands. These factors are more than sufficient to prevent comparison of Peter's factories with artificially forced hothouse plants. And nevertheless the collapse of Petrine large-scale industry is a fact just as indubitable as the other facts we have just stated. The manufactures founded under Peter failed one after another; hardly a tenth part of them dragged out their existence to the second half of the eighteenth century.

A closer examination of this, the first industrial crisis in Russian history, shows that nothing could have been more natural, and that it is to be explained by the very fact formerly assigned as the cause of the rise of large-scale industry in the reign of Peter. It is an absolutely mistaken opinion that political conditions forced the growth of Russian capitalism in the seventeenth and eighteenth centuries; but it is quite true that the political framework of a state that was controlled by the nobles prevented this capitalism from developing. Here, as in other fields, Peter's autocracy could not create anything, but it did destroy much; in this respect the history of the Petrine manufactures supplies a perfect parallel to the picture of administrative havoc so well depicted by Mr. Milyukov in his book.

"The merchantry of Your Majesty are very few, and it may be said that already there are none," as an unknown Russian "who was in Holland" wrote to Peter in 1715. His explanation was the competition of "exalted personages." But, over and above competition, Peter's very method of influencing industry was such as to frighten capital away rather than to attract it. Even in the Muscovite period industry had been hampered enough by monopolies and privileges; but both of these restricted the application of capital negatively, so to speak, by showing it what it could not do. Peter tried to teach capital what it must do and where it ought to go, and he executed his task with the energy and force ever native to him, but with a naïveté that might vie even with the methods of Pososhkov, who made the amount of trading profit depend on the trader's firmness of character. Commands in the spirit of Pososhkov (and in the spirit of mediæval mercantilism in general)—for example, that serfs should wear Russian cloth only and should not dare to wear imported cloth, and in case cloth failed should sew clothes of kersey, or that no one should dare to wear clothes with galloon, "for the English are richer than we, and they do not wear galloon"—were the mildest and most indirect methods employed by Peter to influence the development of industry.

He was capable of acting far more directly and simply. An edict to the Senate (January, 1712) prescribed: "so to multiply plants, and not in one place, so as in five years not to purchase an imported uniform, and to give an establishment to the trading men, having collected a company, whether they are willing or not, and not to assess this plant heavily so that they should have encouragement to earn in that business." We have heard a good deal about serf labour under Peter; but of serf entrepreneurs we have heard far less often, and this type is incomparably more interesting. In 1715 it came to Peter's ears that Russian leather was not thought much of abroad since dampness soon spoiled it, thanks to the Russian method of tanning it. Immediately it was prescribed that the leather be made in a new way, for which purpose craftsmen were despatched through the whole empire; "for this instruction a term of two years is to be given, after which if any one makes leather in the old way, he shall be sent to penal servitude and deprived of all his property."

The results of such paternal care are shown by the well-known fate of the north Russian linen-weavers. As we know, Russian linen and linen-cloth went abroad in large quantities. Foreign merchants chanced to reproach the tsar because the Russians sent them very narrow linen-cloth, which was disadvantageous in use and therefore was priced far more cheaply than if it had been broad. Immediately Peter most strictly forbade the weaving of narrow linen-cloth and linens; but in the huts of the Russian domestic-workers there was no room to set up broad looms, and the domestic weaving of linen languished, ruining many merchants engaged in the marketing of this merchandise. Similar were the results of prohibiting the men of Pskov from trading in flax and flax products with Riga, a measure designed to stimulate the trade of the port of St. Petersburg. That this whole campaign against domestic weaving was intended to support the large-scale manufactories of linen-cloth which were then being established (one of them belonged to the empress) can hardly be doubted.

But Peter lacked the patience to wait until capital began of itself to flow into the business, and he tried to drive capital into the manufacture of linen-cloth with a club. As a result, in place of the tens of thousands of weavers now ruined, he got only the linen-cloth manufacture conducted by a certain Tamesz; it is true, this establishment made goods, as foreigners declared, no worse than foreign goods, but it could make ends meet only thanks to the fact that it was bolstered up by having ascribed to it a large village (Kokhma) of 641 peasant homesteads. A factory that had to be maintained by the labour of serfs was no capitalistic enterprise. It was flaunted before foreign travellers as a nursery of Russian craftsmen, but it does not appear that they later found application for their skill.

Peter firmly believed in the club as a tool of economic development. "Is not everything done by compulsion?" he asked his imaginary opponent in an edict of 1723, as usual passing from the tone of legislator to the tone of publicist; "already much thanksgiving is heard for what has already borne fruit. And such is not to be accomplished in manufacturing by propositions alone, but must also be compelled, and aided with instruction, machines, and all manner of means; and one must be like a good manager, with compulsion in part. For example, it is proposed: where they felt fine sledge-covers, there compel them to make hats (supply craftsmen), so that it is not permitted to sell sledge-covers if the proposed parts of the hats are not there; where they make leather, there hides for chamois and other things made of hides; and when it is established, then it may be without supervision." But this "be without supervision" meant still remaining under inspection, only not of the central authorities but of the "burmisters of that town" where the manufacture was established.

The most European measure in this catalogue of compulsions was the protective tariff; "whatever factories and manufactures are established among us, it is incumbent to impose on such imported articles a duty on everything except cloths." In fulfilment of this desire of the edict of 1723 the tariff, published in the following year, imposed on a large part of the manufactures imported from abroad a duty of 50-75 per cent *ad valorem*. It is evident that the domestic market must have reacted to this tariff, since among the wares subject to a high duty was iron, which for fifty years had been an object of mass consumption. How rationally the tariffs were worked out is attested by an interesting petition of the silk manufacturers, in whose interests silk-weaving had already been subjected to prohibitive duties. They asked that the importation of silk brocade be permitted again, on the ground that their own manufacture "cannot soon come into condition to be able to satisfy all the realm with brocades"; they deemed it more advantageous to get into their own hands control over the trade in foreign silk goods, "in order that we, at our own discretion, might permit the importation of some brocades and prohibit others." Capital, driven into industry with a club, sought permission to go back into commerce. . . .

This petition bears the signatures of three of the greatest personages of Peter's court, Admiral Apraxin, Vice-Chancellor Shafirov, and Peter Tolstoi. Their enterprise, in point of capital outlay, was most likely the very greatest in the Petrine period. Something like a million gold rubles (in modern values) had been invested in it; of this total the treasury had supplied one-third, not counting the fact that it had provided the "company" with buildings, materials (we shall remember that trade in raw silk was a tsar's monopoly), etc. And all this support was lavished on a branch of production that had minimum significance for the domestic market, and in view of Peter's mediævally mercantilistic measures against the spread of luxury among the masses ought not to have had any at all. Meanwhile, in Peter's reign silk factories grew like mushrooms; in Moscow alone there were five of them, and who was there that did not rush into this profitable business! Here we meet ministers of state (like those mentioned above), servants of the tsar's palace (Milyutin), post-masters (Sukhanov), and Armenian sojourners. In view of what we already know of Russia's position at that time in the silk trade of the world, the attractiveness of the idea of selling the West silk products instead of silk is quite comprehensible. But it was a childish fancy for a state in which industry had only just been born to try to compete with Lyons or Utrecht. The warden of the Moscow drapers' market officially declared that silks woven in the fatherland "cannot compare in work with foreign [products], and in price are sold from the factories higher than foreign ones"; and in behalf of all the drapers he asked for free importation of foreign silk stuffs. The whole enterprise was a typical adventure and soon crashed, although the treasury had spent large sums on it, and capital had been diverted from other manufactures.

In a different, but just as unhealthy, way Peter's mercantilism manifested itself in the iron industry; almost prohibitive duties were imposed on iron, and at the same time the treasury plants at Tula were wholly absorbed (from 1715) in the manufacture of the arms needed in such quantities for the army as reformed by Peter. Supply of the popular demand was wholly in the hands of privileged monopolist entrepreneurs

like the celebrated Demidov or the tsar's kinsman, A. L. Naryshkin. It
was more advantageous to the treasury, both politically and financially,
to have its own small-arms and its own cannon than to be dependent on
Holland for them. But probably more favourable for the development of
the iron industry in Russia on a large scale had been the times when
Marselis made poor cannon and good frying-pans.

The intensive and compulsory development of Russian manufactures
under Peter had, of course, a third consequence, one long since noted
by historians; Peter's reign marks the beginning of the bondage factory.
The advantages of free labour in manufacture were as well recognised
then as in the preceding period; Tamesz was bound by contract, like
Vinius and Marselis in their time, "to hire as apprentices and workmen
free men and not serfs, with payment for their labour of a worthy wage."
But when it was a matter of putting a hundred enterprises into operation all at once, including some very large ones (Tamesz had 841 workers; at the Moscow cloth factory of Shchegolin's there were 730; at
another, Miklyaev's Kazan cloth manufactory, 742; at the Sestroretsk
arms plant 682; at the Moscow treasury sail-making factory 1,162; etc.),
the small number of free workers available could not be sufficient. On
the other hand, the monopolist entrepreneur was not much interested
in the quality of his products. The quality did not matter, for there
was no one else to buy from. Hence arose a natural tendency to replace
free labour with substitutes, and the government was willing to meet this
effort half way. "By the edict of February 10, 1719, it was prescribed
to send off to the linen-cloth factories of Andrew Turchaninov and his
colleagues, 'for the spinning of flax, the women and girls, who, whether
by the central offices at Moscow or by other provinces, are punished for
their faults.' By an edict of 1721 this measure was made general; women
guilty of various offences were sent, at the discretion of the Collegium
of Manufactures and Mines, for work in company factories for a certain
term or even for life." The edict of January 18, 1721, permitting
merchants to purchase inhabited hamlets for factories and workshops,
definitely legalised this state of affairs. But if the factory owner could
now carry on his business with the labour of serfs, who prevented the
serf-holder from establishing a factory? Peter's measure brought little
advantage to Russian industrial capitalism, but it was one of the forerunners, remote enough as yet, of bondage, or landlord, capitalism.
Given a uniform character, and consequently uniform quality of labour,
the landlord's factory had every chance of defeating the merchant's;
and so it turned out in the course of the eighteenth century. By drawing
the string too taut, Petrine mercantilism broke it altogether.

But we should be very much mistaken if we ascribed this outcome to
the individual error of the "Reformer." Even the method by which

he introduced industrial mercantilism into Russian life was not a personal peculiarity of his; Pososhkov, a typical representative of the average Russian bourgeois of the time, attached just as much importance to "volitional impulse" and recked just as little of the objective conditions as did Peter himself. Brought up on the tsar's monopolies and surrounded by the conditions of handicraft production, Russian commercial capitalism was very ill-adapted to the wide field of action on which it found itself at the beginning of the eighteenth century, not led thither by its own sweet will so much as driven thither by the pressure of Western European capital; to the latter fell the lion's share of all the profits. Whereas in the seventeenth century the maximum number of ships at Archangel, then the only Russian port, had not exceeded one hundred, in the year of Peter's death (1725) there were 242 foreign vessels in St. Petersburg and besides that 170 at Narva, 386 at Riga, which had now also become a Russian port, 44 at Reval, 72 at Vyborg— only Archangel itself was deserted, whither came only twelve vessels from abroad; from 1718 trade through this port had been hedged about, in the interests of St. Petersburg, by such difficulties that foreigners had begun to avoid it. In general, in point of the number of ships, Russia's export trade had grown in half a century, since Kilburger's times, from eight to ten fold.

Yet the Russian merchantry at this time were "very few, and it may be said that there are none at all, for all the trades have been taken away from the merchants, and there trade in those wares exalted personages and their men and peasants." This expression of the unknown promoter "who was in Holland" was fully supported, indirectly, by the "exalted personages" themselves very soon after Peter's death. In 1727, in the commerce commission of the Supreme Privy Council, Menshikov, Makarov, and Osterman gave an "opinion," in which they agreed that "the merchantry in the Russian realm is almost entirely ruined," and that it was necessary "immediately to establish a commission of good and conscientious men to consider that merchantry and to seek to heal this so necessary nerve of the state from the root and from the foundation."

By way of physic it was proposed to repeal certain arbitrary measures of Peter's, for "the merchantry requires freedom," and in part to return to Muscovite practice by reopening Archangel. But, and this was the chief thing, it was proposed to review the industrial enterprises of the Petrine epoch, deliberating on the factories and manufactures, "which of them are to the advantage of the realm, and which a burden," and for the future to forestall excessive multiplication of such "burdensome" enterprises by forbidding the merchantry "in future to purchase hamlets." "And [forbidding] the landlords *themselves* to trade," the "opinion" diplomatically added; "but rather to bid them to render powerful aid to their peasants in industries and in the multiplication of rural workshops of all sorts." Giving a few sops to the bourgeoisie, it was thus proposed to perpetuate trade by eminent personages through their dependents. Thus appears before us, along with foreign capitalists, another social group reaping the fruits of the "reforms"; this was the new feudal aristocracy, which, under the name the "supreme lords," began to rule Russia the day after Peter's death.

4. *The New Administrative Machinery*

So long as Russia was under the control of the nobility, the work of administration had been directly performed by those who held the political power; in the seventeenth century the vassals of the Muscovite sovereign, the military landholders, had collected taxes, had administered justice, and had maintained a police system just as they had done a century earlier, and as, in reality, they were to do two centuries later if we consider the social meaning of the phenomenon rather than its juridical formulation. The uniform background presented by the régime of the nobility, however, is very distinctly marred at the end of the seventeenth and beginning of the eighteenth centuries; for the shifting of the economic centre of gravity could not fail to affect the apportionment of power among the several groups of society. The springtide of commercial capitalism brought with it something absolutely unprecedented for Muscovite Russia, a bourgeois administration.

Russian historians have long since described how on the border line between the two centuries, in 1699, the nobles' voevoda, a man who, in return for service and wounds, had been appointed to his post to "feed himself to satiety," had to surrender his post to the townsman's burmister, a man who was something between "the responsible financial agent of the government" and (but more like this latter) an accountable steward. But with their customary faith in the miraculous power of the state, these historians have not been arrested by the fact; for why should not the state hand over local administration to the merchants if it suited its convenience? Had not even Ivan the Terrible boasted that from stones he could raise up the seed of Abraham? To make a trader a judge and administrator was many times easier than this. Yet if we remember what a gigantic smash had accompanied the transfer of the administration from the hands of the boyars, *i.e.*, the representatives of large landholding, into the hands of the nobles, *i.e.*, the representatives of middling landholding, we shall be able to understand how great a leap was the transfer of authority, even though only of local authority, into the hands of men who did not belong to the landholding class at all.

There is, perhaps, no better illustration of the revolutionary, catastrophic character of Peter's reforms than this change, which it has become customary to explain by meagre considerations of state convenience.   To deprive one class of power and transfer it to another simply in order "more reliably to regulate financial responsibility" (as Mr. Milyukov explains the reform of 1699)—this is something that not one state in the world has done, simply because not one could do it.

It is true, Petrine Russia did not succeed in making the transfer for long; in less than thirty years the nobles' state had regained the upper hand.   But even the attempt could not have been made had there not existed a very special correlation of forces; it needed that alliance of the bourgeoisie with the foremost members of the landholding class to which we have already referred.   When the new feudal aristocracy had no further use for its bourgeois ally, the latter had to return to its former political insignificance.   But it immediately became clear that without this meagre support the "supreme lords" themselves were quite unable to hold their ground; coming face to face with the nobility, which had been pushed into the background, they rapidly had to give way to it, and the nobles again steadied themselves in the saddle, this time for almost two centuries.

The alliance of the bourgeoisie and the "supreme lords" even antedated Peter.   From 1681 date two projects, rather strange if taken separately: one of them has long been familiar; the other, if we mistake not, was first expounded in detail by Professor Klyuchevsky, though from the "state" point of view.   Both have remained "interesting episodes" of unknown inception and import.   The one aimed at centralising the collection of indirect imposts throughout the Muscovite realm in the hands of the capitalists of the city of Moscow.   The higher grades of merchants at Moscow were to set up customs and liquor-excise officials all over Russia.   We need hardly say that our jurist-historians immediately fell to pitying the poor gosts, who were charged with such a difficult business, and explained the project itself by "the deficiency of state arrangements."   But the gosts, in declining the proffered honour, did not refer to the difficulty of the business but declined on the ground that they knew no men in the province on whom they could rely—a reply the meaning of which we shall grasp if we remember Kilburger's account of the attitude of the provincial merchantry toward the privileged factors of the tsar; the gosts of course knew even better than did stray foreigners that the local merchants had a mind to "wring their necks." In saying that they did not know whom to trust in the provinces, they were really acknowledging that in the provinces no one trusted them. It is possible that they were also disturbed over the indefiniteness of their relations to the local noble administration.

The other project, whether connected with this or not, but advanced at the same time, was a project for the reform of the local adminis-tration. "It was proposed to divide the realm into several palatinates and to set over them available representatives of the Muscovite aristoc-racy with the power of actual and at the same time irremovable pala-tines." The projected palatinates were to coincide with the separate "kingdoms" that had entered into the composition of the Muscovite realm—Siberia, Kazan, etc.—so that they would be "not the petty counties into which the Muscovite realm was divided but integral his-toric provinces." This time the project did not fall through because of the dissent of those upon whom such difficult functions were to have been imposed, but for a different reason altogether; the Church, the guardian of tradition, rose against it in the person of the Patriarch Ioakim. This fact alone ought to show that there was no question of restoring boyar rule, but of doing something absolutely new and, for Moscow, unprece-dented. Twenty years later, when the voice of the patriarch no longer meant anything, this new and unprecedented something was moulded into two institutions, the very names of which negated Muscovite tradi-tion; these were the *ratusha* [town council] and the *guberniya* [province, from the French *gouvernement*].

The project of 1681 was a failure in so far as it was a bold attempt to concentrate the collection of taxes in the hands of the representatives of great commercial capital; yet it did not remain altogether a dead letter. Beginning with the 'eighties, the voevodas and agents of the central bureaux are systematically removed from the financial adminis-tration; not only are the indirect taxes taken from them, but newly introduced direct ones no longer fall to them; such was the fate of the new strelets tax, the assessment of which was fixed by the gosts.

The first extant edict on the ratusha (March 1, 1698) refers to edicts of similar import issued by Tsars Alexis and Fedor II. The language of the edict of 1698 leaves no doubt that it was not merely a question of "financial convenience," but of taking power from one social group and transferring it to another. And in this sense it was understood by both parties, both by the nobles' administration and by the townsmen. In Vyatka, for example, the townsmen not only ceased to pay the voevoda anything at all but did not even want to sell him foodstuffs at the customary price, very indelicately intimating to their chief of yesterday that it was time for him to betake himself out of the town. For their part, the voevodas replied by collective retirement and attempts at obstruction; newly appointed ones refused to go to their posts, and old ones shunned all business, conducting lengthy correspondence with the Moscow bureaux on the topic of what they were to do now. As might have been expected, the poorer townsmen turned out to be on the side of the voevodas. They did not at all like to pass under the authority of the hated gosts, and a number of provincial towns attempted to evade the innovation (33 out of 70, according to Mr. Milyukov's reckoning). The government had to make concessions; in favour of the townsmen they lowered the amount of taxation originally fixed; the voevodas and agents of the central bureaux kept under their administration the localities where serfdom prevailed. In other words, Russia of the nobles remained under the administration of the nobles; bourgeois administration held its own only in the towns, and the countryside fell under its control only where there were no landlords, the whole north of the Muscovite realm being left to the "burmisters." This Dutch name was, it seems, the only thing in the whole reform that belonged to Peter personally; he had then just returned from his trip to Holland.

The principal feature of the project of 1681 was reproduced in full in the edicts of 1699-1700; the administration of bourgeois Russia was concentrated in the hands of the Moscow merchantry, who this time evidently found no objections to the "burden" imposed on them. The Moscow "burmisters" were to control the burmisters of all the other towns, and the Moscow "ratusha" was to serve as a centre for all levies based on the new system. In the hands of the plenipotentiaries of the Moscow bourgeoisie was almost one-fifth of the whole budget, and far more if we count in all the industrial enterprises of the tsar's treasury, which were in fact administered by this same bourgeoisie. The system of monopolies had never attained such development as in the first years of the eighteenth century. The sale of whiskey had never ceased to be an exclusive privilege of the treasury; tavern monies comprised the bulk of the "ratusha's" budget. From 1705 salt likewise became a tsar's monopoly, yielding annually from three to five hundred thousand rubles (three to three and a half millions gold). A little later tar, chalk, train-oil, tallow, and bristles became treasury merchandise.

As Whitworth wrote in 1708, "the court here is turned quite merchant and not content with ingrossing the best commodities of their own country as tar, potash, rubarbe, isingglass, etc., which they buy at low rates, and all others being forbid to sell, put it off to the english and dutch with great profit, but are now further incroaching on the foreign trade and buy up whatever they want abroad under the name of particular merchants, who are only paid for their commission, but the gain and risk is the czar's."[6] In exactly the same way Russian wares were sold abroad direct, the tsar's "gosts," invested with the new name of "high commissioners," being sent even as far as Amsterdam. There is no need to say that, like the gosts of olden times, they traded not only for the tsar but also for themselves personally, without using any special

[6] Whitworth to Harley, April 29, 1708. *Sbornik*, v. 39, p. 262.

care to distinguish the one function from the other. The influence then enjoyed by the merchantry in the financial administration may be judged by the right conferred on the ratusha (1703) to control the distribution of the sums that passed through its hands. As a result, the whole financial apparatus of Peter's army was under the supervision of the burmisters; they distributed the wages in the provinces and checked up on the use of their disbursements by the military authorities.

Nevertheless, even for the Petrine era such a state of affairs was too incongruous to last long. Influential as the bourgeoisie (more foreign than native) was economically, political power was not in its hands. The ratusha with its bourgeois centralisation had long had a rival, in whose name and for whose profit the bourgeoisie was really working. The project of the "palatinates" of 1681 had no more fallen from the sky than had the project of an all-Russian "House of Burmisters." Even in the 1650's we find on the frontiers of the Muscovite realm authorities with extraordinary full-powers, and always drawn from the great aristocracy, close to the tsar's court. Such was Prince Repnin, who ruled first at Smolensk, later at Novgorod; when he went to Moscow for a time, his son assumed the command—just as though it were a question of a real appanage principality. Such were Prince Romodanovsky at Belgorod and the famous B. A. Golitsyn at Kazan, who, in the words of a contemporary, "ruled all the Low [all the Volga country] as absolutely as if he had been the sovereign." As befitted feudatories, they were, in the first instance, military authorities—in modern terminology, commanders of the troops of this or the other area; but, in accordance with feudal usage, the military authorities were the authorities in general. The voevoda of Belgorod administered the towns ascribed to Belgorod, not only in military but also in financial and judicial respects. In 1670 several towns of the Smolensk area were handed over to that of Novgorod, "with all service and with all the revenues of those towns, and with trial and jurisdiction, both pomestye and votchina matters."

To a foreigner contemplating the Muscovite order of things from a bird's-eye view, so to speak, and from whom, therefore, the details of Muscovite administrative technique could not conceal the essence of the matter, the order of things established by the end of the seventeenth century seemed a formal "partition of Rus." The English seaman, Perry, who arrived in Russia in 1698, writes that "such of the chief Lords who were Favourites and commonly were of the greatest Families in *Russia* . . . acted as sovereign Princes under the Czar, in the several Provinces into which the Empire was divided; who had the Liberty to make use of the Czar's Name for their Authority in the issuing forth their Orders, and might be said to have the sole Power of Mens Lives and

Fortunes in their Hands. And for the Examination of Causes, and for the Execution of their Orders, each of these Lords, or Princes, held apart an Office or Court of Justice in *Mosco,* where these great Lords usually resided, and to whom there was an Appeal from the District of all the lesser Towns and Cities in each respective Province. A Bench of *Diacks* (or Chancellors) sate as Judges in each of these principal Offices or Courts in *Mosco,* whose Business it was to hear and determine Matters; and to sign Orders, as well relating to the Treasury, and the Military, as to the Civil Matters; and to make a Report from Time to Time of their Proceedings to their respective Lords, under whose Command they acted, and the said Lords seldom coming themselves in Person to hear any Causes, the *Diacks* represented Matters to them in such Form and Colours, as they thought proper: And beyond which, in case of any Grievance, there was at that Time no higher Court of Appeal. Each of these Lords had the sole Power also lodged in them, to appoint and send Governors to the several Towns and Cities, to which each Province was again subdivided into lesser Districts. . . . These Governors . . . had the Power . . . to return such sums as they collected . . . into the grand *Precause,* or proper Office of each *Boyar,* residing in *Mosco,* where the Account of the Collections made in each Province was made out, (such as was thought fit), with the Account also of what was expended on the several pretended Occasions, for the Service of each respective Province; the rest sent into the office of the great Treasury in *Mosco,* as aforesaid.''[7]

"On Peter's part the organisation of the 'ratusha' was an attempt to counteract" this rending asunder of the state by the "chief Lords who were Favourites"; if we substitute for the symbolic figure of Peter commercial capital, which at the beginning of the Northern War dominated the situation, this appraisal of Mr. Milyukov's is entirely correct. At the peak of its power the commercial bourgeoisie crowded Peter's satraps into the background, and they did not even venture to offer serious resistance (Perry does speak of some kind of opposition of the boyars to the institution of the ratusha). But very soon the "chief Lords who were Favourites" got their way. In 1707 or 1708[8] all the towns except those that were within 100 versts of Moscow were "assigned" among the frontier centres: Kiev, Smolensk, Azov, Kazan, Archangel, and St. Petersburg.

The guiding principle in the "assignment" of towns is clearly stated by Tatishchev, a well-informed contemporary. The "gubernators"

[7] J. Perry, *The State of Russia under the Present Czar,* London, 1716, pp. 187-190.

[8] The year of the institution of the guberniyas is not accurately known—an example of how little even the bare facts of the history of the "period of reforms" has been studied.

tried to get hold of as many as possible of the richest possible towns: thus, for example, Menshikov ascribed Yaroslavl to St. Petersburg "for the wealthy merchantry"; as the person nearest to Peter he received two of the towns in his guberniya, Yamburg and Koporye, outright as personal property. For the same reason, Menshikov had begun to get towns even before the official "assignment" of them by guberniyas; as early as 1706 Peter had handed over to Menshikov the government of "Novgorod, Velikie Luki, and the other towns belonging to them." But the other "gubernators" were also men very close to the tsar; the guberniyas of Azov and Kazan were in the hands of the brothers Apraxin, one of whom, the Admiral F. M. Apraxin, was, next to Menshikov, closer to Peter than any one else; that of Kiev was given to Prince D. M. Golitsyn, who later became so famous as the leader of the "supreme lords" in 1730, and whom Peter especially esteemed; in Smolensk sat the tsar's kinsman, Saltykov.

We should be very much mistaken if we explained this local concentration of authority in the hands of the tsar's confidants by considerations of expediency—by a desire to be better acquainted with local matters, to exercise a more direct influence on them, etc. This was out of the question because it was impossible to be near to the tsar and near to one's province simultaneously. The gubernators were for the most part to be found wherever the centre of power was, and during the Northern War they "usually were with the army." The one who was most settled in his province was Prince D. M. Golitsyn; but in place of Menshikov in "Ingermanland" ruled the "landrichter" Korsakov; in place of F. Apraxin in the province of Azov ruled Kikin; in place of Peter Apraxin in Kazan ruled the vice-governor Kudryavtsev; the governor of Siberia, Prince Gagarin, whom Peter later had to have hanged for an unimaginable robbery, was at Moscow for the most part. The administration through the "Diacks (or Chancellors)" spoken of by Perry thus continued even after the new division of the country among the "chief Lords."

All that Peter demanded of them was that they should share their revenues with the central authorities; re-establishing the money contributions of the mediæval vassal to the mediæval suzerain, the gubernators brought the tsar "gifts." These might be large (up to 70,000 rubles at one time) or small (reckoned in tens of rubles), regular (from year to year) or extraordinary (on special occasions).[9] Of them all, the governor of Kazan, Peter Apraxin, most comforted Peter with his "gifts," sending the tsar in three years 120,000 rubles out of his zeal (in modern gold currency somewhat more than a million); on the other

[9] On the occasion of Peter's wedding to Catherine the gubernators had to send fifty rubles from each town.

hand, under him "were made waste" in the province of Kazan 33,215 homesteads of non-Russian subjects who paid tribute in furs, and thence it soon proved "impossible to collect not only the extraordinary but also the ordinary levies—on account of the great increase in the number of abandoned homesteads." During his administration in the province of Kiev, D. M. Golitsyn collected in "extra money levies" 500,000 rubles (4,500,000 gold), "and by those burdens and by the extra levies the province of Kiev was made a desert." And still Golitsyn was accounted the best governor!

The "chief Lords" had in their time been opposed to the organisation of the ratusha. What was the attitude of the bourgeois ratusha toward the institution of the guberniyas? Here, too, there were attempts at resistance. The chief inspector of the ratusha, the famous Kurbatov, protested bitterly against the "rending asunder" and strove to touch the tsar in his most sensitive spot by pointing to the possible diminution of revenues under the new order of things. Were it not for the ratusha there would be no sinews of war, he threatened. It was hard for Peter to find an answer to his arguments. He who was so soon to create the bureaucratic régime in Russia now cavilled at the bureaucratism of the ratusha, referring ironically to the ten receipts every paymaster must take, and now harped on the outworn theme of the difficulties of absentee rule. This theme was unapt for the very reason that, as we have seen, the guberators were for the most part absentee rulers, although it is true that they gave themselves no trouble about receipts or about accounts in general. Kurbatov's objections merely delayed matters a little. The sole concession to the bourgeoisie was that Kurbatov, the representative and defender of its interests, was made chief of the guberniya of Archangel, the most bourgeois of them all. Commercial capital and the feudal aristocracy thus delimited their spheres territorially, the latter securing nine-tenths and the former retaining only one-tenth of the whole territory and of all authority.

Yet this partition could not make a clean sweep. In the first place, as Mr. Milyukov puts it, Peter "gradually created for himself . . . a special sphere of direct state-economic activity, taking under his personal direction the exploitation of a number of regalia." In other words, as in the seventeenth century, the largest economies of private votchinniks were surpassed by the tsar's economy. Moreover, there remained a city and the region around it not subject to territorial division; Moscow and the adjacent counties could not be included in the partition because they were at one and the same time the centre both of the new feudal aristocracy and of the greatest bourgeoisie. Since geographically Moscow coincided with the centre of the tsar's economy, there was nothing more natural than concentration in the same hands of authority over the

"guberniya of Moscow" and of the management of the tsar's enterprises. If we did not become confused by associations evoked by a state
of affairs much later than 1711, if, besides, we were not under the
hypnosis of names, we should long since have found the correct place in
the history of Russian institutions for the Petrine Senate.

This "rare and strange" creation of Peter's, as the old jurist-
historians deemed it, was primarily an assembly of the tsar's responsible
stewards. This is perfectly clear if we read attentively the famous
"points" of March 2, 1711, by which the tsar, then setting out for the
Pruth campaign,[10] defined the activity of the "ruling" centre he had
just created. There were nine "points" in all; here are the last five:
"check bills of exchange and keep them in one place; inspect and examine the goods whether farmed out by chancellories or guberniyas;
try to farm out salt and take care of the revenue from it; lease the
Chinese trade, forming a good company; increase the Persian trade and
show favour to the Armenians as much as possible and make it easy for
them, as far as is fitting, so that they may desire to come in great numbers." Kilburger's "college of gosts" had fulfilled the same functions
in its time. The fact that this college now included, along with Vasily
Yershov, a former bondsman who had become *"intendant"* of the
guberniya of Moscow, a great number of former boyars (not of the
first rank, it is true), is only additional evidence of how all concepts
were mixed up with the displacement of the economic centre of gravity.
The functions of those boyars who happened to become senators were
perfectly consonant with their new rôle. Of the original personnel of
the Senate, Samarin was *General-Kriegs-Zahlmeister, i.e.,* paymaster-
general of the army; Opukhtin had charge of the silver bazaar, the
Merchants' Hall, etc.; Prince Volkonsky of the Tula arsenals, etc.

Not one of the "supreme lords," such as Menshikov and Apraxin,
entered the Senate; they wrote "edicts" to it, whereas the Senate's
right to send edicts to them was very doubtful. From a number of
Peter's edicts we learn that the gubernators paid not the slightest attention to the orders of the Senate, regardless of the menacing declaration of the edict of March 5: "we have appointed a Governing Senate,
to which, and to the edicts of which, every one will be obedient as to us
ourself, under pain of severe chastisement or of death, according to the
fault." These words of the creator of the Senate have evidently
produced more impression on later historians than on those to whom
they were more directly addressed. Even after this edict the governors
more than once drove Peter to threaten to deal with them "as is meet
for robbers," and they took not the least notice, understanding very

10 After the battle of Poltava Charles XII of Sweden took refuge in Turkey,
whither Peter attempted to follow him in 1711.

well that words accomplish nothing. Historians, paying most attention
to the title of the institution and to the first point of Peter's instructions ("deal out true justice," etc.), have worn themselves out talking
about the rare and strange institution, alleged to have been borrowed
from Sweden. In fact, the Senate of Peter the Great had nothing in
common with the Swedish, aristocratic and genuinely "governing,"
Senate except the name.

It would not have been at all surprising had the tsar's stewards been
invested with wide judicial and administrative powers at the beginning
of the eighteenth century, since at the end of the century it was nothing
to convert the tsar's valet-de-chambre into prime minister. Opposition
to the Senate could appear only in case it, like the ratusha, acquired a
social significance and became a weapon of the bourgeoisie in its struggle for power with the nobility. But the bourgeoisie's centre, such
as the ratusha had been, had by the time of the Senate's appearance
been definitely destroyed; the "supreme lords" had "rent asunder"
among their guberniyas all that the merchant administration had managed to get together. Reform of the Senate itself was necessary only
when the "supreme lords" had entered this institution, in which originally they had not been represented and had been little interested.

But even before this final note in Peter's administrative reforms had
been struck, the fierce hatred of the middling and petty military servitors had been earned by the *fiscals,* an instrument of senatorial
administration possessed of two basic features: in the first place, this
institution was actually, not in name alone, borrowed from the West;
in the second place, a large share of influence on affairs was left, though
indirectly, in the hands of non-nobles. The name "fiscals" is so definitely associated with the idea of secret investigation and espionage
that it is not so easy to discover the real meaning of this institution.
Nevertheless, taking it as it is depicted in contemporary documents,
particularly in the instruction of March 17, 1714, which put the finishing touches on the fiscal's office, it is not hard to see that in Peter's
imagination there was floating, in rather nebulous form, something in
the nature of the modern public prosecutor.

The fiscal was the representative of the *public* interest, protecting
"the people's interests" against encroachments on the part of private
persons. Hence his jurisdiction included not only "extortions and
peculation" but also all cases in which no private person had occasion
to intervene. If a traveller was murdered, or if an estate was left without an heir, the investigation, or the protection of the untended estate,
was the business of the fiscal. In Muscovite Rus the public interest as
such had had no guardian of its own; the nearest approach to the fiscals
were the "guba heads," but they had protected the interests, not of

society as a whole but only of the local population, whose organs they were. But these functions of the fiscals, which had been inspired by acquaintance with European customs, were sloughed off or relegated to the background even in Peter's time, as soon as the office of public prosecutor appeared under its own name [*procuratura*].

In the imagination of contemporaries and in the memory of posterity was far more vividly imprinted the other task of the fiscals, the attempt to increase the tsar's revenue; their method was very original, consisting not in securing new sources of revenue, but in doing away with the drain on the revenue arising from abuses and peculation. Yet the old method of increasing the revenues did not wholly vanish from the practice of the fiscals; the famous Nesterov in his "report" enumerates among his services, not only the disclosure of abuses but also his project of founding a merchant company to protect the interests of the native merchantry from the competition of foreigners. But this is only one of the points in the "report," and the last one at that; in the rest, it is a question of detecting or anticipating stealing, whether from the tsar's enterprises (*e.g.*, velvet entrusted to an agent for sale) or from the state treasury (*e.g.*, from the mint); nor is it evident that this servant of Peter the Great was aware of that imponderable distinction between what was the sovereign's and what the state's under the régime of an absolute monarchy, a distinction which our jurist-historians have drawn with such subtlety. The tsar's fiscal, with the indefatigability of a bloodhound, pursued equally the theft of the tsar's velvet and the bribes that the court judge, Savelov, had taken, striving to convert this hunt for grafters into an hereditary profession. "They are a common company of nobles," Nesterov complains of his colleagues, "while I, thy slave, have been mixed among them alone with my son, whom I am accustoming to the office of fiscal and have as a clerk. . . ." And from this same passage of the "report" we learn, incidentally, that only this one non-noble fiscal took his business seriously; the rest, the "company of nobles," "avoiding service and errands, live themselves like downright parasites in their own hamlets and care about them and not about their duties as fiscals." Granted that this former bondsman was on this occasion finding fault with his former masters, yet Peter's edicts themselves testify that the tsar did not esteem the nobles as guardians of the tsar's revenues.

The office of fiscal was at once thrown open to the bourgeoisie. "Select the chief fiscal, a clever and good man, of whatever grade he be," reads Peter's first detailed command about the new office (the edict of March 5, 1711; in the edict of March 2 fiscals are only mentioned). In accordance with this requirement (to select without reference to grade), the first chief fiscal was taken from among the secretaries of the Preobrazhensk Bureau, Peter's police department. The men of rank immediately adopted obstructive tactics against their superintendent of no standing, and with such success that the new chief fiscal, appointed in April, 1711, by August had no subordinates, no chancellory, not even office room. But Peter, or rather the bourgeois circles that had not yet lost their influence over him, were not deterred, and even the edict of March 17, 1714, requires that at least two of the fiscals attached to the Senate should be of the merchantry; in exactly the same way some of the posts as fiscals in the provinces had to be given to the bourgeoisie. In one of the later edicts of the Senate we actually find that municipal fiscals were to be "elected of the provincial fiscals and *of all the merchant folk of the town.*"

As a matter of fact Nesterov was the last chief fiscal not drawn from the nobility; his place was taken by a noble, a colonel of the Guard. But when the bourgeoisie first appeared in the guise of defender of the public interest and comptroller of the nobles' administration, it inevitably provoked the men of rank to an outburst of rage difficult to describe; only the original words of an orator who had absorbed all the nobility's rancour against the new institution can give any idea of their feelings. In his famous Lenten sermon (1712) Stefan Yavorsky sounded frankly revolutionary notes: "The law of the Lord is pure, but the laws of man mayhap are impure. What kind of a law is it, for example, that sets up a superintendent over a court and gives to him the freedom that whom he wishes to accuse, he accuses, whom he wishes to dishonour, he dishonours; and to lay calumny on a privy judge is free to him. Not so ought it to be: he sought my head, laid calumny on me, and did not bring proof—now let him lay down his own head; he spread a net for me, let him be taken in the toils; he dug a pit for me, let him fall into it himself, the son of perdition. . . . Whatever objection you make to him [the fiscal] he considers as an insult to his honour." This rather original theory of the criminal responsibility of the prosecutor in case of the defendant's acquittal was actually put into practice; the edict of March 17, already cited, provides for fiscals a "light fine" for unintentional mistakes, and a penalty equal to that which the person accused would have been subject to in case of proven malicious intent on the part of the fiscal. But this meant the conversion of the fiscal's inquest into a sort of duel between the investigators of abuses and the "abusers": either you me, or I you. Heroes, fanatics of their fiscal duty like Nesterov, were as rare here as everywhere. This point of the edict of March 17, 1714, was a great victory for the nobility over the bourgeoisie—the beginning of the end of bourgeois administration in general.

Although doomed, this administration was able, if we are to believe certain very authoritative statements, to deal one more blow to the old nobles' administration. Vockerodt, who wrote not more than twelve years after Peter's death (he was, consequently, almost a contemporary and in any case had heard much from contemporaries), thinks Nesterov's reports as fiscal the starting point of Peter's greatest administrative reform, the introduction of the "collegia." He presents the matter as follows: for the first thirty years of his life Peter "cared little or nothing" about the internal administration of the realm, being completely absorbed in the reform of the army and creation of a fleet. It was not foreign policy alone, as we are wont to think, that urged him on in this direction; Peter was conscious, says Vockerodt, "what significance a standing army has for autocratic power." We shall presently see that in this passing observation the Prussian diplomat "briefly, clearly and as usual intelligently" (the characterisation that Mr. Milyukov gives Vockerodt) had noted one of the cardinal lines of Peter's policy. Thus, Peter, who for the first thirty years of his reign had not concerned himself with questions of internal administration, first turned his attention to it when it had become utterly chaotic; and what first opened the tsar's eyes, according to Vockerodt's assertion, was a memorandum composed and submitted by Nesterov in 1714. At that time Peter may have been persuaded that the reform of the army and the fleet on European models had yielded splendid results; it was most natural that he, a military instructor and marine engineer, should conceive the idea that, by applying the same methods in the field of civil administration, he might easily make it a masterpiece just as he had the Baltic fleet or the Preobrazhensk grenadiers. Since Sweden had been the nearest exemplar in military and naval matters, it was no less natural that he should turn thither for models of administration also. So he sends to Sweden (with whom he was then still at war) a trusted man, giving "money on money," to secure, to purloin, so to speak, the statutes and regulations of Swedish administrative institutions, as one might purloin the plan of a fortress or the model of a ship. When this peculiar spy returned to Russia with his booty, the documents secured were hastily translated into the Russian language, and there were created in Russia a number of administrative organs presenting an exact copy of the Swedish ones. Since instructors invited from abroad had played a conspicuous rôle in military and naval matters, they now hastened to find some more instructors; a large number of foreigners, especially Germans, were invited to serve in the newly founded "collegia." It soon developed, however, that those who had been invited were ill acquainted with Swedish technique, and what was still more important, that good administration requires more than technique. Moreover, the new central institutions proved to be an island in the sea

of old "prikaz" Rus, for the provincial administration remained unchanged. All this compelled Peter to bide his time in the further development of the new institutions and even to undo much that he had
done. The "collegia" preserved their names, but their system reverted
in many respects to the former, Muscovite type, while at the same time
Peter energetically set about a re-working of the *local* administration.

This much simplified and even naïve interpretation has been so re-
touched by modern historians as to destroy the classic clarity of the
picture sketched by Vockerodt. We know now that the introduction of
the "collegia" was not such a childishly simple operation as he represented it to have been; that Peter had at his disposal, not only the reports of his spy but a number of detailed projects of divers origin; that
the "collegia" were not introduced suddenly, as though by a military
command; that several years elapsed between the first idea of the "collegia" and the realisation of this idea; finally, that the civil instructors
invited from abroad were no worse than the military ones, and among
them we find such men as Luberas and Fick, on whose administrative
ideas political circles of the time depended long after Peter's collegiate
reform. But, in complicating the picture, in correcting its rough con-
tours, modern scholars have not annihilated Vockerodt as completely as
might seem to be the case. Even now we must acknowledge that the
starting point of the reform was the administrative chaos, which actually did attain its apogee in 1714, and that in the disclosure of the situation to Peter his bourgeois administration, represented by the fiscals,
really must have played a great rôle.

The only enduring result of the reform, as Vockerodt particularly emphasises, was the introduction into Russian fiscal administration of those
methods of strict accountability "which exist in commercial establishments." At the instigation of commercial capitalism the reform had been
undertaken; under its tutelage it was consolidated; to recognise the
"collegia," quite apart from their salaried bureaucratic personnel, as
part of that same "bourgeois administration," it is not necessary even
to refer to the share in their system allotted to the interests of capitalism and capitalists. The "collegia" were the highest organs of the central administration, corresponding to modern ministries; but whereas
under Nicholas II both trade and industry were content with a single
ministry (and until shortly before the Great War with a single department of the one ministry), under Peter not only did there exist separate
"collegia" for trade and industry, but an attempt was made to create
a special ministry of factories, the "Collegium of Manufactures,"
apart from the Ministry, or Collegium, of Mines. If we add that finance
and accounts were allotted three entire central institutions (the Kammer, Staats, and Revision Collegia) or as many as all foreign policy

taken together (Foreign, War, and Admiralty Collegia), but that for public instruction and even for police there were no central institutions at all (among the "collegia" there was none corresponding to the Ministry of the Interior), the comparison with a "commercial house" does not seem overdrawn.

Perhaps there is nothing more remarkable about the collegiate reform than that it grew out of anxieties about trade. A collegium appears under Peter's pen for the first time in the edict of January 16, 1712, which says: "found a *collegium* for commercial matters and administration, in order to bring them into better condition, for which are requisite one or two foreigners (whom it is requisite to make content, that they may show truth and zeal in that) sworn to establish a better order of things, for it is incontrovertible that their trade is incomparably better than ours." For this first Russian collegium Peter's representative at The Hague was charged specially to seek out bankrupt Dutch merchants, since it was assumed that those "to whom any injustice had been done in their fatherland" would, in the first place, more willingly enter foreign service and, in the second place, more zealously serve their new sovereign, having no interest in concealing from him the secrets of the commerce of their fatherland. As a matter of fact, however, they did not succeed in realising this most original collegium of bankrupts, and the Commerce Collegium was organised on the Swedish model, with the aid of the same Fick and Luberas.

That it was the fleet and the army that led Peter to the idea of "collegia" is another point on which, apparently, Vockerodt is not to be corrected; in proof he needed only to refer to the famous edict prescribing that the regulations of *all* the "collegia" should be drawn up on the model of the Admiralty. What is good on shipboard cannot be wrong anywhere. But this subjective aspect of the collegiate reform does not prevent it from having been objectively a tool of the selfsame commercial capital that was served by the whole Petrine reform in general. However, the "collegia" came too late for the bourgeoisie to be able to make use of them. We shall presently see that in contrast to the ratusha, which was in merchant hands for a number of years, the "collegia" were not in them for one moment, and that the "supreme lords" did not have to "rend asunder" the new institutions simply because they immediately became masters in them.

But this was the practical aspect of the matter; it is of exceptional importance that in theory the collegiate reform constituted a great concession to the public opinion of the nobility, so unceremoniously dealt with in 1699. In introducing the new institutions, Peter, as we saw, was consciously guided by technical considerations, and unconsciously was serving the interests of that economic force that was driving Russia into Europe, irrespective of any one's subjective plans and intentions. But when he begins to explain the reform to his own subjects, we hear notes, quite unexpected and in harsh dissonance with all that we are accustomed to expect when we think of Peter the reformer. The fanatical worshipper of the cudgel, confident that everything depends on giving good orders and seeing that they are executed, suddenly begins to worry about what his subjects will say of him. Wherefore are the colleges being introduced? "Lest intractable men should slander and say that the monarch commands this or the other by force and out of caprice rather than by justice and by truth," is Peter's answer through the mouth of Feofan Prokopovich. For thirty years this man Peter had been convinced that by force he could do anything; now he talks of not wanting to be reproached for using violence.

Captivated by his own argument, Peter's secretary (such was, of course, Prokopovich when he wrote this preface to the Ecclesiastical Regulation) launches on nothing more nor less than a critique of personal power in general and a laudation of political liberty. "The truth is more certainly discovered by corporate counsel than by a single person. . . ." And what is most important, "A collegium has the freest spirit for justice: not as under a sole ruler is the oppression of the strong to be feared." But what would have happened to nine-tenths of Peter's edicts without dread of the "oppression of the strong"? What is most interesting is that these were not mere words. In organising the Collegium of Justice, Peter recalled that it "relates to all the realm" and that there might be "reproaches that they had chosen some one out of partiality"; therefore it was prescribed, in the first place, to elect its members "by all the officers whoever are here" and, in the second place, "to pick out a hundred of the better nobles, and they likewise" should elect three members of the Collegium of Justice. When later, in 1730, the nobility talked about "balloting" by all the nobles for the members of the Senate they had a splendid precedent at hand; did the Senate "relate to all the realm" any less than did the Collegium of Justice?

But so far these were only *concessions* in favour of the nobility—and not made by the bourgeoisie; who wielded authority in the new institutions is sufficiently evident from the roster of presidents of the "collegia." At the head of the War Collegium stood Menshikov, of the Admiralty Apraxin, of Foreign Affairs Golovkin, of the Kammer Collegium Prince D. M. Golitsyn, of the Commerce Collegium Peter Tolstoi; if we add to these the most influential senators, Musin-Pushkin, who became president of the Staats-Collegium, and Prince Yakov Dolgoruky, who occupied the same post in the Revision Collegium, then the roster of the "supreme lords" who had been controlling Russia as "gubernators" is almost entirely coincident with the roster of the new ministers. The only exception is the president of the Collegium of Mines and Manufactures, the celebrated Bruce; and this exception is no less to be remarked than was the fact that the "guberniya" of Archangel had been left in the hands of Kurbatov. There still remained a little corner, territorial in the earlier case, organisational in this case, in which the "supreme lords" did not venture to exercise direct control. But Bruce was a more complaisant man than Kurbatov and even easier to get along with. He flatly refused appointment as a member of the "privy council" on the ground that he was a foreigner. And one of Peter's edicts inadvertently reveals why the ministry of factories and works was turned over to this modest man; in 1722, in taking the "collegia" from their former presidents, the emperor remarks that this change should include the Collegium of Mines—"and I know not a man out of the ordinary." Bruce was not a politician but simply a good technician; it was not easy to find any one to replace him, and at the same time he was in no one's way. His presence among the presidents of the "collegia" did not mar the general picture of the "supreme lords" holding sway over Russia through the "collegia."

The "rending asunder" of the national inheritance was bound to be continued without hindrance, although in a different form. The famous case of Shafirov reveals a bit of collegiate economy in the first years after the reform. The introduction of accountability had, as we know, been one of the very strongest points of the reform. But it sufficed to put at the head of a collegium the "Most Serene Prince" for it to be removed from all control; Menshikov promptly demanded for his department everything that was appropriated for the whole army, and to demands that he "give accurate account of receipts and expenditures" he replied with contemptuous silence. Meanwhile, the army never attained its full complement, with the result that each year large surpluses remained at the disposal of its commander-in-chief. But the attempt to penetrate the secret of the use to which they were put almost cost Shafirov his head. Upon his banishment from the personnel of the "supreme lords" the last man retired who both by his origin (Shafirov was of a Jewish merchant family) and connexions stood closest to the bourgeoisie. The feudal character of the supreme administration became purer than it had ever been, while the distinction between the "old" aristocracy, represented by the Golitsyns and Dolgorukys, and the "new," represented by the Menshikovs and Tolstois, never was so great as to create grounds for a political realignment.

But under such conditions the new institutions were bound very soon to become bankrupt, not in consequence of *technical* causes, as Vockerodt thought (the ignorance of the hastily hired German officials and the inadaptability of the central administration to the local), but for purely *social* causes. Recognition of this bankruptcy led to what was, chronologically, Peter's last reform, the reformation of the Senate and "collegia" in 1722. Officially, of course, this change was motivated by considerations of state advantage; the edict of January 12, 1722, begins by describing how difficult is the task of the Senate and of the senators, and how impossible it is to be president of a collegium and a Senator at one and the same time. The direct conclusion following from this, it would seem, was that the presidents must be released from their "labours" in the Senate; this was done in the cases of Menshikov, Golovkin, and Bruce. They were released from the obligation of attending the Senate at the usual time but were left complete masters at home, each in his own collegium. But Golitsyn, Tolstoi, Pushkin, and Matveyev (president of the Collegium of Justice) were rather unexpectedly treated in just the opposite way; they were "released" from command in their "collegia" but were left seats in the Senate. In other words, the real one-man power wielded by each of them (it is hardly necessary to explain to the reader that the "collegiate character" of the Petrine institutions was just as much an empty form as was the collegiate character of the later bureaucratic "board") was taken from them, and they were left one vote each in an institution where the most important questions of state were jointly deliberated. This simply meant, as when in later times a minister was appointed a member of the Council of State, honourable discharge. Those contemporaries who, like foreign diplomats, were closely observing the course of events were never so naïve as to accept, as do modern historians, the edict's explanation at its face value. "The tsar has dismissed from office almost all the presidents of the collegia or councils," the French ambassador Campredon informed his government. "All these lords are senators, and henceforth they will simply sit in the Senate, before which formerly they supported their opinions."

Though he did not realise that the nobility was recovering lost ground, Peter did see one thing clearly: that he could not rely on that group of men with which he was accustomed to deal; that its interests differed in some fatal fashion from the interests of the business he had in hand; that these men were not accelerators but brakes, if not indeed conscious foes of his undertakings; that under his eyes feudalism, revived by the seventeenth-century restoration, was struggling with the new economic forms brought in from without; that of course what was native would assimilate to itself what was brought from the West, and not the other way about; that his whole attempt was condemned to failure in advance. Meanwhile, the requirements of this same business compelled him to go to Persia, two thousands versts away. And it is significant that whereas on going away in 1711 he created an organ of administration—the Senate,—on going away in 1722 he left behind him an organ of supervision —the office of procurator-general.

History has subsequently made of the procurator-general a sort of vizier, a minister of all affairs, or, if you like, the tsar's chief burmister. But this was not at all what Peter had in view for him. His procurator-general, as sketched by the instruction of April 27, 1722, administers nothing. He merely watches, watches diligently the sly and lazy slaves who bear the title of senators and privy councillors—both that they should not waste their time, should work "truly, zealously, and in orderly fashion," and that they should not forget the rules laid down for them by Peter, should act "according to the regulations and edicts," and not in appearances only ("not on the table only should accomplish business but in real action should execute the edicts"), and especially that they should not steal or be venal ("that the Senate in its calling should act righteously and unhypocritically"). In the person of the procurator-general Peter hoped to have a telescope, with the aid of which he might from Astrakhan and Derbent follow the last red cent that fell from the treasury chest into the pockets of the "lords of the Senate." Thus he defined the new office, "our eye," and threatened this living telescope with the most severe fate if it functioned badly. It was no accident that this office was intrusted to a man comparatively young and not particularly outstanding in the ranks of the statesmen, yet on the other hand in unusually close relations with the tsar; this was P. I. Yaguzhinsky, who seems for several years to have occupied under Peter the position which, according to common conviction, Menshikov had earlier occupied. When in France in 1717, Peter had not parted with him for a moment and all the time had not taken his eyes off him.

But the young tsar's favourite was, it seems, too weak for this rôle of universal examiner. Upon his return from Persia, Peter decided to take the business of supervision directly into his own hands. Vockerodt relates that Colonel Myakinin, the new chief fiscal, was established in one of the rooms of the palace nearest the tsar's bedroom, and this chief of the whole inquisitional system was made the chief and constant adviser of the emperor. In long conversations with him Peter insisted on one thing—the rooting out of all abuses. Every one's life hung on a hair, even Menshikov's and Catherine's. But this plan of universal extermination reeked too much of madness to yield any practical results. It merely indicates that by this time it was not Peter's physical health alone that had been worn out, and that the catastrophe of January 28, 1725, came in the nick of time.

CHAPTER XIII

THE REFORMS OF PETER (*Continued*)

5. *The New Society*

THE triumph of commercial capitalism over feudal Russia, however temporary and unstable, was necessarily accompanied by great changes in the customs of Russian society. Superficially the transformation was probably sharper than any that Russian society had experienced in the whole thousand years of its history; it appears particularly striking if we view the Russian social pyramid from above. At its very apex had formerly strutted something in the nature of a living icon, in strict Byzantine style, making its slow and solemn appearances before the eyes of the reverent throng, only to withdraw immediately into the obscure depths of the *terem*. In its place was now seen a nervous figure, active, bustling, in a working-jacket, constantly among men, constantly on the street. Nor was it possible to distinguish where the street ended and the tsar's palace began, for both were equally indecorous, noisy, and drunken; both were frequented by a motley and unceremonious throng, in which the tsar's minister in gilt caftan and ribbon of St. Andrew rubbed elbows with a Dutch sailor come straight from his ship or with a German shopkeeper come straight from behind his counter.

It is true that the further one went from the palace, the less this change was felt. The military servitor donned a German costume rather willingly, and somewhat less willingly shaved his beard; but though he now sat in a collegium of foreign pattern, he was fain as of old to engage in the traditional disputes over precedence. At home he observed the rules of the old decorum; if he ever admitted the street, it was only with great reluctance and at the strict command of the tsar. Below the military servitors came the dense mass of "schismatics and bearded men"; even in their outward appearance they remained unaffected by the changes about them and for a hundred and fifty years, down to the novels of Pechersky and the comedies of Ostrovsky, they preserved their "customs" inviolate. Nor could any change at all be discerned in the multi-millioned muzhik masses; the new order had not lightened the old bondage yoke, while the new "capitalistic" barshchina, with its more subtle means of exploitation, still lay far in the future. The "court" was more affected than was the "town," while the country-

308

side was changed not at all; the "court" was the centre, the "town" the theatre of the economic revolution. We shall, of course, not fall to talking of "Petrine culture" as a new era for the whole Russian people, which was not to be "Europeanised" until the second half of the nineteenth century; yet the task of tracing the influence of this economic change even on "manners" and "customs" is not devoid of interest. It is all the more interesting in that we have here a succession of phenomena which does not constitute a national peculiarity of the Russian people. There is a photographic likeness between what took place in Russia at the beginning of the eighteenth century and what Western Europe had experienced in the sixteenth century. Despite the lapse of two centuries and despite their own ignorance of Europe's past, Peter's Russian contemporaries reproduced, even to details, the Italian and Flemish "Renaissance."

Let us take Taine's classic description of the Renaissance. "The picturesque festivals held in all the towns, the solemn entries, masquerades, cavalcades, constituted the chief pleasure of the people and of the sovereigns. . . . When you read the chronicles and memoirs, you see that the Italians liked to make life a lavish holiday. To them all other cares seemed stupidity." [1] We must not be confused by the general definition, "Italians"; among the examples cited by our author flash the names of Galeazzo Sforza, duke of Milan, Cardinal Pietro Riario, Lorenzo Medici, Popes Alexander VI and Leo X. The "Italians" who were striving to convert their life into a lavish holiday were, once again, the "court" and, in part, the "town"; the Italian peasantry lived then just as it did two hundred years earlier or two hundred years later.

Take the memoirs of any contemporary of Peter's reforms who had opportunity to observe Russia "from above," even though it be the famous diary of Bergholz. It makes us feel that the Russians, like the Italians of the sixteenth century, had decided to make their whole life a continuous festival and to deem all else stupidity. From a rout at the Summer Garden we pass to a ball at the palace; from the ball to the launching of a new ship, worth ten balls; from the launching of the ship to the masquerade on the occasion of the Peace of Nystadt. It is incorrect to say "to the masquerade," for there were several of them, and each lasted several days. A thick pall of vinous fumes hangs over this detailed and loquacious odyssey of the Holstein court at St. Petersburg as related by Bergholz; not without a sigh of relief does he sometimes (so rarely!) inform us that "to-day we were permitted to drink as much as we wished," for usually one was obliged to drink as much as the tsar wished. Lorenzo the Magnificent, vainly striving to procure an elephant for one of his processions, might have envied Peter, at whose

[1] H. Taine, *Philosophie de l'art*, Vol. I, p. 175.

service was a whole menagerie. And probably no Italian prince could have staged such a masquerade as the Russian winter gave Peter when a whole fleet passed through the streets of Moscow on sleighs. The tsar's own carriage presented an exact copy (in miniature) of the newly-launched *Fridemaker,* the greatest ship of the Russian fleet. On it were several young boys executing all the naval evolutions "like the very best and most experienced boatswains." At Peter's command they set the sails as the direction of the wind required, "which proved good assistance to the 15 horses that dragged the ship." It was armed with 8 or 10 real cannon, with which Peter fired salutes from time to time; he was answered from a similar "ship" by the hospodar of Wallachia, who came at the end of the parade. There were about 60 sleighs in all—25 of ladies and 36 of men; the very smallest were drawn by six horses. This "serious" or "genuine" masquerade was preceded by a mock procession of the "prince-pope" with his cardinals and Neptune, the god of the sea. "All things considered, the emperor amused himself in truly regal fashion." We need not inquire how much this pleasure cost the sovereign who liked to say that "a copeck saves a ruble." It was not the first diversion of the kind within a very brief space of time; only a few months before, also in celebration of the Peace of Nystadt, there had been a lavish masquerade at St. Petersburg, likewise lasting several days and taking place alternately on dry land and on the Neva. Some thousand masks participated. The ladies were dressed as shepherdesses, nymphs, blackamoors, nuns, harlequins, scaramouches; they were preceded by the empress with all her maidens and ladies of honour in the costumes of Dutch peasant women. The men went in the costumes of French wine-growers, Hamburg burgomeisters, Roman warriors, Turks, Indians, Spaniards, Persians, Chinamen, bishops, prelates, canons, abbots, Capucins, Dominicans, Jesuits, ministers in silk mantles and enormous periwigs, Venetian nobles, ship-carpenters, miners, and, finally, Russian boyars in high sable caps and long brocade garments, "likewise with long beards and riding on tame live bears." Behind them, closing the train, the tsar's jester, "giving a very natural representation of a bear," whirled in a huge squirrel-wheel; then came an Indian Brahmin, bedecked with cowries, in a hat with the widest of brims, and American Indians covered with variegated feathers. For two hours this procession passed before the eyes of the Petersburgers, who from small to great had gathered on the Senate Square; at its head was the tsar himself, indefatigably beating on a drum, clad now as a Dutch boatswain, now as a French peasant, but not leaving off with his noisy instrument in any costume.

Bergholz many times repeats that everything in the procession was very "natural." Among other masks, for example, was Bacchus "in a tiger's skin, bedecked with the clusters of the vineyard." "He gave a very natural representation of Bacchus; he was an unusually fat, short man with a very full face; they had made him drink unceasingly for three days before, giving him no time to sleep." Here the health of the wretched Bacchus was sacrificed to "art." But Peter loved to jest at others' expense and simply for the sake of the joke, with no thought of consequences. During the river part of the masquerade his renowned "prince-pope" was drawn across the river on a special machine, consisting of a raft on which was placed a cauldron full of beer; in the middle of the cauldron, in an enormous wooden cup, floated the unhappy "mock patriarch," while behind, in barrels, floated the no less unhappy cardinals, more dead than alive. When the "machine" reached the shore, and its passengers had to be disembarked, those to whom the tsar had entrusted this operation overturned, by his special command, the cup with the prince-pope, who received a beery bath. At a dinner at Chancellor Golovkin's "the tsar amused himself with the tsaritsa's chef, who was serving at table; when he put a plate of food before the tsar, the latter seized him by the head and made horns on his head." This was a delicate allusion to the fact that the chef's wife had been unfaithful, a circumstance which Peter had signalised at the time by ordering a pair of stag's horns hung over the door of the chef's dwelling. The butt of the tsar's jests did not take them very patiently, and the tsar's orderlies had to restrain him. He struggled, and not in jest; once he seized the tsar by the fingers so hard as almost to break them. Such scenes were constantly taking place between Peter and this man, Bergholz was told; nevertheless, Peter fell to teasing him whenever he saw him. Twenty years earlier Korb had witnessed a similar but still more expressive scene. The incident occurred at a "sumptuously given feast," with the envoy of the Holy Roman Emperor as host. Among the aristocracy invited along with the tsar was the boyar Golovin, who "nourished an innate aversion to salad and the use of vinegar; the tsar bade Colonel Chambers squeeze the boyar as hard as possible, and himself began forcibly to thrust salad into his mouth and nose and to pour in vinegar until Golovin had a violent fit of coughing and the blood spouted from his nose."

In the sixteenth century the head of the Christian Church in the West had found pleasure in watching "devil's jokes" with Fra Mariano and the presentation of a comedy, the mere subject of which made Rabelais' countrymen blush. At the beginning of the eighteenth century the head of the œcumenical Orthodox realm took special delight in making sport of ecclesiastical rites. We have already made passing mention of the "prince-pope"; his appearance with his College of Cardinals was the very choicest number in the masquerade described by Bergholz. The college consisted of the "greatest and most dissolute drunkards of all Russia, but all men of good birth at that." We shall not repeat the naïve explanations of this ritual which Bergholz borrowed from the lips of Peter's courtiers, namely, that it was something between a satire on drunkenness (the tsar's court of the time might itself well have served as the incarnation of such a satire) and a mockery of the Catholic Church (with which Peter had nothing to do). The testimony of a man who had witnessed the foundation of the "mock college" leaves no doubt that Catholicism was in no way involved. "Now one must not forget to describe in what way the play patriarch was set up," Prince Kurakin begins his description of Peter's pastimes in his *History of Tsar Peter I* [in Russian]. And though Kurakin strives to soften the impression with reservations, such as that "the attire was made in some sort jesting, and not just like the patriarch's trimmings," yet he could not leave unmentioned that "in place of the Gospels was made a book in which were several flasks of whiskey," and that a caricature of the patriarch's solemn riding of an ass on Palm Sunday was one of the chief sports; on that day they rode the "patriarch" on a camel "into the garden by the bank to the French wine-cellar."

Another eyewitness, Korb, has left us a still more vivid description of one of these ceremonies. On February 21, 1699, the "patriarch" consecrated Lefort's palace, reproducing in every detail the Church ritual; instead of burning incense they smoked tobacco, while two pipes placed one across the other served in lieu of a cross during the consecration. This latter circumstance produced an exceptionally powerful impression on the pious Catholic; "who will believe," Korb concludes his account "that a cross thus fashioned, the most precious symbol of our redemption, should be the object of laughter?" But men more familiar with the facts would have believed more than that. Insult to the Gospels and to the cross was the most innocent part of the "mock" ritual. Just as in his time a spectator of a comedy presented in the pope's theatre had not ventured to report its content but had only hinted at the impression it produced on the spectators, so Prince Kurakin did not venture to describe in detail the ceremony of the consecration of the "patriarch." "In such terms," he says briefly, "as we do not find it meet to expatiate on, but we may briefly say,—drunkenness, and lechery, and every debauchery." Yet this author is a great realist in describing the tsar's pastimes and cites examples of Peter's "jests" that it would be unseemly to repeat nowadays. One may imagine what it was that even he found it necessary to be silent about!

Were Peter's "humoristics" simply the fruit of cynicism and coarseness, as the sober-minded German Vockerodt thought? During the Renaissance jests at monks passed into earnest denial of Church tradition.

Men laughed at sacred things because in the depths of their souls they had already ceased to account them sacred. When the popes sensed this, they ceased to play with fire; then the Jesuits appeared, and at the papal court jests at monks disappeared. But humanism was not confined to the papal court; outside of it there was room enough for the triumph of the "secular mood," and its expression was not confined to jests. Did this serious side of religious freethinking affect Peter himself? Contemporaries describe him as a man who, in this field, observed the old customs, did not omit Church services, liked to accompany the chanters in the choir, and never entered a church in a German periwig; this was the only occasion on which the tsar himself forsook the Western fashion he had introduced. But when it was a matter of more than harmless concessions to usage, when usage clashed with practical necessity, Peter proved himself a freer thinker than might have been expected of a man of such conservative habits. During the campaign of 1714 Peter's commissariat deemed it the part of piety to feed the soldiers on lenten fare during the Fast of St. Peter. Contemplating the results of this piety, Peter wrote to Kikin, the man responsible: "Your pious order—for five weeks rotten fish and water—the soldiers have obeyed for two weeks, whence little short of 1,000 men have fallen ill and have been lost to the service; wherefore I have been compelled to stop your law and to give them butter and meat. . . . True, if the Swedes were to be thus fed, matters would be tolerable; but I am not a stepfather to our men."

Toward the *raskolniks* [schismatics], who depicted Antichrist and his host in the uniforms of Peter's Guard, Peter had no reason to be particularly well-disposed. But the schism was powerful among the merchantry, a fact with which the tsar had to reckon, ready as he was to import even bankrupt merchants from abroad. On being informed that Old Believing merchants were "honourable and diligent," Peter expressed a sentiment, abridged perhaps but hardly invented by his historian: "if they are really such, then for my part let them believe what they will; when it is impossible to turn them from superstition by argument, neither fire nor sword will avail; as for being martyrs to stupidity, they are not worthy of the honour, nor will the state have profit." The schismatics of the R. Vyg were given formal permission to worship according to the old books, under the condition of working in the Povenetsky mills; this was probably the first case of religious toleration in Russia in respect, not to "heretical" teaching but to a "sect" arising within Orthodoxy. The declaration in the famous edict of 1702 about the tsar's unwillingness to "constrain the human conscience" was not an empty phrase, and we have an example of what was, for those times at least, the tolerant attitude of Peter and his government toward formal "freethinkers." A Moscow physician, Tveritinov, loudly said—and not only said but wrote and offered his writings to be read—such things as: "An icon is only a painted board without the power of working miracles; if you throw it in the fire, it will burn and will not save itself"; "it is not meet to bow to a cross, which is only soulless wood, having no power at all"; "monkish celibacy is not kept in the sense of Holy Writ." The spiritual authorities, headed by Stefan Yavorsky, guardian of the patriarchal see, of course brought the bold doctor to book. Yet not only was he not burned as a result of the inquiry, as he undoubtedly would have been fifty years earlier, but he even received attestation of his Orthodoxy, after formal penance, it is true. In the Senate, where Tveritinov's case was discussed, his spiritual prosecutors had to listen to things that were very unpleasant to them. "Monkling—rogue!" the senators shouted at the monk who accused the physician, "thou hast sold thy soul for a flask of wine." The Metropolitan Stefan himself was unceremoniously expelled from one session of the Senate on the ground that he was not a senator, and that there was no place for him at the trial (of a heretic, let us note). On the score of monasticism the emperor himself, toward the end of his life, expressed opinions that would probably have been very displeasing to Yavorsky, had he been alive. If not the origin, at least the spread of monasticism he was inclined to attribute to the "bigotry" of the Greek emperors, "and particularly of their wives," and to the fact that, making use of this bigotry, "certain rascals came" to them. "This gangrene among us was to spread at first under the protection of the Church monarchs, but still the Lord God has not so deprived former rulers of blessings, as the Greeks."

The breach with tradition was of course bound to be more strongly expressed in literature than in life. Specialists have long since noted the realism and secular mood of the Russian narrative of the seventeenth century. The mediæval writer, like the mediæval artist, knew only the abstraction, and not the living man; he was interested in examples of good life, not of human personality. Interest in the individual, "individualism," constitutes one of the most marked features of both the art and the literature of the "Renaissance." Russia's artistic literature of the seventeenth and eighteenth centuries was only translation and imitation; the more genuine mood of Russian society may be found only in the historical works of the period. Even the historians of the Troubles, writing in the first half of the seventeenth century—the Pseudo-Palitsyn, Katyrev-Rostovsky, and especially the author of the pertinent chapters in the so-called "chronography of the 2nd edition"—are not interested in their heroes as abstract moral examples but as perfectly concrete beings.

Prince Katyrev-Rostovsky was the first to wish to collect data about the physical appearance of Russian sovereigns, beginning with Ivan the

Terrible, and he tried to characterise each of them individually. Far higher than he in this respect stands the chronography of 1617. In it Godunov, the Alleged Dmitry, and Hermogen are almost living men. You can feel Dmitry's impetuosity and impatience, his loquacity and lively intellectual interests. And in order to sustain the classic type of the "heretic and unfrocked monk," the author—who in the depth of his soul was probably very disturbed because he was writing what was not meet—has to lavish vilification that is absolutely out of harmony with the facts he himself adduces. Over Patriarch Hermogen he could not restrain himself and in place of the stereotyped model of a "sufferer for the truth," gave a portrait which is, it is true, an excellent explanation of Hermogen's fate, but which might well cause scandal even in centuries other than the seventeenth. "Not sweetly speaking," "in manners rough," "not quick to distinguish good and evil, but diligent in flattery and double-dealing," "heeder of rumours"—such realistic features in the physiognomy of a near-saint so troubled one of the later editors of the chronography that he found it necessary to accompany the characterisation with an extended refutation, in which he proved that "this writer wrongly said all these things about this holy man about Ermogen." But fortunately he did not destroy the characterisation itself.

The realism of Kotoshikhin is so well known that we need not dwell on it. From our present point of view he is interesting, among other reasons, in that he is the first to attempt to explain historical changes as the result of the activity of individuals. To him the rise of the Muscovite state is a matter of the personal policy of conquest pursued by Ivan the Terrible; and, if Tsar Alexis was not made to grant a charter limiting his power, it was because of his personal character— "they thought him most quiet." In the writings of the greatest historian of the Petrine epoch, Prince B. I. Kurakin, we find the same method, on an incomparably grander scale. The *History of Tsar Peter I* plunges us fairly into the midst of a "renaissance," just as did Peter's masquerades. Prince Kurakin's passion for Italian citations is quite in keeping with this spirit. When you read his work the image of the great Italian historian inevitably rises before you; and perhaps there is no better way of measuring the relative profundity of the Renaissance and of its remote and unconscious Russian imitation than to compare Machiavelli's *History of Florence* with Kurakin's *History*. The former, despite its seeming dryness and restraint, describes with arresting dramatic effect how the Florentine people gained their freedom—and lost it. The latter, just as soberly, concisely, and accurately, sketches divers "accidental men," seizing power by intrigues and, thanks to the intrigues of others, losing it. In the former, a vast amphitheatre, suited, if you like, to ancient Rome; in the latter, a petty domestic scene. And thanks to its restricted proportions, thanks to the insignificant number of persons in action, the latter was better adapted to treatment from the individualistic point of view. In Machiavelli parties and, still deeper, classes, are too clearly evident behind the individuals; with good reason has he become one of the forerunners of modern "economic materialism."

There is no historian further from the idealisation of reality, more "materialist" in his cosmic philosophy, than Prince Kurakin; but there is no room in his philosophy for economic interpretation. He knows no other motives than the egoistic, no other sources of social changes than personal will. If he has to explain the mutiny of the streltsy, it is, of course, the intrigues of the Tsarevna Sofia. But since Sofia was a "princess of great mind," "never was there such wise rule in the Russian state." Both the economic and the cultural development of the Muscovite realm at the end of the seventeenth century are to be explained by this fact and by nothing else. "The whole realm came during her reign, in the space of seven years, into the flowering of great wealth. Commerce and crafts of all kinds likewise multiplied; and learning began to restore the Latin and Greek languages." Peter loved foreigners; this similarly is due to the personal influence of Prince Boris Golitsyn. "He was the first to consort with foreign officers and merchants. And out of this his inclination toward foreigners he brought them openly to the court, and the tsar's majesty took them into his favour." Men began to wear German clothes; again Kurakin is able to identify this change with an individual's name: "There was an English trader Andrew Krevet, who bought his majesty all kinds of things, ordered them from abroad, and was admitted to court. And from him men first learned to wear English bonnets, such as Sirs wear, and under-jackets, and swords with belts." Might it not seem that there is nothing less individual than drunkenness and debauchery? Yet here, too, Kurakin has no difficulty in finding the culprit. "At that time the so-called Franz Yakovlevich Lefort came into extreme favour and confidence through amorous intrigues. The aforesaid Lefort was a diverting and prodigal man, what you might call a French *debauché*. And ceaselessly he gave dinners, suppers, and balls at his house. And here in this house it began to come to pass that His Majesty the Tsar consorted with foreign ladies, and his first amour was with a merchant's daughter named Anna Mons. True, the girl was passable and intelligent. Here in the house [of Lefort] began debauchery and drunkenness so great as can not be described; for three days, shut up in that house, they were drunk, and it befell many to die therefrom. And from that time to this date and till now drunkenness continues and has become the fashion among great houses." And it does not enter Kurakin's head that it was not from Lefort that the old "prince-cæsar," F. Y. Romodanovsky, was "drunk by the whole day," or the tsar's uncle, Leo Naryshkin, who was "incontinent in drinking," had learned to drink.

This individualism of the period of the reforms found expression in law as well as in literature, or rather, in two laws, both of which may be said to be more literature than law, for both remained dead letters. These are the law of 1714 on primogeniture and the edict of 1722 on the succession to the throne. Undoubtedly both measures were outwardly related since Petrine primogeniture, as is well known, meant not inheritance of the whole property by the oldest son but inheritance by one of the sons at the father's discretion, to the exclusion of the rest. In this right of the father to dispose of his property at his discretion lay, in the opinion of Peter and his councillors, the whole essence of the institution. An extant memorandum, supplying Peter with information about the English system, asserts that "by the common law of the English land fathers can cut off and remove from their children all lands which are not appointed to them by will or otherwise, and they can leave all to one son only and nothing to the others, which keeps children in duty and obedience." The manifesto of 1722 merely reproduces this opinion (absolutely erroneous, it need hardly be said) about the "common law of the English land," when it says: "that always it may be at the will of the reigning sovereign, to appoint the succession to whom he wishes, and to replace the designate again, on seeing any worthlessness, that his children and descendants fall not into such evil as written above, having this curb on them." Here is a correspondence so literal that we do not even need the references in this edict to the law of 1714 to see the connexion; in both cases Peter felt it important to extend the limits of paternal authority, without bothering in either case about the customs operative in the Muscovite realm. In the Muscovite realm neither the hereditary estate nor the tsar's throne could be disposed of at personal discretion. In electing Michael to the throne they had in effect elected the Romanov family, and the oldest son of the family automatically, so to speak, had become sovereign on the death of his father. This automatism seemed to Peter a "bad, old custom," though it was the very thing that lay at the basis of English primogeniture, which he valued for what was not in it; and he strove to convert family property, such as land was in Russia, into personal property, like moveables, chattels and money. In this penetration of bourgeois views into the sphere of inheritance of land and succession to the throne, into the very heart of feudal law, so to speak, lies the enormous cultural interest of both these abortive laws. Nor was the borrowing altogether unconscious; when the edict of 1714 was being prepared, Russian agents abroad had been required to report on the "inheritances and division," not only of "noble," but also of "merchant families."

The "individualism" of the Petrine epoch should, however, not deceive us any more than the individualism of the Italian Renaissance. Literature, which is permitted to idealise everything, may, of course, represent the heroes of the Renaissance, not only as bold and beautiful, but also as refined and elegant, profound and cultured even to the eyes of a twentieth-century reader. The historian has no such right; he has to state that the pleasures of this period were extremely coarse, as we have seen, that the philosophy of the humanists was a mixture of the most naïve prejudices, bequeathed by the Middle Ages, with hastily garnered and ill-digested fragments of classical wisdom, and that the most resplendent signors, though patrons of humanism, sometimes did not know how to write. Fortunately, there are no such prejudices with respect to the level of Petrine culture; indeed, we are accustomed to regard the Academy of Sciences of those days with even more scepticism than it perhaps deserves. The scientific interests of Peter himself—if one may speak of such things —did not go beyond the collecting of "monsters" and "experiments" like the attempt to create a race of tall men by marrying an "exceptionally tall" Finnish woman the tsar had secured somewhere to a French giant who appeared in show-booths for money. To the reformer of Russia the trade of barber, which in those simple days combined the functions of both dentist and surgeon, did not seem beneath his dignity; next to a yachting trip or work with an axe or at a turning-lathe, nothing seems to have given Peter such pleasure as pulling teeth. Since it apparently gave his patients somewhat less pleasure, the tsar's orderlies were charged with the delicate duty of finding him opportunities to exercise his skill as a dentist. Bergholz relates with what difficulty he managed to save his own teeth when he had the imprudence to complain of a toothache in the presence of one of these scouts. The tsar was not at all squeamish about his patients' social status and honoured with his professional visits not only courtiers or foreign merchants but even their servants. No less than pulling teeth did he like to let water from those suffering with dropsy.

The milieu surrounding Peter was still more primitive in this respect. Though to the end of his life Peter's writing was frightfully illiterate, even from the Old Russian viewpoint, he always loved to read, and in languages other than Russian. He followed attentively the Dutch newspapers of the time, noting in them what interested him, and ordered books from abroad. The two persons who stood next to him in rank, Catherine and Menshikov, were most likely wholly illiterate; at least, contemporaries insist that in the art of writing Menshikov had not advanced beyond ability to write his family name; as for Catherine, legend has it that when she had become autocratic empress, her daughter, the Tsarevna Elizabeth, signed her edicts for her. Let us repeat, hardly any one will seek to exaggerate the culture of Petrine society; but it is hard for us to visualise the simplicity of the manners of the time. The titles of ministers, field-marshals, and "cavaliers" involuntary hypnotise us, and we are inclined to see something "European" in Peter's court. Contemporary Europeans, as in the case of the Germans, though they themselves might not have made much progress in external culture, must have easily rid themselves of this illusion. Take, for example, a scene described by that same verbose Holstein gentleman-of-the-bedchamber who was so fond of describing Peter's masquerades. "All the aristocracy of Russia" was assembled at a banquet at Prince Romodanovsky's. After the tsar had left, a quarrel broke out between the "prince-cæsar" and one of his guests, Prince Dolgoruky; one reminded the other of some old offence, and Dolgoruky refused to drink when invited by Romodanovsky. "Then both old men, freely exchanging the most repellent insults, clutched each other by the hair and for a good half hour pounded each other with their fists, while none of those present interfered or tried to separate them. Prince Romodanovsky, who was very drunk, was worsted; then he called the guard and, master in his own house, had Dolgoruky arrested. When the latter was released, he refused to go out from under arrest and, it is said, demanded satisfaction from the emperor. But the affair will, of course, blow over, because such drunken fist-fights happen too often and are not even talked about." In fact, the picture of the tsar's ministers clutching each other by the hair occurs again in the pages of Bergholz's diary; this time the incident happened in the presence of the duke of Holstein, who, understanding the customs of the country, turned away and pretended not to notice. Korb gives us an almost identical scene between Romodanovsky and Apraxin, Peter's future admiral-general; but the latter, under the fresh impression, it must be, of his foreign acquaintanceships, acted more "in European style"; he drew his sword, which terribly frightened Romodanovsky, who was accustomed to having the affair end with fists.

After such scenes as this, we are scarcely impressed by the spectacle of Peter's daughter Praskovia receiving foreign visitors while dressed only in her shift; while the "princess" extended one hand to be kissed, with the other hand she covered her nakedness with a cloak hastily taken from one of the court ladies. On another occasion, in the apartments of the same tsarevna and her sister Catherine, Duchess of Mecklenburg, a king of some kind, who had just received 200 blows with rods, was deemed worthy, as if nothing had happened, of the honour of playing with their Highnesses. The famous "cudgel of Peter the Great" begins to outline itself in its real setting. With men so "simple" other men than Peter would not have stood on ceremony. Contemporaries have noted only cases in which the cudgel affected very noteworthy persons, or when the consequences of its application unexpectedly proved tragic. When the tsar suddenly despatched to the next world a soldier who had stolen a bit of copper during a fire, it caused talk in the city; the incident astounded foreigners, the Saxon resident Lefort, for example, who retails it. But Lefort is scarcely correct in drawing the conclusion that Peter was ''not distinguished by a humane character''; that is, of course, true, but the particular instance was not at all exceptional. The tsar's intimate servant, the turner Nartov, cannot deny himself the satisfaction of recalling how the cudgel used to play along the back of Menshikov and other titled personages. ''I have often seen,'' he relates, ''how for the fault of men of high rank the sovereign prepared a cudgel here [in the turner's shop], how afterwards they came out into other rooms from the sovereign's direction with a merry appearance so that outsiders should not notice anything and on that same day were honoured by admission to his table.'' And a naïve provincial like Syrensky, the burgomeister of Novgorod, who had become acquainted with court life, might let slip the opinion: ''those who dwelt with Christ lost their heads, but those who dwell with the tsar lose both their heads and their backs.'' Yet the members of Peter's court, and Peter himself, deemed the cudgel the very mildest form of punishment or, rather, no punishment at all but, so to speak, a reminder of the possibility of punishment. ''Now for the last time the cudgel,'' said the tsar to Menshikov after one of the ''privy'' scenes described by Nartov, ''in future, Alexander, beware!''

This crudity proves on examination to have noteworthy features. Consider one of the scenes to be witnessed at festivals in the Summer Garden. ''Presently came several evil apostles, inspiring almost every one with dread and alarm; I mean a half dozen or so grenadiers of the Guard, who, in pairs, were carrying on hand-barrows basins of the commonest grain alcohol, which gave off such a powerful odour that many sensed it while the grenadiers were still in another walk, more than a hundred paces away. When I saw that many people immediately fled as though they had seen the devil, I asked a friend standing beside me what had happened to these people that they disappeared so hurriedly. Seizing my arm, he pointed out some advancing youths, whom I had not at first noticed, and we began to run with all our might, which was very prudent, inasmuch as soon afterward I met several men who complained bitterly of their misfortune in being unable to get the taste of whiskey out of their throats. Since I had already been warned that there were many spies to see to it that all received the bitter cup, I did not trust a single person but pretended to be suffering even more than they. But one conscienceless rogue knew how to verify whether I had drunk or not and asked me to exhale. I replied that it was useless since I had rinsed my mouth with water, to which he retorted that I should not tell him such a story; he knew that nothing would help; 'even though you put cinnamon or cloves in your mouth, for not less than 24 hours the mouth would smell of whiskey all the same, and you would not get rid of the taste for a still longer time'; he added that I, too, should experience it in order to be able to tell of these festivals in the best possible way. I declined with thanks, mentioning the fact that I absolutely cannot drink whiskey; all would have been vain, had it not been for my good friend, who was pretending to be a fiscal in order to tease me. But if any one falls into the clutches of a real fiscal, neither pleading nor tears will help him; he must submit, even to the point of standing on his head. Nor are even the daintiest ladies free from this obligation, for the tsaritsa herself sometimes drinks with the others. Majors of the Guard followed the tub of whiskey everywhere in order to compel any to drink who had not obeyed the simple grenadiers. One must drink the health of the tsar from the cup offered by one of the rank and file (it will hold a good beer glass, but they do not pour it equally full for everybody); they call it the 'health of our colonel,' but it is one and the same thing. When I later made inquiry why they use [for this purpose] such a nasty product as this whiskey, they answered that it is done partly because the Russians prefer this common grain alcohol to all the Danzig and French whiskeys in the world. Another reason is love for the Guard, which the tsar cannot flatter enough, for he often says that among his Guardsmen there is not one to whom he could not trust his life freely and without danger.''

The Guard made up the inevitable background of every festival. Both at the Summer Garden, where the court made merry, and on the Tsaritsyn Meadow might constantly be seen its dark green square, variegated with the red collars of the Preobrazhensky Regiment and the blue of the Semenovsky. And in their midst was frequently conspicuous the tall figure of the tsar, regaling himself with the whiskey of his soldiers before they went to regale the ministers and chamberlains with their beverage. To these guests on the Tsaritsyn Meadow Peter was more attentive than to the guests at the Summer Garden. The latter must quietly submit to the tsar's whims—drink what the tsar bade them, dance when he wished it. Very often Peter withdrew from the rout to rest (he always slept during the day) or on some business or other; but on his return he wished to find the merriment in full swing. At all the exits of the Summer Garden were placed sentries of the Guard, who let no one leave on any pretext. During one of these balls under arrest, it rained in bucketsful; the covered galleries were too small to accommodate all the guests, and many of them were drenched to the skin. But whereas at the Summer Garden all had to await the tsar's pleasure, and the ball could not end without his command, on the Tsaritsyn Meadow the tsar had to wait patiently until the whole military ceremony had ended. On his name-day, June 29, 1721, Peter was very distraught about something; his head was shaking and his shoulders twitching, with him always a sign of strong agitation; he scarcely looked at the courtiers assembled to greet him and went straight past to the Guard's square. Nor could he stay long there; he wished to leave when he had heard the first salute. But the Guard was to repeat the salute three times; Menshikov caught up with the retiring tsar and reminded him of the fact; Peter turned and remained till the end of the salute.

In our historical literature is firmly rooted the characterisation of Peter the Great as the "craftsman-tsar." In fact, a tsar in the ship-yards, with axe or plane in hand, is a picture far more unusual and therefore more effective than a tsar on the parade-ground. But if we are not striving for effect, we must admit that Peter became a soldier long before he became a craftsman, and that in his time he had studied the science of the drum with no less zeal than he later studied the trade of ship-carpenter. Nor did the latter ever crowd the former out of his head. Immediately on his return from his first trip abroad, with the memory of the Saardam shipyard still fresh in his mind, Peter set off to inspect his troops before he had seen the tsaritsa and the tsarevich, and as soon as he had arrived in the German Suburb. "As soon as he was convinced how far these hordes were from being real warriors, he himself showed them various gestures and motions, teaching these dis-orderly masses what bodily carriage they must strive for by bending his own body."

To the end of his life the drum remained his favourite instrument. All his pleasures bore a distinctly military stamp; they all "smelled of powder." In proving that the tsar had enough resources to continue the Swedish war in 1710, the Austrian resident Pleyer cites the considera-tion that "for two years not a single powder-mill has been working because there is still a great supply of powder in perfect readiness, despite the fact that in the instruction of recruits, as soon as they learn to handle firearms, there occurs incessant and violent shooting; when the tsar is present, or the heir, or Prince Menshikov, whether at Moscow or in the country, after almost every dinner, at every toast to any one's health, during a ball or a dance, on name-days and birthdays, or on the occasion of the most insignificant victory, muskets are fired incessantly." Descriptions of Peter's lavish fireworks reoccur throughout contemporary memoirs; they were admired, too, by men like Prince Kurakin, who was well acquainted with Europe. Whether the tsar banqueted at Lefort's, or a ship was launched, or there was a masquerade through the streets of Moscow, we hear a ceaseless discharge of cannon. At the New Year festival in 1699 "a salvo of twenty-four cannon marked every solemn toast.'' One of the foreign diplomats regarded this waste of powder on the air as a serious item of expenditure imposing a real burden on the state budget.

Whenever Peter made merry, he was far more the boisterous soldier (the drunken landsknecht, if you like, for we are not so far from the Thirty Years' War) than the tipsy craftsman. Wielding the cudgel when sober, in his cups Peter was prone to reach for the sword. At a banquet at Lefort's, toward the end of the dinner, becoming provoked at the voevoda Shein, ''the tsar became so incensed that, dealing blows indiscriminately with his drawn sword, he reduced all his dinner-companions to terror; Prince Romodanovsky received a slight wound in the finger, another in the head; Nikita Zotov [the 'mock patriarch'] was injured in the arm by a backhand movement of the sword; a far more disastrous blow was preparing for the voevoda, who undoubtedly would have fallen by the tsar's right arm, steeped in his own blood, had not General Lefort (to whom almost alone this was permissible), clasping the tsar in his arms, averted his hand. The tsar, however, fell into violent displeasure that there should be any one who dared to interfere with the consequences of his perfectly just wrath, immediately turned around, and dealt the meddler a heavy blow in the back; there was only one person who could straighten matters out, he who held first place among the Muscovites as regards the tsar's attachment to him. They say that this man was raised by destiny from the lowest milieu to a pinnacle of power envied by all. He succeeded in so softening the tsar's heart that he refrained from murder, confining himself to threats. This violent storm was succeeded by pleasant and clear weather.'' The beneficent sorcerer, whom Korb does not name, was Menshikov; the passage we have cited is one of those on which is based the familiar notion of the character of the relations between Peter and his ''Alexander.''

Were this love for the military and these soldier's habits merely a matter of personal inclination, or do they represent a conscious tendency on Peter's part? We must not forget that the world had not yet known the ''great Frederick,'' who ''made all kings corporals''; the soldier's trade was not yet the king's trade par excellence. Of preceding Russian tsars not one, except the Alleged Dmitry, had liked military things. Peter's childhood must have played a certain rôle, passed as it was under the impression of the long wars of Tsar Alexis, just terminated; most likely previous tsareviches had not had so many military playthings. The struggle for the Ukraine and the war with Sweden were bound to stir deeply the military instincts of Moscow's high society, dormant since the Troubles. Yet, besides instincts, contemporaries or near-contemporaries saw a serious political aspect in Peter's militarism—and not the one usually advanced. We have already made passing mention of

Vockerodt's remark that Peter "was sufficiently convinced from experience what a strong support to monarchical power a regular army offers," and that for this very reason he "devoted himself in particular and with all zeal to the improvement of his troops." Vockerodt assigns only second place to the influence of military needs in the narrow sense. As is well known, the old prejudice that Peter was the creator of a regular army in Russia has long since been abandoned; the first regiments "of foreign order" appeared in Russia under Tsar Michael; during Peter's minority these regiments, together with the streltsy, who also were a standing army rather than a feudal militia, made up the bulk of the Russian army. True, this was an inferior regular army, probably like the Turkish or Persian soldiers of the first half of the nineteenth century. Nevertheless, there were professional soldiers in Russia before Peter's time, and Peter's Guard represented nothing new from the standpoint of military technique. Nor was its establishment connected with military technique. Let us trace its gradual development, as it stands out in strong relief in Kurakin's *History*. At first there were 300 "playmates"; these were organised in sport; it is not likely that there was any serious calculation behind it. But in the collision with Sofia the "playmates" proved to be a force that could be relied on, especially since his opponent's adherents among the streltsy also numbered only a few hundred. Thus, "on his return from the Troitsa campaign of the year 7197 [1689]," *i.e.*, after his flight from Preobrazhensk to Troitsa and the settlement of accounts with Sofia and her supporters, Peter "began formally to recruit his two regiments, the Preobrazhensky and the Semenovsky." For the seventeen-year-old tsar they remained playthings; but for his mother's kindred and for B. A. Golitsyn, the real author of the coup d'etat of 1689, they were a serious military and police force, capable of being opposed, in case of need, to the unreliable streltsy. Ten years later it fell to the lot of the Guard to play this very rôle. From their inception the Preobrazhensky and Semenovsky Regiments were needed against the domestic foe; it was only later that they moved against a foreign foe.

This origin of the Guard explains its significance under Peter. The Guard officers played a rôle very like that of the gendarme officers of the time of Nicholas I. All the more or less intimate investigations into peculation and other abuses committed by persons very close to Peter were made with their assistance. Thus, the fiscal's report against Prince Ya. F. Dolgoruky was examined by a commission consisting of Major Dmitriev-Mamonov, Captain Likharev, Lieutenant-Captain Pashkov, and Lieutenant Bakhmetev. Before the establishment of the procurator-general, Peter had thought of making the staff officers of the Guard into an organ to supervise the whole Senate. Majors of the Guard were to attend sessions of the Senate and see that the senators carried on business properly; if they saw anything "contrary to this," they might arrest the culprit and take him to the fortress.[2] It is not surprising that the members of the Senate "rose from their places before a lieutenant and conducted themselves toward him with servility," as the agent of Louis XV remarked with amazement; he had some ground for finding that the "dignity of the empire" was "abased" thereby.

But the servility of senators before a lieutenant was nothing compared with the position in which provincial administrators were placed. The Guard officers, when sent to the provinces, had the right, in case their demands were not fulfilled, "to chain by the legs the governor as well as the vice-governor and other subordinates and to put a chain on their necks and not to set them free until they prepare" the reports demanded by the Guardsmen. Later a similar right was bestowed not only on officers but even on non-commissioned officers. The picture that Moscow (no backwoods corner!) presented under the yoke of non-commissioned officers is vividly portrayed in a letter of the well-known Petrine diplomat, Count Matveyev. "A non-commissioned officer sent here from the Kammer-Collegium, Pustoshkin by name," he relates, "caused an atrocious commotion and made havoc of the whole chancellory, and all the administrators here, except those of the War and Justice Collegia, he humiliated with chains not only on their legs but on their necks. Among them the local vice-governor, Master Voeikov, merely replied to the commissioner that he was willing to be put in chains but that he should be told his fault; which he, Pustoshkin, dared not do without the order of the War Collegium. Nevertheless, he, the vice-governor, is kept by him, Pustoshkin, in the chancellory of that province just as straitly as the rest. . . . I, visiting those prisoners out of Christian duty, verily with tears did see in the chancellory of the province here a multitude of children and women and honourable individuals, and floods of tears surpassing outright penal establishments." This was at Moscow, and the man chiefly injured was a vice-governor and brigadier, who found an intercessor in the person of an intimate of the tsar, a man who had recently been envoy at the court of one of the great powers, as Holland then was, a man who was almost one of the "supreme lords." What men suffered in remote provinces may be judged from the complaint of a Vyatka official against the "soldier," Netesev. This Netesev, relates the official, "comes into the chancellory drunk at hours not appointed . . . at two or three o'clock at night and beats the corporals of the guard and the sentries with a stick, and, without declaring any fault and without any reason, holds us under arrest in the watch-house and at other times

[2] Even then, according to Vockerodt, the Fortress of Peter and Paul played less of a military than a police rôle; it never defended any one or anything, but it was "a sort of Bastille."

in chains, and, seizing on inhabitants of Vyatka, as well townsmen as countrymen of the better sort, ex-burmisters and [other officials] . . . keeps them under guard beneath the local government office and in chains, where heretofore robbers were kept, and takes bribes." "This soldier," adds Bogoslovsky, from whom we borrow these tales, "had attained a sort of intoxication with authority, which in his case seems to have coincided with intoxication with whiskey. Repeatedly he made boastful speeches that, 'coming to the chancellory, he would fetter and torture to death the chancellor and his secretary; and if they would not put themselves in irons, he would beat them with those irons and break their heads open.' The wife of the secretary he threatened to cut up with his sword into small pieces and swore to fulfil this his intention, kissing the image of the Saviour in the presence of witnesses."

Bourgeois on the surface, Petrine society continued to be military at the core. The mention of "soldiers" may have inspired in the reader the illusion that we were speaking of something new, of a sort of military democracy. Nothing of the sort; the kernel of Peter's Guard was composed of "princes and simple nobles." This vital fact had at once impressed itself on foreign observers, who strove to explain it according to their lights. "He is gracious with all," says the French diplomat Campredon, "and pre-eminently with the soldiers, most of whom are children of princes and lords, who are serving him as a pledge of their fathers' loyalty." In fact, even under Peter, the nobility had begun to elaborate the central organ which was to aid it in resuming authority under his successors. The thin bourgeois veil had no more changed the nature of the Muscovite state than had the German cloak changed the nature of the Muscovite man. When Peter died, only the small group of "supreme lords," devoid of social support among the masses, stood between the nobility and power. The "supreme lords," having failed to create a bourgeoisie, were like a staff without an army, while the old military-serving class, clad in the Preobrazhensky uniform, merely awaited a convenient moment to "break the lords' heads for them."

6. *The Agony of the Bourgeois Policy*

The military force very quickly managed to make itself a political force. Scarcely had Peter closed his eyes in death when the Guard was master of the situation. Without the consent of the Guardsmen no one could ascend the Russian throne, so lately filled by "their colonel."

The impact of commercial capitalism on Russia had cost her very dear; nor were Russia's losses to be measured by her expenditures in men and money. No "active policy" can ever dispense with such outlays, and in this particular Russia in 1725 did not differ essentially from France at the moment of the death of Louis XIV, from Prussia at the close of the

Seven Years' War, or even from England at the end of her struggle with Napoleon. The population had been ruined and had scattered. The effects were felt long before the close of the war; by 1710 the loss of population, as compared with the last pre-Petrine census, has been calcu-lated by Mr. Milyukov as reaching 40% in some places. However unre-liable the statistics of the time (even contemporaries had no confidence in the census of 1710), they give a fairly definite general impression, especially where they are supplemented by comments. Of the province of Archangel the official document remarks that "losses of homesteads and their inmates have appeared because the men have been taken as recruits, as soldiers, as carpenters, to St. Petersburg as workers, as settlers, as smiths." Of the 5,356 homesteads "lost" in the Shekhona country, 1,551 had been abandoned because of conscription for the army or for labour on public works, and 1,366 because of flights. To foreigners it seemed that the central provinces had been absolutely depopulated thanks to the Northern War; and though this opinion must be taken with the same reserve as the assertion of these same foreigners that the clay-soil near Moscow was among "the best lands in Europe," this sum-mary impression was not pure fantasy. A document of 1726, which bears the signatures of almost all the "supreme lords," accepts unquestion-ingly the following "reasons" for non-payment of the soul tax: "since the census many peasants who were able to earn money by their labour, have died and been taken as recruits and run away . . . while of those who now by labour can get money to meet the state taxes there remain but a small number." Nor did the "supreme lords" dispute a reference to the decline of peasant economy: "besides that, for several years now there have been crop failures, and in many places the peasants sow little grain, and those who sow are compelled to sell the grain in the ground to meet state taxes, and hence they go running into far places where it would be impossible to seek them out." Yet in this second quotation we already have an explanation of peasant ruin by other than political factors; for obvious reasons the official document is silent about the social causes, which were, however, clearly evident to foreigners, who, in ac-counting for the depopulation of central Russia assigned to the "savage dealings of the masters" as much weight as to the Northern War.

The bankruptcy of Peter's system lay not in the fact that "at the price of the ruin of the country Russia was raised to the rank of a European power" but in the fact that, regardless of the ruin of the country, this goal was not attained. Foreigners in Russian service rated the might of Peter's empire far lower than did foreigners looking on from a distance, or than later historians have done. Field-Marshal Münnich, in an intimate conversation with the Prussian envoy, Mardefeld, did not conceal from him that the Russian troops were in a very lamentable condition: the officers were good for nothing; among the soldiers were many untrained recruits; there were no cavalry horses at all—in a word, had there appeared another opponent like Charles XII, he might with 25,000 men have settled accounts with the whole "Muscovite" army. And he said this only two years after the Peace of Nystadt, so brilliantly celebrated! The fleet was no better off; only the galleys were worth anything, and while they were very practical for a little war in the fiords of Finland, they were not fit for the open sea. For the sake of speed, ships were built of green wood; they rotted with extraordinary rapidity in the fresh waters of the Kronstadt haven. This was one of the chief reasons for Peter's attempt to transfer his fleet base to Rogervik (later "Baltic Port," near Reval), situated close to the open sea, where the water was salt. But Peter's engineers could not cope with the large waves; every violent storm swept away all the fruits of their toil, so that the construction of Rogervik became synonymous with the labours of Sisyphus. The personnel of the fleet was no better than its materiel. Peter was soon disappointed in his foreign-trained "midshipmen" and by the end of his reign was no longer sending them abroad to study. The condition of the sailors is best indicated by a report one foreign diplomat made to his government, a report made at the very time of the magnificent masquerades in celebration of victory over the Swedes. "By way of anticipating disorders and preserving tranquillity the number of the guard in the residency here was doubled. I was told that the cause of the multiplicity of precautions taken on this occasion lay in the fact that a very considerable number of sailors, whose wages, despite the order given by the tsar before his departure that they should be paid off, had not been paid, and who had not a piece of bread, had conspired to gather in a crowd and loot the houses of the inhabitants of the residency here."

At the same time Russia was on the eve of a new war. Commercial capitalism, which had forced Peter to fight for twenty years for the Baltic Sea, now drove him to the Caspian. Ere the Peace of Nystadt was concluded, Peter had already prepared a new detailed map of the latter sea, for which the French Academy elected the tsar to membership. The officers who made the map brought, as foreign diplomats said, the important information that the chief centres of silk production lay near the border of the tsar's dominions. "Here they all flatter themselves with the hope that since the Persians have not a single naval vessel, it will be possible to attract a great part of the silk trade here and to extract great revenue from it," the Prussian envoy wrote to his king. It was only the Prussian diplomat who discovered this America; the Russian court had of course never forgotten that "greatest trade in Europe" after which there had been so many seekers in the seventeenth century. Peter's Persian campaign was the inevitable complement to the silk manufactories he had planted. A year later it was being talked of quite definitely. "The tsar wishes, for the safety of his trade, to have a port and fortress on the other side of the Caspian Sea and desires that the silks, which are usually sent to Europe through Smyrna, should henceforth go to Astrakhan and Petersburg," wrote another diplomat in 1722; soon afterward he heard a similar explanation from the lips of Peter himself, except that the tsar naturally spoke, not of seizure of the silk trade by the Russians but of "freedom" for this trade.

Hardly had the military operations against the Swedes been brought to a close than the troops engaged in them began to be drawn off toward Moscow, and thence onward to the banks of the Don and the Volga. On the latter rapidly grew up a military and transport fleet, for service of which 5,000 sailors were transferred from Kronstadt through Moscow to Nizhny Novgorod. As usual, there was no lack of pretexts for war. At Shemakha the tsar's "gosts" had been robbed of anywhere from fifty thousand to five hundred thousand rubles; later three million was mentioned. Moreover, the tsar's "gost" was so near to being a government official that it was impossible not to view the incident as downright disrespect for the dignity of the Russian sovereign. True, the plunderers were rebels against their own sovereign, the shah of Persia; but all the less reason had he to be angry at the appearance of Russian troops in his dominions. It was for him, in the last analysis, that they were restoring order; he was bound to appreciate this fact, and at the Russian court it was even hoped that perhaps the shah would freely assign the silk monopoly to Russia, out of pure gratitude.

All these iridescent hopes, however, were bound soon to fade. If not the Persian government itself (which at the time it was not easy to find, as several pretenders were struggling for the throne), then its vassals on the shores of the Caspian Sea, in alliance with the mountaineers of Daghestan, offered the Russians desperate resistance. The Caspian fleet turned out no better than the Baltic; most of it was destroyed by storms. The climate was a foe deadlier than storms and the Persians; diseases and horse murrain raged in the Russian camp. Peter, who had set out on the campaign in the spring of 1722, returned to Moscow in the following January; his very meagre conquests had cost "15,000 horses, more than 4,000 regular troops, without counting a far greater number of cossacks and a million rubles." But these immediate losses were nothing in comparison with those the future threatened.

Russia's rival for the silk trade, Turkey, understood Peter's Caspian expedition as a direct threat to her; one war involved another, and that incomparably more dangerous. "I can, as it seems to me, assure Your Majesty," Campredon wrote to Louis XV in April, 1723, "that, however the Russians boast and with whatever obstinacy they throw dust in one's eyes, they are unable to support a war against the Turks, whether on the Persian front or on that of Azov. The Russian finances are bad, and hunger is making itself ever more strongly felt. The cavalry is without horses, for they all perished in the last campaign, and the troops have not been paid for 17 months, something that never happened in the last war." The fact of non-payment of wages to the troops, at first sight improbable, is fully borne out by Russian documents; on February 13, 1724, the Senate reported to the sovereign that "many officers, mostly foreigners, but likewise Russians with small estates or none at all, on account of non-payment of their wages for the past year have fallen into such straits that they have consumed their own equipment." By the end of the reign even those on whose account the whole country was starving were themselves starving!

On men inclined to pessimism, such as the Saxon resident Lefort, for example, Peter at this time produced the impression of a man who had renounced everything and had taken to drink from grief. "I cannot understand the state of this realm," Lefort wrote six months before the emperor's death; "for the sixth day the tsar has not left his room and is very unwell because of a spree on the occasion of the laying of the corner-stone of a church, which they christened with 3,000 bottles of wine. . . . The masquerades are near at hand, and men are talking of nothing but pleasures, while the nation weeps. . . . They pay neither the troops nor the fleet nor the collegia nor any one whatsoever; every one is grumbling terribly."

The death of the reformer was a worthy finale to this festivity in the midst of plague. As is well known, Peter died of the effects of syphilis, probably contracted in Holland and ill-cured by the doctors there. For that matter, given the Homeric drunkenness of Peter's court, the best doctors could scarcely have helped him. For the tsar death came quite unexpectedly, though outside observers had long been prepared for the catastrophe; and the temper which he displayed may very well shake the legend of "men of iron." "In the course of his illness, he fell off strongly in spirit, feared death frightfully, but at the same time expressed sincere repentance," writes the French envoy in his detailed relation of Peter's last days. "By his express command they set free all those imprisoned for debt, most of whom he ordered discharged out of his personal resources. The rest of the prisoners and all in penal servitude, except murderers and state criminals(!), he likewise ordered set free; he ordered prayers for himself in all churches of divers religions and received the Sacrament three times in one week." He was ill long enough to have been able to draw up a will, which would have been the logical sequel to his law on the succession to the throne. But his fear of death was so great that he lacked the spirit to set about it, and those around him to remind him of it. They recollected it when Peter was already almost in his agony, but in the scrawls produced by his trembling hand they could distinguish only two words: "give all. . . ." To whom remained unknown.

Thus, the day after the death of the first emperor of Russia the throne became elective. Neither in theory nor in practice was there so much novelty in this as we might suppose. The first tsars of the House of Romanov had usually been "elected" to the throne by a zemsky sobor; at least the formality of election was preserved even at Peter's accession to the throne. When the "Holy Synod and the High Governing Senate and the Generality in unison bade" the Russian people bear obedience to the widow of the deceased, the Empress Catherine I, it was not so much a new form as simply new words to designate an assembly of essentially the same composition as the one which in 1682 had elected Peter himself, and which had consisted of the "Holy Synod," the "boyar duma," and the "Moscow estates." The innovation lay in the fact that previously, from Alexis on, the election had been really only a form because the heir was known to all; now, although there was no lack of an heir, in passing him over they elected a person who had no rights to the throne at all. And those who did the electing were not those who by tradition had the power and in whose name the manifesto was written, but, once more, persons who had no formal right of election. "Senate, Synod and Generality" was written at the dictation of the Guard, which at this moment of universal dissatisfaction was the most dissatisfied and most dangerous force.

Foreign diplomats are in general agreement in their versions of the events that took place in the palace on the night of the 27-28th of January, 1725. When the Guard officers took leave of their colonel, who had already lost consciousness, their seniors (according to some reports, on their own initiative; according to another version, led by the "reichs-marshal," Prince Menshikov) betook themselves to Catherine and "took an oath of loyalty" to her. That this was not an oath as loyal subjects is clear from the fact that Peter was still alive at that moment; the "oath" evidently consisted in the promise of the Guardsmen not to forsake their lady colonel. Reassured by this promise, she acted in accord with the dictates of expediency; for even after the visit of the Preobrazhenskys to Catherine, which was of course immediately echoed in court circles, there were bold men who asserted that the lawful heir was the son of the executed Tsarevich Alexis and grandson of the first emperor, the future Peter II; and among these men were the great majority of the "supreme lords." Only Menshikov, Tolstoi, and Admiral-General Apraxin were resolutely opposed to his candidacy; and if Tolstoi's position may be easily explained by his sombre rôle in the affair of Alexis, the conduct of

the chief of the land army and of the commander-in-chief of the Russian
fleet can hardly be reduced to personal motives alone. They were driven
in a definite direction by the public opinion of the groups they headed.
What the army expected from Catherine becomes absolutely clear as soon
as we learn the promises she gave in exchange for the Guardsmen's
"oath of loyalty." "The empress declared from the very beginning that
she would pay them their wages out of her own treasury." More than
that, she "took the precaution in advance to send money to the fortress
to pay wages to the garrison, which, like the other troops, had not received them for sixteen months. . . . In order to make them still better
disposed toward her, the tsaritsa ordered distribution of moneys to all
the regiments over and above their wages; soldiers engaged on various
labours were ordered to cease their labours and betake themselves to their
stations, supposedly to pray God for the sovereign."

The skill with which Catherine conducted herself at this odd auction
for the moment roused foreign observers to extraordinary enthusiasm
and inspired them with an exceedingly exaggerated notion of the capa-
bilities of the new sovereign. She "may in all justice be called the
Semiramis of the North and an astonishing example of miraculous good-
fortune," Campredon wrote of the event of January 28. "Without high
birth, without any support except her personal deserts, unable even to
read or write, she has through long years enjoyed the love and confidence
of the most august monarch, a man least of all mortals subject to any
lasting influence, and after his death she has been able to make herself
autocratic sovereign, to the general enthusiasm of all and without the
least shadow of opposition, at least so far, to her good fortune." To
oppose would have been very risky, when Prince Menshikov frankly
threatened to slay any one who dared to oppose the proclamation of
Catherine as reigning empress, and "the Guard officers, intentionally
stationed in a corner of the hall" where the Synod, Senate, and Generality were holding counsel, "said the same thing."

The personal rôle of the sovereign began to seem less significant, even
to the most enthusiastic, when they inspected her administration more
closely. Of all Peter's functions that which suited his widow best was,
strange as it may seem, the rôle of colonel. Here she strove with exceptional energy and not without success to replace the late emperor. When
her daughter Anna was married to the duke of Holstein (they had been
betrothed in Peter's lifetime), Catherine did not attend the wedding
because of mourning; but mourning did not prevent her from appearing
at the military part of the ceremony. On foot she made the circuit of
the ranks of the Guardsmen, drawn up as usual on the Tsaritsyn Meadow,
of course drank whiskey to their health and distributed roast beef to
them. The soldiers "greeted her with enthusiastic shouts, throwing up

their caps." But gradually contemporaries began to find that the empress was attracted overmuch by this side of her task. Six months after her accession, Campredon, who had been so enthusiastic about her, began to find that the empress might lose "both the respect and the advantage merited by her great gifts," thanks to her "distractions." "These distractions consist in almost daily carouses, lasting all night and a good part of the day, in the garden with persons who on account of their service obligations have to be always at court." Catherine rarely went to bed before four o'clock in the morning, and her constant condition of drunken stupor excluded all possibility of busying herself with "affairs of state."

Foreign men of affairs, who had had occasion to observe Peter closely during his trips abroad, had not had a high opinion of the efficiency of the reformer himself in this field. The French official put in charge of Peter during his journey to Paris could not understand when the Russian tsar busied himself with politics, and finally came to the conclusion that among the Russians political questions were probably decided during dinner, over a bottle of wine. In reality, these matters had been decided by the "supreme lords" quite independently; if the matter did not relate to the army or the fleet, Peter interfered only sporadically, chiefly at moments when the machine had begun to squeak badly and threatened to stop altogether. To expect even such sporadic interference from Catherine would have been nonsense. The necessity for a real sovereign along with the nominal one was recognised by men who knew the empress, apparently even at the very moment of her accession; even then there were rumours of some kind of a "special council, vested with a certain authority," which would prevent Catherine from being "entirely autocratic." At that moment, however, she was supported by the army and the fleet, by Menshikov and Apraxin; talk of a "council" was not energetically supported by any one. But Peter's autocracy had offered too negative results for men to put up readily with a simple continuation of it when the official wielder of it was manifestly incompetent to maintain even outward decorum.

Not at all in the name of a return to tradition, as it is usually presented, but, on the contrary, in the name of the "Europeanisation" of political forms, the opposition which had smouldered in Peter's time burst out in bright flame in the reign of Catherine I. If during the reformer's lifetime matters had not gone beyond bold speeches, such as the declaration of a captain of the fleet that the tsar, properly, had no right to give orders without consulting the zemsky sobor, his successor had to deal with far more than simple talk. During military salutes, of which in the empress' presence they were as liberal as in the reign of the late emperor, balls began to whistle from muskets "accidentally" loaded; men fell killed and wounded, and, as though by design, at two paces from Catherine. In the torture-chambers they were constantly torturing some one, whether soldiers of the Guard, or "two aristocratic ladies, brought from Moscow in fetters," or the brother of the Grand Duke's tutor. Romodanovsky, son of the "prince-cæsar," who had inherited from his father the office of chief of the secret political police, told his cronies that he was no longer able to bear the horrors he had to witness. It was impossible to place unconditional reliance even on their chief support—the army. Besides individual officers and soldiers, whole armies fell under suspicion, like the Little Russian army, whose commander, Prince M. M. Golitsyn, very popular with his subordinates, was deemed one of the most untrustworthy; in February, 1726, they had to change the garrison in the Peter and Paul Fortress. They had to conciliate at least some of the malcontents and try to mollify the discontent of the rest. In this setting arose an institution, the significance of which has hitherto not been very intelligible to Russian historians, though contemporaries understood it perfectly and at once—the Supreme Privy Council.

The "points" presented to the Empress Anna in 1730 were clearly foreshadowed in February, 1726. The well-known "opinion not in edict," which supplied the constitution of the Supreme Privy Council, really puts matters more generally and more simply than do the celebrated "points." In place of enumerating the cases in which the empress cannot act independently, the "opinion" generalises all possible cases: "no edicts shall be issued until they have been absolutely settled in the privy council." Edicts were to be issued with the formula: "given in Our Supreme privy council"; in the same way all kinds of "reports, memoranda, or presentations" must be subscribed, "for submission to the Supreme privy council." Thus, in the eyes of the subjects power was locked up in a very solid casket, and the public had gradually to get used to the fact that the sovereign did not rule directly, and that the sovereign's commands had force only when clothed in a certain constitutional form.

From the very beginning, however, it was perfectly clear that in itself this form could not satisfy any one. Menshikov agreed to the formation of the Council without much dispute, it seems, because he valued the reality of power far more than the parade; as one making a concession, he demanded full autonomy for himself at home in the War Collegium, where formerly the Senate had wearied him with its attempts at supervision and control. But just because matters had not changed much in comparison with the preceding period, such a change was not enough for the public. In order to accustom it to an aristocratic constitution on the English model, it was necessary to demonstrate its practical advantages.

Otherwise its "English" form could only compromise it. From the very first day, it may be said, the "supreme lords" [3] could not but sense that the Council would have to fight for its existence. Officially the Council was established on February 9, and an edict about it was sent to the Senate; the Senate did not receive the edict and had its usher in the most insulting way "throw" it into the chancellory of the new institution. This was one of those moments when even in dry chancellory correspondence is felt the tempo of drama—or rather of comedy: for the moment when the secretary of the Council thrust the edict into the bosom of the Senate's usher undoubtedly belongs to the latter genre.

The social group closest to the supreme lords in point of its official position, Peter's "generality," manifestly did not desire to recognise the "English" constitution, which made a few men, who only yesterday had sat in their midst, their masters. Harsh measures were applied to the Senate; it was deprived of the title of "Ruling" and remained only "High"; what was far more important and more noteworthy, the Senate was deprived of an independent military force; under the pretext of economy (it was then a universal pretext) the "Senate Company" was abolished, 10 couriers being left to the Senate; finally, a number of new senators were appointed, as in England new peers are appointed to subdue a disobedient upper house, and appointed without reference to their hierarchical rank or to the dignity of the Senate. In official correspondence the Senate was gradually equated with "the other collegia"; and for any negligence on the part of senators their pay was withheld just as it was from the small fry of the chancellories. In a word, the Council exacted full satisfaction. But the collision with the Senate was merely symptomatic of the general state of affairs. Neither the "supreme lords" nor the "generality" directly represented any social class; the significance of the Supreme Privy Council and its fate become clear to us only when we discover the class implication of its policy. Then we shall see that the régime of the "supreme lords" was the finale of the Petrine reform. During Dmitry Golitsyn's administration of Russia [4] the wave of bourgeois policy reached its last crest. From the moment of the fall of the supreme lords sets in a continuous ebb-tide; by his constitutional projects Golitsyn himself testified to the fall of the system of which he was fated to be the last representative.

The bourgeois policy of the Supreme Privy Council was very early evident—even before the fall of Menshikov. As early as December 20,

---

[3] As members of the Council were appointed Menshikov, Apraxin, Golovkin, Tolstoi and D. Golitsyn; Ostermann was added a little later. The duke of Holstein substituted for Catherine. Yaguzhinsky, who attended the first meetings, soon left and became the sworn enemy of the supreme lords.

[4] He was in fact the head of the Privy Council in the two-year interval between the banishment of Menshikov and the death of Peter II in 1730.

1726, on the initiative of Menshikov, Ostermann, and Makarov, it was decided to organise a commission to consider the condition of the Russian merchantry and to devise means of improving it "to the profit of the realm." And as an earnest of the great and rich favours that the merchantry might expect from this commission, the empress, on the report of the same persons, "was pleased to decree: for the sake of developing the merchantry every one shall be permitted from the coming year 1727 to trade to the town of Archangel without interdiction." The reasons for the measure were set forth in detail in the "opinion" submitted to the Senate by the Kammer and Commerce Collegia and by the Chief Magistracy. This "opinion" is one of the most intelligent documentary expressions of Russian mercantilism of the early eighteenth century. In great detail it proved that in the province of economics Peter's cudgel had merely compelled superfluous and unproductive expenditures and, consequently, had served no purpose except to retard the accumulation of capital. "Commerce ought to be in all freedom; whatever merchants are able to trade to any port ought not to be forbidden to do so"; any one who can make a profit by transporting his wares to St. Petersburg will take them there in future, and if any artificial pre-eminence can be created in favour of the capital, it is by making the import duties everywhere lower than at "the town" (as the document very remarkably calls Archangel, which to the pre-Petrine bourgeoisie was "the town" par excellence). To forbid the importation of wares into "the town," as Peter had done, was sheer nonsense. The official document of course did not express itself so definitely; but the idea was precisely that. It is worth remarking one detail; among the wares that enter Archangel the 'opinion" has grain in mind. "In return for such exported grain great capital came into the Russian realm from foreign countries because of the peasants' labour"; Peter's prohibition of grain exports had deprived of this "capital" the "peasants who in certain littoral towns and in Vyatka paid their taxes for the most part by selling grain." So early appears an anticipation of agrarian capitalism, and, what is most noteworthy, in the region where there was no serfdom; in converting themselves into factories for the production of grain for export, the landlords' estates of the second half of the eighteenth century were only following in the footsteps of the "black plough" [state] peasantry.

It need hardly be added that abolition of the privileges of St. Petersburg in the matter of exports was from the economic point of view a progressive, not a reactionary, measure, all the more so since we know that St. Petersburg had been founded out of military, not commercial, considerations. But Menshikov's policy was by no means focused on bourgeois interests, and we shall be able to form a real estimate of it only if we acquaint ourselves with a series of measures the Supreme Council took relating to the soul tax. This financial innovation of Peter's, as is well known, had meant not so much a revolution in financial technique as an extraordinary intensification of the tax burden. The fact that the tax was now assessed on souls of male sex instead of on homesteads would be very expressive of Peter's individualism, had the money been collected from the "soul," if, in other words, the tax had been individual. But such was not the case at all; the tax was, as of old, imposed in gross on the whole hamlet, and within the hamlet was distributed according to the number of economies there; only the total amount was determined by the number of "mouths" of male sex in the hamlet, not excepting decrepit old men and nursing babes. This method of reckoning simplified matters in the extreme; no disputes such as those that had formerly taken place under the homestead census (over what was a homestead, what not) were possible; there could be no dispute about the number of workers, the relative strength of the taxable homesteads, and such like, for every male paid whether he was a worker or not.

The psychological explanation of the reform must then be sought not in the domain of bourgeois economy but in a circle far closer to Peter—the army. The whole male population of the country was divided into serving soldiers and paying soldiers; according to Peter's idea, the latter must support the former directly. To this end the collection of the soul tax in each "guberniya" was concentrated in the hands of the military authorities; from each regiment in a definite locality was detailed a "command," headed by an officer, which exacted the tax with military despatch and punctuality. These military peculiarities of the new financial system were the most grievous to the population.

When the Supreme Privy Council, influenced by the considerations of which examples were given at the beginning of this chapter, decided to carry out a "relief of the peasantry in the payment of the soul tax," it began by removing the military collectors from the hamlets. "Whatever staff officers and subalterns and men of the rank and file are in permanent quarters for the collection of the soul tax and on expeditions for various levies . . . shall go to their commands immediately," says the journal of the Supreme Council for February 1, 1727. Officially the collection passed from the hands of the military into the hands of the civil authorities—from the "staff officers and subalterns" to the "voevodas," who under Peter had lost the last vestiges of their former significance and had preserved a purely etymological connection with military (voenny) affairs. But the voevoda could not replace the military collector, who had travelled through the province and exacted the soul tax from the peasants directly; herein had lain the burdens of the former system. The civilian authorities could retain only general supervision; to whom the functions of the "staff officers and subalterns" really passed,

is stated with absolute definiteness in an edict of February 22 of the same
year, which sums up all the "favours" shown by the Supreme Council.

By this edict a special commission was empowered to examine the
question of the soul tax and to change the rate; but the tax imposed on
the peasants "the landlords themselves shall collect, and in their absence
their stewards [and other agents] shall be constrained to pay." One of
the most important of the landholder's rights, the right which had been
so effective in enserfing the peasants but which, thanks to Peter's financial reforms, had become a fiction, once more became a reality. The
military landlord, who for twenty years had been regarded as cannon
fodder, became once more the "financial agent of the government," as
modern historians delicately and elegantly express it; it would be more
correct to say that once more he became a sovereign in miniature, for so
long as serfdom existed there could be no control over the way in which
this "agent" collected the taxes from his peasants. Of course, Peter
had not intentionally pared down the powers of the nobility in this
respect; theoretically the local authority of the nobility was even increased in his reign.

But how could these theoretical rights be put into practice by the
military landlord, who on account of the "active policy" served "without
leave" until overtaken by senility, without seeing his home for years at
a time? Under Peter retirement had been permitted only in case of utter
inability to continue service. All served "without leave," from the
highest to the lowest; the septuagenarian field-marshal, B. P. Sheremetev,
several times asked the sovereign to let him go to Moscow to arrange his
affairs but was not even honoured with a reply. If Peter was so strict
with a field-marshal, it is easy to imagine what the service of simple men
of no rank was like. Not only was service burdensome; to the noble of
those days, with his habits, it seemed humiliating as well. In the Muscovite period he had offered himself for service with a detachment of
armed bondsmen, whom he commanded; if he was subordinate to the
senior commander, the latter was always a fellow noble. Peter's statute
forbade men to be made officers and given command unless they had
previously served in the ranks and "knew the soldier's business from the
foundation." The noble newly taken into service had to pull in the collar
along with his own serfs, and sometimes fell under the command of one
of them who had been made a non-commissioned officer for distinguished
service. Service alone did not suffice for promotion; one had to study.
Non-fulfilment or poor fulfilment of service obligations was punished
most severely; Peter's phrases about "sharp torture for negligence"
must be understood quite literally. Noteworthy in this respect are the
memoirs of one military servitor of the time, Zhelyabuzhsky, a genuine
martyrologist of the military-serving class. There we find on every page

notes, such as: Colonel Moksheyev was beaten with a knout because he had released a schismatic; in 1699 Divov and Kolychev were beaten with lashes because Divov had given Kolychev 20 rubles in money and a cask of wine to escape reporting at Voronezh for shipbuilding. In 1704 Prince Alexis Baryatinsky was beaten with lashes at Preobrazhensk for not reporting men eligible for service, while Rodion Zernovo-Velyaminov was beaten with rods for not registering in time. Non-appearance on service was punishable, under a law of 1714 by confiscation of all one's property, under a law of 1722 by "political death." No regard was had for person, and prompt punishment was exacted for violation of the statutes, whether small or great. In the same year, 1704, according to Zhelyabuzhsky's diary, the voevoda Naumov was beaten unmercifully with rods for having failed to shave his beard.

This is the reason why with the "favour" to the peasants, at which the peasants were perhaps not the most delighted, there was closely linked a promise of favour to the nobles, who undoubtedly appreciated it at its true value. "When circumstances permit, two parts of the officers and sergeants and rank and file, who are of the nobility, shall be dismissed to their homes in order that they may inspect their hamlets and bring them into proper order"; their duties were meanwhile to be performed by foreigners and men without service estates. This idea of exempting the military-serving nobility was ascribed by foreign diplomats to Menshikov. The commander-in-chief of the military force was, perhaps unconsciously, representing the interests of the military class.

The fall of Menshikov was, then, much more than a court revolution of little interest for the historian. An exceptionally typical representative of "primary accumulation," Menshikov combined in his own person the powerful feudatory and the great entrepreneur, and it seems the latter frequently predominated. In the documents of the period we incessantly find "His Serene Highness," now selling pitch, now coining his old silver, at enormous profit to himself; he had several factories; he farmed the fisheries in the White Sea. At the same time he was surrounded by a sort of court (the papers relating to his exile mention Menshikov's free followers) and had his own soldiers, who evidently caused some anxiety to those who banished the prince. But it does not appear that these soldiers, or any soldiers and officers at all, stirred in favour of the banished man; the army, it seems, was too well aware that its generalissimo was most concerned with filling his own pocket. Since there was, among his opponents, no lack of popular generals, like M. M. Golitsyn or V. V. Dolgoruky, it was natural enough that the military-serving nobility decided to play a waiting game and see what the "supreme lords" would do when they had got rid of the real autocrat.

The removal of Menshikov was bound to establish a formal oligarchy, for at this time the Russian throne was only nominally occupied. The long foretold death of Catherine I was not long in coming; Peter II, who replaced her in May, 1727, and who as early as 1725 had been the candidate of a majority of the supreme lords, had, in the words of the English diplomat, Rondeau, one dominant passion—hunting.[5] The fact that this thirteen-year-old boy, who looked all of eighteen, matured very early, offered an additional means of ruling him—through women. Here the supreme lords—or their daughters—had only one rival; the Tsarevna Elizabeth, daughter of Peter the Great, pleased the young emperor better than did any one else around him. But they had little cause for worry; at that time Elizabeth (she herself was only eighteen) had one dominant passion—to say nothing of others—the passion for dress. Politics were absolutely foreign to her; at the most critical moment she thought only of sending to her political rival to complain that the court chef did not send her cooks pepper and salt. Menshikov had made the first attempt to supply Peter II with a wife who would watch over the interests of her family; but he went about it so crudely, and the princess was so uninteresting that the attempt was an utter failure, and, it seems, even hastened on the catastrophe which it had been designed to ward off. Dolgoruky almost succeeded where Menshikov had failed; his plans were thwarted by a pure accident, for in 1730 Peter died of smallpox on the eve of the day appointed for his wedding with Princess Catherine Dolgoruky. This event necessarily terminated the attempts of the supreme lords to secure themselves by "family" means; they had to resort to other courses. Here success was wholly dependent on the attitude of the noble public toward the rule of the Supreme Privy Council. This attitude in its turn was determined by the policy pursued by the supreme lords during the reign of Peter II.

The real head of the Council during this period was, as already mentioned, Prince Dmitry Golitsyn, former "gubernator" of Kiev, later President of the Kammer Collegium, and one of the most important of the "supreme lords" of the Petrine period. Contemporaries deemed him the head of the "Old Russian party"; modern scholars, correcting this mistake, have begun to emphasise his education on the Western model and his Western acquaintanceships. That Golitsyn was not the head of an "Old Russian party" is, of course, true; no such party existed. But it is noteworthy that he, one of Peter's closest aids, did not like foreign languages, though he could make himself understood in them, and his celebrated library in the village of Archangelskoye, near Moscow, was filled with manuscript translations of European jurists and publicists made specially for him. Likewise is it noteworthy that at the time when

[5] "Certain other of his passions it is not meet to mention," adds the cautious diplomat.

he enjoyed the greatest influence a manifest attempt was made to return the capital to Moscow. Peter II spent the greater part of his reign there and died there. During this time all the central institutions were moved thither, among others the mint, which foreigners thought a mark of the permanence of the change; under pain of the severest punishment it was forbidden even to speak of the court's return to the banks of the Neva. We cannot but see in this a further forward step of the policy which had once more "opened" Archangel for trade.

The bourgeois tendency that Prince Golitsyn represented in the Supreme Council was nearer to pre-Petrine than to Petrine mercantilism, a fact, however, which did not make it reactionary; for after the collapse of Peter's enterprises it was too obvious that the natural development of the germs of capitalism existent in the seventeenth century would yield far more results than all the attempts to drive the Russian bourgeoisie into the capitalistic Eden with a cudgel. "Emancipation of commerce" was made the slogan of the economic policy of the Supreme Council in the reign of Peter II. The series of "free-trade" measures began with the edict of May 26, 1727, abolishing the greatest of the treasury monopolies—that in salt; the tariff published in the same year diminished the customs duties on a whole series of foreign wares by one-half. But the real stream of "bourgeois" legislation begins after the banishment of Menshikov. From September, 1727, the protocols and journals of the Supreme Privy Council take on a very strange hue; we might think we were in a realm where trade was the soul of everything, and where merchants and mill-owners ruled. On September 16 (just a week after the exile of Menshikov) was permitted free establishment of mines in Siberia, without licence from the Collegium of Mines. On the same day trade with Khiva and Bokhara, which had been broken off after Peter's unsuccessful campaigns, was "re-established." On the same day was published an edict on the free sale of tobacco; another of the great treasury monopolies had disappeared. On September 27 the treasury factories began to go the way of the monopolies; the Yekaterinhof linen manufactory was released. On the same day the working of mica was declared free. On October 20 were abolished the dues on "merchant folk and their workers" going to and from Siberia, and it was ordered that they be given passports free. On December 30 was published a salt statute, reducing to practice the abolition of the salt monopoly, in principle already effected in May. On March 18 of the following year the potash monopoly was abolished. On August 19 were abolished the last restrictions securing exports to the port of St. Petersburg; exportation of goods from the provinces of Pskov and Velikie Luki to the ports of Narva and Reval was authorised. On the same day was abolished the regulation Peter had introduced in the construction of merchant vessels. The exaction from the merchants of customs dues owing for the past year was deferred; the excise on foreign wines was likewise deferred. On May 16, 1729, was published a statute governing bills of exchange, and on the same day an edict on the construction, free of duty, of ships of Russian material and by Russian entrepreneurs, even though intended for sale to foreigners. We have enumerated only measures of a more general character; these journals and protocols swarm with private exemptions and sops to Russian factory-owners. On that same famous day, September 16, 1727, a series of exemptions was granted to the paper manufacturer Solenikov. On August 9, 1728, was deferred recovery of a loan given to the "director of the linen factory," John Tamesz; and an order was issued to give 5,000 rubles for four years without interest to the Zatrapezny. Merchants suffering from a fire in the port of St. Petersburg were given a treasury loan to cover the damage. Even merchants who had smuggled foreign goods were deemed worthy of the favour; they were promised pardon if they declared the hidden goods before a fixed date. During the whole reign of Peter I no greater blessings had poured out on the merchantry of All Russia than in the brief reign of his grandson!

A modern scholar has defended Golitsyn's political projects from the reproach of having a "personally selfish" character; in this scholar's opinion they were not even of a "class-selfish" character. We shall presently see how far this praise is applicable to the fruits of Prince Dmitry Golitsyn's political creative genius, which was not purely personal either; the projects we know about undoubtedly represent the result of a compromise between the diverse tendencies existing amongst the supreme lords, which, unfortunately, are not more intimately known to us. But the compliment is perfectly applicable to the economic policy of the Supreme Privy Council in 1727-1729, which he did inspire; it was not "class-selfish." The supreme lords were not serving the interests of their own little group but were serving the interests of that same commercial (and only in part industrial) capitalism, which had made the "reformer of Russia" its tool, and were serving it better and more intelligently than he had done. Some time or other closer acquaintance with the economic documents of the period will permit of an answer to the question: What evoked this "second childhood" of the Petrine reform? Meantime we have to establish only the existence of the fact itself.

Yet even now it is possible to estimate its political consequences. At this time, as also earlier, the bourgeoisie was not the dominant political force in Russia. The master of the position at court was the Guard, i.e., the nobility armed and organised. How far did Golitsyn's policy correspond to the interests of the nobility? The nobility, of course, also drew some profit from the "free trade" of the supreme lords. As salt became cheaper, every one benefited, including the nobility, too; nor could the nobility lose by the lowering of prices on tobacco and foreign wares. The return of the court to Moscow was bound to be especially popular in noble circles. Landlords serving in the Guard could still get all necessaries from their own hamlets, situated mainly in the central provinces; it was one thing to transport linen and provisions 50 or 100 versts, another thing to transport them 600. The difference was perceptible even for those who bought most of their supplies; foreign diplomats were struck by the relative cheapness of everything at Moscow, especially at first, before the presence of the court had inflated prices.

But all these advantages were offset by one natural consequence of the "bourgeois" and free trade character of Golitsyn's policy. The dues and monopolies abolished by the Supreme Council had constituted an important part of the government's revenue; the loss could be made up only by increasing the direct imposts. From the very outset the new régime sought to abolish the exemptions from payment of the soul tax made under Menshikov; nominally Menshikov was still sitting in the Council when, on August 31, 1727, an edict was published commanding that "in order that there be no deficiency in money in the maintenance of the army and garrisons, arrears of the soul tax for the past January third, likewise for the coming September third, shall be collected immediately according to former decree." Remarkably enough, this edict once more restored the military commands for the collection of deficits which, in the preceding period, had been regarded as the chief evil; to assist the gubernators and voevodas were detailed "from every regiment a subaltern and soldiers . . . who shall aid the zemsky commissars in the collection of the soul tax, and shall constrain them to despatch reports." Of the right the landlords had just reacquired—the right to collect taxes independently in their hamlets—there remained only a very unpleasant residue—personal responsibility of the master for default by his peasants. The edict of March 21, 1729, required the voevodas "by virtue of their instructions" to send expressly to hamlets in arrears and "take to the town for correction, if they have no stewards and elders, the landlords themselves"; an exception was admitted only for "eminent men," for whom their stewards were answerable.

By the time of the death of Peter II the fate of the supreme lords might be deemed decided; the catastrophe, therefore, followed swiftly. All the conditions which in 1725 had prevented them from seizing power were in existence in January, 1730, to deprive them of power. As in 1725, the nobility were offended because their interests were subordinated to those of the bourgeoisie. The elementary mind of the noble of those days conceived of the Westernising bourgeoisie in the guise of "Germans," as a South Russian peasant of to-day conceives of the bourgeoisie in the guise of a Jew; nothing therefore could better illustrate the temper of the nobility than the German pogrom organised by the Guard as early as May, 1729—scarcely a year before the fall of the Golitsyn régime.

A conflagration broke out in the German Suburb; "as soon as the fire was noticed," reported the French resident, "all the soldiers of the tsar's Guard ran thither with axes in their hands; they usually use this tool in such cases to pull down the neighbouring houses and thus stop the spread of the conflagration. But these soldiers, without trying to extinguish the fire, rushed like madmen on the houses threatened by the conflagration; with blows of their axes they smashed down the walls, then broke open the coffers, cupboards, and cellars, and looted everything in them; the owners who wished to oppose this violence they threatened to brain with their axes. And the most abominable thing about it was the fact that all this happened under the eyes of all the officers of these same troops, who did not dare or rather did not desire to stop the tumult; some were heard to make such remarks as, 'Let them massacre these Germans.' In a word, the pillage was no less dreadful than if a whole legion of barbarians had invaded a hostile country. They were to be seen even cutting the well-ropes in order to prevent the drawing of water. What stronger words could be used to describe the savage character of this people? And yet men talk about their being ready to change their manners and convictions!"

In fact, when we survey this scene (let us not forget that at that time the majority of the soldiers of the Guard were nobles), it is difficult to picture its heroes debating projects for a Russian constitution. "Liberal" historians have tried to read into the drafts subscribed by the nobility the ideology of the late nineteenth century. Far nearer to historical truth was that sober and tranquil Englishman who reported to his government: "I have seen several projects submitted to the Supreme Council, but they all seem ill digested. . . . Accustomed to obey blindly the will of an autocratic monarch, none of these nobles have any clear idea about the limitation of authority." When the authors of the projects themselves, including men such as the historian Tatishchev, evidently were unable to distinguish a constitutional from an absolute monarchy, what could be expected of the brave captains and lieutenants, scratching their names either on this paper or on that, depending on who shoved it under their noses? We shall therefore not burden the reader with a detailed analysis of the "ill digested" projects, which has no place in a general history of Russia. Here we are interested only in class tendencies, which were bound to find expression in the projects, whether intentionally or not, and however confused the political philosophy of their authors.

Nearest to realities was the scheme that first entered the heads of the supreme lords, dazed by the unexpected disappearance of the symbolic figure so indispensable to all their combinations. The Supreme Council was a council under the emperor, and he was dead; in whose name was it now to speak and act? To judge by the allusions of certain foreign diplomats to a sort of "republic without a head" [*république sans chef*], somebody had expressed the opinion that the Council might rule in its own name. The futility of this idea may be judged from the fact that their most savage foes, like Feofan Prokopovich, later tried to attribute this very purpose to the supreme lords. The members of the Council themselves were of course well aware of this, and it is therefore wrong to speak of a "republican" project. The first realistic idea was much simpler. If there is no emperor, one must be invented; a new person must be found immediately, capable of serving as a living symbol like Peter II,—and a person just as compliant. Minority or, at least, extreme youth, seemed to be the capital qualification for the nominal wielder of power; preferably the immature sovereign should be taken from "their own family." The boy-emperor was dead; why not set up a girl-empress? The betrothed bride of Peter II was 17 years old; in point of age she was very suitable. Her rights were, so to speak, only one degree less than the rights of Catherine I had been; the latter had been wedded, the former only affianced; but on the other hand, the latter had been of God knows what origin, while the former was a Russian princess of the blood of Rurik. To re-enforce her rights her kinsmen did not hesitate even to circulate rumours that she was pregnant by the deceased emperor; nor would this have been so scandalous then, for most men regarded both the daughters of Catherine I as born out of wedlock, a fact which did not prevent them from being princesses and tsarevnas.

Yet it was the bayonets of the Guard, not her rights, that had gained the throne for Catherine I; could the Princess Dolgoruky count on their co-operation? Her relatives, being practical men, deliberated which of them should be lieutenant-colonel and which major in the several Guard regiments; especially close to the candidate, apparently, were the men of the Preobrazhensk regiment, who with loaded weapons had surrounded the young couple on the day of their betrothal. The order had been given by their commander, Ivan Dolgoruky, brother of the sovereign's bride and favourite of the emperor; had he been a man of the temper of Gregory Orlov, we should undoubtedly have to record an attempt to enthrone the Princess Catherine and, perhaps, not an unsuccessful one. But the good-natured and weak-willed drunkard, Prince Ivan, went no further than to forge a will of Peter II, and even that he left in his pocket. The member of the family best able to have acted, Field-Marshal Prince V. V. Dolgoruky, had looked askance on his niece's betrothal to the sovereign; he refused most decidedly to assist in putting her on the throne. Still less co-operation in the founding of a Dolgoruky dynasty could be expected from the supreme lords of other families; the Golitsyns especially had always been very jealous of the influence of the Dolgorukys. D. M. Golitsyn was the real president of the Council; and the military influence of his younger brother, the field-marshal, had been felt even in the days of Menshikov. From the first step, then, the "designs of the supreme lords" were checked in their own midst, which promised no good to the "designs."

With the collapse of the attempt to settle matters in a "family way"—the most primitively feudal method—more complicated methods had to be devised. Apparently guided by some personal calculations, Prince V. L. Dolgoruky [6] advanced the candidacy of the niece of Peter I, Anna Ivanovna, Duchess of Courland, who had little more right to the Russian throne than had Princess Catherine Dolgoruky. The candidacy was readily accepted, for Anna was a stranger to them all. But she was no girl and might be expected to make independent moves (later she fully justified such expectations); most important was the fact that she had at Mitau her own court, a nest of rivals to the men then ruling Russia. It seems that fears inspired by this Courland court gave rise to the celebrated "conditions," which are too familiar to merit detailed attention here. It was no accident that the one point of the "conditions" that attracted the most attention was that which forbade Anna to give court rank to foreigners. It was twice debated, and the original bald edition was replaced with a more complicated and "decent" one: "neither Russians nor foreigners shall be given court ranks without the counsel of the Supreme Privy Council." They evidently did not wish to make Anna's Courland friends rebel against them at once; even then the name of Biron was circulating in public gossip. The other conditions, which, as the Swedish historian Jerne has shown, had merely been adapted from corresponding Swedish documents, fully justified the remark of Feofan Prokopovich that the supreme lords "had no mind to introduce popular sovereignty but assigned all power to their Council of eight members." Throughout, the conditions speak of the rights of the Council, systematically omitting the estates which, in their Swedish model, everywhere figured along with the Council. There was no question of any new limitation of autocracy; the aim was simply to secure to the personnel of the Supreme Privy Council the position which in fact it had held under the deceased emperor.

Yet juridical guarantee of the existing order had more than formal significance. Hitherto very few had known how Russia was ruled; for

---

[6] Officially D. Golitsyn was the first to intrigue for Anna. But V. L. Dolgoruky's rôle is clear from all the known facts, even without considering the definite mention of it by Prince Shcherbatov, who had heard the stories of contemporaries.

the masses the sovereign's name had covered everything. Now the
masses were bound to learn that the real rulers were the Golitsyns
and Dolgorukys and their brethren. Had the rule of the Supreme
Council given universal satisfaction, this imprudent lifting of the veil
might perhaps have had no effect. But when people are discontented,
such disclosures supply most convenient justification for their discontent.
"Neither the civil nor the military ranks receive their pay," wrote the
Saxon envoy Lefort two months before the death of Peter II. "There
are few regiments whose pay is less than a year in arrears; as for the
generality and the civil officials, they have not received pay for ten and
eight years. What has happened to the money? I don't know." The
nobility knew well; the supreme lords had stolen the money. While the
Council was still in power, two Dolgorukys were tried for extortion and
embezzlement. But if the others had hoped to ransom themselves with
these heads, they were cruelly mistaken. When, writes the same diplomat,
"Field-Marshal Dolgoruky proposed to the Preobrazhensk Regiment that
they take oath to the tsaritsa and to the Supreme Privy Council, they
replied that they would break his legs if he came to them once more
with such a proposition. This compelled them to change the form of
the oath."

Perhaps men who knew of no other methods than "breaking legs"
or "smashing heads" were not directly dangerous to such skilled
politicians as were Prince Dmitry Golitsyn or V. L. Dolgoruky. But
they soon found at their service men no less dexterous politically
than were the supreme lords themselves. Some of them, indeed, were
members of the Supreme Council, though in an inconsiderable minority
there; such was Golovkin, the former chancellor of Peter I. Some were
men who considered that they had every right to be members of the
Council but, to their surprise and fury, were left without the pale;
typical of these was Peter's former procurator-general, Yaguzhinsky.
These men had constituted a "very formidable" party, and had been
preparing for a struggle with Golitsyn and the Dolgorukys as long as a
year before the death of Peter II. Could this "very formidable" party
let slip such a moment as the present, when the supreme lords were
forced to balance over an abyss? Yaguzhinsky had made an attempt to
upset them while the "conditions" were being drawn up. Put rudely
aside, he countered by sending Anna a letter which opened her eyes to
the real state of affairs. After this, it was futile to arrest him and put
him "under guard"; the blow had been dealt and had hit the mark.
Yaguzhinsky was supported by the serried ranks of Peter's "generals,"
each of whom had some grievance or other against the supreme lords.
The cleverest of the latter, Dmitry Golitsyn, very quickly realised that

for him and his colleagues honourable capitulation was the only escape; the question was whether it would still be accepted.

Prince Dmitry Golitsyn devised a most ingenious form of capitulation; it shows how far he was above the average level of the "supreme lords" of that time. Golitsyn decided to save the Supreme Privy Council by ransoming it from the nobility—by a constitution. Considering the average political level of the nobles of the time, this was, of course, a rather demagogic proposal; it is even possible that Golitsyn counted on finding among the lower strata of the nobility docile "voting cattle," who might in a crisis be directed against the supreme lords' real rival, the "generality." However that might be, the very idea of such a "European" weapon against his political opponents could never have entered an ordinary head in a country where, even long afterwards, the palace conspiracy, relying on the bayonets of the Guard, was the sole and universal resource. The earliest sketch of the Golitsyn constitution is to be found in the English despatches, where it appears as early as February 2, only two weeks after the death of Peter II, not only before Anna had reached Moscow but only two or three days after her acceptance of the conditions was known. Evidently the supreme lords risked no loss of time; they were too painfully conscious of their critical position.

In the project, the essence of which the English resident reported very accurately, two basic ideas are manifest. In the first place, the circle of men directly participating in the government was to be widened by increasing the membership of the Supreme Council to 12 men (there had been 8 of them); this should satisfy the leaders of the opposition. Alongside the Council was to be established, as a peculiar "lower house," a Senate of 36 members, "considering matters before they are introduced into the Privy Council"; here all the "generals" at all prominent were to find scope for their ambition. But Golitsyn did not propose to drown the supreme lords in this sea of generals; they retained two anchors of safety in the shape of large assemblies, one of 200 men from the "petty nobility," the other bourgeois, in which merchants were to participate.

Neither of these assemblies was to have any direct share in the government, but they could interfere in case of "violation of rights" and "oppression of the people." In other words, the minority of the supreme lords had in these assemblies [7] a ready point of support in a struggle with the majority, which would inevitably be composed of their opponents.

The opponents were not to be so easily snared. They very quickly adopted without dispute that part of the Golitsyn constitution which gave them a share in power. Tatishchev's project, opposed to Golitsyn's

[7] To Golitsyn, it must be emphasised, the bourgeois one was of special importance.

by the "generality," provided for two houses under the names of "upper" and "lower" government; they were to have even more members than Golitsyn's (21 and 100 respectively), so that the personal influence of the supreme lords was bound to be further weakened. But the project of the "generality" did not mention houses of the lower nobility and merchantry; it relied on buying over the lesser nobility by a less costly means. In place of pressing on them political rights for which they had as yet no great desire, the "generality" promised to satisfy those daily needs of the petty landlords about which the nobility had been long and fruitlessly clamouring; it promised abridgement of the term of military service to not more than twenty years and emancipation from service in the lowest ranks. When the lesser nobility found itself in a position to express its own desires, it had nothing to add except demands that pay be issued punctually; the houses of lesser nobles and merchants thus remained a feature peculiar to the project of the supreme lords themselves. The nobility did not accept Golitsyn's political gift; it expressed, and absolutely definitely, public lack of confidence in him, demanding that the newly appointed members of the Supreme Council be balloted on by all the nobility. The middling and petty landlords were tired of the reign of the new feudal aristocracy and desired to have their own government; once it had been elected, of course, they would leave it to do what it liked. The nobles' projects did not anticipate any form under which the nobility might permanently influence matters of state. One petition set forth Tatishchev's personal idea that the "new form of government" should be deliberated by a sort of constitutional assembly of the nobles, but this was subscribed by a very few; these modest men were ready to leave all political matters to their commanders.

Such was the situation when Anna arrived at Moscow and the "restoration of autocracy" took place. In fact, the leaders of the "generality" merely replaced the supreme lords; the conditions lapsed automatically, for they were artificial props, necessary to the "frost-killed tree," the supreme lords, but not to the real masters of the situation. It cannot be denied that Anna personally displayed great talent for adapting herself to the situation, a fact which assisted her allies' game. Her first meeting with the Preobrazhensk Regiment ended in a whole battalion throwing itself at her feet "with cries and tears of joy," while, in direct violation of the conditions, she declared herself the chief of the regiment. "Later she summoned to her chamber a detachment of the Horse Guards, declared herself commander of the squadron, and poured each a glass of wine with her own hand." The worthy soldiers of the Guard, who during the reign of the child-emperor had become unused to Petrine manners, thought they saw Mother Catherine reincarnate. Here, of course, is the psychological explanation of the scene enacted within the walls of the Kremlin palace on February 25, 1730, when the Guard officers threw themselves at Anna's feet, promising to exterminate all her ill-wishers.

Yet the political outcome was not "restoration of the autocracy" but replacement of the Supreme Council, now abolished, by the Senate, once more "Governing," as in the days of Peter I. This resurrected institution took in all those whom the supreme lords had jealously excluded from their circle, chief among them being, of course, Yaguzhinsky. At the same time, the minority of the supreme lords, who had betrayed their colleagues, received their due; Chancellor Golovkin, who had had the foresight to bring with him to the palace on February 25 the conditions which Anna then and there tore up, ranked first among the newly appointed senators. Yet, at least nominally and at first, they did not venture to exclude even their enemies; Dmitry Golitsyn and V. L. Dolgoruky were also appointed senators. Vengeance overtook the Dolgorukys several months later; Golitsyn had a few years' respite. The loss of political power did not at once deprive the "supreme lords" of their importance as a social force. Whether their successors would become a social force depended on the political course the new institution might steer. And here the nobility soon found it had long yet to wait for full satisfaction of its interests.

I. KIEVO-NOVGORODAN RUS (to 1500)

II. MUSCOVITE RUS (1500-1682)

Conquests of Peter the Great from Sweden.

Conquests of Peter the Great from Persia.

III. RUSSIA (1600-1730)

GLOSSARY AND NOTES

ACADEMY OF SCIENCES—planned by Peter the Great in imitation of Western models and opened in 1726; its first members were imported, principally from the Germanies.

AGE OF CATHERINE—the reign of Catherine II ["the Great"] (1762-1796).

AKSAKOV, CONSTANTIN (1817-1860)—one of the chief representatives of Slavophil scholarship; *cf.* Slavophils.

ALEXANDER III—emperor of All Russia (1881-1894).

ALEXANDER "NEVSKY"—so-called because of his victory over the Swedes on the ice of the Neva in 1240 while prince of Novgorod; he later became grand prince of Vladimir (1252-1263).

ALEXIS—tsar (1645-1676), second tsar of the Romanov dynasty; father of Peter the Great; his reign was marked by the drafting of the Ulozhenie, the ritual reforms of Nikon, and the annexation of the Ukraine, involving wars with Poland, Sweden, and Turkey.

ALEXIS (PETROVICH)—tsarevich (1690-1718), only son of Peter the Great to reach maturity; fled abroad; induced to return by Peter Tolstoi on promise of immunity; sentenced to death and died suddenly in prison; father of Peter II.

Altyn—an old coin equivalent to 3 copecks.

ANASTASIA—tsaritsa, daughter of Roman Zakharin-Yuryev, founder of the Romanov family; first wife of Ivan the Terrible and mother of Tsar Fedor (I); died in 1560 under circumstances which led Ivan to believe she had been poisoned by the boyars.

ANDREW BOGOLYUBSKY—prince of Suzdal in succession to Yury Dolgoruky (1157); sent an army against Kiev which sacked the "mother of Russian towns" in 1169; assumed title of grand prince without going to Kiev; murdered by his subjects (1174).

ANDRONOV, FEDOR—merchant; supported Second Dmitry at Tushino; joined Sigismund of Poland at Smolensk (1610); hanged at Moscow by victorious forces of Prince Pozharsky (1612).

ANNA IVANOVNA—empress of All Russia (1730-1740); daughter of Tsar Ivan V, half-brother of Peter the Great; married duke of Courland; invited to return to Russia as empress on condition of accepting the "points," which she subsequently repudiated.

ANNA PETROVNA—tsarevna (1708-1728); daughter of Peter the Great and Catherine I; married Charles Frederick, duke of Holstein; mother of Peter III.

APPANAGE—the customary, though inaccurate, translation of *udel;* the Russian, like the German, custom of inheritance was equal division among all the sons; hence, each son of a prince received an *udel,* a portion of his father's territory with full sovereign rights, not *en apanage.* The practice was particularly characteristic of the period from the twelfth to the fifteenth centuries, which Klyuchevsky distinguished as a special "appanage period." *Cf.* also text, p. 28, n. 14, and pp. 89 *et seq.*

355

ARISTOV, N. YA. (1834-1882)—professor of history; author of *The Industry of Ancient Rus* (1866) [in Russian].

Ataman—an elected cossack chieftain.

AUGUSTUS II—[Frederick Augustus I, elector of Saxony (1694-1733)], king of Poland (1697-1704 and 1709-1733).

Barshchina (*corvée, Frondienst*)—obligation to labour for the lord (*barin*).

Baskaks—tax-gatherers of the Mongol khans.

BATHORY, STEPHEN—prince of Transylvania (1571-1575), king of Poland (1575-1586); after his election Poland prosecuted the Livonian War with greater success, forcing Ivan to accept a humiliating peace in 1582.

BATY—nephew (?) of Jenghiz Khan; conqueror of Rus in 1237-1240; first khan of Golden Horde.

BELYAEV, I. D. (1810-1873)—professor of the history of Russian law in the University of Moscow; strongly influenced by Slavophils.

BERGHOLZ, FRIDERICH WILHELM VON (1699-1765)—son of a general in Russian service (d. 1717); page to Charles Frederick, duke of Holstein, who married Peter's daughter, Anna; gentleman-of-the-bedchamber to the latter's son [the future Peter III] (1742-1746). Cf. *Tagebuch, welches er in Ruszland von 1721 bis 1725 als holsteinischer Kammerjunker geführet hat*, in *Magazin für die neue Historie und Geographie angelegt von D. Anton Friedrich Büsching, Neunzehnter Theil* (Halle, 1785).

Berkovets—a Russian measure equal to 10 puds (361 lbs. avoirdupois).

BIRON, ERNST JOHANN (1690-1772)—a Courlander, favourite of Empress Anna; made duke of Courland by her.

BOGOSLOVSKY, M. M. (1867——)—professor of history in the University of Moscow to 1925; member of the Academy of Sciences (1921); author of a number of studies on Peter the Great; now writing a detailed biography of Peter.

BOLESLAW I—king of Poland (992-1025), supported Svyatopolk "the Accursed" against Yaroslav "the Wise."

BOLGARS OF THE VOLGA—a branch of the same Asiatic people that has given its name to the Slavs of the Lower Danube. Their capital city stood on the Volga near the confluence of the Kama. They were important in commercial relations with the East and were subjugated by Baty in 1237.

BOLTIN, IVAN NIKITICH (1735-1792)—official of War Collegium, interested in wide range of subjects; one of first to attempt to understand Russian history as an integral process in accordance with law, being strongly under the influence of Montesquieu; interest in history aroused by Leclerc's *L'histoire de la Russie*, on which he published two volumes of comment; sometimes called "the first Slavophil" because he noted certain dark sides of blind imitation of the West.

BOYAR (*boyarin*)—free follower of a prince; member of highest social and political class in Russia until Peter the Great established the "Table of Ranks" (1722), which made rank technically dependent on service position (as it had already become in fact); those boyars descended from Rurik, Gedimin of Lithuania, or other sovereign rulers bore title of Prince (*knyaz*); the rest were untitled, but should not be confused with military servitors of lesser standing, nobles (*dvoryane*) and knights (*syny boyarskie*).

BRUCE, ROMAN (1668-1720)—grandson of an emigrant from Scotland (1647), who had served as a major-general under Tsar Alexis; made a count by Peter.

Burgomistr or *burmister*—a title, corrupted from the Dutch, applied by Peter in 1699 to the slightly remodelled office of *zemsky starosta* which was at the same time subordinated to the *ratusha* (*q.v.*).

BUSSOW, CONRAD—a German employed by Sweden in Livonia; attempted to betray Sweden's interests; welcomed to Moscow by Godunov (1601); supported Second False Dmitry; failing to find employment under Sigismund, retired to Riga (1612), where he began his *Relatio, das ist summarische Erzählung vom eigentlichen Ursprung dieses itzigen blutigen Kriegs-Wesens in Moscowiter Land oder Reussland, u.s.w.*, one of the most important sources for history of Troubles.

CAMPREDON—the despatches of French diplomatic and consular agents in Russia from 1715-1730 are printed in the original in *Sbornik russkogo istoricheskogo obshchestva*, vols. 34, 40, 49, 52, 58, 67, and 75.

CASIMIR IV—grand prince of Lithuania and king of Poland (1445-1492).

CATHERINE I—empress of All Russia (1725-1727); a Livonian peasant girl; second wife and successor of Peter the Great; mother of Anna, duchess of Holstein, and Elizabeth, later empress, both born out of wedlock.

CHANCELLOR, RICHARD—commander of one of three vessels under Sir Hugh Willoughby sent by Edward VI of England to find a northeastern passage (1553); Willoughby was frozen to death in the Arctic, but Chancellor made his way to Moscow, thus discovering the trade route round Norway; in 1555 Chancellor was sent again to Russia, this time as envoy of Mary and Philip; he was drowned off the coast of Scotland on the return voyage (1556).

CHARLES IX—king of Sweden (1604-1611).

CHARLES XI—king of Sweden (1660-1697).

CHARLES XII—king of Sweden (1697-1718), youthful antagonist of Peter the Great in the Northern War.

Chet or *chetvert*—a land measure equal to ½ desyatina.

Chetvert—a dry measure equal to a little less than 6 bushels.

CHIEF MAGISTRACY—virtually a collegium, established in 1720 and given authority over the urban population and its elective officials.

CHRISTINA—queen of Sweden (1632-1654).

Chronography of the second edition or *of 1617*—a popular compendium of universal history, composed in Russia by a Serb in middle of fifteenth century and reworked to suit the times.

Collegia—the name given by Peter the Great to the reorganised *prikazy*, or administrative bureaux; nominally boards; actually the president exercised full control; remodelled by Alexander I into ministries.

COLLINS, SAMUEL (1619-1670)—Englishman, court physician to Tsar Alexis, author of *The Present State of Russia, in a Letter to a Friend at London; Written by an Eminent Person residing at the Great Tzar's Court at Mosco for the space of nine years.* London, 1671.

COMMERCIAL CAPITALISM—this term is used with the consent of the author though he would prefer to reserve the word "capitalism" to denote what is currently known as "industrial capitalism"; the term "commercial capitalism" is, of course, used to characterise that phase of economic organisation in which capital is employed in large-scale trade to yield a profit, in contradistinction to "industrial capitalism," which arises with the Industrial Revolution (*i.e.*, in Russia, only at the end of the nineteenth century).

CONSTANTINE PORPHYROGENITUS—the Byzantine Emperor Constantine VII (911-959), whose treatise *On the administration of the empire* is a valuable source for early Russian history.

Copeck—a Russian coin; $\frac{1}{100}$ part of a ruble.

COSSACKS (*kazaks*)—often romantically described as freemen who would not tolerate yoke of serfdom and went out into the open steppe to build a new world where all were equal, where there were neither lords nor serfs; actually a frontier population, accustomed to bear arms and engaged in hunting, fishing, apiculture, agriculture, and raiding, embracing all social strata from landholders and boat owners to labourers; bore no fixed relation to government and were not clearly marked off from other classes; wealthier and more influential cossacks (the "elders") really members of landholding class; rank-and-file threatened with enserfment; cossacks were found on Dnieper (*e.g.*, the Zaporozhians), Don (where they retained a special status until the revolution of 1917), Volga, Ural, etc.

COURMENIN, DES HAYES—French envoy to the Holy Land, ordered to go by way of Moscow, where he negotiated a treaty of commerce (1630).

CRIMEA, KHANATE OF—a Tatar principality founded in the fifteenth century when the Golden Horde was dissolving; their raids made Russian occupancy of the steppe dangerous in the sixteenth and seventeenth centuries, occasionally endangering Moscow itself, as in 1571; the inaccessibility of the Crimea and the protection of the Turkish sultan made reprisals difficult.

DEMIDOV, N.—granted extensive privileges in connection with iron works founded by him (1702); founded a dynasty of ironmasters in the Urals.

Denga—an old Russian coin equal to $\frac{1}{100}$ part of a ruble.

DE RODES—a seventeenth-century Rigan merchant; his *Bedenken über dem russischen Handel im Jahre 1653* are printed in J. P. G. Ewers, *Beiträge zur Kenntnis Russlands und seiner Geschichte* (Dorpat, 1816).

Desyatina—a land measure equal to 2.7 acres.

DMITRY DONSKOI—prince of Moscow (1359-1389); successfully asserted right to title of grand prince (1363); regarded as a national hero for his victory over the Tatars under Mamai at Kulikovo on the Don (1380), though Tokhtamysh exacted full vengeance (1382).

DMITRY OF UGLICH—younger son of Ivan the Terrible; murdered at Uglich in 1591 (*cf.* text, pp. 169-171). Subsequently appeared a series of False Dmitrys (*q.v.*).

Druzhina—a retinue of free men (later known as boyars) serving a prince or other magnate); analogous to the *comitatus* of the Germans. *Druzhinnik*, member of a druzhina.

Duma (of boyars)—the prince's council (*dumat* [to think]), the chief organ of government until its position was shattered by the oprichnina and the Time of the Troubles; its power passed to the zemsky sobor and to the tsar, and the duma ceased to exist under Peter the Great. Its membership was divided into several grades—boyars, okolniches, nobles of the duma, and dyaks.

Dvor (*Hof* or *cour*)—in absence of an English equivalent, the word has been variously rendered in the present text; *e.g.*, *krestyansky dvor* (*Bauernhof*) has been translated as "peasant homestead"; *cf.* p. 16, n. 3.

Dvorishche—the primitive commune of Western Russia; *cf.* text, p. 9.

Dvoryanin—a member of the landholding class obligated to perform military service, but ranking below the boyars; the word has been translated throughout as "noble" (*q.v.*); *cf.* text, p. 133, n. 1.

Dyak—a minor official (clerk) attached to the duma or to an administrative organ.

DYAKONOV, M. A. (1855-1919)—Russian historian, professor of the history of Russian law; author of several important studies on the sixteenth and seventeenth centuries.

ELIZABETH—tsarevna, later empress of All Russia (1741-1762); daughter of Peter the Great and Catherine I, born out of wedlock; passed over on death of Peter II in favour of her cousin, Anna.

FALSE DMITRY—a series of persons, each alleged to be son of Ivan the Terrible; First Dmitry (*cf.* text, p. 180) enthroned at Moscow (1605-1606); Second Dmitry (*cf.* text, p. 200), unable to take Moscow, established himself at Tushino; subsequent False Dmitrys of lesser significance (*cf.* text, p. 206, n. 1).

FEDOR I—tsar (1584-1598); son of Ivan the Terrible and last of the dynasty of Rurik; succeeded by brother-in-law, Boris Godunov.

FEDOR II—tsar (1676-1682); oldest son and successor of Tsar Alexis.

Feeding—*cf. kormlenie.*

FEODOSY—founder of Pechersky Monastery (*q.v.*)

FILARET—patriarch of Moscow (1619-1633); oldest son of Nikita Romanov and cousin of Tsar Fedor (1584-1598); protégé, later rival, of Boris Godunov, who forced him to take the tonsure. Installed as patriarch at Tushino by Second False Dmitry; helped negotiate Treaty of Smolensk (1610) with Sigismund; installed as patriarch at Moscow on return from captivity in Poland (1619) in succession to Hermogen (d. 1612); co-tsar with his son Michael.

FLETCHER, DR. GILES—ambassador of Queen Elizabeth of England to Tsar Fedor of Moscow (1588); published treatise, *Of the Russe Commonwealth* (London, 1591).

Funt—a measure of weight equal to 9/10 lb. avoirdupois.

GERMAN SUBURB—village on River Yauza on outskirts of Moscow, where foreigners in Russian service were concentrated.

GODUNOV, BORIS—tsar (1598-1605); brother-in-law of Tsar Fedor and regent during his reign (1584-1598).

GAUTIER, YU. V. (1873——)—Russian historian and archæologist; professor, University of Moscow, 1915-1925; chief librarian Rumyantsev Museum, 1909-1924; author of several works on the economic and social history of the seventeenth century.

GOLDEN HORDE—Mongol-Tatar principality established by Baty at Sarai on Lower Volga after his conquest of Bolgar and Russian principalities (1237-1240); at first dependent on Great Horde of Karakorum, breaking up of which in fourteenth century was soon followed by breaking up of Golden Horde; chief principalities into which Golden Horde dissolved were khanates of Kazan, Astrakhan, and Crimea; some of lesser Tatar princes recognised suzerainty of Moscow, and Ivan III ceased paying tribute (1480).

GOLITSYN, PRINCE V. V.—chief adviser and intimate of Sophia during her regency (1682-1689); not to be confused with earlier Prince V. V. Golitsyn, prominent during Time of the Troubles.

Golova [head]—chief officer of guba (*q.v.*); in Peter's time replaced by land-rath; also known as starosta.

GOLUBINSKY, YE. YE. (1834-1912)—professor, Moscow Ecclesiastical Academy; member Academy of Sciences (1904); author of *History of the Russian Church* [in Russian], 2 vols. (1880-1904 unfinished), especially valuable for criticism of sources.

Gost—member of higher stratum of merchantry, trading beyond bounds of own principality and endowed with special privileges; *cf.* text, particularly p. 36, n. 4, and p. 268, n. 4; word also equivalent to German *Gast; gostit* means both "to visit" and "to trade."

Guba—the *guba,* or police unit, was administered by an elective board (or college); the gubnoi golova, or starosta, was elected from local nobility, the tselovalniks from rest of population; *cf.* text, p. 128.

Gubernator—title given by Peter the Great to governor of his new administrative unit, the guberniya.

Guberniya—new administrative unit, embracing a number of counties, introduced by Peter the Great and continued until after the Revolution; corrupted from French *gouvernement.*

HAGARENES—the Crimean Tatars, who as Mohammedans were presumed to be descended from Ishmael, son of Abraham by Hagar.

HAHN, ED. (1856———)—German economic historian; author of *Die Entstehung der Pflugkultur* (1909); *Von der Hacke zum Pflug* (1914), etc.

HEGEL, G. W. F. (1770-1831)—German metaphysician, professor in University of Berlin from 1818; his concept of a succession of "historic" nations, each destined to dominate the world in order to make its contribution to civilisation, profoundly influenced Russian historical thought in the 1830's and 1840's; too patriotic to follow their master in believing that German-Protestant culture represented the culminating form of civilisation and in classifying the Slavs as an "unhistoric" nation, Russian Hegelians turned to Russian history to solve the riddle of the future, dividing into the warring camps of Westerners and Slavophils (*q.v.*).

HERMOGEN—patriarch of Moscow (1606-1612); alleged author of letters appealing for a national uprising against the Poles.

HORDE—the camp of a migratory Tatar tribe, figuratively used as name of Mongol government; the capital of the Great Horde was Karakorum; its subsidiary, the Golden Horde, was established at Sarai on the Volga.

IGOR—grand prince (912-945); son of Rurik and successor to Oleg; succeeded by his widow, Olga.

Initial Chronicle—the basic Russian chronicle, compiled at the beginning of the twelfth century and incorporated into later continuations of the chronicle; the oldest extant copies are found in the *Lavrentyevsky* and *Ipatyevsky* Chronicles; *cf.* Louis Leger, *Chronique dite de Nestor traduite sur le texte slavon-russe avec introduction et commentaire critique,* Paris, 1884.

Ipatyevsky Chronicle—one of the two basic versions of the *Initial Chronicle* written by a continuator at the turn of the fourteenth century, and found in the Ipatyev Monastery at Kostroma.

IVAN I—prince of Moscow (1325-1341), called "the Purse" (Kalita); with aid of Tatars wrested title of grand prince of Vladimir from prince of Tver (1328); induced metropolitan to transfer his see from Vladimir to Moscow; founder of Muscovite branch of dynasty of Rurik.

IVAN II—prince of Moscow and grand prince of Vladimir (1353-1359); younger son of Ivan Kalita and father of Dmitry Donskoi.

IVAN III—grand prince of Moscow and of All Rus (1462-1505), called by Karamzin "the Great"; during his reign the "gathering" of the various Russian principalities under headship of Moscow virtually accomplished; conquered Novgorod; ceased paying tribute to Tatars; married Sophia Palaiologa and assumed Byzantine insignia.

IVAN IV—grand prince of Moscow and of All Rus (1533-1584), assumed title of tsar (1547); called "the Terrible"; Karamzin and other Russian historians have divided his reign into two periods: the first, or "beneficent" period, embraced his minority, and the period of the "reforms" characterised in text; in the second period, after his break with Silvester and Adashev, Ivan is usually painted in the blackest colours.

IVAN V—co-tsar with Peter the Great (1682-1696); weak-minded son of Tsar Alexis; passed over at death of brother Fedor (1682) in favour of half-brother, Peter I; enthroned by mutiny of streltsy; used as figurehead for rule of sister Sophia (1682-1689).

IZYASLAV MSTISLAVICH—prince of Galicia-Volhynia, grand prince of Kiev (1146-1154); from him descended rulers of southwestern Rus, while from his uncle and rival, Yury Dolgoruky, descended the grand princes of Vladimir in the northeast; not to be confused with Izyaslav Yaroslavich, grand prince of Kiev (1054-1078) temporarily expelled by revolution of 1068.

JENGHIZ KHAN, (d. 1227)—Mongol conqueror; founder of Great Horde; nephew Baty conquered Rus (1237-1240).

KALITA—cf. Ivan I of Moscow.

KARAMZIN, N. M. (1765-1826)—conservative landlord, greatest Russian historian of his day; his History of the Russian State was based on belief that "secret hand of Providence" decides the fate of nations through chosen hero-sovereigns; believed that Russia had originally been a united state, had fallen apart, and been "gathered" together again by the princes of Moscow. Cf. Karamzin, Histoire de l'empire de Russie (to 1606), 11 vols., Paris, 1819-1826.

KARDIS, PEACE OF (1661)—treaty concluding war with Sweden in the triangular struggle of Russia, Poland, and Sweden brought on by Russian intervention in the Ukraine and Swedish claims to Polish crown.

KAZAN, KHANATE OF—Tatar principality on middle Volga, founded in fifteenth century when Golden Horde was dissolving; conquered by Ivan the Terrible (1552), as was also khanate of Astrakhan (1556).

KHAN—Tatar title for their rulers, sometimes called tsar by the Russians; applied also to rulers of other Turco-Tatar peoples and of the Mongols.

KHAZARS—Turkish people who held sway in the steppe from seventh century to tenth, when remnant of their power was destroyed by Svyatoslav.

KILBURGER, J. P.—author of Kurzer Unterricht von dem Russischen Handel wie selbiger mit aus- und eingehenden Waaren 1674 durch ganz Russland getrieben worden, published in Magazin für die neue Historie und Geographie, angelegt von D. Anton Friedrich Buesching, vol. III, pp. 245-342 (Hamburg, 1769).

KLYUCHEVSKY, V. O. (1840-1911)—professor of history in University of Moscow; greatest of successors of Solovyev; researches on boyar duma and interest in economic aspects of Russian history contributed to break down theories of Solovyev and "historical-juridical school," substituting theory of "the struggle with the steppe" as chief formative force in "the binding of the classes," etc.; revived Storch's theory of trade origin of early Russian towns; author of *A Course of Russian History*, 5 vols. (4 vols. only edited by Klyuchevsky), written with consummate literary skill; translated into English by C. J. Hogarth, 4 vols., London, New York, 1911-1926.

KNIGHT—this word has been reserved to render the Russian *syn boyarsky* (*cf.* text, p. 23, n. 10).

Konets—literally "end"; name given to the five wards of which Novgorod was constituted.

KORB, J. G.—secretary of Austrian legation; author of *Diarium itineris in Moscoviam;* English edition translated and edited by Count Mac Donnell, 2 vols., London, 1863; *cf.* also German edition of F. Dukmeyer.

Kormlenie—administrative post as provincial or district governor in Muscovite Rus; sometimes alleged to be derived from the verb *kormit* [to feed] because profits of administration accrued to holder of post; *cf.* text, pp. 119 *et seq.*

Kormlenshchik—holder of a kormlenie; frequently appointed as reward for service in the field, not with an eye to efficient administration.

KOSTOMAROV, N. I. (1817-1885)—professor in University of St. Petersburg; removed from his chair but remained a legal and respected writer on history; particularly interested in ethnography in connexion with early period; attracted attention to popular participation in the veche republics, in the Troubles, in the revolt of Stenka Razin, etc.

KOTOSHIKIN, G. K. (c. 1630-1667)—podyak in Muscovite Foreign Office; fled to Sweden (1664), where he wrote a description of the Muscovite state, first published in Russia in 1841 and regarded as one of the most important sources for the period; executed for murder.

Kremlin—a fortress serving as the citadel in a Russian town; specifically, the Moscow Kremlin.

KULIKOVO—a meadow on banks of Don where Dmitry won his appellation, "Donskoi."

Kupets—consistently rendered as "merchant"; for higher stratum of merchants term *gost* (*q.v.*) has been retained.

KURAKIN, PRINCE B. I. (1676-1727)—diplomat; intimately associated with Peter in his youth; his *History of Tsar Peter I* virtually an autobiographical chronicle.

KURBSKY, PRINCE A. M. (d. 1583)—boyar associated with Silvester and Adashev in the "elected council" during "reform" period of reign of Ivan the Terrible; commander-in-chief of Muscovite armies in Livonian War; his desertion to Lithuania was almost immediately followed by establishment of oprichnina; author of *The History of Grand Prince of Moscow*, which provoked the "correspondence" between Kurbsky and Ivan the Terrible.

Kurgan—a prehistoric burial-mound.

Last—a dry measure equal to 12 chetverts or 8⅔ quarters.

Lavrentyevsky Chronicle—oldest extant version of *Initial Chronicle*, with a continuation written in 1377 by "the wretched, unworthy, and sinful slave of God the monk Lavrenty" for the prince of Suzdal and preserved in the Rozhdestvensky Monastery at Vladimir on the Klyazma.

LEFORT, FRANCOIS (1656-1699)—Genevan Swiss adventurer who finally settled down as a colonel in Muscovite service; had great influence on the young Peter the Great.

Life of Feodosy—an outstanding early example of Russian hagiography attributed to Nestor.

LIKHACHEV, N. P. (1862———)—author of numerous works on palaeography and diplomatics.

LITHUANIA—a non-Slavic principality, at first pagan, later Orthodox, which in fourteenth century, under Gedimin and Olgerd, absorbed many Russian principalities; under Jagello was effected a dynastic union with Poland (1386), opening way to Polish and Catholic influences; with growth of Moscow's power, Lithuania forced into closer dependence on Poland (Union of Lublin, 1569).

LIVONIAN ORDER—the Knights of the Sword, a German crusading order founded in 1201 for conquest of pagan Livonia; merged with the Teutonic Order, founded in Palestine in 1190, for conquest and conversion of whole southeastern Baltic coast (1237); in 1521 Prussia and Livonia were separated, former being secularised in 1525; during Livonian War (*q.v.*) Order ceased to exist; dominions of Order broken up, Sweden annexing Esthonia, and Lithuania annexing Livonia, while Courland became a vassal duchy of Lithuania.

LIVONIAN WAR (1558-1583)—initiated by Moscow's attack on declining Livonian Order, which put itself under Polish protection, Sweden also intervening; by peace with Poland (1582) and Sweden (1583) Ivan the Terrible abandoned his conquests and even surrendered his former holdings on the Baltic coast (Yam, Koporye, Ivangorod) to Sweden.

Low land—cf. Suzdal.

MAKHMET—one of a number of Tatar khans ruling simultaneously during the days of the decline of Golden Horde; captured Grand Prince Vasily III (1445) and held him for ransom; not to be confused with Peresvetov's Makhmet, sultan of Turkey.

MAMAI—successful pretender to khanate of Golden Horde; defeated by Dmitry Donskoi at Kulikovo (1380); soon afterward overthrown by Tokhtamysh.

MARDEFELD, BARON VON—Prussian envoy to Russia under Peter the Great; his reports are printed in the original in *Sbornik russkogo istoricheskogo obshchestva*, vol. 15.

MARGERET—French adventurer, veteran of Wars of Three Henries and Turkish wars; entered service of Boris Godunov in 1600 as captain of a German company; given command of bodyguard by First Dmitry; sent home by Shuisky with rich present; wrote *Estat de l'Empire de Russie et Grand Duché de Moscovie avec ce que s'y est passé de plus mémorable et tragique, pendant le règne de quatre Empereurs; à sçavoir depuis l'an 1590 jusque en semptembre 1606* (Paris, 1607); returned to take service at Tushino, transferring to Poles under Zolkiewski; offer to return to Russian service not accepted.

MASSA, ISAAC A. (1587-??)—envoy of Netherlands to Moscow (1600-1608) and again under Tsar Michael from 1614; documents in connection with Dutch negotiations of 1630-1631 printed in original in *Sbornik russkogo istoricheskogo obshchestva*, vol. 116.

MERRICK, SIR JOHN—principal agent of English Russia Company at Moscow from 1596; employed on numerous missions to and from Russian court; knighted by James I and sent as ambassador (1615) to negotiate Peace of Stolbovo (1617) between Sweden and Russia.

Mestnichestvo—system of "places" (*mesta*) which governed appointments to offices and safeguarded political power of boyars (*cf.* text, p. 126); it is to be noted that offices were not hereditary but could be filled only from a limited circle of men possessing requisite hereditary service relationship to other office-holders (*otechestvo*—*q.v.*).

MICHAEL—tsar (1613-1645); first of Romanov dynasty; elected by zemsky sobor summoned by Prince Pozharsky after recovery of Moscow from Poles; succeeded by son, Alexis.

MICHAEL—prince of Tver (1365-1399); rival of Dmitry Donskoi for title of grand prince; grandson of another Michael of Tver, grand prince of Vladimir (1304-1319).

MIKLASHEVSKY, I. N. (1858-1901)—professor of political economy and statistics in University of Kharkov.

MILYUKOV, P. N. (1859——)—professor of history of Russian law in University of Moscow; leader of Cadets (Constitutional Democrats) in Duma; Foreign Minister in first Provisional Government (March-May, 1917); now an émigré in Paris; author of *Essais sur l'histoire de la civilisation russe* (Paris, 1907); *Russia and its crisis* (Chicago, 1905); *Russia to-day and to-morrow* (New York, 1922), etc. As a historian, insisted on the "complete antithesis" between Russia and West in the past and on a uniform "internal law of evolution" bringing them together in the future.

MININ, KUZMA—a merchant of Nizhny-Novgorod, who played a prominent rôle in organisation and equipment of the force which, under the command of Prince Pozharsky recovered Moscow from Poles in 1612; a statue of Minin and Pozharsky stands in Red Square in Moscow.

Mir—literally "world"; popular name for peasant commune (*obshchina*).

MONGOLS—a nomadic people of eastern Asia who under Jenghiz Khan and his successors subjugated China, the Turco-Tatar peoples of central Asia, Persia, Mesopotamia, Russia, etc.

MONOMAKH—*cf.* Vladimir Monomakh.

MONTH COURT—once in four years metropolitan or his representative went to Novgorod to hear appeals from court of archbishop, remaining there for a month, during which he collected not only judicial revenues but gifts; revenue of metropolitan of Moscow from this source has been estimated at 200,000 rubles (in pre-war currency); in 1385 the Novgorodans swore to submit no more appeals to the metropolitan; the futile anathema of patriarch of Constantinople and the military force of grand prince of Moscow were employed to secure recognition of metropolitan's appellate jurisdiction, but financial results proved unsatisfactory.

MSTISLAV THE BOLD—prince of Toropets, an appanage offshoot of principality of Smolensk; figured prominently in feuds of princes in early thirteenth century as free-lance—a "belated dry-land Viking"; not to be confused with other Mstislavs.

Namestnik—local agent of prince administering a town and district round it; *cf.* kormlenshchik.

NATALIA [NARYSHKIN]—tsaritsa (d. 1694); second wife of Tsar Alexis; mother of Peter the Great.

NESTOR—monk of Pechersky in second half of eleventh century; alleged author of *Initial Chronicle* (*q.v.*); perhaps actually author of portion of it; for a discussion of his identity *cf.* Kluchevsky, V. O., *A History of Russia*, v. 1.

NICHOLAS I—emperor of All Russia (1825-1855).

NICHOLAS II—emperor of All Russia (1894-1917).

NIKITSKY, A. I. (1842-1886)—professor in University of Warsaw; specialist on history of Novgorod and Pskov; author of *History of the economic life of Great Novgorod*, 2 vols. [in Russian] (1883).

NIKON—patriarch of Moscow (1652-1667); effected reforms in ecclesiastical ritual which caused a schism (*raskol*) in Orthodox Church; quarrelled with Tsar Alexis (1658) and deposed by a Church Council (1666-1667). While endorsing Nikon's reforms, council, attended by the four Eastern patriarchs either in person or by proxy, asserted supremacy of tsar over patriarch.

Nikonovsky Chronicle—digest of earlier Greek chronographies and Russian chronicles, compiled in middle of sixteenth century.

NOBLE—this word has been reserved to render the Russian *dvoryanin* (*q.v.*). It is to be remembered, therefore, that "the nobility" is used, not to include but to contrast with the boyars (*i.e.*, the high nobility); loosely the term "noble" coincides with "pomeshchik" (*q.v.*); military servitor is more inclusive, embracing both boyars and knights (*q.v.*) as well.

NORTHERN WAR (1700-1721)—begun by Peter the Great in alliance with Poland and Denmark against Sweden under Charles XII; after initial defeat at Narva (1700), Peter reformed army while allies were being crushed by Charles; in attempt to effect junction with cossack hetman, Mazeppa, Charles advanced too far from his base and was defeated at Poltava (1709), taking refuge in Turkey; Peter attempted to follow him across the Pruth (1711) but was compelled to restore Azov to Turkey; war dragged on until 1721, when it was concluded by Peace of Nystadt (*q.v.*).

NOVODEVICHY MONASTERY—monastery on outskirts of Moscow, whither Boris Godunov retired on death of Tsar Fedor, remaining until his election as tsar; later place of confinement of Tsarevna Sophia, half-sister of Peter the Great.

NYSTADT, PEACE OF (1721)—treaty at end of Northern War (*q.v.*) by which Russia annexed Esthonia, Livonia, Ingermanland, and a strip of Karelia.

Obrok—consistently translated as "dues"; until sixteenth century and even later paid in kind; in contradistinction to barshchina or labour obligation.

Ognishchan—a member of wealthier social classes in Kievan-Novgorodan Rus; exact meaning of term unknown.

OLEARIUS, ADAM (d. 1671)—*magister* of Leipzig University; visited Russia several times as secretary to embassies sent by Frederick, duke of Holstein, and was invited to accept employment there; wrote a description of the Muscovite state. *Cf., The voyages and travells of the ambassadors sent by Frederick duke of Holstein to the great duke of Muscovy, and the king of Persia, 1633-39. Faithfully rendered into English by John Davies of Kidwelly* (London, 1669). *Cf.* also *Die erste deutsche Expedition nach Persien (1635-39), nach der Originalausgabe bearbeitet,* von Dr. Hermann von Staden (Leipzig, 1927).

OLEG—grand prince of Rus (879-912); successor of Rurik owing to minority of latter's son, Igor; transferred his capital from Novgorod to Kiev.

OLEG SVYATOSLAVICH—prince of Chernigov (1076-1115); rival of Vladimir Monomakh, to whom he was genealogically senior; his descendants, the Olgoviches, were ultimately excluded from the succession to the throne of the grand princes.

OLGA—wife of Igor and regent during minority of son, Svyatoslav (945-964); privately converted to Christianity and hence canonised by Russian Church.

OLGERD—grand prince of Lithuania (1339-1377); chief rival of Dmitry Donskoi of Moscow for hegemony over the other Russian principalities; frequently in league with Tatars.

Oprichnik—man who served in oprichnina.

Oprichnina—weapon of Ivan the Terrible in destroying power of boyars; *cf.* text, pp. 142 *et seq.*

ORLOV, GREGORY—favourite of Catherine II; with brother, Alexis, headed conspiracy that overthrew Peter III (1762).

OSTERMANN, ANDREW [HEINRICH] (1686-1747)—son of a Lutheran pastor in Westphalia; entered service of Peter the Great (1703), rising rapidly to high office; influence survived all vicissitudes until accession of Elizabeth (1741).

OSTROVSKY, A. N. (1823-1886)—dramatist.

Otechestvo—hereditary rank determined by a man's genealogical place in his family and by family's historic service-relationship to other families (cf. mestnichestvo, rodoslovets, and razryadnaya kniga).

OTREPYEV, GREGORY (GRISHKA)—a monk attached to Romanov household, who fled to Poland; frequently identified with First False Dmitry.

-ov (-ev)—a possessive suffix, in family names indicating ancestry (approximately equivalent to the prefixes Fitz-, O', Mac-, or the suffixes -son, -sen, etc.); the diminutive form (-ovich, fem. -ovna) is used in the individual personal patronymic: thus, Nikita Romanovich Yuryev means Nikita, son of Roman and descendant of Yury; in later generations "Yuryev" is replaced by "Romanov."

PALITSYN, AVRAAM (c. 1550-1626)—forced to take tonsure (1588) for participation in revolt of 1587; became cellarer of Troitsa under Shuisky (1608); sent on embassy to Poland (1610), but returned to take active share in nationalistic agitation; after Peace of Deulino (1618), retired to Solovetsky Monastery, where he completed his *History for the Memory of Future Generations* (begun in 1601).

Paterik, Pechersky—a thirteenth-century collection of Lives of Saints of the Pechersky Monastery.

PAUL—emperor of All Russia (1796-1801); murdered by a conspiracy of nobles, some of them holders of high office (*e.g.,* Count Pahlen, Military Governor of St. Petersburg.

PAVLOV-SILVANSKY, N. P. (1869-1908)—Russian historian and archivist; author of *Feudalism in Ancient Rus* [in Russian] and of *Reform Projects in the Writings of Contemporaries of Peter the Great* [in Russian], etc.

PECHENEGS—a Turco-Tatar people who succeeded Khazars in control of the steppe; from their first attack on Kiev (968), were a constant menace to the Russian principalities and particularly to Russian trade with Constantinople until they were themselves superseded by the Polovtsians in middle of eleventh century.

PECHERSKY MONASTERY (MONASTERY OF THE CAVES)—most famous monastery in Russia; founded at Kiev in eleventh century; more austere monks hollowed out subterranean cells, in which they sealed themselves up, leaving only small apertures through which to receive sustenance; the Mecca of Orthodox Russians.

PECHERSKY, ANDREW—pseudonym of P. I. Melnikov (1819-1883), belle-lettrist and ethnographer.

Pechishche—primitive commune of north Russia; *cf.* text, p. 9.

Peter—metropolitan of All Rus (1305-1326); sided with Ivan Kalita in struggle with Tver; virtually transferred ecclesiastical capital of Russia to Moscow.

Peter I—called "the Great," tsar (1682-1725); formerly, until Solovyev and Klyuchevsky, treated as the "reformer" whose "Westernising reforms" marked a break in Russian history; first tsar to go abroad (1697-1698 and 1717); waged Northern War (1700-1721); assumed title of emperor (1721).

Peter II—emperor of All Russia (1727-1730); only grandson of Peter the Great in male line; passed over in 1725 in favour of Catherine I; ascended throne at age of twelve and died without direct heirs.

Plano (or Piano) Carpini—a Franciscan monk who passed through Russia in 1246 on a mission from the pope to Mongol khan at Karakorum; has left a description of his journey in his *Liber Tartarorum.*

Platonov, S. F. (1860——)—Russian historian, member of Russian Academy of Sciences, distinguished for his original researches on sixteenth and seventeenth centuries; only his high-school text has been translated into English, as *A History of Russia* (New York, 1925).

Podyak—an assistant dyak.

Pogrom—a devastating raid.

"Points"—conditions on which Anna was invited to ascend imperial throne in 1730.

Polovtsians—a Turco-Tatar people who succeeded Pechenegs in control of steppe in middle of eleventh century; more formidable than their predecessors, they were themselves superseded in middle of thirteenth century by Tatars, under Mongol leadership.

Poltava, battle of (1709)—defeat of Charles XII by Peter the Great during Northern War.

Poltina—a Russian monetary unit equal to one half ruble.

Pomeshchik—a man holding land on temporary (pomestye) tenure in contradistinction to the votchinnik (*q.v.*); the two types of tenure were gradually fused into one; in modern usage term "pomeshchik" means simply "landlord" (*cf.* text, p. 229, n. 3); in sixteenth and subsequent centuries roughly equivalent to "noble" (*q.v.*), though a boyar, a knight, or a cossack might also be a pomeshchik.

Pomestye—an estate held temporarily on condition of discharging military or other service; speedily assumed an hereditary character and ultimately became fused with the votchina (*q.v.*).

Posad, posadskie—portion of town outside walls of the kremlin called *posad* (*faubourg* or suburb), its inhabitants *posadskie;* a walled town was called a *gorod,* its inhabitants *gorozhane.* Both *posad* and *gorod* have been translated as town, *posadskie* as townsmen, *gorozhane* as burghers.

Posadnik—chief official of early Russian towns, generally appointed by prince (who might be non-resident); at Novgorod in thirteenth century the veche secured the right to elect the posadnik, bishop, and other officials.

Pososhkov, Ivan Tikhonovich (165?-1726)—prosperous peasant of village of Pokrovskoe, near Moscow; from a hostile schismatic he was converted into an ardent admirer and partisan of Peter the Great; author of *On poverty and wealth,* and other writings.

Pozharsky, Prince D.—leader of the army that recovered Moscow from Poles in 1612; summoned zemsky sobor, which elected Michael tsar (1613); a statue of Minin and Pozharsky stands in Red Square in Moscow.

Pozhiloe—a fee paid by peasants for use of their homesteads.

Pravda, Russkaya—the earliest monument of Russian law, formerly attributed to Yaroslav the Wise but now recognised as the product of a process of gradual accretion. Various extant versions may be reduced to two forms, a long and a short: the former is found first in a thirteenth-century ecclesiastical code of Novgorod, subsequently in other ecclesiastical law books; the short form is found first in a copy of the Novgorod chronicle of the end of the fifteenth century, and subsequently in other, so to speak, literary productions having no legal significance.

Precept OF VLADIMIR MONOMAKH—composed for moral edification of his children; a French translation may be found in L. Leger, *Chronique dite de Nestor* (Paris, 1884).

PREOBRAZHENSK—a village on outskirts of Moscow whither Peter the Great and his mother were banished during regency of Sophia (1682-1689); its name was given to one of the regiments of the Guard.

PRESNYAKOV, A. Y. (1870-1931)—professor of history in University of St. Petersburg; *The princely law of early Rus* was his doctoral dissertation.

Prikaz—a command or order; the function a boyar was ordered to discharge; the administrative organ developed for the permanent discharge of such functions, *i.e.*, a bureau. A boyar might be charged with widely different administrative functions simultaneously; his prikaz continued to be charged with these functions, introducing hopeless confusion into administrative system. The bureaux were replaced by or absorbed into the collegia of Peter the Great.

PRINCE-CAESAR—a mock title bestowed on Prince Romodanovsky, head of the Preobrazhensk Bureau (secret police).

PRINCELINGS (*knyazhata*)—descendants of appanage princes who had entered Moscow's service; as scions of formerly sovereign families entitled to title of Prince, though not necessarily boyars.

PRINCE-POPE (ALL ROWDIEST AND MOST MOCK PATRIARCH OF MOSCOW)—title bestowed on Nikita Zotov, who had been Peter's tutor. Associated with him was a conclave of twelve cardinals, with a suite of bishops, abbots, and even abbesses, bearing scandalous nicknames; they were carefully organised as the "maddest, most mock, and most drunken synod," Peter himself having the rank of archdeacon. The first commandment was never to go to bed sober. *Cf.* Kluchevsky, V. O., *A History of Russia*, vol. IV, chap. 2.

Pud—a Russian measure of weight, equal to 40 *funt* or 36 lbs. avoirdupois.

RANDOLPH, THOMAS—sent by Queen Elizabeth of England as ambassador to Ivan the Terrible (1568); negotiated grant of commercial charter of privileges to English Russia Company; on return to England (1569) addressed special memoir to Privy Council.

Raskolniks [schismatics]—those who held to "Old Belief," refusing to accept ritual reforms of Nikon.

Ratusha—town council of Moscow set up in 1699 and given jurisdiction over burmisters of provincial towns; authority destroyed by decentralisation involved in establishment of guberniyas.

Razryadnaya kniga—official record of service, used as basis of mestnichestvo calculations.

Rodoslovets, Gosudarev—official record of Muscovite genealogies, used in determining otechestvo (*q.v.*).

ROMANOVS—old boyar family, not of princely origin; known variously in successive generations as Zakharins, Yuryevs, Romanovs, and Nikitiches. The family first became prominent with marriage of Anastasia (*q.v.*) to Ivan the Terrible (1547); her brother, Nikita Romanov, had five sons, the Nikitiches. The oldest of these, Fedor, better known under his ecclesiastical name of Filaret, was father of Michael, elected tsar in 1613.

ROZHDESTVENSKY, S. V.—author of *Service landholding in sixteenth century* (St. Petersburg, 1907).

ROZHKOV, N. A. (1868-1927)—materialist historian; in 1905 served on editorial staff of Bolshevik paper, *Pravda,* and played "Danton" in December uprising at Moscow; exiled to Siberia, whence he returned after 1917 revolution, no longer a Bolshevik; author of numerous studies on economic and sociological history of Russia, particularly in sixteenth century; his most ambitious work was *Russian history in comparative historical light (Foundations of social dynamics),* 12 vols. [in Russian] (1919-1926).

RUBLE—legal monetary unit until replaced by *chervonets* in 1922; the gold ruble was equal to 2s. 1½d. or 51 cents.

RURIK—by tradition, first grand prince of Rus and ancestor of the dynasty which became extinct on death of Tsar Fedor in 1598; according to *Chronicle* "invited" by Slavs of Lake Ilmen (*i.e.,* Novgorod) to rule over them in 862 and died in 879; succeeded by Oleg, regarded as first genuinely historical prince.

SAPIEHA—Polish chancellor in reign of Sigismund.

Sazhen—a Russian measure, equal to 7 feet.

SCHISMATICS—*cf.* raskolniks.

SCHLÖZER, A. L. (1735-1809)—German scholar, fascinated by wealth of content and poetical language of Russian chronicles, study of which he continued while professor at Göttingen; first to apply scientific critical methods in study of Russian history; chief work in this field was *Nestor* (1802-1809).

SERGEYEVICH, V. I. (1837-1911)—professor of history of Russian law in University of St. Petersburg; author of *Russian juridical antiquities* [in Russian] (1890-1896); interested in comparative historical method of Freeman.

SHCHERBATOV, PRINCE M. (1733-1790)—widely read in literature of Enlightenment; disciple of Montesquieu and defender of privileges of nobles; wrote *History of Russia* in 15 vols. [in Russian] (1770-1792), ending with Time of Troubles.

SHUISKYS—prominent boyar family descended from once independent princes who had accepted suzerainty of Moscow and entered its service. Most important member of family was Tsar Vasily (*q.v.*).

SIGISMUND—king of Poland (1587-1632) and Sweden (1594-1604); invaded Russia in reign of Vasily Shuisky; by Treaty of Smolensk (1610), his son, Vladislav, became tsar of Moscow.

SIMEON THE PROUD—prince of Moscow and grand prince of Vladimir (1341-1353), son and successor of Ivan Kalita.

SKURATOV, MALYUTA—notorious oprichnik, whose daughter married Boris Godunov.

-SKY (or -SKOI)—adjectival ending, in family names approximately equivalent to French *de,* German *von,* etc. (*eg.,* Prince Shuisky = prince of Shuya); similarly found in sobriquets (*e.g.,* Dmitry Donskoi, Alexander Nevsky)

SLAVOPHILS—literary group of 1840's and 1850's influenced by Hegelian concepts and insisting on root difference between history of Slavs and of Western Europe; urged as peculiarities of former: (1) Slavs received Christianity from Byzantium, not Rome; (2) Slavonic society based on commune as opposed to German principle of individual liberty and property rights; (3) Russian state founded by agreement, not conquest, thus obviating Western "hostile demarcation of classes." The West is perishing, with socialist revolution imminent, whereas in Russia communism is already attained, with no proletariat. Leading Slavophils were Aksakovs, Khomyakov, brothers Kireyevsky, Samarin; their views influenced Herzen and development of Narodnik thought; reflected philosophy of landholders whose economy rested on peasant commune, and who were fighting penetration of Russia by capitalism and transfer of power to bourgeoisie; hence denunciation of "work of Peter," in opposition to "Westerners" (*q.v.*).

Smerd—a peasant; *cf.* text, p. 58, n. 3.

Sobor—an assembly, whether ecclesiastical (synod) or lay (*cf.* zemsky sobor); also used for Russian equivalent of cathedral, assembly of churches under one roof.

SOPHIA, TSAREVNA (1657-1704)—half-sister of Peter the Great; regent (1682-1689); imprisoned by Peter in Novodevichy Monastery.

SOPHIA VITOVTOVNA—daughter of Vitovt, cousin of Jagello of Poland-Lithuania and virtually independent ruler of Lithuania (1392-1430); became wife of Vasily II (the Dark) of Moscow.

SOLOVETSKY MONASTERY—one of greatest monasteries in Russia, situated on island in White Sea; now used as place of exile for political offenders.

SOLOVYEV, S. M. (1820-1879)—professor of history in University of Moscow; greatest Russian historian of nineteenth century; profoundly influenced by Hegelians and by German Historical School; one of founders of Russian historical-juridical school; interpreted Russian history in terms of transition from primitive "clan life" to "state life"; first to attempt (in later writings) to explain reign of Peter the Great without making it a break in organic evolution. In partial agreement with Buckle on rôle of natural environment; rarely attributed phenomena to economic influences, stressing laws rather than realities. Author of *History of Russia from the earliest times* [in Russian] 29 volumes (to second half of eighteenth century), still greatest detailed exposition of Russian history, despite weakness of theoretical concepts.

SOMBART, WERNER (1863———)—German economist; professor in University of Breslau; author of *Der moderne Kapitalismus*, etc.

Starosta [elder]—for *gubnoi starosta* (or *golova*) *cf.* guba: for *zemsky starosta cf.* zemsky.

STOLBOVO, PEACE OF (1617)—treaty with Sweden at end of war brought on by Troubles; confirmed Russia's exclusion from Baltic at end of Livonian War.

STORCH, H. F. (1766-1835)—economist, disciple of Adam Smith; much interested in Russian history and economics; first to advance opinion that origin of early Russian towns was to be assigned to trade between Byzantium and northwestern Europe via the Black Sea, Dnieper, Western Dvina, Volkhov, and Baltic Sea; theory resurrected and given new basis by Klyuchevsky. Author of *Historisch-Statistisches Gemälde des russischen Reichs*, 9 vols. (Leipzig, 1797-1803).

Streltsy—semi-professional soldiers living in special Strelets Quarters with families and engaged in industry and petty trade; first organised by Ivan the Terrible; most efficient part of army until importation of foreign officers to train Russian regiments was begun under Michael; revolts in 1682 and 1698 led to abolition by Peter (1699).

STROGANOVS—wealthy family of merchants and salt-boilers; in 1560 granted extensive lands on Kama, which they colonised; engaged largely in exploitation of fur, and later mineral, resources of Urals. Yermak, cossack ataman who in 1584 overthrew khanate of Siberia, was employed by them to collect tribute in furs from native peoples.

Sudebnik—law code; first Sudebnik drawn up in 1497; second, or Tsar's Sudebnik, in 1550. The code drafted in 1649 is known as the Ulozhenie.

SUZDAL—in early times largest town in the mesopotamia (northeastern region between Upper Volga and Oka); name loosely used to distinguish this area from older areas of Slavonic settlement in basin of Dnieper and round Lake Ilmen; also called "the Low" because downstream for traders from Novgorod (Nizhny Novgorod means Novgorod the Low).

SVYATOSLAV—grand prince (945-972); under regency of Olga to 964; a pagan; under younger son the Rus were officially converted to Christianity.

TATARS—Turkish peoples of central Asia, subjugated by Mongols under Jenghiz Khan in thirteenth century; first appeared in Russian steppe under Mongol leadership in 1223, inflicting defeat on combined forces of Russians and Polovtsians. *Cf.* Golden Horde.

TATISHCHEV, V. N. (1686-1750)—a noble; attracted to history by interest in geography; wrote *History of Russia* [in Russian] (to the Troubles), published posthumously in five volumes, valuable only because much of material on which it was based has since been lost.

Terem—private living-quarters of tsar.

THOUSAND-MAN (*tysyatsky*)—high military and judicial official in Kievan Rus; *cf.* text, pp. 42-43.

TOKHTAMYSH—superseded Mamai as khan of Golden Horde; inflicted dire vengeance (1382) on Moscow for Dmitry's victory at Kulikovo (1380).

TROITSA MONASTERY (MONASTERY OF THE TRINITY)—strongly fortified monastery about forty miles northeast of Moscow, founded by Sergius in fourteenth century; chief centre for pilgrimages in Suzdal (*q.v.*).

TSAREVICH—any son of a tsar, not necessarily the heir apparent.

TSAREVNA—daughter of a tsar.

TSARITSA—wife of a tsar.

Tselovalnik [juror]—*cf. guba* and *zemsky.*

TUSHINO—village near Moscow where Second False Dmitry (the "knave") established his headquarters; the name is used also symbolically of the noble-cossack rebellion.

TVER—appanage principality, from whose princes Moscow, with aid of Tatars, Church, and Novgorod, wrested title of grand prince of Vladimir in fourteenth century.

Tyaglo [*taille*]—direct tax paid by townsmen and peasants, the clergy and military servitors being exempt.

Ukraine—a frontier or frontier province. There were a number of ukraines, *e.g.,* Volhynian (later Polish), Seversk, *Polskaya* (*i.e.,* Field—also called the Wilderness), etc. With the disappearance of the frontier the name has come to be synonymous with Little Russia, roughly equivalent to the area transferred in 1569 from Lithuania to direct rule of Poland and in part conquered by Moscow in long war (1654-1667) that grew out of revolt of Zaporozhians.

Ulozhenie—law code drafted in 1648-1649 with collaboration of zemsky sobor to replace Tsar's Sudebnik of 1550.

UNFROCKED MONK—the First False Dmitry, so-called in allusion to belief that he was really Gregory Otrepyev.

UZBEK—khan of Golden Horde (1314-1341).

VARANGIANS (VARYAGS)—members of bands of Northmen organised [*var*= oath] for plundering expeditions; at least as early as ninth century such bands, using the great Volkhov-Dnieper waterway, found their way to Constantinople, where many entered service of emperor; others established themselves at strategic points along "water road," thus founding the Russian principalities; *cf.* Rurik, Oleg, and text, p. 12.

VASILY I—grand prince of Moscow (1389-1425).

VASILY II—grand prince of Moscow (1425-1462), called "the Dark" because blinded by enemies in course of only feud waged within family of princes of Moscow.

VASILY III—grand prince of Moscow (1505-1533).

VASILY (SHUISKY)—tsar (1606-1610).

Veche—town assembly in early Russian towns; *cf.* text, pp. 43 *et seq.*

Verst—Russian measure equal to two-thirds of a mile.

VLADIMIR—town in Suzdal founded by Vladimir Monomakh; residence of Grand Prince Andrew Bogolyubsky and his successors; in fourteenth century possession of Vladimir and title of grand prince seized by princes of Moscow.

VLADIMIR MONOMAKH—grand prince of Kiev (1113-1125); transferred from throne of Pereyaslavl in violation of rights of Oleg Svyatoslavich; famous for debt legislation and *Precept* addressed to children; last outstanding ruler of Kiev; father of Yury Dolgoruky; idealised in chronicles and by most historians, especially in text-books.

VLADIMIR, SAINT—grand prince of Kiev (980-1015); son of Svyatoslav; won throne by wars with brothers; effected conversion of Rus to Christianity; father of Yaroslav "the Wise."

VLADISLAV (LADISLAS)—tsar of Moscow (1610-1612); son of Sigismund of Poland; accepted as titular tsar under Treaty of Smolensk in succession to Tsar Vasily (Shuisky); succeeded father as king of Poland (1632-1648).

VOCKERODT—secretary of Prussian legation at St. Petersburg under Peter; wrote memoirs in 1738. *Cf.* Hermann, E. (ed.), *Zeitgenössische Berichte zur Geschichte Russlands: Russland unter Peter dem Grossen.*

Voevoda—a military commander; in the seventeenth century also a provincial governor.

VOLODAR AND VASILKA—princes of Galicia (1080-1124), involved in a feud with Grand Prince Svyatopolk.

Volost—in early times the area under the jurisdiction of a town (generally translated "province"); in later times an administrative subdivision of the *uyezd* [county], translated as township (not to be confused with town).

Volostel—governor of a volost, *i.e.*, a kormlenshchik.

VSEVOLOD "BIG NEST"—grand prince of Vladimir (1176-1212); brother of Andrew Bogolyubsky and ancestor of almost all the families of princes in Suzdal.

Votchina—an estate held unconditionally, though the holder might on other grounds be held liable for the discharge of military or other service; gradually fused with the pomestye (*q.v.*).

Votchinnik—holder of land by hereditary (votchina) tenure, in contradistinction to the pomeshchik (*q.v.*).

WESTERNERS—literary opponents of the Slavophils (*q.v.*) in the 1840's and 1850's; influenced by teachings of Hegel, sought to discover how Slavs might become a "historic nation" and found answer in "reforms of Peter," who rescued Russia from her Asiatic past; advocated further "Westernisation of Russia." Chief writers—Granovsky, Solovyev, Kavelin, Chicherin. Their views, in modified form, gained ascendancy in academic circles; reflected philosophy of bourgeois interests, advocating rapid development of capitalism in Russia.

WHITWORTH, CHARLES—English envoy at court of Peter; his despatches are printed in the original in *Sbornik russkogo istoricheskogo obshchestva*, vols. 39, 50, 61.

YAROSLAV "THE WISE"—grand prince of Kiev (1019-1054); younger son of St. Vladimir; won throne in feud with brothers; traditionally credited with authorship of oldest articles in *Pravda;* after his death, dynasty divided into numerous branches (*e.g.*, the Olgoviches and the "stock of Monomakh").

YAVORSKY, STEFAN (1658-1722)—a Little Russian, metropolitan of Ryazan; on death of Patriarch Adrian (1700) Peter, unwilling to appoint another Great Russian opponent of his reforms and afraid to appoint a Little Russian because their orthodoxy was suspect, compromised by naming Yavorsky to discharge duties of patriarch without bearing the title.

YEFIMENKO, ALEXANDRA Y. (1848-1919)—historian of common law, communal landholding, and the Ukraine—killed by Petlurists. Author of *Peasant landholding in the Far North,* etc.

YURY (DANILOVICH)—prince of Moscow (1303-1325); son and successor of Daniel (son of Alexander Nevsky and founder of first permanent dynasty of appanage princes of Moscow); with Tatar aid usurped title of grand prince of Vladimir (1319), precipitating Moscow's long struggle with Tver.

YURY DOLGORUKY [Long Arm]—prince of Suzdal (1096-1157); son of Vladimir Monomakh; seized throne of Kiev (1154); father of Andrew Bogolyubsky and Vsevolod Big Nest.

ZABELIN, I. Y. (1820-1908)—Russian historian; attributed rise of Moscow, not directly to economic influences he described but to support of people to prince who best managed economic activities. Author of *Russian life from the earliest times* [in Russian], *History of the city of Moscow* [in Russian], etc.

Zakup—peasant bound to the soil by debt.

ZAPOROZHIAN BROTHERHOOD—an association of cossacks with headquarters beyond (*i.e.*, below) the rapids (*za porozhe*) of the Dnieper. The spread of serfdom in the Ukraine after the Union of Lublin (1569) and the efforts of the Polish government, in the interest of good relations with Turkey, to check cossack raids on Turk and Tatar settlements on Black Sea coast provoked series of disturbances; in 1648 the Zaporozhians, under their elected ataman, Bogdan Khmelnitsky, raised the whole Ukraine in revolt; the intervention of Moscow (1654) brought on a long war which ended in the annexation of Kiev and the left bank of the Dnieper by Moscow (1667).

Zemshchina—that portion of Ivan's realm not taken into oprichnina and left under rule of the boyars.

Zemsky—roughly equivalent to German *Land-*(in contradistinction to *Reich-*). The zemsky reform means the reform of local government on autonomous principles; elected *zemsky starosta* [elder] assisted by elected *zemsky tseloval-niks* [jurors], presided over *zemskaya izba* [local government office]; *cf.* text, p. 129.

Zemsky sobor—Russian counterpart of Western estates-general, parliament, diet, etc.; *cf.* text, p. 150.

ZHDANOV, I. N. (1846-1901)—professor of history of literature in University of St. Petersburg; made researches on Stoglav Sobor.

Zolotnik—a Russian measure of weight equal to 2.4 drams.

INDEX

INDEX

A

Adashev, Alexis, 134, 135, 136, 138, 139, 164

Agriculture, primitive, 4-9; Muscovite, 112-113, 116-119, 151-152; after Troubles, 227-236; see also Landholding and Peasants

Aksakov, K., 47, 355

Alexander (Yaroslavich) Nevsky, 72, 80-81, 355

Alexandrovsk, 143, 144, 146

Alexis, metropolitan, 99, 100, 164

Alexis (Mikhailovich Romanov), tsar, 231, 240, 241, 248, 250, 251, 252, 264, 268, 283, 291, 315, 323, 331, 355

Alexis (Petrovich Romanov), tsarevich, 331, 355

Alleged Dmitry (First), 180-199, 201, 206n, 207, 210, 214, 223, 315, 323

Alleged Dmitry (Second), 199-211, 217, 223-224

Anastasia (Romanovna), tsaritsa, 138, 355

Andrew (Yuryevich) Bogolyubsky, 65, 66, 67, 68, 79, 82, 90, 355

Andrew (Ivanovich) of Staritsa, 111, 139, 144

Andronov, Fedor, 218-219, 221, 241, 249, 355

Anna (Ivanovna), empress, 334, 346-350, 355

Anna (Petrovna), tsarevna, 332, 355

Apiculture, 3, 6, 8, 9

"Appanage period," 13, 28n, 32, 89-90, 91, 355

Apraxins, 240

Apraxin, F., 280, 286, 295, 297, 304, 319, 331, 333, 335n

Apraxin, P., 295

Arabs, 6, 7, 8, 33, 36, 74

Archangel, trade through, 115, 154, 245, 259-260, 262, 265, 267-268, 273, 274-276, 288, 336

Aristov, 35, 356

Astrakhan, conquest of, 132

Augustus of Poland, 275, 356

B

Baryatinskys, 201

Baryatinsky, A., 339

Baryatinsky, F., 204

Bathory, 153, 356

Baty, 70, 356

Bekbulatovich, 155, 176

Belsky, Bogdan, 162-163, 164, 166, 183

Belsky, Ivan, 141

Belyaev, 2, 228, 356

Berestov, assembly of, 59

Bergholz, 309, 310, 311, 312, 318, 319, 356

Biarmiya, 38, 77

Biron, 346, 356

Blood vengeance, 10, 55

Bogolyubsky, see Andrew (Yuryevich)

Bogoslovsky, 326, 356

Boleslaw, 52, 356

Bolgars, 7, 8, 33, 36, 39, 64, 79, 92, 356

Bolotnikov, 198, 199, 203, 204, 212, 223n

Boltin, 1, 356

Boris of Nizhny-Novgorod, 27-28, 100

Boris, tsar, see Godunov, Boris

Bourgeoisie, in Kievan Rus, 53-56, 66-67; and Tatars, 70-73; in Novgorod, 83-84, 85-86; in Moscow, 93-95, 103, 114, 129-130; under Ivan IV, 122, 129-130, 131-133, 144-145, 150, 154-155; and Godunov, 166-168, 178, 186-187; and Alleged Dmitry, 188, 191-192; and Shuisky, 192-193, 195-196, 200-201, 203-206, 211-212; and Vladislav, 217-218, 220-222, 224-225; in seventeenth century, 242-247, 254; and Peter, 288, 293, 294, 296, 298, 300, 308, 317, 326; after Peter, 335-336, 341-342

Boyar, 356

Boyars, in Kievan Rus, 15-17, 26-29, 110-111; in Novgorod, 84-86; and rise of Moscow, 91, 95-97, 102; and Ivan IV, 109-111, 118-119, 119-121, 126-128, 131, 139, 141-142, 145-149; and Godunov, 161-164, 165-168, 176, 183, 185, 186; and Alleged Dmitry, 187-188, 190-192; and Shuisky, 192-195, 201, 207-208, 209-212; and Vladislav, 215-216, 218-219; in seventeenth century, 250-251

Boyar duma, see Duma

Bruce, 305, 306, 356

Buchinsky, 187

Bureau of Secret Affairs, 242, 252

Bussow, 193, 357

C

Campredon, 306, 326, 329, 332, 333, 357

Capitalism, commercial, 357; in Kiev, 56-58; at Novgorod, 79-80, 84; in Muscovy, 114-116; in seventeenth century, 257-276; under Peter, 286-288, 291, 302, 341; see also Bourgeoisie, Money economy, and Monopolies

Casimir IV, 43, 101, 357